DP
270
•P7

Preston, Paul

Spain in crisis:
the evolution and
decline of the
Franco regime

DATE DUE

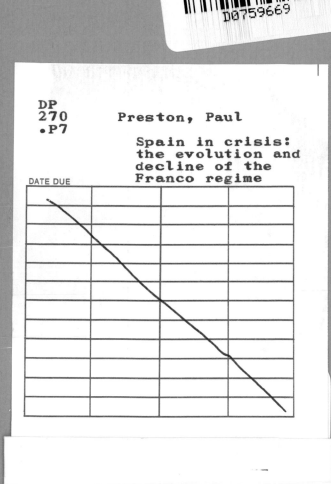

SPAIN IN CRISIS
*The Evolution and Decline
of the Franco Régime*

SPAIN IN CRISIS

The Evolution and Decline of the Franco Régime

Editor Paul Preston,

*Lecturer in History,
Queen Mary College, London*

BOOKS
10 East 53d St. New York 10022
(a division of Harper & Row Publishers, Inc.)

First published in USA by
HARPER & ROW PUBLISHERS, INC
BARNES & NOBLE IMPORT DIVISION
10 East 53rd Street, New York 10022
ISBN 0 06 495711 X

Copyright © 1976 The Harvester Press Limited

Typeset by Input Typesetting Ltd., London SE1
and printed in Great Britain by
Redwood Burrr Limited, Trowbridge, Wiltshire

Contents

Contributors

Herbert R. Southworth was educated at the University of Arizona and Columbia University. He wrote his first article on the Spanish Civil War in 1937 in the *Washington Post*. Since that time he has contributed articles to *The Nation, New Statesman,* and *Foreign Affairs* amongst others. He is the author of the classic *El mito de la cruzada de Franco* (Paris, 1963), *Antifalange* (Paris, 1967) and *La destruction de Guernica* (Paris, 1975), to be published in English by the California University Press.

M. García is a young Spanish sociologist, educated at the University of Madrid and in Great Britain. He is currently working on a full-length study of the Spanish armed forces.

Norman B. Cooper was educated at the University of Birmingham and subsequently did post-graduate work at the Universities of Bristol, Salamanca and Reading. He is head of the Spanish Department of Merton Technical College, and author of *Catholicism and the Franco Régime* (London, 1975).

Juan M. Esteban was educated at the Universities of Barcelona and Oxford. He is lecturer in economics at the Universidad Autónoma in Barcelona. He is co-author of *Capitalismo español: de la autarquía a la estabilización 1939-1959* 2 vols (Madrid, 1973).

Eduardo Sevilla Guzmán was educated at the Universities of Madrid and Reading. He is Professor of Rural Sociology at the University of Córdoba. He has published several articles on the problems of Spanish agriculture and the peasantry in the twentieth century.

Paul Preston was educated at Oriel College, Oxford. Having previously lectured in Madrid, Rome (the Centre for Mediterranean Studies) and the University of Reading, he is presently lecturer in Modern History at Queen Mary College, University of London. He has published several articles in scholarly journals on the coming of the Spanish Civil War and on the Franco régime. He is also a regular contributor to *New Society, The Times Literary Supplement* and *The Nation*.

Sheelagh Ellwood was educated at the Universities of Essex and Reading. She is presently engaged upon a doctoral thesis on the decline of the Falange.

Salvador Giner was educated in Barcelona, Germany and Chicago. He has been a lecturer at the Universities of Barcelona, Puerto Rico, and Reading, and a Fellow of King's College, Cambridge. He is presently Senior Lecturer in Sociology at the University of Lancaster, and the author of several books on sociological theory, many articles on Spain, the best-selling *Sociology* and a forthcoming study, *Mass Society*.

John Llewelyn Hollyman was educated at the Universities of Manchester and Reading. He is currently Senior Lecturer in Spanish at Bristol Polytechnic. He has published articles on ETA and on press censorship in Spain.

Norman L. Jones was educated at Brasenose College, Oxford, later doing post-graduate work at the Universities of Reading and London. He is presently Senior Lecturer in Spanish at Oxford Polytechnic, and is the author of the forthcoming study *The Catalan Left*, while also preparing a doctoral thesis on the *Esquerra* during the Second Republic.

Introduction: The Crisis

PAUL PRESTON

In the two years following the assassination of Admiral Carrero Blanco on 20 December 1973, Spain has witnessed more dramatic political activity than was ever permitted during the previous thirty four years of the Francoist dictatorship. Yet this has not signified a relaxation of the régime's repressive machinery. Indeed, throughout 1974 and 1975, repression in the form of widespread arrests, torture and executions, as well as the ready resort to firearms by the police and the Civil Guard, have increased to a level not seen since the late nineteen forties. Nevertheless, the régime has been unable to prevent the assassination of a prime minister, massive strikes paralysing entire provinces, a savage guerrilla war in the Basque country and sporadic violence by activists of both the ultra-right and the ultra-left in Madrid and Barcelona.

The Franco régime is clearly undergoing a crisis. And perhaps what is most significant about it is that the threats to the survival of the dictatorship have not only come from the traditional opposition. Once-reliable pillars of the Francoist establishment also seem to be giving way. Open conflict between Church and State is at an unprecedented level. In the higher echelons of the Army, there is an increasingly apparent friction between ultra-reactionary generals and relatively liberal 'modernizers' who would like to play down the Army's political role. For the first time since the Civil War, dissident middle-rank officers have been arrested, accused of belonging to an alleged Democratic Military Union. There have been mounting demands from within the Francoist political élite for democratization. The government of premier Carlos Arias-Navarro has been largely neutralized, caught in the cross-fire of these 'liberalizers' and what has come to be known as the bunker [1], the hard-line Falangists, entrenched in the bureaucracy, the police, the

Army, who would defend the dictatorship to the bitter end. The forces of order have not been slow to seize the initiative – hence the vicious circle of growing repression and growing demands for reform.

It is in the internecine squabblings of the régime that the seriousness of the crisis lies. The division between those in the bunker and the erstwhile Francoists who have decided that their own survival can best be assured by opting for liberalization becomes ever more apparent. One of the most vocal members of the reactionary group, Luis María Ansón, recently commented bitterly: 'the rats are going to leave the régime's ship . . . the cowardice of the Spanish ruling class is truly suffocating . . . already it has reached the beginnings of the 'sauve-qui-peut', of the unconditional surrender'.[2] His venom was directed against those ex-servants of the régime who are now calling for a democratic reform – the *Tácito* group of Christian-Democrat high-level functionaries who took part in recent mass resignations, Manuel Fraga, José María Areilza and others who prefer to concede a little rather than lose everything. And among those who have benefitted from the régime, it is not just the shrewder bureaucrats who are calling for change. Joaquín Garrigues-Walker, one of the most significant figures in Spanish capitalism and one-time representative of several multi-national corporations, has led growing calls from the financial and industrial oligarchy for change. He has expressed the liberalizing position with great clarity: 'It is only by taking the risk of possible change . . . that one can control the change. Otherwise, the social forces which are bringing pressure to bear on the institutions of the state will end by triumphing as did Ho Chi Minh in Saigon. By rubbing out everything and starting afresh'.[3]

It was to provoke just this kind of contradiction within the régime that the assassination which opened the crisis period was carried out. The ETA communiqué accepting responsibility makes this quite clear: 'Luis Carrero Blanco, a hard man, violent in his repressive attitudes, was the key which guaranteed the stability and continuity of the Francoist system. It is certain that without him the tensions within the government between the Falange and the Opus Dei will now intensify'. Carrero Blanco represented a link between two clear tendencies within the ruling élite. He was eminently acceptable to the bunker, being a survival of hard-line nineteen forties Francoism. His first political assignment was to attend the Rome celebrations of the twentieth anniversary of Fascism in 1939.[4] Thirty-one years later, he could write, using the pseudonym Ginés de Buitrago, that to attempt to liberalize Spain was as reprehensible as to offer a reformed alcoholic a drink.[5] Yet, at the same time, he seemed acceptable to the modernizers, since it was he who, at the end of the 1950s is reputed to have persuaded Franco to abandon autarchic policies and let neo-capitalism have its head. In fact, it seems unlikely that Carrero Blanco could long have averted the clash between the advocates of reactionary politics and the champions of modern economics. It is certainly the case that tensions emerged rapidly after his death.

In a sense, the régime came through the confusion surrounding the assassination of the Admiral rather well. The ease with which the necessary constitutional mechanisms functioned and the absence of any major breach of public order were obviously the basis of the self-congratulatory tributes to the 'political maturity' of the Spanish people made at the time by official spokesmen.[6] However, all was not so easily resolved. It seems that the Director of the Civil Guard, General Carlos Iniesta, attempted a coup. He ordered his local commanders to seize the provincial capitals and to shoot left-wingers at the first sign of demonstrations. It was the joint initiative of the more liberal Chief of the General Staff, Manuel Díez-Alegría, and the Minister of the Interior, Carlos Arias-Navarro, in taking control which prevented bloodshed.[7]

Arias-Navarro was named soon after as Carrero-Blanco's successor. He followed up his actions against the ultras by a declaration of intent to liberalize the régime. His celebrated speech of 12 February 1974 came out in favour of wider political participation for Spaniards, although within the limits of the strictest order. A limited programme provided for the election, as opposed to the government appointment, of mayors and senior local officials. Parliament was to become about 35% elective as opposed to the existing 17%. The vertical syndicates were promised more bargaining power. Political associations, although not parties, were promised.[8] It amounted to little, but this was still the most liberal declaration ever made by a minister of Franco. In the following two years, it was systematically whittled down by the efforts of the bunker.

That the ultra-right should react in such a way was not surprising. What was remarkable was that the prime minister should choose to challenge a powerful faction of the régime – indeed a faction to which he was thought to belong. Arias had been nominated by *La Vanguardia* of Barcelona as the hardest man in the previous cabinet. An expert in matters of internal security, he was for a long time Director General of Security under the notorious hard-liner, General Alonso Vega.[9] During his six months as Minister of the Interior, from June to December 1973, there was a major offensive against the opposition: on ETA – nine militants shot in clashes with the police; on the Communists – several regional networks broken up; on the Workers' Commissions – regular harassment. Why then did Arias adopt a seemingly liberal policy?

The short answer is growing opposition and impending economic crisis. Working class militancy has been steadily increasing in recent years. Although economic growth means that workers are now much better off than in the nineteen fifties, they still suffer from long hours, poor conditions and a very high accident rate. Minimal social, health and education services do little to compensate. The régime's readiness to use violence against strikers has not prevented strikes spreading. One of the most significant features of strikes in the seventies was the way in which their scope began to widen beyond the limited economic demands of specific groups. In September 1972, a stoppage at the Citroën plant in Vigo spread to other factories and even to local shop-keepers. In the summer of 1973, the entire city of Pamplona was affected by a general strike. When Arias came to power, the winter of 1973 had already been intensely conflictive. After a year of rampant inflation, the Carrero Blanco government took a series of 'stabilizing' measures in November, including a freeze on wage increases over fifteen per cent. Almost immediately, there were strikes in the Asturian mines, the Basque iron foundries and the Catalan textile industry. To these problems inherited from Carrero, there had to be added the immense complication of the energy crisis. One of the prices paid by Spain for her rapid growth was a gigantic increase in energy imports. [10] Apart from the problems of meeting her own energy bill, Spain was also likely to suffer from the wider effects of the oil crisis. The European recession was soon to take its toll of the two main sources of Spanish income, tourism and remittances from emigrant workers. The prospect of increased unemployment and lower living standards heralded growing militance. Limited political reform seemed to be a reasonable concession to avoid a serious challenge to the entire structure of power in Spain.

Spain in fact survived the worst consequences of the recession. Nevertheless, there still exist major contradictions between the attempt to maintain economic modernization within the context of a political system whose proudest boast is that it has eliminated the enlightenment from Spain. If the Francoist system once suited the needs of the economic oligarchy, it is now increasingly a hindrance. This is the root of the divisions now apparent in the Spanish ruling élite. In other words, the crisis facing Arias-Navarro and Franco's heir, Juan Carlos, is a crisis of the obsolescence of the political forms of Francoism. The way in which Spain has developed since 1939 illustrates this.

The Civil War was won by a rightist coalition which arose in response to the attacks on the prevailing socio-economic balance of power made during the Second Republic of 1931-1936. Accordingly, the first objectives of the new régime established by that coalition were the maintenance of the existing structure of landed property and the strict control of the recently defeated working class. These tasks were carried out by a politico-military bureaucracy made up of those members of the middle- and working classes who might be deemed the service class of Francoism.[11] For whatever reasons, geographical loyalty during the war, conviction, opportunism, they threw in their lot with the régime and were tied to it by networks of corruption and complicity on the great repression during the years of hunger. These are the groups which today make up the bunker.

The Falange, as a fascist organization, might have been expected to attempt to mobilize the working class. However, as Herbert Southworth shows in chapter one, after a victorious war the ruling classes had no need for such an operation. Falangist bureaucrats still mouthed anti-capitalist rhetoric, but they dutifully served their masters by disciplining the working class and the peasantry within the corporative syndicates. The Falangist bureaucrats themselves clearly stated the class nature of the régime. José María Areilza declared that the state protected capital from internal as well as external aggressors. José Solís admitted that 'when we speak of transformation or reform in the countryside, no one should think that we intend to harm the present owners'.[12] A system of safe-conducts and certificates of political reliability turned the defeated into second-class citizens. The oligarchy no longer suffered from the pre-war militance of the workers and peasants. Indeed, economic survival for the lower classes tended to be so linked with ostensible political apathy[13], that a slow accumulation of capital became possible. This was not the only benefit of forcible stability. When the world economic conjuncture changed, Spain was tremendously attractive to foreign investors.

The corporative syndicates and the weight of the forces of order were clearly a considerable asset to the economically dominant classes. Yet the economic development which they partly facilitated was gradually to remove the need for them. Growth has solved some structural problems such as the land-hunger which previously characterized the southern estates. The needs of a complex economy have created a new working class with relatively high levels of skill and income. Sophisticated productivity agreements are nearer to the needs of Spain's economic progress than police terror. Relative prosperity has altered the nature of the working class threat to the industrial oligarchy. Many members of the economic élite have hopes of integrating the working class into the capitalist system by means of a reward-based economy. They feel that their hopes will be frustrated as long as the only method of expressing political preference open to workers is the strike.[14]

A further reason for the dissatisfaction of the economic oligarchy with the political forms of Francoism is that they constitute a major obstacle to further economic development. The most obvious way in which this is the case is with regard to Spain's relations with the EEC. Although certain industries would wither under the consequent competition, it is widely felt among the industrial community that continued development is dependent on entry into the Common Market. Already, 43% of Spain's consumer goods exports, 53% of raw materials and 56% of food exports go to the EEC.[15] Entry into Europe requires democratization. A growing number of economists in Spain are also convinced that the health of the economy necessitates an expansion of the public sector in order to finance a more adequate infrastructure. The necessary fiscal reform would only be possible within a democratic structure.[16]

Thus, a situation has arisen in which the traditional pressure of intellectuals, students, workers and peasants for a liberalization in Spain is now being reinforced by similar pressure from sectors once thought to be within the régime. In a sense, the function of Carlos Arias has been to try to adjust the régime's political forms to the changed situation. In almost every respect, he has failed. The bunker has managed to block reform and in doing so intensified the crisis.

It was in an attempt to molify the bunker that Arias became involved in the famous clash with Mgr. Añoveros, the Bishop of Bilbao. On 24 February 1974, he issued a pastoral letter appealing for recognition of the cultural and linguistic identity of the Basque people. He was accused of making subversive attacks on national unity. Arias was eventually forced to make a humiliating retreat on the issue and succeeded merely in accelerating the Church's withdrawal from the orbit of the régime forces, described in chapter three by Norman Cooper. This, and the execution of the anarchist, Salvador Puig-Antich, in the face of an international outcry, destroyed the credibility of the liberalizing operation. The attempt to adapt Spain's institutional framework to social realities seemed to be working in one sphere only – the relaxation of censorship by the Minister of)nformation, Pío Cabanillas. The reaction of the ultras was rapid. On 28 April 1974, José Antonio Girón, an old-guard Falangist, attacked Cabanillas and the other relatively liberal member of Arias' cabinet, the Minister of Finance, Antonio Barrera de Irimo.[17]

This *Gironazo* was only the most celebrated of a whole barrage of attacks made by figures of the ultra-right throughout 1974 on those who were trying to give the régime a face-lift. The verbal offensive was accompanied by a series of solid triumphs. On 13 June, the 'liberal' Chief of Staff, Manuel Díez Alegría, was removed from his post. On 15 June, when Arias announced his scheme for political associations, it was qualified by an announcement that they would not alter the permanent spirit of the Franco régime. The most savage attack of all preceded the greatest triumph of all. On 27 September, Blas Piñar, the most vocal member of the bunker, launched a virulent tirade against Arias from his magazine, *Fuerza Nueva*. Then in October, the ultras had gained sufficient influence with Franco himself to precipitate the dismissal of Pío Cabanillas, on the grounds that he had opened up the press and the media to the 'reds'.

It was precisely this victory of the ultras which showed up the real crisis of the régime. For it convinced many within the régime that they must opt for reform if they were to guarantee their own survival and it convinced many of the economic oligarchy that there was little future in the régime as it stood. The immediate consequences showed the extent to which the odds are weighed in favour of an evolution towards some kind of bourgeois democracy. The most important development was the resignation in sympathy with Cabanillas by Barrera de Irimo. As ex-president of the Spanish subsidiary of ITT, he could be seen as an excellent barometer of opinion within the financial community. Indeed, the stock market plunged immediately. This unprecedented resignation by a minister of Franco was followed by a major withdrawal from important posts in the civil service by the conservative Christian Democrats of the *Tácito* group.

Thus, a situation was emerging during 1974 as a result of which significant sectors of the Spanish oligarchy were coming to emulate the traditional opposition demand for democracy. During the spring, there were virtually open meetings between prominent industrialists and financiers and figures from the tolerated opposition. One of these meetings took place in the Hotel Ritz in Barcelona; the other was at the home of Joaquín Garrigues at Aravaca near Madrid. Garrigues has significantly resigned his many company directorships in order to devote his efforts to the creation of a political party. This activity on what is popularly called the 'civilized right' has coincided with a major move towards unity on the left. It all seemed to coincide with the Communist Party conviction, analyzed in chapter six, that the bourgeoisie would support the peaceful transition from the outmoded political forms of Francoism to a more advanced bourgeois democratic régime. It is worth noting that from the beginning of Franco's fatal illness to the handing-over of the headship of state to Juan Carlos, the value of shares on the Spanish stock market rose by seven per cent.[18]

This then is the nature of the crisis in Spain. The chapters of this book attempt to show how the forces of the régime and their opponents arrived at the present situation. They can only serve as possible indicators of future development. The crisis of the régime has created a coincidence of interest between part of the economic oligarchy and the opposition. But if history should be on their side in the advance towards democracy, it must be remembered that the members of the bunker, entrenched in the Army and the forces of order, have access to superior firepower. The crisis will have to be resolved by Juan Carlos.

He faces a interesting dilemma. There is much to be said for the benefits of democratization and by opting boldly for such a solution, Juan Carlos would be assured of wide support and would have a good chance of isolating the bunker. Yet if he were to do so, he would be denying the purpose of his inheritance and his training – the continuation of the Francoist dictatorship. Even assuming a will to encourage reform, something Juan Carlos has still to show, success for the monarchy depends largely on its ability to seem politically neutral. As Blas Piñar has recently declared: 'this is no monarchical restoration but the installation of a new Francoist monarchy which has no other thought behind it than the Nationalist victory in the Civil War'.[19] Franco destroyed any neutrality Juan Carlos might enjoy just as he undermined the monarchy's other two attributes of continuity and legitimacy, by excluding it from Spain for forty years and by his temerity in nominating his own royal successor.[20] It remains to be seen whether Juan Carlos can break out of the dilemma. It would be an unwise king who chose retrograde solutions at a time when Spanish capitalists are itching to get into Europe.

Notes

1. The phrase was coined by 'Luis Ramírez', 'Morir en el bunker' in *Horizonte Español 1972* Vol. 1 (Paris 1972).
2. *ABC* 20 May 1975.
3. *ABC* 5 June 1975.
4. Joaquín Bardavío, *La crisis: historia de quince días* (Madrid 1974) pp. 25-6.
5. *ABC* 2 April 1970.
6. *La Vanguardia* 25 December; *Ya* 26 December 1973.

7. *Washington Post* 27 December 1973; *Le Monde* 5-8 January 1974; Bardavío, *Op. cit.* pp. 111-6.
8. *La Vanguardia* 13 February 1974.
9. For Arias-Navarro's previous career, see *Mundo* 5 January 1974.
10. Charles F. Gallagher, Spain, *Development & The Energy Crisis* (American Universities Field Staff Report, AUFS West Europe series, Vol. VIII No. 11) (New York 1973).
11. This concept is developed in some detail in Eduardo Sevilla & Salvador Giner, 'Absolutismo despótico y dominación de clase: el caso de España' in *Cuadernos de Ruedo Ibérico* No. 43-5, 1975.
12. Amando de Miguel, *Sociolgía del franquismo* (Barcelona 1975) pp. 47, 59
13. Juan Martínez Alier, *La estabilidad del latifundismo* (Paris 1968) pp. 131-47.
14. Cf. Fernando Claudín, 'Dos concepciones de la vía española al socialismo' in *Horizonte Español 1966* Vol. 2 (Paris 1966).
15. *Cambio 16* No. 202, 20 October, No. 209, 8 December 1975.
16. Ramón Tamames, *Un proyecto de democracia para el futuro de España* (Madrid 1975) pp. 41-2; *Cambio 16* No. 203 27 October 1975.
17. José Oneto, *Arias entre dos crisis* (Madrid 1975) pp. 85-92.
18. Based on figures in *Cambio 16* thoughtout October and November 1975.
19. *Cambio 16* No. 206 17 November 1975.
20. Rafael Calvo Serer, 'Juan Carlos après son père?' in *Le Monde* 29 January 1974; José Luis Aranguren, *La cruz de la monarquí española actual* (Madrid 1974) *passim*.

Preface

Earlier versions of some of the chapters in this volume were read at a conference on Franco's Spain held at the Graduate School of Contemporary European Studies, University of Reading on 16-17 December 1974. The conference attracted many visitors and the debates which took place during its sessions were of considerable value to the scholars concerned. Nevertheless, this book does not constitute the proceedings of that conference so much as the long-term fruition of the weekly graduate seminars on Spain since 1939 held at the Graduate School between 1972 and 1975. After the assassination of Admiral Carrero Blanco in December 1973 and the consequent disarray of Franco's plans for his succession, the notion grew that the time had come for a serious study of the evolution and decline of the francoist regime. The intention was for a book which broke with current fashion by being neither a day-to-day narration of the doings of the Madrid government nor a biographical study of the Dictator. Rather it was hoped to bring together much monographic research in progress on various aspects of the regime and the opponents to it. That is why the book is divided into two parts: the first deals with the various components of the reactionary alliance which won the Civil War and with the economic and social policies that they have pursued; the second deals with the groups excluded from the narrow circles of power and who, in one way or another, have tried to oppose or change the regime.

When members and guest speakers of the seminar were approached with this conception of a collective work, they greeted it with enthusiasm. The conference was a useful method of getting all the authors together to test the results and discrepancies of their work before a wider audience. In that sense, it was a great success. I would like, therefore, to take this opportunity to thank a number of people who contributed to that success and to the eventual appearance of the book, without for that reason wishing to implicate them in the book's shortcomings:– Professor Hugh Thomas, Chairman of the Graduate School, for his support; Mrs. Pat Sales and Mrs. Pat Tucker for comforting words at moments of apparently impending disaster; Teresa Lawlor and Irene Cunningham for help in correcting often indecipherable proofs; Hartmut Heine for preparing the index and many friends and colleagues – particularly those in Spain – for their continuous encouragement.

Queen Mary College,
December 1975

Part I   The Régime

1

The Falange: An analysis of Spain's Fascist Heritage

HERBERT RUTLEDGE SOUTHWORTH

Most studies of fascism in Spain are marred by the failures to furnish the reader with a clear, general idea of what is meant by fascism.[1] I shall, therefore, before dealing with the subject of fascism in Spain, define fascism as it is considered in this chapter. There exist a goodly number of definitions of fascism, ranging from that of Mussolini, the founder,[2] through the significant appraisal of Dimitrof pronounced at the 13th Plenary Session of the Executive Committee of the Third Internationals,[3] to that recent one by the German professor, Ernst Nolte.[4] Fascism, for the purpose of this chapter, is defined as follows:

> Fascism is that manifestation of capitalism which made its appearance, within the geographical limits of Western and Central Europe and within the temporal limits of that period which began with the Russian Revolution and ended with the decolonization struggles that followed the Second World War, in the form of a modern, highly organized attempt to save the menaced capitalist structure in certain vulnerable countries through the subversion of the revolutionary élan of the workers, channelling this élan away from the class struggle and toward an enterprise of class collaboration, necessarily and inevitably debouching into an adventure of imperialist conquest.

Fascism is not one of the great social and political inventions of our time, but merely an ephemeral solution to a capitalist crisis, severely limited to certain countries and to a precise moment of history.[5] Such solutions for the crises of capitalist society are a constant in the history of this century, and indeed before. To diminish social tension and promote class collaboration, the political thinkers of the possessing classes are forever obliged to advance new ideas (or old ideas with new names) to persuade the mass of the workers that a solution to the social crisis of the day has been finally

1

discovered. Thus, in the United States, the 'New Deal' of Roosevelt, the 'New Frontier' of Kennedy, the 'New Society' of Johnson, or in France, the Gaullist programme of *participation* or *concertation*, Edgar Fauré's proposal for a 'Nouveau Contrat Social', have all been attractively packaged concepts aimed at solving the problems posed by the class struggle. Fascism, in its day and in its place, was just such a fugitive solution. This is not to say that the US or French programmes referred to above are fascist programmes, but rather that fascism played a similar role in the class struggle of its own time and place. These are all formulae conceived by elements of, or aspirants to, the possessing classes, which are intended to cope with the crisis of the hour and diminish the ferocity of the class struggle and achieve a maximum of class collaboration.

Fascism in Spain was just such a political movement, brought to birth by the class struggles of its epoch. From the basic doctrinal texts of Spanish fascist leaders, an outline of the proposed seizure of the Spanish State by the Spanish fascists has been constructed. The first phase of this programme was *the formation of the movement*. It had to have a national organization, form leaders and militants. It had to establish bases for propaganda, through meetings and printed matter (handbills, pamphlets and newspapers). It had to find sources for financing. These were activities common to all political groups with national ambitions in Spain. One difference between Spanish fascists and more traditional Spanish political movements lay in the narrow gamut of the methods that would be employed to organize the movement. These were three: 1. violence and direct action; 2. youth; and 3. ultra-nationalist propaganda. The prototype of a pre-Civil War Spanish fascist would be an excited young man, brawling in the streets and shouting fiery nationalist slogans. [6]

After this first phase of the plan had been completed, after the movement had been organized, the second phase, *the conquest of the State*, would be undertaken. This State was to be a totalitarian State, each Spaniard was to be situated in the place where he could best serve this State. The totalitarian State was to be solidly anchored on the rock of Spanish unity. For the founders of Spanish fascism, Spain was disunited, territorially, politically and socio-economically. The Spanish fascist movement, in the process of conquering the State, would unify the country.

Spain was to be unified *territorially*. This meant the strengthening of the central power in Madrid, and the ruthless suppression of the movements for regional autonomy in Catalonia, the Basque country and Galicia.

Spain was to be unified politically. This meant that there would be no more political parties; there would be no Left, no Right, no

2

Centre; there would be no effective parliament; there would be but the fascist movement, embodying the totality of the political energies of the country.

Spain was to be unified socio-economically. The class war would be outlawed and a new era of class collaboration would be ushered in. The existing trade-unions, of both marxist and anarcho-syndicalist inspiration, would be abolished, and national-syndicalist 'vertical' unions would be formed to take their place. A worker would then be closer to the owner of his factory than he would be to the workers in another factory. All international bonds uniting the workers would be sundered.

But finally what differentiated the Spanish fascists from other elements on the Right side of Spanish politics, from Dr Albiñana, an excited nationalist who led his uniformed youths into street battles; from Gil Robles, the Catholic spokesman, who opposed the class struggle with imitations of Nuremberg rallies and a Christian-fascist vocabulary; from Calvo Sotelo, the monarchist leader, who fought against regional autonomy with the contraband *afrancesadas* ideas of *Action Française* brought back from his Paris exile, was the specific purpose for which the Spanish fascists employed violence, youth and ultra-nationalist propaganda, the specific purpose for which they sought a totalitarian State for a nation unified territorially, politically and socio-economically: *to subvert the revolutionary élan of the Spanish masses into an imperialist adventure.* Dr Albiñana did not dream of a new Spanish empire; Gil Robles had no intention of expanding the frontiers of Spain; Calvo Sotelo did not attempt to seduce the workers of Spain, but to crush them. The difference between the Spanish conservative solution of the capitalist crisis and that of the Spanish fascists lies in the programme of imperial expansion.

Fascist movements never knew consistent successes in countries other than Italy and Germany. The history of Spanish fascism is the story of the Spanish movements which developed in *imitation* of Italian Fascism and German National Socialism.

Fascism never knew success in the four European countries with colonial empires: England, France, Holland and Belgium, although there were fascist movements in all these countries which sought to conquer the State.

In Spain, the fascist movement never gained control of the State, but the Spanish fascist movement did know successes and conquests unrealized in any other country except Italy and Germany. Cannot we, therefore, conclude that there existed something potentially fascist, something inherently favourable to fascism, in the political background of Italy and Germany – and also Spain – something which was lacking in the colonial powers? This element can be

3

identified as regrets for lost glories, nostalgia for past greatness. This factor was present in the political life of Italy, Germany and Spain; and it was lacking, and for good reason, in the political life of the European colonial powers.

It is an easily documented fact that countries which have lost empires, whilst neighbouring countries have kept theirs (or won new empires), suffer for long periods in trying to accommodate spiritually and psychologically to their new and lessened dimensions. The humiliation of the defeat of 1898 at the hands of the young American republic weighed on the Spanish soul. A generation of Spanish writers and intellectuals was called 'The generation of 1898'. The man who most influenced the beginnings of Spanish fascism was not of that broken generation, but a son of 1898, the political philosopher, José Ortega y Gasset. He was fifteen years old in 1898 and was thus branded with the mark of Cuba in his youth. In 1921 he wrote a book entitled *Invertebrate Spain*. It was still another inquest into the subject that was fascinating Spanish intellectuals: Spanish decadence.

The violent young ideologues of Spanish fascism, Ernesto Giménez Caballero, Ramiro Ledesma Ramos and José Antonio Primo de Rivera, all had known in their formative years, the profound influence of this political thinker, Ortega y Gasset. It was from reading his essays that they concluded that only through a foreign policy of great dimensions could a country hope for a fruitful interior development; it was from his books that they learned to associate territorial losses with national decadence. Before the melancholy picture which he drew of a disintegrating and disunited 'invertebrate Spain', these young men reacted with hallucinations of a new Spanish Empire.

Ernesto Gimenez Caballero – he called himself a 'grandson of 1898' – wrote a book in 1932 entitled *Genio de España,* in which he chided his master, Ortega y Gasset, for having the political behaviour of a magpie, chanting his religious panic in Geneva, at the League of Nations, but laying his eggs in the fascist nest. *Genio de España* was built around the symbolism of 1898; each loss of Spanish territory through the centuries was an 1898. The first 1898 of Giménez Caballero was in 1648, the Peace of Munster, by which the Spanish Empire first lost territory; in the sixth 1898, that of 1713, Gibraltar was lost; in the twelfth, the real 1898, Cuba, the Philippines, Puerto Rico. There was a thirteenth 1898, the 1930 Pact of San Sebastián, where elements of the Spanish Left and the Spanish Republicans agreed to grant an autonomy statute to Catalonia.

Giménez Caballero accepted Ortega's analysis of Spanish history,

4

but refused Ortega's dismal conclusions. Whereas Ortega was saddened by what he foresaw in Spain's future, his disciple Giménez Caballero optimistically perceived a turning back in the path ahead. He prophesied that the thirteenth 1898 – the Pact of San Sebastián – would be the last 1898 and that now Spain would take the fascist road, the road that led back to the Empire.[8]

The foremost ideologue of Spanish fascism was Ramiro Ledesma Ramos. In 1935, after he had left the *Falange* movement, but not his fascist faith, he wrote a book, essential for any understanding of Spanish fascism, *Discurso a las juventudes de España*. This work, like Giménez Caballero's *Genio de España,* was inspired by meditations on Spanish decadence. Ledesma Ramos, like Giménez Caballero, accepted Ortega's pessimistic analysis of the last three hundred years of Spanish history, and, like Giménez Caballero, he rejected Ortega's vision of the future. Spain was not decadent, he proclaimed. Spain had been defeated in battle. To redress this situation, it was but necessary to vanquish the enemy, victorious for three hundred years.

'But if the interior victory should take place', he wrote, 'if Spain should overcome its present crisis in a manner favourable to its national recovery, then the international perspectives would be limitless. Spain would dare all, and it could dare all. To recover Gibraltar. To unite in a single destiny the whole Peninsula, unified . . . with the great Portuguese people. To trace a wide line of African expansion (all of the North of this continent from the Atlantic to Tunisia has buried many Spanish illusions and a great deal of Spanish blood). To carry out an economic and cultural rapprochment with the great Hispanic bloc of our America. To imagine for Europe itself a continental order, firm and just . . .'[9]

No one has expressed more clearly or more cynically the basic programme of Spanish fascism than did Giménez Caballero in a footnote to a new 1938 edition of *Genio de España.*

'There has existed in the world but one effective system of overcoming this eternal war of the classes. This is to translate the social struggle to a different plane, to remove it from the national to the international scene. The poor and the rich of a nation can get together only when both are decided to attack other peoples or lands where wealth and power exist – to be shared by all the attackers. The feeling of *social equality,* which is at the base of all class struggle, is overcome only by carrying this equality into the attack against other countries which are unequal to ourselves.'[10]

The need for an atmosphere of past and lost glories in the development of fascist movements has been mentioned above. There is another indispensable element for fascist growth: *the favourable*

5

conjuncture. In order for a fascist movement to conquer the State, it is not only necessary that the conservative possessing classes be genuinely frightened of the possibility that the Left seize control of the State, it is also necessary that these possessing classes have lost confidence in the political efficacy of the political groups which have in the past defended their interests. This postulate must be kept in mind in order to understand the vicissitudes that accompanied the Spanish fascist movement in its course toward the Conquest of the State.

We shall now observe the attempts of the Spanish fascists to organize their movement. The first attempt took place in February 1931, when eleven young men, among them Giménez Caballero and Ledesma Ramos, met in an ill-furnished, badly-lighted room in Madrid and signed a manifesto ambitiously but correctly called 'La Conquista del Estado'.[11] During the seven or eight months that followed, this small group published a weekly newspaper, fought in the streets, tried to get their new ideas before the public. Their weekly publication, *La Conquista del Estado,* was frequently seized by the police of the new Republic and Ledesma Ramos and some of his comrades spent at one time ten days in jail. The Spanish Right was disoriented, but it had no funds available for the Spanish fascist movement. In June, *La Conquista del Estado* cut down the number of its pages from six to four.[12] When Ledesma Ramos called upon the internationally known Catalan financier, Francisco Cambó, in Madrid's Ritz Hotel to talk about money, the rich man thought the postal employee to be in possession of 'a harsh, dangerous theory'.[13]

In the summer of 1931, another young man, Onésimo Redondo, formed a fascist group in Valladolid, *La Junta Castellana de Actuación Hispánica.* In the pages of the Junta's weekly, *Libertad,* Redondo called upon the youth of Spain to take up arms for the social revolution and for a 'great Spain'.[14]

In October 1931, these two groups fused into a new fascist movement called *Juntas de Ofensiva Nacional-Sindicalista.* The Spanish fascists now had a name for their ideology: National-Syndicalism, a name as Spanish as National-Socialism was German. They had an emblem: the yoke and the arrows. They had a slogan: For the Fatherland, Bread and Justice. But they had very few members and sympathizers, very little money. Their activities were constantly harrassed by the republican-socialist government. In Madrid the J.O.N-S had barely twenty-five members in 1932 and could not pay the hundred pesetas monthly rent to maintain its headquarters.[15] Onésimo Redondo was forced to flee to Portugal, where he lived with his family from August 1932 until November 1933, at which time the electoral campaign permitted his return to Spain.[16] During

6

the two years of republican-socialist government, Spanish fascism stagnated. The Spanish fascist movement was not yet organized.

However, a new impulse was to be given to Spanish fascism. During the 1933 electoral campaign, José Antonio Primo de Rivera, son of the former dictator, announced the creation of a new fascist movement, *Falange Española* (the initials 'FE', which also spelt 'faith' in Spanish, were originally the initials of *'Fascismo Español'*).[17] The statement which doubtless most touched his Right-wing audience at the founding meeting on October 29, 1933, on the eve of the elections after two years of Republican and Socialist rule, was the following:

> And we wish, finally, if this programme is to be achieved at some moment by violence, that we shall not draw back before the prospect of violence. For who has said – in speaking of 'everything except violence' – that the supreme hierarchy of moral values resides in being amiable? Who has said that when they insult our feelings, rather than react as men, we are obliged to be amiable? It is very well, yes indeed, that the dialectic serve as a first instrument of communication. But there is no other dialectic admissible than the dialectic of fists and pistols when offense is given to justice or to the fatherland.[18]

Primo de Rivera's social position – he was a Spanish grandee – gave considerable impetus to fascist activities in Spain. Primo de Rivera himself was elected to the Cortes, but not as a fascist; he was a conservative candidate in a conservative district. Early in 1934, the *Falange Española* group joined forces with the *JON-S*, but this marriage of two small movements did not greatly increase fascist strength in Spain. In fact, a number of Rightist personalities, attracted to the *Falange* by the Primo de Rivera name, now abandoned the new coalition, *Falange Española de las JON-S.*[19]

In October 1934, a general strike took place in several large cities; in Barcelona, regional autonomists proclaimed a Catalan Republic in a federal Spain, and an armed insurrection broke out in Asturias. The Asturias revolt was violently put down by the military, with the aid of Moroccan troops from Africa. Leaders of the Left parties and the labour movements either fled the country or were imprisoned. Thousands of militant Leftists and trade-unionists were jailed.

It must be underlined here that the Spanish fascists supported the Right-Centre government in putting down the strikes and revolts of October 1934.[20] In making this choice, in constituting the Phalangists into auxiliaries of the brutal repression, in accepting this traditional method of capitalism in dealing with workers' revolts, the Spanish Phalanx, being an as yet unorganized movement, did itself a disservice. In the Cortes debates which followed, Primo de Rivera sought to set things aright, insisting that for the Spanish fascists the 'separatist' demands of the Catalans were far more dangerous for

7

Spain than were the social demands of the Asturian workers. [21]

It is frequently asserted that capitalists are but waiting to enforce fascism on a prostrate people. This theory is not borne out by Spanish events of 1934. After October, the Spanish working class organizations were badly beaten and the Red Menace was under control, but the resulting situation was *not* favourable to the development of fascism in Spain. After the 'victory' of the army over the workers in Asturias, the Spanish Right felt not fear of the workers but confidence in its own strength. The owners of Spain, the bankers, the landholders and the industrialists, with the military and the clergy, felt at this time no urgent need to call upon young Primo de Rivera and accept his offer of 'fists and pistols'.

The year in which José Antonio Primo de Rivere placed his own mark on the Spanish fascist movement was 1935. Early in that year, his chief rival, Ledesma Ramos, separated from the *Falange* and went his own fascist way. The movement set up its specialized branches, precursors of a totalitarian organization: a student syndicate, a women's auxiliary, an imitation of a trade-union. The *Falange* held meetings in Madrid, where, reportedly, great crowds came to hear the new evangel. When Primo de Rivera spoke in Salamanca, Miguel de Unamuno walked down the street with him to the meeting place, listened to the speech and then had luncheon with the fascists. [22] Young Primo was invited to address Madrid's industrial and commercial community at the Círculo Mercantil. Some came out of curiosity, some to hear the son of the former dictator, others to hear the fascist doctrine. [23] But converts were few.

The harsh fact is that the Spanish Right during 1934 and 1935 looked with indulgent indifference on the strange behaviour of this young aristocrat, and made their financial contributions to other political causes. On 18 January 1935, the Salamanca Phalangist leader, Francisco Bravo, had written to Primo de Rivera:

> As for our Salamanca enterprise, you cannot imagine the hostility that surrounds us . . . We have no powerful friend to give us a helping hand. The centre and its upkeep costs us two hundred pesetas a month and where shall we find them? . . . the people with money, selfish in their own interests, will not give us a penny. [24]

Primo de Rivera kept the movement going with personal funds, occasional contributions from his wealthy friends, and with a monthly subvention from Mussolini. [25] Efforts of the *Falange* to find the money for a daily newspaper were failures. [26] A six-page weekly was launched on 21 March 1935. It was harrassed by the Right-Centre government, reduced from six pages to four, and then suspended by the authorities on 4 July. It was not allowed to publish again until 31 October. Another example of the political isolation of

8

the Spanish Phalanx: its Seville headquarters were kept closed by the conservative government for 442 days, despite repeated démarches by Deputy Primo de Rivera.[27]

During the five years between February 1931 and February 1936, the Spanish fascists had not succeeded in organizing their movement. Any honest observer must today admit that the fascists in Spain had fared no better under a Right-Centre régime than they had under the Republican-Left government. At no time during this period had the conjuncture been favourable for fascism in Spain.

New elections for the national legislature, the Cortes, were to be held on 16 February 1936. In spite of the newly-found Popular Front unity of the Leftist and Republican parties, the Right, captained by the Catholic leader, Gil Robles, was supremely confident of victory. The monarchist forces had also found new vigour with the return of Calvo Sotelo from exile in France, where he had absorbed Maurrasian ideas.[28] Calvo Sotelo, a former minister of the dictator Primo de Rivera, disliked the son of his dictator, and the feeling was reciprocated.[29] Gil Robles thought the young Primo de Rivera lacking in political ambition.[30] The Spanish Rightist coalition refused to give to the Spanish fascists the safe seats in the Cortes that would have, through the parliamentary immunity of its leaders, permitted the movement to survive and prosper from 16 February to 18 July 1936.[31] Gil Robles spent money on a scale unknown in previous Spanish elections. There was little money available for Spain's fascists.

On the morning of election day, if the Spanish Right wasted a thought on Spain's fascists, it was one of irritated tolerance. This attitude was to undergo an immediate change, for the *Frente Popular,* to the consternation of the Rightist forces, won the elections. Political weight shifted heavily and quickly from Gil Robles to Calvo Sotelo, and on to the Phalanx. Now was the great moment come for the Spanish fascists. For the first time in Spain the conjuncture was favourable for fascist development. The conservative elements were panic-stricken by the Popular Front victory, and had, in the course of forty-eight hours, lost their faith in the capacity of the political groups which had in the past defended their interests. Catholic youths who but a few days before had been screaming '*Jefe! Jefe! Jefe!*' at every appearance of Gil Robles, now abandoned in droves the catholic youth organization,[32] the JAP, and for the first time viewed with interest and wonder the fascist solution in 'the dialectic of fists and pistols', for their 'justice' and their 'Patria' had been insulted by the victory of the Left.

But this opportunity was to be lost for the Phalanx. Even that small progress made toward organization in 1935 was now undone

9

by the Popular Front government, which proceeded to suppress the Phalangist press, close its centres and headquarters, and imprison its chiefs. On 14 March, the leadership in Madrid, including Primo de Rivera, were arrested. Under these circumstances, the Phalanx could not take advantage of the favourable conjuncture and when the Civil War broke out in the Peninsula on 18 July 1936, what little fascist organization had been achieved in Spain from February 1931 to July 1936 was in a shambles. The chief activity of the Spanish fascists, during the period between the electoral victory of the *Frente Popular* and the outbreak of the Civil War, was street fighting, anti-Communist propaganda and political assassination.[33] Such activities had their value, for they kept alive the theme being propagated in the Cortes by Gil Robles and Calvo Sotelo, that Spain was already in a state of chaos and anarchy; and it showed to Spain's conservatives, young and old alike, that the *Falange* was ready to protect their interests against the Oriental Menace from Moscow.

In April, after the deposition of President Alcalá-Zamora, the Madrid catholic organ *Ya* asked its readers their preference for a new president. To the probable surprise of the editors, the Catholic Gil Robles came in fourth, with J. A. Primo de Rivera at the top of the list.[34] This radical change in the Rightist point of view is exemplified by a run-off (new?) election held in Cuenca Province in May. The Right wanted to consider this a new election, with the consequent right to name new candidates. As the first name on their new ballot, the conservatives wanted Primo de Rivera, the very man no responsible Rightist had wanted in February. Had he been on the ballot, and had he been elected, Primo de Rivera would probably have been released from prison. The Popular Front Government refused to accept this manoeuvre, but there is little doubt that, nevertheless, thousands of Rightist votes went to the imprisoned Primo de Rivera in the Cuenca balloting on 3 May.[35]

A military conspiracy to overthrow the *Frente Popular* Government by force began almost immediately after the elections. Primo de Rivera, despite his imprisonment easily kept himself aware of the military plans. Up until the actual outbreak of the revolt the issue was debated by members of the *Junta Política* of the *Falange*: Should Spain's fascists join the military in the uprising? Primo de Rivera came from a military family and he distrusted the social aims of any insurrection fomented by the Spanish army that he knew. Late in April he wrote a long letter addressed to the military in general, calling upon them to save Spain from the Red Menace, which came from without the country, a fact that in itself, he told them, justified the intervention of the army against this exterior enemy. But he

10

pointed out that the military institution had no right to use its force on behalf of 'a new reactionary policy' or 'for the profit of narrow interests' or 'to come to the relief of an economic organization that is in many ways unjust.'[36]

Primo de Rivera's continuing hesitations concerning possible collaboration with the military conspirators are seen in an order he addressed to *Falange* leaders in the provinces on June 24. It should be pointed out that the twenty-seventh and final point of the Phalangist programme stated that the movement would fight alone 'with the forces subject to our discipline' and continued: 'Only in the final battle for the conquest of the State will the leadership accept the necessary collaboration, but always on condition that our supremacy be assured.' Primo de Rivera feared that this principle risked being forgotten in the military insurrection.

'The participation of the *Falange* in one of these premature and ingenuous projects', he told his lieutenants, 'could constitute a most heavy responsibility and would bring about *its total disappearance even in the case of victory.*'[37]

He also wrote prophetically:

> Let the comrades reflect to what point it is offensive for the Phalanx to be asked to take part as a figurant in a movement that is not going to lead to the establishment of the national syndicalist State, that is not going to represent the dawning of the immense task of national reconstruction outlined in our twenty-seven points, but is to reinstate a conservative bourgeois mediocrity (of which Spain has known so many examples), garnished for greater mockery, with the choreographic accompaniment of our Blue Shirts.[38]

Nevertheless, despite these misgivings, inevitably the Phalanx was pushed into collaboration with the military plotters. Like them, the Phalangists wanted to overthrow the government which had taken such decisive steps against them, and given the sociological composition of the Spanish electorate, and the evident determination of the Popular Front deputies of the new Cortes to eliminate *caciquismo* from Spain's political life (as evidenced by the sessions of the *Comisión de Actas*), the overthrow of this government was not likely to take place in the voting booths any time soon. The only apparent means by which the *Falange* leaders could leave their prison cells in the near future lay in the success of the military conspiracy. Thus it was that on 29 June instructions were given by Primo de Rivera to territorial and provincial chiefs of the Spanish Phalanx concerning the manner in which they might collaborate with the military conspirators,[39] and on 17 July he placed himself and his fascist followers on the side of the rebellion in a manifesto.[40]

The Spanish fascists were unable to seize upon the opportunity

11

given them by the post-electoral turnabout of the conservative classes, and consolidate their organization during the five months that followed 16 February 1936. The *Falange* thus entered the Civil War in disarray, without having even completed the first phase of their political programme. But the Spanish fascists were now given what appeared to be a second chance.

In those provincial capitals where the military rebels were able to seize power during the first hours of the uprising, arms were immediately distributed to the Phalangist militants, an action due in great part to the liasion work carried out with the military during the weeks preceding the revolt by one of the few working class *jefes* of the *Falange*, Manuel Hedilla.[41] (On the other hand, in cities, especially Madrid, where the Republicans kept power, endless debates went on concerning the wisdom and legality of arming the workers.) Once the fronts were stablized after the first days of the insurrection, and some semblance of provisional government had been set up behind the Rebel lines, it became evident that a vast political void existed in Nationalist Spain. The electoral disaster of February had washed away the hopes of Gil Robles and his followers. Gil Robles was not even *persona grata* in the Rebel Zone. The adherents of Alfonsine monarchy aroused no popular enthusiasm. The two political formations which seemed to stand out in the territory controlled by the military were the Carlists and the Phalangists. But the followers of Don Carlos preached a rude dogma; proselytizing was difficult and probably not always desired. On the other hand, the Phalanx welcomed recruits, and workers caught behind the Insurgent lines found anonymity and an easy disguise by putting on a Blue Shirt of the *Falange*.

By December 1936, in provincial capitals under Rebel control, where, before the war, the Spanish fascists could not count a score of militants, *Falange* headquarters had enrolled thousands of dues-paying members. For the first time in its history, the Phalanx had members and money in the cash-box. Where before the war the Phalanx had rented a couple of rooms, it now 'owned' entire buildings. *Falange* leaders had automobiles and chauffeurs at their disposal.[42] For the first time, the Phalanx had a daily newspaper of its own, and not just one, but a score of them. For the first time now the *Falange* was being organized; it was realizing the first step on its march to the Conquest of the State, to the Conquest of the Empire.

But this movement which before the war had leaders and few members, now had members and few leaders. In June, Primo de Rivera had been transferred from the Cárcel Modelo in Madrid to a prison in Alicante, where he remained until he was shot by an execution squad on 20 November 1936. Most of the other members of the *Junta Política* were also in prison when the revolt broke out. Onésimo Redondo, jailed in Avila, was released by the triumphant military during the first hours of the insurrection, but he was killed in the fighting a few days later.[43] Ledesma Ramos who, despite his separation from the dominant fascist movement, remained a significant figure in Spanish fascism, was arrested in Madrid in August and executed on 29 October 1936.[44] The hierarchically important figures of the movement who slowly made their way to the Rebel capitals of Burgos and Salamanca were second rate and mediocre.

The *Falange's* lack of leaders of stature during the crucial months that followed the military outbreak was the result of two factors: first, the incapacity of Spanish fascism to effect an organization during the years of the peacetime Republic, and, secondly, the decision of the Popular Front government to destroy the movement after the 1936 elections. During the first weeks of the rebellion, no central Phalangist organization existed. Provincial chiefs, finding themselves for the first time with money and influence, tended to concentrate their labours in their local satrapies. But slowly a semblance of national headquarters was set up in Salamanca, and the Phalanx, with tens of thousands of new adherents, and constantly growing, could be considered to have carried out its primary task of organization.

The organization of the Spanish fascist movement was, after more than five years of effort, but the first step in the *Falange* programme. It had been achieved, but at a fatal cost; it had been achieved by means of a long civil war. It is instructive to note here that neither Mussolini nor Hitler had had to take recourse to such a drastic measure, merely to organize their movements. Two and a half years after Mussolini had founded the *fasci di combattimento* he had more than 300,000 followers. A year later he was Prime Minister. Mussolini enjoyed three and a half years of constant progress in which to organize, under an incompetent conservative government in which the owning classes progressively lost faith, and with the trade-unions 'still sufficiently active to frighten /but/ too weak for effective opposition',[45] that is, the conjuncture was favourable for his movement during his period of organization, as it had never been for the Spanish fascists. Mussolini never had to confront the Left in control of the government, as did the Spanish Phalanx.[46]

(Hitler's rise to power was slower than was that of Mussolini, but he also never encountered the resolute opposition that disrupted the progress of the Spanish Phalanx in the Spring of 1936. It is true that Hitler spent nine months in prison after the beerhall putsch of 1923,

13

but it must be plain to everybody today that the judges who sentenced him did not really try to break up his movement, as was the intention of the Spanish Popular Front in dealing with the Phalanx in 1936. When Hitler came out of prison in 1924, with the manuscript of *Mein Kampf* under his arm, he immediately set to work to complete the organization of his movement. 'The going was slow, but each year some progress was made; 39,000 members in 1926, 72,000 in 1927, 108,000 in 1928, 178,000 in 1929.' [47] In 1928, Hitler had a dozen men in the Reichstag. In 1923, ten years before he took power, he owned a daily newspaper, and as early as 1923, the Nazi movement was receiving large sums from industrialists. Even the economic crisis that followed 1929 helped Hitler, for the industrialists and the lumpenbourgeoisie saw in him a possible barrier to communism.)

The Phalanx' lack of first-class men permitted, in April 1937, a take-over of the movement in a manoeuvre carried out by Franco's brother-in-law, Ramón Serrano Suñer. Through a decree of unification, promulgated by Franco on 19 April, 1937, the Traditionalists (Carlists) and the Phalangists (and all the other political elements of the Rebel zone) were merged into a conglomerate called *Falange Española* Tradicionalista y de las JON-S. The Carlist and Phalangist dogmas were theoretically equal, but the *Falange* programme was decreed the basis of the New State – minus the 27th point which specifically forebade such conglomerations.

The *Falange* was now apparently on the road to the Conquest of the State. Everybody wore a Blue Shirt. *Falange* emblems – the Yoke and the Arrow – were on every wall, in every window. Everybody obligatorily gave the fascist salute. Every mouth echoed Phalangist slogans. When the Civil War ended, on 1 April 1939, any casual observer could justifiably have concluded that the Spanish fascists had now effectively conquered the State. This assumption would have been wrong. The Phalanx was indeed close to the Conquest of the State, but that victory was not yet won.

The basic tenet of Phalangism, as has been shown, was the subversion (persuasion?) of the revolutionary élan of the masses into an imperialist adventure. This conception of a solution to the problem of class warfare differed fundamentally from the classic repression of this revolutionary élan by the ruling classes. The Phalangist idea was built on the factor of national unity, indispensable for the imperialist adventure. Both Mussolini and Hitler had enjoyed this national unity. But Spanish fascism encountered on its road to the Conquest of the State obstacles which neither Italian nor German fascism ever knew. The only Spanish

14

political element favourable for fascism was the subjective one of nostalgia for the lost empire. The objective elements: the unpropitious climate for fascist organization, the electoral victory of the Popular Front and the consequent dismantling of the fragile fascist formation that existed, the outbreak of the disunifying civil war in which the Phalanx had to participate, the lack of Phalangist leadership which permitted the violently imposed Unification – all of these elements were unfavourable to Spanish fascism.

The Spanish Phalanx had not won the Civil War. The Civil War had been won by the conservative-reactionary elements that had owned Spain before the war. The revolutionary élan of the working masses had not been subverted in preparation for a great adventure; it had been bled to death on the field of battle and against the patio walls in the grey Castilian morning and in the desolate marches to exile. The social situation in Spain at the official end of the Civil War, on 1 April 1939, was comparable (if we except the economic ruin of the war), in the calculations of Spain's reactionary owning class, to that which had followed the military victory over the workers in the Asturian uprising of 1934. Nay, it was far better, for a whole generation of social protest had been wiped out in blood.

Every day of civil warfare had seen the Phalangist banners flying higher in the skies of Rebel Spain, and every day had seen the *Falange* farther away from *its* victory. The Phalanx programme of imperial conquest could not begin to be put into execution until the Spanish fascists had gained control of the State and unified the country, and three years of civil warfare between the classes and pitiless class repression had divided Spain into two camps of mutual hatred.

Had the *Falange* seized control of the State? In my opinion it had not and never did. By the Unification Decree, Francisco Franco had won ascendancy over the Spanish fascist movement, and Franco was not, intellectually, or by social class, a fascist. His relations were conservative relations; his ambitions for himself and for Spain were conservative ambitions. Yet he had been obliged, by the political bankruptcy of the conservative parties in February 1936, to exploit the possibilities of Spanish fascism, and to endow Spain with a totalitarian administration structured on the fascist model. Thus, when the Civil War ended, Spain had a totalitarian fascist administration, without fascist conquest of the State.

This situation was unfortunate for Spain's fascists, for the dread hour of destiny was approaching. If Spanish fascism was going to profit from the international political conjuncture, it was absolutely necessary that Spain be ready to march at the side of the Axis in the inevitable adventure that was to upset the European empires and

15

open the gates to their imperial successors.

Ramón Serrano Suñer, now the leading Phalangist personality, and Foreign Minister, was favourable to the enterprise of hazard,[48] and Franco, ever the opportunist, had not closed off his options in that direction. But the Civil War had not only left the country divided by hatred, it had left the economy in dire straits.[49] Agricultural production had fallen off badly; rail and other means of transport were in poor condition; the labour force had diminished. Any country in these conditions could hardly enter voluntarily into a war of European, perhaps world-wide, dimensions. If only Spain could have a respite of two or three years to repair the ravages of war and bind up the wounds of internal dissension, then it might be able to envisage taking up the march to imperial conquests, at the side of Nazi Germany and Fascist Italy. Serrano Suñer went to Italy in the summer of 1939 and received assurances that the Second World War for colonial redistribution would not break out in 1939.[50]

But Hitler had other ideas and the war did break out. As the battles raged, far from Spain, near the frontiers of the Soviet Union, Franco waited, and the hungry Spaniards listened to the mounting cries of 'Imperio! Imperio! Imperio!' Then came the Battle of France. Franco, profiting from the Falange organization, kept in high visibility, changed his declared position from 'neutrality' to 'non-belligerancy', occupied Tangier as the first step to Empire, and on the very day that Mussolini declared war on defeated France, dispatched a messenger to Hitler. Franco wrote to the Führer that he too was willing to enter the war on the side of the Nazis – on certain conditions: 1. that Spain's economy, its productive capacity greatly lowered because of three years of Republican resistance, be helped with supplies of wheat and petroleum products, its rolling stock replenished, its armament renewed, etc., and 2. that the Falange ambitions be realized, that Spain be given Morocco, the Oran region of Algeria, new territories in the Spanish Sahara hinterland, and an aggrandizement of its possessions on the coastal region of Spanish Guinea.[51]

Did Franco want to enter the Second World War? It is unlikely. He has never shown a taste for taking risks. But we cannot accept the argument that he did not overtly participate in the war, that he did not openly declare war, because of his 'will' to stay out of the war.[52] He did not have the means, without massive economic help, to enter the Second World War, had he had the 'will' to do so. The arguments which he presented to Hitler did not represent the wily artifices of a skilful gamester; these arguments were based on facts.

The reality of the situation was that Spain's economic structure had greatly suffered from the long Civil War and that Spain was a

16

politically divided country (not only because of the civil war, but also because of the savagery of the post-war Nationalist repression).[53] These were the facts and not the baseless arguments of a clever manipulator. They were not the results of Franco's 'will', but the results of three years of Republican resistance to Franco and to fascism. Franco's role was to protect the interests of Spain's (underdeveloped) capitalism, a role easy to define during the Civil War. The problem during the Second World War was more complex. Where lay the interests of Spain's possessing class? Was it not to recover from the Civil War and stay clear of the World War? However, in the case of an Axis victory, the economic forces represented by Franco had an interest to participate in the spoils of that victory, that is, in the realization of the *Falange* programme.[54] Franco, ever instinctively the opportunist, maintained the *Falange* to keep open an eventual option on joining the Axis.

For reasons which do not form an essential part of this essay, Hitler and Franco did not reach an agreement on Spanish participation in the fighting on the western front of the Second World War.[55] When Germany attacked the Soviet Union in the summer of 1941, Franco sent the Blue Division to the Russian front, as a symbol of his anti-Communist sentiments. But the great day of Phalangist decision came on 8 November, 1942, when the American and British forces landed in North Africa, on territory which, in the great colonial redistribution envisioned in Phalangist imagination, was to belong to Spain. This was the hour to react, now or never. Spain did not, *could not*, react to this occupation and with that Spanish silence disappeared once and for all time the dream of the Blue Phalangist Empire.

The watershed date of 8 November 1942 was not, of course, immediately apparent. But with each new retreat of the Axis forces – the encirclement of the German armies at Stalingrad, the Italo-German withdrawal from North Africa, the Allied advance into Italy, the deposition of Mussolini, the landing in Normandy, the Soviet offensive on Berlin, the execution of Mussolini, followed by the suicide of Hitler, and ending with the final surrender of the remnants of the Axis armies – it became increasingly clear to those who had seriously believed in the Phalangist Conquest of the State and the March on the Empire that all was lost.

The fulfilment of the Spanish fascist plan was never earnestly considered save as an action carried out in collaboration with the Italian and German fascist movements; its success, in the imaginings of its prophets, was always as a subsidiary, subsequent achievement to the earlier triumphs of the Italian and German programmes. The objective bases of Spanish fascism were thus

17

faulted from the beginning. Italian fascism sought a solution to Italian problems through Italian territorial expansion. German fascism sought a solution to German problems through German territorial expansion. Each was dependent essentially on its own power. When Mussolini attacked Ethiopia, he went in alone. When Hitler took the Rhineland, Austria and Czechoslovakia and began the Second World War, he acted independently. When Spain took Tangier, it was merely lapping up the crumbs under the table.

The Fascist Internationale never existed. Fascist governments were by nature competitors, not cooperators. The history of recent years has shown us that if in theory a Communist, or Socialist, Internationale is viable, its realization is nevertheless beset with enormous difficulties. Theoretically, a Fascist Internationale is impossible, its very existence is contrary to nature. Yet the Spanish fascists, from the beginning naively believed in the premise that Fascist Italy and Nazi Germany were one day going to help a fascist (*Jonsista*, Phalangist) Spain regain a colonial empire.

The Spanish historian, Angel Viñas, has presented us with a persuasive argument to show that Hitler did not decide to help Franco, on the night of 25-26 April 1936, in order to set up a fascist government in Spain, that Hitler did not make his decision to intervene in Spain for ideological reasons, but for 'strategic considerations'.[56]

Hitler, thinking of the Franco-Soviet Pact, wanted to neutralize Spain, so as not to have in Spain an unfriendly government, a government that might help France, on the day when Hitler struck at the Soviet Union.

There is no proof that Hitler wanted a fascist régime in Spain. It can be argued that no fascist government in Europe actually ever wanted another fascist (aggressive, ultra-nationalist) government in Europe. A competing fascist government limited the room for manoeuvring of each other fascist government. This situation can be seen in 1940 and 1941, when Franco offered to help in the attack on Gibraltar, on condition that he be recompensed with territory in North Africa, territory claimed at that same time by the Vichy French government. Mussolini also demanded a part of North Africa. And finally, Germany itself wanted facilities in Morocco, and even in Spanish territory.[57] And although the Spanish régime was nearer to the fascist model than was that of Vichy, Hitler did not let ideological considerations sway him in favour of Franco Spain. At the end, everybody lost, and it is worth observing that with the loss of all the colonies by the European powers, there is far less rivalry among them.

When Italian Fascism and German National-Socialism were

annihilated, Spanish National-Syndicalism (fascism) was emptied of its *raison d'être*. This conclusion is borne out by the fact that those intellectuals most thoroughly impregnated with Phalangist culture, such as Dionisio Ridruejo, Santiago Montero Díaz, Antonio Tovar, Pedro Laín Entralgo and others, during these decisive years signaled their awareness of the Phalangist ideological collapse by their gradual separation from the movement. [58]

These Phalangist intellectuals had no longer any hope, for they understood that Spanish fascism had now lost its last chance. They understood better than others the ephemeral nature of fascism, a solution for the crisis of a given moment, of that moment and of nothing more. Significant are the words of Enrique Sotomayor, young Secretary General of the Phalangist student organization, the SEU, spoken in November 1939, two years before he was to be killed on the Russian front:

> It is time to march! . . . In six years of struggle we have obtained that which God denied us for centuries: an occasion on which Spain can be definitely won or lost . . . Either the Revolution or the Empire. Left and Right throughout History. Today we are living in the possibility of gaining both enterprises at the same time. God is knocking now at our gates! The moment has come to raise in parallel the two banners and to follow after them. The watchword that brought us into war has sounded again. Now or Never! [59]

When the defeat of the Axis was written on the wall, the true believers in National-Syndicalism knew that 'Now' had passed them by forever, and that they must live with 'Never' for the rest of their lives.

We have now come to another difference between the fascist movements of Italy and Germany, and that of Spain. Spanish fascism was not wiped out in blood and fire as were the other two, who had more easily made the Conquest of the State, and who had been able resolutely to undertake the March on the Empire. Spanish fascism had never quite conquered the State and its March on the Empire was limited to the apologetic occupation of Tangier. Spanish fascism had no conquests to surrender. It had established a totalitarian State; it had created an artificially united Spain, through a civil war, followed by a pitiless repression; it had crushed the regional autonomy movements; it had outlawed the political parties and created a parody of parliament; it had wiped out the trade-unions. It had created a Phalangist bureaucracy, a fascist administration. This administration had no need for ideological content to perpetuate itself.

Mussolini was not overthrown by the Italian people; Hitler was not chased from power by the German people. They were dragged

19

down from power by a military defeat, inflicted by foreign armies. No such determined effort to bring down the fascist structure in Spain was ever attempted from without, unless we so assess the pious, ambiguous utterances at times heard from the conquerors of the war against fascism.[60] Neither the 1945 declaration of Potsdam concerning Spain, nor the statement of 4 April 1946, of Paris, London and Washington, condemning the Franco Government, nor the United Nations' resolution of December 1946, did more than leave in the hands of the unarmed Spanish people the formidable task of demolishing the solidly entrenched totalitarian (authoritarian?) régime.[61]

We have seen that when the Civil War ended in 1939, the owning classes of Spain, who had confirmed this ownership in winning the war, had no urgent need of the help of the FET y de las JON-S in keeping down the defeated Spanish workers. But, because the political vacuum in Rebel Spain had been filled by the Spanish fascists, and no other suitable political instrument was at hand, and because the international situation led many of the proprietary class to think of the possibility of a fascist Europe (in which the Phalanx could claim charter membership), the Phalanx and its totalitarian projects for organizing the control of the Spanish people were kept in place.

Now in 1945 the Second World War ended with a crushing defeat of the Axis Powers and the demolition of Fascism and Nazism. The Spanish fascist movement, though emptied of its ideological content, was left untouched, for it might still be of utility to the ruling class. The seekers of position, the holders of place, those who from 1937 on had formed the cadres of the Movement, continued to administer. Those who had dreamed of 'sweating the burnouse' in Marrakech were, after all, just as content to stay within the Peninsula and make the Spanish people sweat.

It is evident to any rational man that nobody in Spain really continued after 1945 to believe in the possible fulfilment of the programme of Spanish fascism. But although this programme had been inexorably abandoned by the forces of History, the unhappy fact that the morbid fascist tissue remaining in the Spanish body politic was not cauterized made possible in Spain the scenes of a useless tragedy that would be presented nowhere else in the world. No other fascist movement than the Spanish, having drawn so near to the Conquest of the State, having established its totalitarian State, its necessary conception of territorial, political and socio-economic unity, had then been left to wither away, its top lopped off by the grim reality of History, much as a giant cedar standing erect but nevertheless dead, incapable of growth, occupying space merely to

20

prevent a more vigorous plant from taking root. The validity of this figure of speech can be verified by the fact that for thirty years all other efforts at political plantation in the shade of the *Falange* have failed.

Epilogue

A review of these thirty years will show that each time that a timid effort has been made to recover a small part of the lost liberties of the Spanish people, the effort has slowly spent itself, leaving nothing, because the surgery necessary on the sick body politic of Spain has never been applied. Franco has remained in control, and his control of Spain has never harmed the primary interests of Spain's dominant class. Franco has announced 'changes' from time to time, manoeuvring in a narrow stretch of territory, but his 'changes' have changed little.

Franco and his backers made concessions to the post-war anti-fascist climate. The Spanish occupation of Tangier was ended. The fascist salute was no longer obligatory. An exercise in casuistry was launched to prove that the Franco State had never been 'totalitarian', that J. A. Primo de Rivera had never, never intended to set up a 'totalitarian' State, that the *Falange* had never been a 'fascist' movement. [62] The blue gradually faded from the Blue Shirts. The visible *Falange* was an embarrassment. The 'totalitarian' organization which the *Falange* had erected to control every facet of Spanish life, to guide the thoughts and acts of the very young, the adolescents, the students, the women, and so forth, little by little became obsolescent. These were not violently suppressed. They dried up. This happened in part because such groups were in competition with those of an older-rooted conservative organization, also adept at guiding thoughts and acts, the Catholic Church. Pressure from the Army and from the business-industrial community also had its effect. However, one Phalangist-inspired formation was kept alive, the *Sindicatos Verticales,* to keep a watchful eye on the working class.

Is fascism really dead in Spain? Or is it after all still alive? All efforts to change the Franco system from 1945 to 1975 have been brought to a halt, if not by the living force, then by the inertia, of the 'Movement', the *Falange*. The artificial unity imposed by the Phalangist ideologues during the Civil War, is still strangling Spanish life. It is symbolized in 1975 by: 1. opposition to regional autonomy, as seen in the violent war being carried out against the Basques, and to a lesser extent against the Catalans; 2. opposition to political parties, as evidenced by the recent failure to enact a Law of

21

Associations which would allow even a smidgin of free political thought; and 3. opposition to any recognition of the existence of the class struggle, as shown by the fact that although the grim sentences given to the Carabanchel Ten in 1973 were lowered in February 1975, a worker can still spend six years in a Spanish prison merely for organizing discussions on labour problems outside the official structure of the government trade-unions, of Phalangist origin.

Is fascism dead in Spain? Or is it after all still alive? Juan J. Linz wrote in 1970 of 'the bureaucratized and lifeless structures' of the Movement.[63] The tree is dead, but it is still standing. It was dead in 1945. If no valiant woodsman has come to chop it down, it is because the owners of the property are afraid of what might grow up in its stead. But if the owners of the property are afraid to cut down the tree, it is certain that the vital and courageous forces of Spain which are more and more in rebellion against the shackling, fraudulent unity of the *Falange*, who are seeking regional, political and social liberties, will some day soon cut down the dead tree, and even a dead tree which falls during the tempest can cause incalculable damage to the property of its shortsighted owners.

2

The Armed Forces: Poor Relation of the Franco Régime

M. G. GARCIA

Of all things in Spain, the military always make news. The declaration of an officer or the mere rumour of a disagreement between generals are interpreted by observers with the same attention as a Cabinet crisis in a parliamentary democracy. A book which is not manifestly political, written by a general, becomes a best seller. An attempt by the Spanish Government to buy war material is capable of sparking off a bitter discussion in the British House of Commons. However, contrary to popular belief, if we consider statistical information which has been used in international comparisons (bearing in mind that it is very difficult to define similarities in questions of Defence) the Spanish Armed Forces appear neither numerous nor powerful.[1] According to propagandists of the Franco régime, the ratio between the Forces and total population has never been as low as it is at this moment.[2]

In the first years after the Civil War military costs became the most important item of Government expenditure; in 1940 the budgetary allocation for the three military ministries represented approximately one-third of the total. Added to this, there was also the cost of the paramilitary police forces, who received their allocation from the Ministry of the Interior.[3] In spite of the importance of the share of the budget which the military institutions received, it remained static for many years. The country lacked a policy of offensive ambition and even a serious defence policy. Moreover the large portion of national income set aside each year for military expenses did not stimulate economic activity. With little growth or development of the means of defence or offence, the military remained on the fringe of the decisions about economic policy. The size of military expenditure was due to the increase in the professional officer corps. Many of the officers who had been mobilized during the Civil War did not return to their former civilian profession but were assimilated instead into the ranks of the professional junior officers. [4]

The number of officers or Generals in an army should not be interpreted in absolute terms nor even in proportion to the number of troops, but in relation to the need for them in a specific situation. Rationalizations about the Spanish Army have frequently been made, attributing the increase in officers in the postwar period to needs deriving from the Second World War, being fought all around Spain. Yet half the provisional officers who entered the active ranks of the Army, were incorporated between 1945 and 1948, when the World War was over. This measure can thus be interpreted as a political rather than a military move. [5] This situation, with an abundance of soldiers, without any imminent warlike activity, is one which has repeated itself at intervals since the beginning of the nineteenth century, as after each civil or colonial war it has been thought preferable to incorporate the provisional officers into the professional officer corps, rather than using them as a reserve in preparation for future mobilization. [6] Once again, the decision was taken to spend the military budget on pay for the veterans rather than rationalizing resources for the Armed Forces. This may well have been a successful political measure, since it kept a large group satisfied, with their pay and their honours. In military terms it was probably a mistake since such a high saturation point means that officers have to wait much longer before being promoted and the Generals are too old to command in a modern war.

The material which the Armed Forces have had at their disposal was for years limited and much of it out-of-date. At the beginning of the fifties the situation of the Forces is captured in a paragraph from the memoirs of J. A. Ansaldo, nationalist war hero turned monarchist opponent of Franco:

> The military, like children, need toys, boats, planes, guns and new tanks. Hearing that the armies of Western Europe are going to have self-guided rockets and submarines which can do 30 knots . . . the Spanish officers suffer in silence like poor lads in front of a shop-window on Christmas Eve. [7]

In a speech given on 4 May 1970, General N. Ariza, the Director of the School of General Staff, strongly attacked the Government's military policy, criticizing the situation in which the Armed Forces found themselves, with poor resources and badly paid. He then added to his remarks, made in the presence of Prince Juan Carlos de Borbón, that by allocating such a small part of the national budget to defence, the Forces were becoming the poor relation of Spanish economic development. General Ariza was immediately dismissed, but his speech was not just the reflection of his own discontent but of that of a certain sector of the military thirty years after the Civil War.[8] Once again the complaints by the military of the Government's lack of attention were raised, as in 1898 and 1921.

In fact, throughout Franco's régime, the attention of observers has been focused, rather than on the war potential of the Spanish military organizations, on two fundamentally political facts: on the one hand that the present political system in Spain was the consequence of a military uprising, and on the other that the Forces have been one of the fundamental pillars of political power and many suspect that they will continue to be so when the moment of political change arrives.

The Role of the Military in the Franco-ist State

Besides the soldiers' specific function of internal and external defence of State, since 1939, Spanish military men have obtained numerous posts both in the Government and in other institutions of political life in spite of the fact that the victorious régime was not organized as a military junta. High-ranking soldiers have headed various departments in the different cabinets of General Franco; to begin with they have had the monopoly of the military ministries since 1939, when the Ministry of Defence, which had functioned throughout the Civil War, was split into three independent branches, Army, Navy and Air Force. There is no legal impediment preventing civilians from becoming Minister of one of these, but this has never happened. Most of the officials in the military ministries are also members of the forces. In addition, many of the military, especially those who retired under special laws in 1958 and 1964, have occupied posts in the bureaucracy.

Apart from their commissions in the ministries, military men also have had posts in other political bodies: the Council of the Realm, the National Council of the Movement, the Council of the State and the Cortes.

Soldiers have frequently occupied non-military ministerial posts in the different cabinets of Franco's régime. If we examine the professions of the 120 men who have been ministers, we see that 42 of them were professional military men. This proportion of 35 per cent is considerable, and from this fact it has been often concluded that the military institutions have partaken of political power in Spain. However, the problem which arises, when interpreting this information, is to see whether soldiers became ministers just because of their military positions or whether other factors were involved. Did Jorge Vigon, who was a retired artillery officer during the

25

Republic, owe his post to the fact that he was a member of the military or as a representative of the political group *Acción Española*? In the case of Luis Carrero's long years of collaboration, was the deciding factor his position in the Navy or his friendship with Franco? There are also problems of whether to classify José Solís, Tomás Garicano or Carlos Arias as military men, since all of them, despite being famous as civilians, are high officials in the Military Juridical Corps.

If we are to examine by means of this numerical information the influence which the military group had on the Government, some qualitative considerations must be added. Half of the group of the military who have been ministers occupied the post in departments traditionally reserved in Franco's Cabinet for the military (22 in all) and the remaining 20 had civil portfolios. Since the fifties the military ministries have been occupied by men of no special political significance, who did not have key posts during the Civil War either.

Only one of the generals who had met in Salamanca in September 1936 and who had named F. Franco as Head of the forces which had participated in the military uprising, reached the position of Minister, General F. Dávila Arredondo. Some heroes of the Civil War remained in the Government until the fifties (Admiral S. Moreno until 1957; A. Múñoz Grandes was Vice-President of the Government between 1965 and 1967) but the era of the victorious warriors in the Government was limited to the period 1939-51 (Juan Yagüe, Enrique Varela, Carlos Asensio, Juan Vigón). On the other hand members of the military who formed a close personal relationship with F. Franco, like A. Suances, L. Carrero or Camilo Alonso Vega, remained in the Government for years.

During the Civil War and in the period immediately afterwards, all the generals who had been Franco's peers in 1936 disappeared from the political scene. By the fifties hardly any of them were still alive. José Sanjurjo, Emilio Mola and Miguel Cabanellas died during the Civil War; Antonio Aranda, Gonzalo Queipo de Llano, Juan Yagüe, Alfredo Kindelán and Enrique Varela lost their prominence in political purges; José Solchaga, Andrés Saliquet, Miguel Ponte, Luis Orgaz and José Moscardó remained submissively in posts with no political distinction. The victorious generals received many honours but very little political power. Franco rewarded many of them with titles of nobility (Moscardó, Queipo, Kindelán, Saliquet and Yagüe). All of them were given the opportunity of rich financial rewards during the years of scarcity which followed the Civil War and many of them seized upon it. [9]

Probably the military élite have been kept contented by their participation in political power and by other advantages of a

26

privileged group; but from the end of the Civil War the role of most professional officers in the political life of the régime has been, with certain nuances, to accept rather than to demand, and to obey rather than govern. The pay of the military was not low in the postwar period compared with the income of other Spaniards, but their income has not kept up with the rate of increase of salaries during the sixties. Many members of the military have had to look for extra money working in civilian occupations in their spare time despite a law, which is not enforced, forbidding them to undertake any job not connected with the military. According to the results of a survey carried out among officers from the Staff corps, 64 per cent devoted part of their time to working in a second profession.[10] Throughout Franco's political era it has been only by the pressures of the accelerated development of Spanish society that a special sensitivity has developed among the military as a result of living in a society which is becoming daily more used to technology. The barracks, without many resources, receive new recruits who are used to handling sophisticated machines and see the equipment of foreign armies each night on television. Each day the officer is faced with a more uncomfortable position with his soldiers because of the contradictions between the image which he would like to maintain and the resources at his disposal to do so.[11]

With a diminished participation of the military in the bodies of political power and scarce means for warfare, the role which has been reserved for the Spanish Armed Forces has been, even more intensely than ever before in the nineteenth or twentieth centuries, that of maintaining the political status quo. As a clarification of the task of the Forces within the State apparatus it has been said repeatedly that they are the 'backbone of the country'. Franco clarified the meaning of this statement when he said:[12]

> The sacred mission of the armies of a nation consists in maintaining order and it is this mission that we have carried out.

Specialization of the Spanish Forces in the job of repression is not really an invention of the Franco régime; already in 1890 the leader of the Conservative Party, A. Cánovas, clearly expressed the political mission which corresponded to the Army:[13]

> The Army will remain for long, perhaps forever, the robust support of the social order and an invincible dyke against the illegal attempts of the proletariat, which accomplishes nothing by violence but the useless shedding of its own blood.

The Armed Forces will continue-presumably to play the same part of coercive tool of the State after the end of Franco's régime. General M. Diez Alegría, one of the soldiers most respected by Spanish democratic opposition, agreed on this aim for the armed

27

institutions 'in order to oppose subversion and violence and ensure that the laws are carried out'.[14]

The State specializes the Armed Forces in the maintenance of the status quo. This task is not an historic innovation, nor does it belong exclusively to the Spanish State. What is interesting about the case of Spain since 1939 is the way in which the Armed Forces have been used by the State to maintain its security. During the first years of its political life, the régime tried to use the Forces as a model for social organization, and throughout the period it has used them as an image of authority to support direct repressive measures.

The victorious classes in the Civil War knew the effectiveness of military command and had confidence in it. Thus, once the struggle was over, their political aim was to prolong military rule over society for as long as it took to 'purify and elevate' Spanish political life.[15] They relied on military action to carry out a double task: on the one hand using the Forces as a public image of authority, on the other, something more intangible and sophisticated, to put 'Spanish military virtues' into practice in society at large.[16] The *Fuero del Trabajo*, which was the first constitutional step in the new state, taken in 1938, already mentions the ideological militarization of civilian life:

> The National State (. . .) undertakes the task of carrying out, in a military fashion (. . .) the revolution which Spain has not yet accomplished.[17]

Thus, the régime which grew out of the Civil War used the ideology of militarization to signify order, submission to the political power in a hierarchical society.[18] This ideology of discipline, as understood by the military organization, was applied fundamentally to the organization of production in the new State by means of trade unions with a hierarchical structure; at work, employees were not to argue with their 'hierarchical superiors' but simply to obey them. However, the use of militarism as an ideological pressure did not in any way signify that the military participated in economic decisions, which remained in the hands of the old oligarchy.[19] The *Instituto Nacional de Industria*, the State holding company, was a special case of a 'militarized' body since there were many members of the military at the top of the organization and the General Staff was partly responsible for fixing its programmes in accordance with defence needs. Nevertheless the existence of INI cannot be considered in any way to be an attempt to place the economy under military control or to nationalize it. There were never any conflicts with private interests in the running of INI.[20]

In practice, the bureaucratic measures which resulted from this half-hearted attempt at social militarization contributed to economic failure. It had to be dropped, since to escape from economic stagnation it was necessary to resort to a more flexible kind of social relations. Moreover the period in which an attempt was made to organize life in accordance with military patterns of discipline also gave rise to increasing corruption at all levels of administrative machinery, which bestowed on the Government a public image far from Spartan.

Despite the régime's own statements about the Army as the pillar of order, the use of the Army against the civilian population has been a last resort, kept in reserve but rarely used. According to Spanish law, military forces will be used against civilians when the civil authorities are incapable of maintaining the public order, and this has not occurred since 1939. In serious political crises such as the violent death of Premier Luis Carrero Blanco in 1973, or during periods of armed struggle throughout Spain in the forties or in the Basque country now, specialized armed bodies have done this job.

The Armed Forces, in accordance with the 'Organic Law of the Spanish State' consist of four bodies: Army, Navy, Air Force and Forces of Public Order.[21] These forces of 'Public Order' are made up fundamentally of two armed groups, the Civil Guard and the Armed Police. In some of their organizational aspects they appear simply to be a part of the Army with a different specialization. Each of them is commanded by a General from the Army and some of the officers in the Armed Police come from the Army; however, most of the officers in the Civil Guard are trained in a specialized Academy. In peace-time both forces come under the orders of the civil authorities. Nevertheless, it is worth recalling that Spain is one of the few countries in the Western World where the police on their normal patrols are armed with infantry weapons and ready to use them at any time. When interpreting the fact that a relatively low proportion of the budget is allocated to the military in Spain, it must not be forgotten that other expenses are to be found in the allocation to the Ministry of the Interior. These are the expenses of maintaining these specialized forces which keep order within the country and whose numbers range between 90,000 to 100,000 men.[22]

All members of both these armed organizations, the Civil Guard and the Armed Police, are professionals, as opposed to the conscripts in the Army, Navy and Air Force. The Armed Policemen are much more like the volunteer professional ranks found in other Western armies; they are effective and well-disciplined, but they lack the special mystique and tradition which distinguish the Civil Guard.

In spite of the importance of the paramilitary police forces in

29

maintaining order, the Spanish State has in fact become progressively less of a police state since 1943. A complicated system of social control has been devised by the Establishment, of which the Civil Guard and the Police are only one part.[23] The bloody repression during the Civil War and the postwar years played a significant role in achieving the subsequent social calm in which the régime has lived. Nevertheless, the use of the Military Law against political offenders, with its very severe penalties, continued for many years after the Civil War. In April 1947 the period of martial law, which had begun in 1936, came more or less to an end. From then onwards certain non-violent political crimes have come under the jurisdiction of civil magistrates. But for many years, and even today, the military tribunals have retained jurisdiction over areas which are normally reserved for civilian courts in other countries. The Code of Military Law, published in 1943, continues to be applicable to crimes which threaten the security of the State, and until 1963 included offences of expression and opinion and strikes.[24] The Law of Banditry and Terrorism, to pursue political violence, was passed in 1943 and was brought up to date in 1960; it was made less harsh in 1963 with the creation of Public Order Courts, and tightened up yet again in 1968.[25]

The most significant recent event in which Military Law was put into practice was in 1970, when the Government, using the Law of Mobilization, placed the striking Madrid underground transport workers under military jurisdiction. The Basic Law for National Mobilization of April 1969 is a rationalizing measure which in a wartime situation puts civilians, and especially industrial workers, under military authority in order to simplify the task of national defence. In 1972 the same repressive measure was taken against the workers in the Bazan shipyards in El Ferrol, and in 1973 Post Office workers and the staff of the nationalized Compañía Telefónica were also threatened in the same way. In this situation, under military law, all workers who declare a strike or remain on strike are charged with rebellion and judged by military courts.

Not surprisingly then, the military have shared the ideology of the state in Franco's Spain more than at any other period in the recent history of Spain, whatever their percentage in the ministries and in government organizations. This sense of identity has been so strong that for many years it overrode the problem of lack of resources and even adverse political decisions such as that of relinquishing the colonial territories in Africa. The military institution has remained silent, or at least has muffled its discontent, without in return being granted any warlike activity or even a seriously articulated defence programme enabling them to fulfil their basic role of being ready for war, and with very little political power and few economic advantages.

In an attempt to support the generalized interpretation offered in the previous pages of the role of the Armed Forces in the Franquist political regime, it is convenient to classify the activities of this long period into different sections. (a) From the Civil War to the pacts with the USA in 1953. (b) Between 1953 and 1965, when, after a renewal of the agreements, a long-term military reorganization was initiated. mc) From 1965 up to the most recent information.

1936-1953. Scarcity

It was fear of revolution which impelled the conservative right to seek support from the armed forces in 1936; it was only with their help that they could put an end to the Republican régime whose development distressed them so. It is widely accepted that a political change directed by the Right needs a fascist type movement with widespread popular support; if it does not have this, then it must necessarily seek the support of the military.[26] This was the case in Spain, where the Fascist movement, even in the first few months after the 1936 elections, was extremely weak. In the February 1936 elections, the Falange obtained only about 44,000 votes, approximately 0.7 per cent of the total.[27] In spite of its aggressiveness, this small base did not offer the Falange sufficient strength to gain political power, even considering that, according to the Spanish fascists, the country was ripe for a Fascist revolution.

Ramiro Ledesma, a fascist capable of lucid analysis of the political situation, wrote in 1935 that in the case of Spain the only alternative to a Left-Wing revolution would be the seizure of power by the parties of the Right which had adopted totalitarian ideas, helped by the military. By converging, these forces, representative of the interests of high finance, industrialists and large landowners, would be able to make good the absence of a Fascist force and thereby oppose the violence of the revolutionary Left.[28] One of their leaders, José Calvo Sotelo, made a compelling appeal to the military. From the Cortes he announced the imminence of the clash between the 'revolutionary hordes' and the 'principle of authority'. The armed forces were not only the target of the conspirators' speeches but also, above all, of their activities, because for them the Army was 'the most august embodiment of authority'.[29] The extreme conservative-minded group *Acción Española* launched the famous phrase defining the Army as the 'backbone of the country' which has been repeated so many times years later in Franco's Spain.

31

The conservative Right had many reasons for expecting the support of the armed forces. Politically their nationalism coincided with the predominant ideology of the Forces, socially the officers belonged to the classes that supported the Right-Wing solution. Fear of revolution was also common and was used as the ultimate argument to bring about the *pronunciamiento*. This horror of revolution is explicit in the writings of those who headed the military uprising. General Emilio Mola is rationalizing his fear of revolution in his account on the seizure of political power by the Liberal bourgeois Republic in April 1931.[30] General Francisco Franco expresses this same fear, with far less literary talent than the former: he does so almost viscerally, transforming the social climate in which the events took place into the background of a film script.[31] These two are not the only examples; they express a latent social phobia of the middle classes, which impelled them to defend the social hierarchy.

In July 1936 the armed forces as a whole did not respond to the call of the civil and military conspirators. Some of the officers of the Army and Navy rose, but others did not; the same happened with the forces of the Civil Guard, the Assault Guard and the Carabineros. Generals, senior and junior officers joined the rising, while others, sometimes from the same ranks, corps or even the same family, remained faithful to the Government of the Republic, and most of them kept their allegiance until the end of the Civil War.[32] The individual analysis of each case and underlying motivations adds nothing to the character of the rising, though it could perhaps serve as proof of the difficulty of achieving a rising of an army against the status quo in a politically developed society. It seems that the Armed Forces are characterized by such conservatism towards the status quo that it is very difficult to convince them to rise unanimously against the Government even in support of the conservative classes.

The Army represented the real strength in the rising of July 1936 and continued to do so during the Civil War and even for some time after the war. This was strength in the most literal sense; without a political programme of its own this fact helped considerably to facilitate the political manoeuvres of the interest groups who had encouraged the conspiracy.[33] The first body of the uprising was the military Junta, created on 24 July 1936, presided over by the most senior of the Generals who had taken part in the uprising, General Miguel Cabanellas. On 29 September 1936 the Junta put all its powers into the hands of one man, General F. Franco, who thereby became Supreme Commander of all the forces which had participated in the rising and provisional Head of the new State.[34]

32

In April 1937 General F. Franco assumed the 'most absolute authority' and declared himself responsible 'before God and History'.

The political model of European dictatorships at the time, and the immediate task of the Civil War, made the legitimization of power possible through the creation of the figure of a man who had been called to lead the rising. Once the messianic figure had been created, it was no difficult task to achieve the personification of the military in the *caudillo* Franco, and for this all means were employed from the staging of mass rallies for special audiences to corruption and relentless persecution.

With the victory in the Civil War and in an international environment in which the ideology of aggressive violence predominated, it seemed obvious that militarism would develop in the direction of efforts to increase the size of the country, simply by means of war. On 19 May 1939, after three years of civil war, Madrid saw the first military parade celebrating the victory. 120,000 men took part, as a sample of the total of more than one million victors. This powerful military force was spread, as regards the Army, over 61 divisions; it was well-equipped and compared very favourably with the European armies, ready to fight, just three months before the outbreak of the Second World War.

Years later, when the Second World War was over, the United Nations discussed what measures should be taken against the Spanish Government. In April 1946 Oscar Lange, the delegate from Poland, described Franco's Government as a threat to world peace. According to a report prepared by the Republican Government in exile, Spain had a mechanized force of some 250,000 men ready to invade France. It was also stated that German scientists who had taken refuge in Spain were helping to prepare this Army, and even that they were working on the production of an atom bomb, which is doubtful.[35] The presence of German military and technicians after the Second World War has been established. The most important collaboration which the Spanish Government relied upon was that of W. Messerschmitt and his team who continued to design planes in Spain.[36] International rumours about the strength of Spanish forces and their preparations for war continued throughout 1947, at a time when it would appear, in fact, that there was the greatest lack of resources for another war. Unlike the Second World War and the enormous developments it produced, even by 1941, shortly after the end of the Civil War, the offensive capabilities of the Spanish forces were out-of-date.

In 1940 the German command had many doubts abou the Spanish forces. According to a report, the Spanish Army numbered

33

about 340,000 men, with the possibility of reaching half a million in the event of war. This force was organized into 20 divisions in the Peninsula and 7 more in Morocco and the islands. Out of all these, only one division was motorized. The main problems pointed out in the report are the lack of ammunition and shortage of industrial capacity for supplying it. With regard to the military command, the Germans showed a marked lack of confidence in the ability of the Spanish military chiefs to direct a modern war.[37] There were probably many factors which prevented Spain's entry into the Second World War. Despite the desire for territorial empire there was the weakness of the Armed Forces who without foreign aid could not maintain a war of uncertain duration; thus the Government preferred neutrality with all its different nuances. Spain's only participation in the war, apart from the sale of raw materials, was limited to the symbolic despatch of a division of volunteers, including a few pilots, known in Spain as the Blue Division.

Between August 1941 and October 1943, these 40,000 Spaniards went to the Russian front. The despatch of these troops had a very different meaning for the Spanish Government than it had for the Germans: for the former it was intended as an internal propagandist move and an escape valve to channel the energy of many Falangists who called for action. For the German command the Spanish force was simply one more combat group, the 250th Division, which was organized and armed with German material and whose members had to swear allegiance to the Führer, without any mention of Franco or Spain.[38] The head of the Division during most of the campaign was General A. Muñoz Grandes, and his responsibility at the front was limited to obeying orders and carrying out the plans of the command of the Army Corps into which the Division had been integrated. The Blue Division fought in a sector of the Leningrad front and remained there for two years, hardly moving at all. For this service by the Spaniards, the German Government had to pay the bill: the total amount came to more than 42 per cent of the total debt Spain had incurred with Germany for her help in the Civil War.[39]

Far from the war, pressure from some of the generals was successful in controlling the radical activism of the Falangists. During these years the friction between the radicalism of the Falange and the conservative political position of the Movement in general expressed itself in the very high tension which existed between the Falange and the Army. The Falangists had few supporters among the military even in these first years after the Civil War; the enrolment of all the military in the Party was a mere formality. General J. Yagüe was the only high-ranking officer who defined himself as a Falangist and even took part in a conspiracy against Franco.[40] In September 1942 the paramilitary Falangist militias were dissolved. After their reorganization in 1940 their aim had been to give military instruction to Spanish males between the ages of 18 and 55, in open competition with the military; in spite of this, the restoration of the Captaincies General in 1940 had given the Generals more effective control of civilian society, in the face of competition from the Party.[41]

Certain individual officers had links with the monarchist opposition out of traditional loyalty, of resentment of Falangist arrivistes, and of anxiety for the future after Franco. In the main, however, with the Civil War won and public order assured, officers had little or no interest in politics. After all, one of the reasons for the military rising of 1936 had been to do away with conventional politics. Accordingly, the 'political' stance of the Armed Forces as a whole was extremely conservative. Violently hostile to the groups of the Left, the officers opposed not only the radicalism of the Falange but even the pseudo-democratic line opportunistically assumed from time to time by the Pretender to the throne. Most of the officers remained loyal to Franco's leadership when in March 1945 Don Juan de Borbón attacked the Franco régime and demanded the immediate restoration of the monarchy. The danger of a monarchist military coup did not shake the stability of the régime but a few prominent generals, such as A. Kindelán, were sent away from Madrid in 1946.

In the forties the Spanish Forces had a large but new officer corps; hardly 20 per cent of the total number of officers from before the Civil War still had their posts. In addition to the losses incurred in the war, the Army was completely purged of those who had been on the losing side: between 1942 and 1943 a total of about 3,000 officers were removed from the Forces. The new officer corps was composed of young men trained on the battlefield and loyal to the new order. The main body of officers retained their identification during these years with the National Movement, even at the time of international loss of prestige and internal economic chaos.

As the Second World War was ending, the Spanish Forces remained increasingly in a passive situation even when a guerrilla war was beginning in Spain, about which there is very little information available. The struggle was partly against resistance groups from the Republican Army who had not surrendered, and was partly aggravated from 1944 by the movement across the border from France of armed groups of Spaniards, veterans of two wars. The fiercest fights took place in the Pyrenees, but the activity of

35

these guerrilla groups spread to large areas of the Peninsula. The peak of the struggle was reached in 1946, 1947 and 1948 when, according to official sources, more than 5,000 guerrillas were captured or killed.[42]

The Army took a secondary role in counter-insurgency, especially after November 1944, which marked the end of an attempted invasion in the Valley of Arán in the Pyrenees by the so-called Republican Army of Liberation, with 10,000 men. The Civil Guard was employed as the principal anti-guerrilla force because of the double effectiveness of this body. From the military point of view the Civil Guard was better equipped to fight against small groups of men. Moreover, by using the Civil Guard, counter-insurgency was given the character of a struggle between the forces of order and groups of bandits, which for propaganda purposes was much more effective than the recognition of a new civil war.[43]

Spain at the beginning of the fifties still had an important military force despite this lack of immediate internal and external functions. The Army was composed of 22 divisions, including an armoured division created in 1943, but very short of material in practice; indeed at the Victory Parade in May 1944 tanks did not take part because of the severe shortage of fuel in the country. Military instruction of the forces rarely extended beyond drills carried out in open spaces near the barracks. The few military manoeuvres which took place during this long period were the unavoidable ones involving troops stationed in the Pyrenees, and never included large units. There were really no large-scale manoeuvres until 1955 – economic problems prevented this kind of expenditure. Moreover, throughout this period the abundance of uniforms and the frequency with which decorations and military honours were granted bore no relation to the power of the military, who were poorly equipped and trained and lacked modern arms and transport.[44] Of all the Armed Forces, the Air Force possessed the most modern resources during this period. It relied on planes based on German models constructed in Spain. The development of aviation throughout the world was so rapid, however, that although the material was not in particularly short supply, it soon became obsolete.

1953-1965. American Help

Whether it was because Franco's government deliberately ignored the needs of the Armed Forces or because the resources available did not permit otherwise, the fact is that, at the beginning of the fifties, the military situation had reached its limit. However, before resentment could crystallize and drive the Army out of its lethargic apoliticism, worldwide political tensions created by the Cold War

36

and sharpened by the Korean conflict gave the Spanish Government the opportunity of escaping from such a gloomy prospect. Relief came in the form of the US interest in using the Iberian Peninsula for strategic territorial support. In exchange, a veil was drawn over Franco's past alliances with the losers of the Second World War. The escape from international ostracism was a considerable prize, yet the basis of the agreement with the United States was no more than strategic: the geographical situation of Spain and its islands in the zone of European conflict. This was practically all that Spain could offer to the Western military organization.

In fact, reports from the United States, like the German ones before them, showed little hope of being able to count on the Spanish military to play any significant role in the military balance of power. Again it was considered that Spain's military resources could do little more than maintain internal order, and at most defend Spanish territory in the event of an invasion. [45] Problems of communications were no less serious: there were few railway lines and these had large sections of single track, narrow roads and few telephone connections. It was necessary to give everything a complete overhaul before it could serve the needs of a modern army, and the cost of such a job was reckoned in 1953 at approximately one billion dollars. [46] Of course the cost of the logistic infrastructure and military bases would have to be paid for directly by the US. Thus the role of Spain in an alliance had to be that of a poverty-stricken ally. Nevertheless in 1953 the strategic needs of the Western powers overcame the difficulties and the cost, in exchange for permission to take advantage of Spain's geographical situation.

In 1940 when the German Minister Ribbentrop asked his Spanish colleague R. Serrano Suñer to allow him a military base in the Canary Islands, the latter, according to his memoirs, flatly refused him because the islands were part of Spanish national territory. [47] Twenty years later it was not so difficult for the Americans to obtain the desired bases – simply the time it took to agree on the price they should pay. The pact between the United States and Spain was signed on 26 September 1953. In synthesis, the agreement granted the United States permission to construct and use, for a minimum of twelve years and a maximum of twenty, air bases in Torrejón near Madrid, Zaragoza and Morón de la Frontera, some 25 miles south-east of Seville; a large depot of material at the aerodrome of San Pablo, at Seville; a naval and and air base at Rota, near Cadiz; supporting naval installations in El Ferrol, Barcelona and Cartagena; seven radar posts in different parts of the Peninsula and Mallorca, and an oil pipeline 485 miles long between Rota and Zaragoza, joining the principal bases. [48]

In spite of the presence in Spain of an American military force of 12,000 men and of the agreements themselves, most Spanish military men accepted the new situation with satisfaction. They put their desire to overcome the deficiencies of the Spanish military organization, their lack of material and the absence of any programme before any nationalistic qualms. The Americans supplied the hope of modernizing their Armed Forces which were in a distressing situation, and this was to become increasingly the first priority of the Spanish military to the exclusion of the political preoccupations normally attributed to them. Accordingly, the units which would have priority in receiving American material were speedily decided on. To begin with it was decided to equip 3 divisions and support elements for an Army corps. The first item on the list of demands was armoured cars. The material which the Americans sent was, in the main, secondhand; the tanks, lorries and artillery had been used in Korea or in Europe. The ships were only on loan and the planes were not very numerous. Nevertheless, this material constituted the only possibility of having an armed force worthy of the name for the first time in many years, and was therefore accepted. Probably the Air Force was the sector which underwent the biggest transformation, both organically and with regard to material. In 1955 the first jet fighters were ready at the base at Manises (Valencia), and from 1958 an air defence force functioned in coordination with the American network in Spain. [49] In the Army the evolution was much slower; the first important reform of the units was not carried out until 1960.

During the fifties the most important measures were aimed at reducing the number of officers, who were too large a group and difficult to adapt to the recommendations of the American military advisers. The reserve laws of 1953 and 1958 granted very good economic conditions to those who agreed to retire. However, the expected results were not achieved, and the officers in the Army continued to be more numerous and less young than rationally desirable. Above rationality, however, in this period, was the weight of established privileges and political concessions which the Government did not try to abolish, and in this respect the Americans were neither willing nor able to make too many demands. This is in a way typical of state–military relations in Franco's Spain during this period. Perhaps remembering the Army discontent in 1917 over pay and conditions and the 1936 rising, Franco, being both soldier and rebel, pursued an ambiguous policy. While expenditure on equipment was systematically reduced – perhaps to prevent an effective military challenge against the state – every effort was made to keep the officers' pay and privileges at a level which precluded their ever questioning their loyalty to the system.

The reforms carried out in the fifties had little effect on the military forces stationed in Africa, although once again during this period they were to play the main part in military actions. In Morocco, the military had almost total political power in their hands. The highest authority of the Protectorate, the High Commissioner, was a member of the military, and the Army of Morocco provided the most brilliant and best-paid future that a young officer could hope for. The select body of the Spanish Army, the Foreign Legion, was created specifically for Morocco in 1920 and remained so.

The Spanish Government adopted an anti-colonialist policy in spite of its African colonies. As a result of this somewhat machiavellian attitude, when the French Government unexpectedly recognized the independence of Morocco in December 1955 the Spaniards had no justification for continuing to maintain their zone, and in April 1956 they were obliged to grant independence as well. Many Spaniards who had interests in Morocco, including, of course, the Forces, wanted to remain, but were incapable of making their discontent effective.[50] The Government's concern about this bad feeling created among the military was reflected in the explanations given about the need to withdraw and in simultaneously attempting to draw the officers' attention to the reforms intended to modernize the armed forces. Franco's speech to the Armed Forces in Seville on 26 April 1956 was a good example of this. The fundamental need to keep the officers happy was seen in the award of salary increases in July 1956.[51]

Spain's problems about remaining in Africa were not solved with the independence of Morocco, but rather became more acute. This was especially so in the territories of Ifni and the Western Sahara, where a guerrilla force attacked Spanish targets from November 1957 to March 1958. Military defence of the territories was not easy and the garrisons did not seem specially prepared to face an attack. The attacking forces were able to obtain supplies easily from Morocco, whereas the Spanish supply base was the Canary Islands, some 200 miles away. The town of Sidi Ifni did not have a port, and all the supplies had to come ashore in landing-craft. For weapons, transport and aviation the Spaniards had to rely on their own resources, since the American material was not at the disposal of the African forces.[52] Finally in February 1958 measures were taken to resolve the situation with the help of French troops from Southern Algeria and Mauretania.

During the conflict, the Spanish Government could not call on their military allies for help, and had instead to resort to military collaboration with the French, their traditional rivals in North Africa. At the time the United States had assumed a friendly position with regard to the Arab League, as they had demonstrated by not supporting the British and French occupation of Suez in October and November 1956.

As the time to renew the 1953 pacts approached in 1963 there did not seem to be many problems to trouble the friendship between Spain and the United States. The Spanish Government did not raise any objections to the installation of atomic weapons at the air bases, and the new Polaris submarines used the naval base at Rota quite normally, while in other European countries, which were members of NATO, such weapons were refused entry. Only one problem emerged: the demands of the Spanish Government. These demands, centring on military equipment, reached $500,000,000 at the first estimate, made in 1960. This amount was considered unacceptable by the American Government. The Senate, for its part, considered that Spain had already received more than enough compensation for bases. Even a second request for $250,000,000 seemed excessive. After three years of debate a new agreement was signed whereby Spain received $150,000,000 in military aid. At the same time Spain became an 'associate' rather than a 'landlord' with regard to the bases, which were to be for the use of both countries. This did not mean, however, that this became a defence treaty with equal rights, for which it would have been necessary to obtain the approval of the United States Congress, where there was a great deal of opposition to an alliance with Spain. [53]

The economic situation has changed in Spain since 1953 and the interests of the Government and the ruling classes incline them to look more and more towards Europe. This will have important repercussions on the development of the equipment and organization of the Armed Forces. Back in 1964 an attempt was made to buy warships in the United Kingdom, but opposition from the Labour Party in the House of Commons prevented the transaction from going through. The Spanish Government was more successful with France in 1965, when a defence pact was signed. The first order was for two submarines, but the contacts between the Armed Forces of the two countries developed and they began to carry out joint manoeuvres in the Pyrenees and the Mediterranean.

1965-1975. The Rise of a New Generation

1965 was an important year for the Armed Forces. For the Army it was a time of great organic reorganization, and for the Navy, the beginning of the first serious programme of shipbuilding after the Civil War.

The Law of the Reorganization Plan for the Army referred for the first time since 1939 to the importance of military expenditure as a 'profitable investment'. This was not just a point made by the military; industrialists, interested in manufacturing weapons and military equipment, declared that planning for the needs of defence should form part of the overall economic plan. Concerning the organic structure, the 1965 Plan aimed at specializing the Army, not just to act as a satellite to its big American ally but also to attend to more limited military encounters. The primary idea was the reduction of numbers: fewer units but more efficient ones. The total peacetime strength was to be just one Army Corps with full support units and services. This reorganization, which is still in force at the present time, groups the forces into two categories: a task force and a territorial defence army, in accordance with the French model. The Army units continued to be unevenly distributed over the country, the greatest concentration of troops being found in the area around Madrid which includes the forces of the Armoured Division, the Parachute Brigade and part of the forces of other units.[54] This is of more significance for a tradition based on the danger of internal subversion than external defence.

The renewal of the pacts with the United States in 1970 brought the Spanish Government $68 million for defence aid. For the Forces this payment for the bases meant new equipment. This war material was a fresh disappointment for the military in the seventies. It has even been compared to the consignments of powdered milk which had been sent by some charitable organizations twenty years previously.[55] This dissatisfaction was shown on several occasions: in 1973 the Navy, for example, refused three destroyers which were part of the military aid, considering them unacceptable.[56] The period in which American cast-offs filled the Spanish military with pleasure would appear to be at an end. American defence aid no doubt continues to help to save public expenditure, but the military no longer accept this saving of public money at their expense, and there are also other interests to support their dissatisfaction. In these circumstances it will be more than ever difficult to renew the pacts in 1975. Politically the United States no longer seems to be an indispensable ally, and militarily there is little more that they can offer. For the Spanish soldiery the United States no longer has the role of catalyst with regard to the improvement of the Forces. The Spanish Government is now looking in other directions. In June 1970, the agreements with France were renewed; these are based more specifically on cooperation rather than on military aid. After 1970 the Spanish Government acquired a consignment of Mirage fighter planes, as well as a large order for armoured equipment

41

(AMX tanks) which apart from technical characteristics had been partly manufactured in Spain. The good relations with European suppliers are not limited to France, but extend also to Germany, and at last it is to be possible to procure British equipment, the vertical take-off Harrier made by Hawker Siddeley.

For many years the United States have been interested in the possibility of integrating Spain into the Atlantic Alliance, to put an end to the often uncomfortable bilateral pacts. This interest was made particularly clear at the Summit in Brussels in May 1975. Once again, the Spanish Government was rejected as a full ally in the Western defence system. Among the alternatives, a situation of neutrality is not unthinkable, as a response to the political rejection of the Spanish régime by most of the members of NATO.

In military circles the general wish is to put an end to dependence on American material as soon as possible, and there is even a hope of trying to become self-sufficient. The Navy has gone ahead in this connection: the second stage of the plan to renew the Fleet (1972-79) is based on the construction of vessels in Spanish shipyards, although foreign patents will be used. Interest in the process of modernizing the military equipment has reached a dynamic phase, and criticism from industrialists of the lack of expenditure on materials has increased. [57]

Throughout an extended period the budgetary allocations for defence have decreased proportionately in Government expenditure. On some occasions the Government has justified the agreements with the United States solely in terms of the saving which American aid implies in defence expenditure. [58] The average proportion of the budget allocated to defence during the period 1962-72 was 15.9 per cent, but in 1973 it represented 13 per cent within the Government's plans for expenditure. [59] The Defence budget for 1973 was just 1.9 per cent of the GNP, which means $32 per capita. An international comparison of these figures would seem to indicate that the military structure is not excessively heavy on the Spanish taxpayer. [60] The Government, faced with the need to spend more money in certain sectors, has traditionally taken the decision to reduce military expenditure rather than obtain a large increase in public revenue by increasing taxes, which would require considerable fiscal changes. In Spain the income from taxes reaches only 13 per cent of the GNP, in comparison with the countries of the EEC where it is 22 per cent. [61] A fiscal reform would have to concentrate on increasing direct taxation, especially income tax, since up to now most of the revenue is obtained from taxing consumer spending. An increase in taxes would not be kindly received by the ruling and middle classes, even if it did mean an improvement in the power of the State's defence machine. That consideration has not weighed with the most progressive political élites within the Establishment, who are prepared to back a process of rationalization of the military as part of the evolutionary process desired for the régime.

The military is a group which is continually being renewed: by 1969 the officers who had been trained since the Civil War were more numerous than either those from before it or those who had been trained during the hostilities.[62] Nevertheless, most of the men in the highest posts on the active list were the provisional officers of the Civil War. It is important to bear this factor in mind when interpreting their position on the problems they face; often they adhere more strictly to the system that they founded than does the Government itself. This group of high-ranking men, sometimes known as 'azules', support reactionary political solutions and have received the approval of those who defend political intransigence. Largely because of strong opposition from this powerful group of the military, who are those who sit in the parliament, the new National Defence Law has not been passed in the Cortes.[63] They are particularly opposed to the creation of a centralized organization of all the Armed Forces, which is the first goal of the liberal military advocates of rationalization. Extreme rightist Generals such as T. García Rebull, A. Campano, or retired ones like C. Iniesta or R. Perez Viñeta, cannot, however, be strictly considered ideologically as Falangists. It is nevertheless clear that they have political connections with the groups which more or less clandestinely in the last few years have carried out demonstrations shouting 'Power to the Army', an increasingly frequent occurrence in the larger towns. These 'blue' officers are the political residue of the victorious forces of 1939, who have not followed the evolution of the ruling classes' expectations through the long life of the régime. Their aim is to maintain a political situation which their allies of 1936 now find to be out-of-date. The social strata who support the conservative generals are also a political residue; they are mainly the bureaucratic middle classes who embraced the 1939 victory as their own and whose interests have remained static, themselves mere spectators of the change which Spanish society has undergone. The Brotherhood of *Alféreces Provisionales*, founded in 1958, appear as the most representative group showing these interests. In 1964 it combined with other veterans associations to form a political association. The resultant federation asserts that its members number almost half a million.[64] One of the aims of the component groups is to gain the support of the military, and they direct their political proclamations towards the Forces for this reason.

Another sector of the military, holding high positions, has

43

adopted views which correspond more closely to the political flexibility which has been pursued by some sections of the ruling classes as their best means of survival. These members of the military are more percipient and 'liberal' than their colleagues, and they receive evidence of support from different groups who are interested in the political evolution of the system. These groups, either within the régime or from the moderate opposition, look to the military stratum for sympathy. The *Asociación Católica Nacional de Propagandistas*, for instance, counts many of the military among its members. In the official list of members for 1958, 42 were from the military and two of these were Ministers.[65] On the other hand, there do not appear to be many members of the military in the *Opus Dei*, at least according to the meagre information published about that society. Even illegal political forces like the Socialist and Communist Parties claim that they too have some military support. Whether or not the latter is true, the Government has tried to prevent this kind of political courting of the military. The traditional speeches of the military ministers in the New Year focused in 1975, not altogether by chance, on the same theme: the military must keep out of 'politics'. The replacement of successive military generations following changes in Spanish society generally, held out no hope for the maintenance of the traditional identification between Government and Forces. In fact, most of the officers who have been trained since the Civil War no longer perceive their identity to be with the régime. The response of the Government is to try to inspire the Forces with the aim of professionalism, which in theory should coincide with the demands made by the liberal sectors of the Forces.

Power to the Army?

Franco allowed many years to elapse before he defined a concrete constitutional solution for the succession. For this reason, once he disappeared only a military power could have filled the gap in political power until an agreement had been reached about the type of government which was to succeed him.

During the summer of 1974 F. Franco was seriously ill, and because of his age everyone expected him to die. The military leaders, however, played a very secondary role in this crisis. For 35 years the institutionalizing process of the Spanish régime has slowly evolved, and has achieved some minimal guarantees for its political continutiy on the death of Franco. The existence of a Crown Prince and of a President of the Government meant that, at least in formal terms, there would not be a political void. A military junta would have to impose itself by force at the expense of the civil political

44

institutions which ensure political continuity.

In December 1973 the President of the Government, L. Carrero Blanco, lost his life by assassination. During the first moments of confusion not only did the Army not assume power, but the actions of some of the military leaders were decisive in maintaining civilian authority in control of the situation. The impulsive and extremist reactionary head of the Civil Guard at the time, C. Iniesta, wanted to occupy the cities with forces under his orders. Such a display of force would not really have been necessary since the political power was hardly shaken by the killing.

The political set-up of the last week of 1973 was illustrative: an 'understanding' General, M. Diez Alegría, was able to show an intransigent General, C. Iniesta Cano, that it would be superfluous for the Army to take over the country since there was no sign of popular revolt. The frustration of the 'blue' General and of other old diehards was probably only comparable to the satisfaction of the 'modernizing' elements of the Spanish ruling classes at being able to show Europe such an example of political maturity.

After the military *pronunciamiento* in April 1974 in Portugal, it was rumoured that many people had sent monocles to General Diez Alegría – a symbol from anonymous admirers to encourage him, as Head of the Supreme Military Staff, to follow the example of General Spínola. The parallel between the end of Salazar's régime and the closing stages of Franco's should probably not be taken so far. The social conditions and political forms of both Iberian authoritarian régimes were not the same. The situation of the Armed Forces in the two countries is also different: the existence of a long colonial war in the case of Portugal and of the Civil War in the case of Spain are strong differentiating factors.

Looking to the future, the development of the new Portuguese political system could have an important influence on the different strata of Spanish society who are closely watching its development. Many of the military will be both pleased and hopeful if they see that the Portuguese have succeeded in establishing coherent political forms, whether or not they follow the political model of the formal democracies. After all, it is easy to prove the sympathy which exists in Spain for régimes such as the one led by General Velasco Alvarado in Peru.

Much of the energy which the Portuguese officers expended in carrying out their *pronunciamiento* was derived from their professional frustration and from the conviction that they were being used by a minority group who were ruling the country, without having anything in common with the aspirations of this group. A similar feeling of discontent has been experienced by the Spanish military many times during the twentieth century. After the Civil War the Armed Forces found themselves, to all appearances, in a privileged position within the State apparatus. It seemed that the discontent which had given rise to the protest movement in 1917 known as the *Juntas de Defensa* had been overcome.

Thirty-five years after the Civil War, this internal satisfaction of the military does not seem to have been maintained. The economic resources allocated to military defence have been insufficient; the supply of material still continues to depend on the American protectors, to a large extent, and its quality and quantity do not satisfy the military. Besides this, defence policy is very vaguely defined. The honours and advantages of being part of the military after a successful Civil War remain available to the soldiers of that period, but there are many officers nowadays without any privileges at all.

Scandals such as Matesa, in which members of the Government are implicated, must necessarily make these men restless; having been trained to respect a sense of honour they are forced to witness the corruption which pervades Government minorities. [66]

Although the figures for applicants to the Military Academies do not present a problem up to the present moment, an ever-decreasing interest in military activities can be observed in the country. This is hardly surprising. Life in the garrisons is dull, except perhaps for the very few élite corps. There are fewer African territories to encourage adventures and in those which remain, there are few opportunities for brilliant military action. There are several symptoms which denote the frustration of the officers; many are indifferent, apathetic and even alcoholic, while others adopt an aggressively assertive tone concerning the army. Some members of the military use their spare time to study in the University, coming into contact with a very conflictive area of civilian society and with its expectations. [67] Yet is is very unlikely that there will be a military *pronunciamiento* as a result of this frustration. As for more than 150 years in Spain, and in Portugal a year ago, the military will not rise alone; they will use the support of other social forces, whether it is a left-wing or a right-wing conspiracy. It is very difficult to contemplate a move towards the left by the new generation of the Spanish military; they tend to derive from lower social groups than before the Civil War, but it is hard to imagine that in this long period of peace they have been able to rise above the very conservative training which they received in the Military Academies. Moreover, there is an efficient information service in their barracks, like a secret police force, watching both rank and file and officers, in order to anticipate possible surprises.

In 1936 part of the Armed Forces declared itself again the Republic, giving to and drawing support from part of civilian society. It was precisely this alliance which gave the rising its effectiveness. Without the financial aid of the ruling classes, the legitimizing ideology of the Church and the popular support of sections of the middle classes, the Army would probably have achieved little. Nowadays, these three allies are drifting away from the Franco-ist system. The economic oligarchy, which in 1936 anxiously sought an authoritarian government, is now placing its hopes on a democratic evolution and some kind of link with Europe. The Church is adopting an increasingly radical position, and the middle classes, with whom the military come most into contact, are in the present situation in Spain less aggressively right-wing than ever before. Given this re-orientation of its allies towards a modernization of the Franco-ist system and the pre-eminence of 'liberal' elements within the Forces, it is likely that military support could be assured for gradual reform. This is certainly the hope of Socialists and Communists. But it is even more likely that if the changes envisaged involve fundamental principles verging on revolution or on any alteration in the system of public order, then the Armed Forces will once again take up arms against the Spanish working classes and the bourgeois liberals.

3

The Church: From Crusade To Christianity

NORMAN COOPER

Introduction

The Catholic Church in Spain has long been regarded as one of the pillars supporting the edifice of Francoism. In 1939 the Spanish Church was under the leadership of the fascist sympathizer Cardinal Isidro Gomá y Tomás. Thirty-six years later its principal leader is Cardinal Vicente Enrique y Tarancón whose image, at least, is that of a supporter of liberal democracy. The Church of the 'Crusade' has been transformed into what is virtually a Church in opposition. This chapter is an attempt to trace this evolution through a consideration of five periods.

(1) The first period, 1939-45, was characterized by the establishment of the Church in an unparalleled position of privilege and dominance and ended with the appointment as Foreign Minister of Alberto Martín-Artajo, a prominent figure in the Catholic Action movement. (2) This nomination can be said to have inaugurated a second period, 1945-53, which culminated in the Concordat of 1953, and during which the régime attempted to use the Catholic Church as a legitimizing force to combat the ostracism of Spain following the Second World War. (3) During the years 1953-62 division began to appear in the previously monolithic structure of Spanish Catholicism. The ultra-conservative Opus Dei became dominant in government while more progressive Catholic militants were becoming alienated from the régime. This period ended with the Second Vatican Council. (4) The years 1962-71 saw the Spanish Church gradually split into two main factions: those favouring strong links with Francoism and those clergy, laity and bishops, inspired by Vatican II, who championed the underprivileged and advocated a break with the authoritarian

48

régime. (5) A climactic point of alienation from the State was reached in 1971 with the Joint Assembly of Bishops and Priests, beginning a period in which the majority of the hierarchy firmly, if prudently, adopted a posture of opposition, although a vocal pro-Franco minority still flourishes. The study ends with a consideration of the Bishops' Collective Letter in April 1975, a cautious document whose main theme is reconciliation.

The Background

The involvement of the Catholic Church with anti-democratic rightist governments has long been a controversial issue. However, it is surely clear that for the Church, survival is the fundamental aim. Believing itself to be the unique means of human salvation, it must insist on its right to teach, proselytize and administer its sacraments. The exact nature of the temporal régime in any one country remains secondary to these basic objectives. Only when this is borne in mind do the seemingly extreme changes of the Church's position under Francoism become explicable.

Of course, certain types of régime are preferred to others. The Spanish Church had been traditionally a fervent supporter of monarchy. During the nineteenth century it tended, naturally, to support Carlism, a doctrine that reflected the ultramontane character of Spanish Catholicism itself.[1] In Spain the Church stood for the integrist position insisting on a dominant role in education and regarding freedom of worship for non-Catholics as unacceptable.[2] It was largely unaffected by the modernist ideas influencing Church attitudes elsewhere. Pope Leo XIII's *Rerum Novarum* of 1891, a tentative exposition of a more liberal outlook, was regarded in Spain as a revolutionary document.[3] Throughout the century the Church had fought a rearguard action against the onslaughts of the modern world as represented by the liberal anti-clericalism of succeeding governments.[4]

However, following the defeat of Carlism, the Church had no alternative but to come to terms with the new economic order and with the Alfonsist dynasty.[5] Its privileges were respected by the Dictator Primo de Rivera, 1923-30, and it seemed as if traditional Spanish Catholicism could regain its dominance, but the year 1931 came as a disaster for the Church. Its liberal enemies were again in power, now with the system of government most feared and abhorred by the Church – a Republic.

The first attack came within a month of the declaration of the Republic in the form of a Pastoral issued by Primate Cardinal Segura. Almost simultaneously came Pius XI's Encyclical

49

Quadragesimo Anno which appeared to support Segura's view, adopting a distinctly anti-democratic tone and praising the virtues of the corporate state.[6]

With the anti-clerical clauses in the new Republican Constitution Church hostility grew.[7] Many Catholics began to plot to overthrow the Republic. Others, however, seemed to be working within the system and to what extent the CEDA party was prepared to go along with the new democracy has remained a subject of controversy among scholars to this day.[8] What is beyond doubt is that these Catholic militants flocked to the rebel colours following the outbreak of Civil War.[9]

Apart from the Basque clergy, ecclesiastical support for Franco was overt. Of particular importance was the 1937 Collective Letter of the Spanish hierarchy addressed 'To the Bishops of the Whole World'.[10] The Church was committed to the victory of the rebels and when the end came it was greeted with relief.

1939-45 – The Victorious Church

On 31 March 1939 a telegram sent by Pope Pius XII to General Francisco Franco read: 'Lifting up our heart to God we give sincere thanks with your Excellency for Spain's Catholic victory.'[11] The Spanish Church had attempted to justify the rebellion as a 'Holy War' waged by the champions of Christian civilization to free Spain from the chaos of liberal democracy with its attendant evils of atheism, communism and Freemasonry. The Civil War had, therefore, been a 'Crusade', a word that became part of the standard vocabulary of the victorious opponents of the Republic.

The Pope's telegram was followed by a statement over Vatican Radio.[12] He welcomed 'con immenso gozo' (with immense joy) the success of the Spanish defenders of the faith, stating that it was the duty of the victors to carry out their task of 'pacification' in accordance with Christian principles. Pius XII, inevitably, maintained a discreet silence regarding Basques and other Catholics who died for the Republic, and avoided mention of the help received by Franco from Hitler and Mussolini.

It is important to note that there was a crucial difference between the Church's relationship with Franco and that with other 'fascist' powers. However attractive authoritarian conservative governments might seem to the Church, the aggressive nationalism of such régimes could eventually clash with evangelical aims. Elevation of the State above the Church – the heresy of 'Statism' – had led to two Encyclicals directed at the régimes of Mussolini and Hitler. These documents *Non Abbiamo Bisogno*, 1931, and *Mit Brennender Sorge*, 1937, had attacked the Fascist and Nazi dictatorships for attempting to subject Catholics to the exigencies of the totalitarian State.[13] No such declaration was necessary regarding Spain. Franco was shrewd enough to tame any anti-clerical tendencies in the ranks of the Falange and Church privileges, particularly in education, were established as never before.[14] At last the Church appeared liberated from the attacks which had characterized the nineteenth century and had culminated in the laic legislation of the Republic. The Church accepted the position of legitimizing authority which was to preside over the coming decades of Francoism. Indeed Church and State became so closely linked that a form of 'National Catholicism' was created. Franco was to stake the long-term future of his dictatorship on this ideology rather than on totalitarian Falangism. The new FET y de las JONS was very different from the organization envisaged in the fascist conception of the original founders.[15] In its first postwar National Council allegiance to the Church was emphasized.[16] The new catechism by the pro-Falangist priest, Fr. Menéndez Reigada, gloried in the imperialist aspirations of Falangism, with Spain placed by God in the centre of the world and with imperial Catholicism as its mission. However, other catechisms were restored, such as the Ripalda, which said nothing of the new order but enjoined the faithful to return to true Christian values which had been lost during the eighteenth and nineteenth centuries. Church domination of education was extended in 1943 to the University and a new Act laid down that all instruction should be adapted to Catholic dogma. Church publications were also exempted from the new rigorous censorship. This seemed an easy price for Franco to pay for total Church support for his régime. However, later it was to prove a source of serious trouble. Franco did exact from the Church an important concession: in June 1941 an agreement was reached with Rome renewing for the Spanish Chief of State the ancient right of Spanish monarchs to nominate bishops.[17]

Inevitably, the Spanish hierarchy were firmly in support of Franco. The most significant exception was Cardinal Vidal y Barraquer, Archbishop of Tarragona, who did not return to his See in 1939. He had refused to sign the 1937 Collective Letter and was clearly persona non grata in postwar Spain.[18] Cardinal Segura did return, now as Archbishop of Seville, and remained a hostile critic of 'pagan' Falangism. The death of Franco's ally, Cardinal Gomá y Tomás, left a vacancy in the Primatial See of Toledo. This was filled in November 1941 by another friend of the Caudillo, Mgr. Enrique Plá y Deniel, who, as Bishop of Salamanca, had been in close touch

51

with the rebel leadership when Franco's headquarters were situated in that city during the Civil War.

There remained the problem of the hostile majority – the defeated. A distinction might be made between the anti-clerical middle-class intellectuals on the one hand and the masses of workers and landless peasants on the other. Many of the liberal intelligentsia were able to flee Spain. Of those who remained few escaped retribution. Indeed, the necessity to re-Catholicize the teaching profession meant that a purge of liberal teachers was unavoidable.[19] With regard to the masses, Church attendance became virtually compulsory. Evidence exists that the defeated Andalusian rural workers were forced to attend Mass in order to obtain work.[20] Chaplains invaded the jails to attempt to convert political prisoners. The success or otherwise of this operation is difficult to determine. Some accounts survive of life in Franco's prisons in the forties, and of the role played by the Church. Inevitably, many of these are written with great emotion and this must be taken into consideration. Descriptions exist of how religious observance was forced upon prisoners. Mass was obligatory, and success in religious tests necessary if any form of remission was to be achieved. In the jail at Alcalá de Henares an exception was made one day and Mass was made voluntary. Of over a thousand prisoners, only eight chose to attend on this unique occasion.[21] Other reports tell of violent behaviour against prisoners by clergy; the truth may never be known, but it requires an extremely blind faith in Franco to assert that force was rarely used.[22]

The Church's missionary zeal was not confined to the captive sectors of the conquered population. Obligatory military service afforded an opportunity to proselytize in the barracks. In addition, a movement of popular missions was initiated to attempt to win for the Church the allegiance of the poorer socio-economic groups. Towns experienced an influx of missioners accompanied by much public display of religosity, prominent roles being played by members of the hierarchy, the army and the local (frequently Falangist) civil authorities.[23]

The pulpit was even used as a 'means for the propagation of the national language' in an effort to stamp out Catalan. A belligerent anti-Catalanist campaign in the 'Crusade' spirit was undertaken by the Apostolic Administrator of Barcelona Bishop Díaz Gómara.[24]

The isolation of Spain during this period facilitated the propagation of nationalism but the Franco régime did not repeat mistakes made by its Italian and German counterparts. The Church was made to feel that it was as important as the State. When Axis defeat was imminent, Franco reduced even more the role of the

Falange and it was now the clerical right, much abused by old Falangist rhetoric, who were confirmed in power.[25] Catholic Action, controlled by the hierarchy, performed a crucial role in the construction of Francoism. Spanish Catholic Action by the early forties could count on over three hundred thousand militants.[26] Its elite leadership was drawn from the membership of the *Asociación Católica Nacional de Propagandistas* (henceforth ACNP) founded in 1909 by the Jesuit Fr. Angel Ayala. It is arguable that this organization has been the most important of all the pressure groups that have vied for power within the so-called 'limited pluralism' of the Francoist system.[27] In this respect its influence has exceeded that of Opus Dei and the Falange. The ACNP preceded Francoism, presided over its course and will probably survive its demise.

The dominant figure in the history of the ACNP was Angel Herrera Oria, a clever journalist and propagandist who exerted enormous influence through his newspaper *El Debate*. During the thirties the ACNP developed into an organization able to embrace all shades of rightist opinion.[28] Above all, the ACNP dominated the conservative *Acción Popular,* the most important element of the CEDA coalition.[29] Many ACNP members were enthusiastic supporters of the corporatist ideology in vogue at the time, and were natural supporters of the military rising. Many indeed associated with the extremist *Acción Española* group, and were active in the conspiracy against the Republic.[30]

At the end of the war the total membership of the ACNP was a mere 580 but the association soon established a strong power base within the régime.[31] Membership was by no means incompatible with Falangism. Fernando María Castiella, co-author of the rabidly falangist *Revindicaciones de España* was prominent in both organizations.[32] To a certain extent the ACNP and Catholic Action became superficially 'falangized' just as the FET itself had been diluted and given a religiose aura. The 'Crusade' myth was a joint creation of these twin pillars of the new régime. The fascist José Antonio Primo de Rivera was presented as a sort of Christian martyr, his name engraved on the walls of churches as a reminder to the faithful of their deliverance from atheistic communism. Herrera himself had spent the Civil War years in Fribourg studying for the priesthood. His return in 1940 restored to the ACNP their charismatic leader. Organization of the ACNP had been left in the able hands of Fernando Martín-Sánchez Juliá who, together with Alberto Martín-Artajo and Joaquín Ruiz-Giménez, provided Herrera with the support which enabled him to win for the ACNP an invulnerable position in the structure of Francoism. It also exerted a strong influence over the *Editorial Católica,* a publishing

53

organization whose newspapers included *Ideal* of Granada, the famous weekly *Dígame* and, above all, the Madrid daily, *Ya*. Herrera's journalistic experience was invaluable in the field of the information media.

The ACNP also successfully attempted to spread its influence in Education and obtained many University Chairs during the war years. The *Consejo Superior de Investigaciones Científicas* (henceforth CSIC), formed in November 1939, provided another means for the spread of influence. Interestingly, Opus Dei was also prominent in these areas at this time and was in certain respects an organization allied to the ACNP. It was not until some years later that the two groups became rivals.

1945-53 – Towards Concordat

With the inevitable decline of the Falange at the end of the Second World War, the ACNP reached the zenith of its power with the appointment of Martín-Artajo as Foreign Minister in 1945. Franco was forced to put up a brave front following the Axis defeat, but the emergence of 'Christian Democracy' in Italy and Germany proved conclusively that the Caudillo had been right in basing his faith on Catholicism rather than Falangism. The Falange was left seething in the wings while triumphant clericalism occupied centre stage. The Cardinal Primate of Spain, Archbishop Plá y Deniel, now condemned totalitarianism [33] but some other prominent clergy, such as the Bishop of Madrid-Alcala, Mgr. Eijó y Garay, remained unrepentantly fascistic. [34] During this period intensive proselytization continued. The *Cursillos de Cristiandad* provided a vehicle for evangelisation, especially among the intelligentsia, and the *Centro Pio XII*, created by Herrera Oria and Martín-Artajo, served both as a centre for internal evangelism and as a means to attract the attention of foreign sympathizers. [35]

In spite of the continued isolation of Spain following the United Nations boycott, the Spanish Church maintained its efforts to win respectability for Spain from the Western powers. Martín-Artajo and Ruiz-Giménez hoped to make friends among Western Christian democrats by stressing the righteousness of Franco's anti-communist 'Crusade'. Pope Pius XII, however, was by no means convinced that Francoism would survive. His lifelong anti-communism made him sympathetic, but he had to be sure before committing himself to the Concordat so much desired by the régime. [36] The Cold War atmosphere of the early fifties was the deciding factor. In 1952 the 35th World Eucharistic Congress was held in Barcelona. A special Mass was celebrated by Mgr. Herrera

54

Oria, now Bishop of Málaga, for Catholic Action members who had died fighting on Franco's side. The Caudillo himself addressed the Congress and consecrated Spain to the Holy Sacrament.[37] Meanwhile, the United States was approaching Franco to discuss the possibility of establishing military bases in Spain.

The American overtures were not welcomed wholeheartedly by the Spanish Church, though Primate Plá regarded them as the work of Divine Providence.[38] Many integrist prelates were preoccupied lest pagan influences should sully the purity of the new pseudo-theocracy they imagined existed in Spain. However, the recognition of Franco by the West gave powerful support to those who were striving to achieve the Concordat. In fact, much had already been negotiated in the meantime. Franco now had a say in the nomination of Deans and Chapters as well as of bishops, and could even veto the appointment of parish priests on 'political grounds'.[39]

The post of *Vicario General Castrense* (Chief Military Chaplain) carried the status of an archbishop, illustrating how closely linked were religion and militarism under the régime. Priests were, of course, exempt from military service.

The Concordat, which replaced that of 1851, was signed on 27 August 1953, one signatory being the ex-Nazi sympathizer Castiella, now Ambassador to the Holy See.[40, 41] It confirmed the gains already made, but one important exception remained. Franco's right to nominate was confined to permanent appointees, i.e. residential bishops and archbishops. The Vatican itself would appoint Apostolic Administrators to cover Sees temporarily vacant, and titular bishops to act as Auxiliaries. These seemingly minor appointments were to assume great political significance later.

The Concordat appeared of mutual benefit to both parties. In return for concessions over the appointment of bishops (Clauses 7-10) the Church enjoyed large financial benefits from the State (Clauses 19 and 20). The very first Clause asserted that the Catholic religion was to have exclusive right to proselytize, and freedom of worship was impossible for Spaniards in reality, although 'freedom of conscience' was permitted, as stated in the 1945 *Fuero de los Españoles*. Clauses 26-31 re-affirmed the clerical grip on Education. Outstanding was Clause 34, allowing the hierarchy to organize Catholic Action independently in all matters concerning its apostolate. Thus, many religious periodicals were exempted from the rigid press censorship controlled by the Information Minister, Gabriel Arias Salgado. The prayer for Franco to be said at Mass recognized him as victorious Christian leader chosen, as it were, by God Himself.

The régime was well pleased with the new treaty whose tone indicated wholehearted Vatican support for Franco. In few modern states has comparable status been achieved for the Church. Nevertheless, enthusiasm was not unanimous; such close links with the State might some day hinder rather than assist the Church in its evangelical mission. Already some clergy were worried by the apparent strengthening of ties between the Church and the victorious ruling oligarchy. This more liberal voice was muted during the rightist euphoria following the Concordat, but currents were beginning to stir which were eventually to divide the Spanish Church into bitterly antagonistic factions.

1953-1962 – Dissent Begins

The gradual emergence of a less intransigent spirit within the Spanish Catholic world can be seen in two main areas: (1) the intellectual debate following the publication of various books propounding a less integrist view of the role of the Church and (2) the identification of certain elements of the clergy with the struggles of the oppressed working-class.

With regard to the former, it may be considered ironic that many of the intellectuals identified with the new more thoughtful and less fanatical stance were, in fact, themselves Falangists. Among these were Pedro Laín Entralgo and José Luis Aranguren. In 1956 Laín published *España como problema*, an expansion of an essay originally composed as early as 1949. Aranguren was responsible for various works including *Catolicismo y protestantismo como formas de existencia*, 1952, and *Catolicismo día tras día*, 1955. He critically analysed Spanish Catholicism and attempted to open the eyes of Spanish Catholics to the more humane Catholic attitudes held abroad. In 1955 was founded the *Propaganda Popular Católica* (PPC), a publishing house which was to do much to change the image of Spanish Catholic theology. Its founder was Fr. Antonio Montero Moreno, later auxiliary Bishop of Seville. It produced various periodicals such as *Incunable* and *Pax*, a fortnightly review which was the predecessor of the powerful liberal Catholic periodical *Vida Nueva*. Others associated with these more progressive elements were Fr. José María Javierre and Ruiz-Giménez himself, by now Franco's Minister of Education, and Dionisio Ridruejo, once, like Laín Entralgo, a Falangist extremist, but now evolving towards a more democratic posture.[42] The integrist right were quick to retaliate. Fr. Javierre soon aroused the ire of his ecclesiastical superior, the virulently reactionary Bishop of Madrid-Alcalá, Mgr. Eijó y Garay, and was banished to Munich where he became Director of the Spanish

56

College. There he worked for a dialogue with exiled socialists to such effect that Franco himself intervened to have the dissident priest removed from his position.[43] Javierre was to reappear on the scene during the sixties as a champion of the new ecumenical Catholicism of Vatican II.[44] As for Laín Entralgo, he had already clashed with Rafael Calvo Serer, Opus Dei ideologue and author of *España sin problema*, 1949, a defence of the spirit of the Franco 'Crusade'. Calvo Serer now attacked not only so-called 'leftists' within the Falange, but also the 'Christian Democrats' who constituted the liberal wing of the ACNP. A 'third force' was needed, he argued, which would combine complete identification with Franco's victory, and yet capitalize on the opportunities for economic advancement provided by the pact with the USA. In *España despues de los tratados,* Calvo Serer advocated the new aggressively capitalistic economic philosophy of Opus Dei, to be put into practice when the Opus entered the government in 1957.

The mid-fifties saw Spain torn by a series of crises. There was a strike wave and the universities became battlegrounds between old-style Falangists and their opponents. It is here that we see the second element in the new progressive Catholicism emerging. This was the Catholic Workers' Movement. Elsewhere in Europe, Catholic trade unions had been formed in accordance with the social teachings of the Papal Encyclicals. This was impossible in Spain where the workers all were rigidly confined to the fascist-style vertical syndicates. However, Article 34 of the Concordat allowed Catholic Action freedom to conduct its activities without State intervention and when Catholic workers' associations were formed outside the *sindicatos*, their legal status under the Concordat gave them a unique position.

Three powerful organizations were formed: *Hermandades Obreras de Acción Católica* (HOAC), *Juventud Obrera Católica* (JOC) and *Vanguardias Obreras Juveniles* (VOJ).[45] Although these organizations aroused the hostility of the Sindicato bureaucracy, the authorities were reluctant to move against them for fear of contravening the Concordat. Cardinal Plá defended these organizations and objected when their members were harassed. However, he was clearly disturbed by what their militancy might lead to and he urged bishops to exercise careful surveillance.[46] This did not prevent many priests from supporting strikers in 1956. Indeed, many Catholics became so identified with the Opposition that they formed themselves into the *Frente de Liberación Popular* (FLP), a movement whose policy was overtly revolutionary. The FLP propagandist Ignacio Fernández de Castro states that the organization was inspired not so much by Catholicism but by a form of primeval

57

Christian egalitarianism and that many members were former anarchists 'converted' in prison ostensibly to Catholicism, but in reality to militant revolutionary Christianity.[47] Members of the HOAC, JOC, VOJ and FLP played their part in the great strike wave of 1962 working together with Marxist workmates in the emerging *Comisiones Obreras*. In twenty years the role of Catholic Action had been transformed. Whereas previously it had supported the 'Crusade' with virtually a unanimous voice, it was now divided. The alienation of many ACNP intellectuals from the régime coincided with the emergence of a new pressure group which was to exert an all-powerful influence on the political and economic establishment – Opus Dei.[48]

The ACNP and Opus Dei were both nurtured during the Republic by the clique surrounding the personality of Herrera Oria and *El Debate*. They sought to make their influence felt by infiltrating the universities and by developing means of propaganda through the communication media. The principal difference between the ACNP and Opus Dei can be said to be one of emphasis, the ACNP stressing the importance of social and political activity and Opus Dei of economic power. Also, the ACNP was capable of containing within its ranks a wide spectrum of political opinion from the extreme right to the centre-left; on the other hand, Opus Dei was almost exclusively dominated by the intransigent right. Opus Dei, of course, constituted the 'third force' advocated by Calvo Serer. The founder of Opus Dei, Mgr. Escrivá de Balaguer, preached a doctrine of leadership and discipline. His aim was to take over the institutions left by the defeated Republican intelligentsia and to invert them so as to serve the aims of an inflexible anti-democratic clericalism which would be allied, for the first time, with a takeover of the centres of economic and political power. Although a strict integrist in theology, Escrivá did not wish, in the manner of his Carlist forebears, to undermine the achievements of the Industrial Revolution. On the contrary, he wished to harness them. Weber's Protestant work ethic was to be combined with the most orthodox Catholicism. Although the latter may teach that one cannot serve God and Mammon, Escrivá and his followers were determined to make the attempt.

The medium through which Opus Dei began their rise to power was the CSIC. They were greatly assisted in this by Franco's postwar Minister of Education, José Ibáñez Martín, a member of ACNP and former associate of Acción Española.[49] The CSIC was a state organization and therefore gave the Opus a great opportunity to infiltrate the machinery of the régime. During this period the Secretary-General of CSIC was José María Albareda Herrera, one of the founders of Opus Dei. The CSIC had taken over the role of the Republican *Junta para Ampliación de Estudios,* responsible for the allocation of grants for higher education. By this means Opus Dei could select people favourable to their ideology and build up a cadre of leaders within Francoist Spain in accordance with the instructions given by Escrivá in the Opus handbook, *Camino.* Like the ACNP, the Opus Dei were successful during the forties in obtaining many university chairs, thanks to the 1943 University Act which gave the Minister of Education the power to nominate three of the five members of the Tribunal which would supervise the tests (*oposiciones*) required for selection. Among those who became University professors were Calvo Serer himself and the future Ministers Laureano López Rodó and Alberto Ullastres Calvo. The period of Opus ascendancy in the University ended when Ibáñez Martín was replaced as Minister of Education by Ruiz-Giménez in 1951. It was then that the Opus made its assault on government.

One of the first members of the hierarchy to recognize the importance of Opus Dei was Mgr. Eijó y Garay, who granted it the title of 'Pía Unión'. Then in 1947, after intense activity in Rome by Escrivá and his lieutenant Alvaro del Portillo, Pope Pius XII issued the Bull *Provida Mater Ecclesia* which created a new form of religious organization, the Secular Institute. The Opus Dei was the first such Institute to be recognized.

Opus members fit into four general categories: Numerarii, who are celibate members, clerical or lay, Supernumerarii, who hold the same high status but are not celibate, Oblati, celibate members who do not fulfil the high academic requirements necessary to become Numerarii and, perhaps most important, the Cooperatores, who are merely required to work for the good of the organization and to have Opus priests as Confessors.[50] Inevitably, the aura of secrecy which surrounds the Opus Dei is due, to a large extent, to the existence of this last category. It is difficult to ascertain whether or not any person is a Cooperator of the Opus and in *Camino* we find members being exhorted by Escrivá to be discreet with regard to their association with the Society.[51]

In 1951 Admiral Luis Carrero Blanco had been made Sub-secretary of the Presidencia del Gobierno. This appointment marked the entry of Opus into the orbit of government and established a close link with the person of Franco himself as Admiral Carrero was an old comrade-in-arms of the Caudillo. The Opus also gained control of the Banco Popular Español which provided access to the profitable world of the new capitalistic expansion which was soon to transform Spain. In publishing, the Opus had already established RIALP and SARPE, organizations for the publishing of

59

books and periodicals respectively. The Cold War atmosphere in Europe assisted the Opus in their quest for power. An aggressively rightist, anti-communist, capitalistic yet superficially non-fascist organization ideally fitted the requirements of post-Concordat Spain. Among the hierarchy the Opus found an ally in Bishop López Ortiz, a reactionary who later became Archbishop Chaplain-General of the armed forces.[52] It was also at this time that the Opus can be said to have parted company with the 'Jesuit' ACNP. In fact, the ACNP and Opus had now become rivals in the struggle for power within Francoism.

The single-minded toughness and united front put up by the Opus was indeed remarkable. From the mid-fifties onwards their advance was inexorable. Envious of the Jesuit Deusto University, which had produced so many of the ACNP elite, the Opus set up their own university college, the *Estudio General de Navarra,* later to achieve full university status.[53] The 'leftist' HOAC and JOC were reviled by the Opus, who also demanded a hard line against student militants in 1956.[54]

Opus ascendancy was finally contested by the Falange itself when José Luis Arrese presented his plan for a refalangized Spain. The Church hierarchy were horrified and urged Franco to choose Opus rather than Falangist government. The Caudillo made his choice and the Government of 1957 contained Alberto Ullastres (Commerce) and Mariano Navarro Rubio (Finance) who joined Carrero Blanco and other Opus sympathizers to form the most powerful bloc within the Cabinet. Moreover, Carrero's chief aide was to be Laureano López Rodó. The first brainchild of Opus Dei in government was the Stabilization Plan of 1959 which was to provide the base for the entry of Spain into the developed neocapitalist world of the West.[55]

The end of autarchy meant a radical economic liberalization, but by no means a relaxation in the anti-democratic committment of the régime. The new Interior Minister was General Camilo Alonso Vega, sympathetic to the Opus and fully in agreement with their repressive attitude towards political opposition. For the next fifteen years the Opus were to dominate the government of Franco.

1962-71 – The Divided Church

Meanwhile, Spain opened her frontiers to millions of tourists while, at the same time, allowing the exit of thousands of workers.[56] Spain had ceased to be isolated from the secularizing influence of modern Europe. The new philosophy of 'desarrollo' (economic development) did not fit in well with the monolithic religiosity which the Church

60

hierarchy had encouraged during the preceding years. The death of Pope Pius XII in October 1958 was also crucial. Cardinal Angelo Giuseppe Roncalli, now Pope John XXIII, at first appeared to the Spanish hierarchy as a man after their own heart. He had asserted that salvation was only possible through the one true Catholic faith and this was bound to gratify the Spanish hierarchy. However, his first Encyclical *Mater et Magistra* (May 1961) must have bewildered them. It omitted the normal encouraging tirade against 'atheistic communism', advocated pluralism and 'freedom of choice' and finally put to rest the traditional claim of the Church, upheld by the Curia, to control the laity on temporal as well as spirtual matters. Ullastres, however, was able to find comfort in it. It reaffirmed established teaching, he stated.[57]

The next Encyclical *Pacem in Terris* (April 1963) was less ambiguous. It stressed the necessity for the basic civil rights of association and expression and the freedom of the people freely to elect those put in authority in the secular sphere. It spoke up for ethnic and linguistic minorities. It even advocated peaceful co-existence with communism. The shock for the bishops of the 'Crusade' must have been devastating.

The liberal minority among the Spanish clergy were at last finding support from on high. Catholic writers such as Alfonso Carlos Comín and Fr. José María González Ruiz, author of *Marxismo y cristianismo frente al hombre nuevo* could now feel that the changes taking place in the Church had to affect Spain.[58] Tourism continued to increase, and this could not only have a secularizing effect but also a liberalizing influence on younger Spanish Catholics, meeting for the first time correligionists from abroad whose attitude to the faith was not that inculcated into the average Spaniard.

The event that was to give most cause for hope among progressive Spanish Catholics, and for dismay among the Francoist hierarchy, was the inauguration of the Second Vatican Council in October 1962. Only the Civil War itself has had more effect on the Spanish Church this century.

To the Vatican Council proceeded Spanish prelates of varying rank, among them Cardinal Primate Plá y Deniel and Cardinal Herrera Oria, together with other older Church leaders who had given unconditional support to the 'Crusade'. These would, therefore, most likely side with fellow conservatives on such subjects as Church–State relations, ownership of property and freedom of worship.[59]

On Church-State relations a significant Spanish contribution was that by Bishop López Ortiz, then Bishop of Tuy-Vigo, later to become Chaplain General of the armed forces. He objected to the notion that Church and State must always be independent and that the State should not be allowed to pass judgment on religious matters. This was against the traditional teaching that when a country is almost unanimously Catholic, the State, by declaring itself confessional, is only showing its obedience to Divine Law – Franco Spain being the obvious example.[60] This speech occurred during the discussions on religious freedom, naturally a subject of particular interest to those seeking to defend the correctness of the Spanish 'Crusade' mentality. The argument centred around a draft text which recognized freedom of worship as a basic human right. It was, of course, to lead to the significant Council document *Dignitatis Humanae*. The integrist Spaniards fought a rearguard action. The Arch-bishop of Santiago de Compostela, Cardinal Quiroga y Palacios, asked why the traditional teaching regarding the evils of liberalism should now be refuted. He demanded that the declaration on religious liberty be completely revised.[61] He was supported by the Archbishop of Tarragona, Cardinal Benjamín de Arriba y Castro, who affirmed that only the one true Church should be allowed to officiate publicly. Bishop Cantero Cuadrado agreed. Religious liberty should be confined to private conscience, and proselytization should be forbidden for non-Catholics.[62] A less extremist position was adopted by Cardinal Bueno y Monreal of Seville. He did not dispute the theological correctness of the text, but supported the right of a Catholic government to prevent the 'spread of error'.

Some significant speeches were made on the subject of the ownership of property. The Bishop of Lérida, Mgr. Aurelio Pino Gómez, stated that property is a way of honouring God. The absurdity of some of his arguments did, in fact, evoke some derision on the floor of the Council.[63] Cardinal Arriba y Castro, like Bishop Pino, presented the age-old stance against communism and objected to the term 'The Church of the Poor'.[64] It was again Cardinal Bueno y Monreal who adopted a less reactionary approach. Coming from the latifundio area of Andalucia and associated by many with the southern oligarchy, the Cardinal was aware of the problems arising from the traditional link between the Church and the richer, more powerful groups in society. He stated that the ownership of property should not be so bound up with the doctrines of the Church and regretted the absence from the draft text of any declaration in favour of redistribution of wealth.[65]

Some interesting statements came from other bishops. One that casts a significant light on what was to come in Spain was made by the ultra-conservative Bishop Pildaín y Zapaín of the Canary Islands. He stressed that decisions made by Conferences of bishops should not be binding. What counted was the Magisterium from above. The right wing were clearly concerned lest pseudo-democratic procedures be allowed to dictate policy.[66] During the discussion on Evangelism, Cardinal Herrera Oria recommended the use of trained sociologists to assist in the training of parish priests.[67] A journalist by training, he was in favour of harnessing the power of the communication media and the methodology of modern social science.

When the Council ended it was plain that the Church was in the throes of a transition; it was also clear that the Spanish hierarchy were ranged firmly on the right, so the Council documents when published must have proved even more disturbing than the Encyclicals of John XXIII.[68] Two documents in particular must be mentioned: The Constitution of the Church in the Modern World (*Gaudium et Spes*) and the Declaration of Religious Freedom (*Dignitatis Humanae*). It is ironic that these were the very documents which were to form the basis of many of the arguments later put forward by those bishops who wished to see an end to the link with Francoism.

Meanwhile a rift was developing in Spain between the progressive and conservative wings within the Church. At first progressivism was confined almost entirely to the lower clergy. The famous declaration by 339 Basque priests in 1960 against police brutality brought upon them the anger of the Episcopate.[69] Dom Aureli Escarré, Abbot of Montserrat, spoke of the two opposing trends within the Church but Cardinal Herrera Oria denied the existence of any serious division of opinion, stating that the majority of priests were docile and obedient.[70] The Cardinal's statement was clearly wishful thinking. He was himself involved in 1961 in controversy over the progressive teachings of his subordinate Fr. González Ruiz, Canon of Málaga Cathedral. González Ruiz was charged with false teaching and dismissed from his post. In many ways he represents the new spirit among the forward-looking clergy. His sermons at Málaga had contained references to oppression by the landlords, condemnations of capitalism and advocacy of dialogue with Marxism. His articles in *Juventud Obrera* continued this theme. In his book, *El cristianismo no es un humanismo*, 1966, he preached a more personal religion rebelling against the institutional Church.

The HOAC and JOC often involved the younger clergy in strikes and even conservative bishops stated that the causes of industrial unrest were often low pay and poor working conditions rather than 'international Communist agitators'. Cardinal Plá y Deniel, Cardinal Bueno y Monreal and Bishop Gúrpide Beope of Bilbao were among those who seemed to prevaricate on these issues.[72] The pressure from below appeared at least to be having some impact. An independent voice was that of Dom Aureli Escarré whose monthly review *Serra d'or*, carried critical comments in Catalan of the state of affairs in Spain. In November 1963, in a Press interview with *Le Monde* about the forthcoming celebrations of '25 years of peace', he asserted that the attitude of those in power in Spain was not truly Christian; they were, in fact, celebrating not peace but 25 years of victory.[73] A brother Benedictine, Fray Pérez de Urbel, Abbot of the Valley of the Fallen and a close friend of Franco, responded by trying to obtain the dissolution of Montserrat with the help of another old ally of Franco, the former Nuncio Cardinal Antoniutti, now a leading member of the Curia. His efforts met with some success: although Paul VI refused to dissolve Montserrat, Escarré retired 'for reasons of health'. However, his successor, Dom Cassia Just, was later to become even more critical of the régime than was Escarré.

Paul VI, formerly Cardinal Giovanni Battista Montini, Archbishop of Milan, had been elected Pope in 1963. In the previous year he had clashed with Franco when he appealed for clemency on behalf of young anarchists sentenced for acts of terrorism. The Spanish Vice-Consul in Milan was, in fact, kidnapped for two days and there were demonstrations outside the Spanish Embassy in the Vatican. Inevitably, relations between the Cardinal and the Spanish government* were strained.[74] In 1967 Paul VI produced his Encyclical *Populorum Progressio* which denounced imperialism and called on Catholics to play their part in the worldwide attack on poverty. Franco welcomed the Encyclical stating that it supported with its doctrine the solutions he had brought to the problems of Spain.[75] In spite of these words, this Encyclical marks the beginning of a rift between the Francoist State and the Holy See. In the mid-sixties the split within Spanish Catholicism became more marked. It can be seen epitomized, above all, in two controversies: one within Catholic Action and the other regarding the confessionality of the State.

Catholic Action was still firmly under the control of the hierarchy led by the Archbishop of Madrid, Mgr. Casimiro Morcillo González in his capacity as President of the Episcopal Commission of Secular Apostolate.

Mgr. Morcillo had moved from Zaragoza to Madrid in 1963 on the death of his mentor, the fanatical Mgr. Eijó y Garay, under whom he had served as Auxiliary from 1943 to 1950. Morcillo then was a typical rightist Spanish prelate whose ties with the régime were strengthed by his nomination by Franco to the Cortes. He insisted that Catholic Action remain firmly under episcopal control

64

and resisted attempts by the HOAC, JOC and other progressive elements among the laity to win more power within the organization. In this he was supported by his even more reactionary Auxiliary Bishop José Guerra Campos, also soon to become a Franco nominee in Cortes. The 1966 Catholic Action Congress was suspended and in 1967 Spain sent two separate delegations to the World Council of Secular Apostolate in Rome, one representing the progressive laity and led by Joaquín Ruiz-Giménez, and the official delegation dominated by the right and including the flamboyant figure of Blas Piñar López, who had founded the journal *Fuerza Nueva* in January 1967. Piñar was soon to become a household name in Spain as representative of the forces of violent reaction. The controversy within Catholic Action ended temporarily with a victory for the right, and Guerra Campos was firmly installed in charge. However, membership dropped dramatically from one million in 1966 to a mere one hundred thousand in 1972. [76]

With regard to the confessionality of the State, the 1966 Episcopal Conference declared that they were ready to renounce rights and privileges in accordance with the wishes of the Pope and did, in fact, decide to give up the fiscal advantages enjoyed by the Church under the Concordat. [77] It was becoming gradually clear to the bishops that the time was approaching when it would be difficult for them to reconcile post-conciliar papal policy with close ties with Francoism. However, the bishops supported the 1966 Organic Law and urged a 'Yes' vote in the subsequent referendum. Bishop Gúrpide Beope of Bilbao suspended all HOAC and JOC members in his diocese who had signed a Manifesto urging a 'No' vote. [78] Such sanctions soon became commonplace against laity and liberal priests.

Many Catholic Action publications were sequestrated. *Aún* was banned permanently and the entire editorial staff of *Signo* dismissed following its advocacy of a dialogue with the Communist Party. Many priests were in fact already working with Communists within the Workers' Commissions and a special prison was established for priests at Zamora since the Concordat stipulated that priests were to be given separate treatment in such circumstances. Many priests, however, demanded to be treated in the same way as other workers. In April 1966 there occurred the occupation of the Capuchin Convent of Sarria. Priests were beaten up by police who thus made themselves liable for automatic excommunication under Canon Law 2343. Such scenes were to be repeated all over Spain, but particularly in Catalonia and the Basque country, where Bishop Pablo Gúrpide Beope had often been in conflict with progressive clergy in his diocese, ever since the priests' declaration in 1960. [79] Many Basque priests went on hunger strike in support of persecuted workers. On 30 May 1968 five priests occupied the episcopal offices at Bilbao. They were later given sentences of from ten to twelve years' imprisonment. [80] In August, forty more priests were ejected by police from the same offices, and fifty priests staged a sit-in at the nearby seminary of Derio. A further anti-régime demonstration occurred in October at the funeral of the former Bishop of Vitoria, Mgr. Mateo Múgica, who had refused to sign the pro-Franco Collective Letter in 1937.

With the death of Bishop Gúrpide in November, a vacancy arose at Bilbao. Under the Concordat Franco could not participate in the appointment of Auxiliary Bishops and Apostolic Administrators and therefore was unable to resist the appointment of Mgr. José María Cirarda Lachiondo, the new Bishop of Santander, as Apostolic Administrator of Bilbao. The significance of the appointment however is to be found in his previous activities as Auxiliary Bishop of Seville. Conditions in the south were still very bad for the labourers. Nearly 90 per cent of these could be classified as anti-clerical, according to a HOAC survey. Similarly, 50 per cent of male Andalusians never attended Mass, and the majority of young men did not make their First Communion until forced to on reaching the age of military service. [81] The Andalusian bishops were clearly anxious to win more allegiance from the impoverished working-class. Bishop Cirarda spoke out against the low wages of agricultural labourers. An even stronger voice was that of the Bishop of Cádiz-Ceuta, Mgr. Antonio Añoveros Ataún. Añoveros coupled his condemnation of low wages with an attack on the Latifundistas. In a pastoral letter in November 1968, reprinted in *Ecclesia,* he analysed the causes of the appallingly low standard of living suffered by Andalusian 'braceros'. [82] The Bishop revealed that even the inadequate minimum wage of 102 pesetas per day was not being paid to many. The average working day was twelve hours and unemployment had doubled in the province of Cadiz from 1962 to 1968. Añoveros called for a radical redistribution of wealth, using as his main support a speech of Paul VI delivered in Bogotá at that time, also referring to the Vatican Council document *Gaudium et Spes.* This attack on Latifundismo was not supported by the hierarchy as a whole who, therefore, tacitly sided with the landowners. However, Añoveros was backed up by the Bishop of Guádiz-Baza, Mgr. Gabino Díaz Merchán, who in a pastoral letter revealed that 41 per cent of braceros and their families lived in caves in the Guádix area. [83] He insisted on the right of the Church to attack injustice and lamented the depoliticization of the working-class. However, Díaz Merchán's liberalism did not extend to advocacy of political parties. He reaffirmed the Falangist cliche of family, municipality and syndicate as means of representation. He visualized a system of associations within the structure of the Francoist system.[84] Perhaps most outspoken of all was the new Bishop of the Canary Islands, Mgr. Antonio Infantes Florido, who had succeeded to the See at Las Palmas on the death of the diehard Bishop Pildaín y Zapaín. It is difficult to imagine a greater contrast.[85] More than any other bishop, Mgr. Infantes constantly refers to the Council documents and Encyclicals of John XXIII. A typical example is his pastoral of June 1969 which insists upon the right to freedom of association and full participation in public life.[86] The Church may teach that authority comes from God, but many régimes fail to measure up to this standard. Public order is not synonymous with tyranny and every citizen has the duty to resist oppression either passively, like Martin Luther King, or indeed actively. The demand for political pluralism is repeated in *Vida Nueva,* and the Bishop has established himself as one of the most radical in his denouncement of repression and political discrimination.[87, 88]

In Catalonia a crisis had arisen with the death of Bishop Modrego Casaus, causing a vacancy in the crucial See of Barcelona. The new appointee was Mgr. Marcelo González Martín, Bishop of Astorga. The appointment of this Castilian caused a furore.[89] Franco had followed a systematic policy, backed by the Castilian hierarchy, of assigning Castilians to Catalan Sees.[90] The Vatican clearly was of the opinion that such nominations were no longer appropriate, and in 1968 appointed four Catalan Auxiliary Bishops, including Mgr. Ramón Torrella, once suspended by Mgr. Eijó y Garay for supporting strike action.[91]

An Act of legislation which demonstrated the divisions within the Spanish church was the Law of Religious Liberty, June 1967. This freedom, held to be mortal sin until comparatively recently, was now accepted as inevitable by even the extreme right of the hierarchy. The Vatican Council document *Dignitatis Humanae* made a return to the old intransigent integrism an impossibility.[92] However, the régime was successful in making the law as ineffectual as possible. The liberal clergy and the Protestant minority expressed their dissatisfaction. Pastor José Cardona, the unofficial leader of Spanish Protestants, organized a successful boycott of the local authority registers of Protestant churches which the new law demanded. The law was welcomed by rightists such as Archbishop Cantero and Bishop Laureano Castán Lacoma of Sigüenza-Guadalajara. Perhaps most significant of all were the statements made by the two greatest champions of clerical Francoism – Blas Piñar called the law 'a triumph of the spirit of Vatican II' and Bishop Guerra Campos stated on television that the régime had every right to give special support to one particular religion.[93, 94] Bishop Guerra was now beginning his career as 'El Obispo de la televisión', a position which was to provide the conservative clerics with a useful means of propaganda.

In the North the situation continued explosive. In addition to the nomination of Mgr. Cirarda as Apostolic Administrator of Bilbao, Franco was obliged to accept the moderate Mgr. Tabera y Araoz to the Archbishopric of Pamplona. Mgr. Tabera had spoken out in March 1969 against the imposition of a State of Emergency stating that it was futile to adopt draconian measures without attempting to remedy the causes of discontent.[95] In 1969 Mgr. Tabera was a surprise choice for elevation to the College of Cardinals, a clear indication of Vatican thinking with regard to the Spanish situation.[96]

The death of Cardinal Plá y Deniel in July 1968 left a vacancy in the primatial See of Toledo. Among eligible candidates were three active Spanish Cardinals Quiroga y Palacios, Arriba y Castro and Bueno y Monreal. The first two were obviously acceptable to the régime but in view of the difficulties with the Vatican the nomination of either might have been provocative. Cardinal Bueno, on the other hand, clearly lacked the tact required for the position. He had declared himself against Franco's role in appointing bishops and had stated that the spirit of Vatican II was not being adequately enacted.[97] He was thus a candidate unacceptable to the right. However, as a disciple of his predecessor Cardinal Segura, and in view of his association with the Andalusian oligarchy, he was also viewed with suspicion by the emergent liberal elements, who still remembered that he had received his Cardinal's hat in 1959 from the hand of Franco himself. Thus, a compromise candidate was necessary. In February 1969 Mgr. Vicente Enrique y Tarancón, Archbishop of Oviedo, became the new Primate of Spain. This quiet, learned theologian was by no means a radical, although a clear supporter of the *Aggiornamento* initiated by John XXIII, and continued by the Second Vatican Council. He was above all, completely loyal to Pope Paul VI and can be described as the instrument for papal policy in Spain. This meant that he became the catalyst in the gradual withdrawal of Vatican support for the Franco régime.

Identification with the régime, however, still remained strong among many bishops. The leaders of the pro-Franco faction were the four ecclesiastical nominees in Cortes: Archbishop Morcillo González, and his Auxiliary Bishop Guerra Campos, Bishop Luis Almarcha Hernández of León and Franco's old ally, Archbishop Cantero Cuadrado of Zaragoza. The Francoists showed their strength by electing Mgr. Morcillo President of the Bishops'

68

Conference, defeating the new Primate Mgr. Enrique y Tarancón.[98] However, the liberals were pressing for more independence from the State and urging the Bishops to renounce their seats in Cortes. Finally, Archbishop Morcillo decided to renounce his seat, perhaps thinking thereby to curry favour with the Vatican and to enhance his changes of a Cardinal's hat – which he never received.[99] The permanent Commission of the Bishop's Conference, dominated by Morcillo and Guerra, issued a statement in February 1969 approving the State of Emergency which had been declared by the régime.[100] The Pope, however, expressed his anxiety with regard to the situation in Spain in a speech to the College of Cardinals in June 1969.[101] A great polemic followed in the Press. His Holiness had previously written to Franco in April 1968 requesting the the Chief of State renounce his right of patronage regarding the nomination of bishops. Franco, however, insisted that the right was established under the Concordat and implied that only a new Concordat could materially change the situation.[102]

The problem of confessionality was still a major source of controversy. More and more Church leaders were speaking out in favour of disestablishment. Franco's end of year message in 1969 stated that the traditional confessionality of the State corresponded with the deepest convictions of the great majority of the Spanish people. This statement must be balanced against a survey published in 1970 by *Vida Nueva* which found that only 5 per cent of Spaniards wished to continue the status quo; 31 per cent wished to see the Concordat drastically revised and no fewer than 61 per cent to see the Concordat ended altogether.[103]

In May 1969 the X Bishops' Congress was a victory for the conservatives led by the President Archbishop Morcillo and the Secretary Bishop Guerra Campos, the communiqué stressing the excellent relations between Church and State. The following Conference, however, which took place in December 1969, showed a shift away from the régime towards the Vatican position.[104] This advance by the liberals had been largely brought about by the general dissatisfaction regarding the proposed Ley Sindical.

The VII Assembly of July 1968 had committed itself to advocacy of freedom of association in accordance with the teachings of the Vatican Council.[105] Six basic points had been put forward regarding freedom of trade unions. The sixth point was of crucial importance in that it affirmed the right to strike for economic ends. The failure of the proposed law to measure up to these standards made it inevitable that the XI Conference would express its hostility. The following year the Permanent Commission for Social Apostolate, a committee which included Díaz Merchán, Infantes Florido and the

69

prestigious Archbishops Emilio Benavent Escuín of Granada and Felix Romero Menjíbar of Valladolid expressed its opposition to the new law in even stronger terms.[106] It seemed as if the Ley Sindical debate was to be a major cause of the rift between Church and State. The Falangists had made their position quite clear in their IV Syndical Congress in Tarragona in May 1968. Solis Ruiz stated that whatever the bishops might say, Spanish syndicalism had spoken in Tarragona and there was nothing more to be said. However, the bishops of that very province issued a statement for May Day 1969 attacking the new law, denouncing the evils of capitalism and reiterating the legitimate right of all workers to free trade unions.[107]

The polemic continued against the background of increasing industrial unrest. Workers were having to resort to the occupation of churches as a means of publicizing their claims; Mgr. Infantes Florido was naturally among those who pointe out that they had little other recourse. Mgr. Díaz Merchán, now Archbishop of Oviedo, added his voice, supported by his progressive Auxiliary Mgr. Elías Yanes Alvarez, demanding fundamental transformation in the economic structure of Spain and defending priests who helped strikers.[108]

In July 1970 there occurred a strike of building workers in Granada. The police opened fire and three strikers were killed. The Falangist press attacked the clergy for inciting the workers. A general strike followed. On 28 July, Archbishop Benavent Escuín issued a pastoral letter. The Archbishop, a disciple of Herrera Oria, was thought by many to be a conservative. But now he spoke out firmly against the police brutality, defended worker-priests from those who wished to label them as 'instigators of violence' and demanded adequate media through which workers could solve their legitimate grievances.[109] Granada Cathedral had provided a sanctuary for strikers. Church buildings came more and more to be used by left wing organizations either for cover or for the organization of meetings. When the police moved in to church property to disperse such gatherings, they violated the Concordat, thus providing the clergy with the opportunity to point out the illegality of such procedures.

A typical example occurred on 1 June 1970 in Bilbao. Mgr. Cirarda issued a pastoral stating that although he was against the continued existence of the Concordat, it must be observed for as long as it lasted. Repression of the liberty of the Church was part of the general repression in Spain.[110] Cirarda had been forced to act by the accusations made on 16 May 1970 by 187 Basque priests who were imprisoned. They criticized their bishops for compromising with the régime. Bishop Cirarda had certainly adopted an equivocal posture.

He had authorized the trial and imprisonment of five priests in Bilbao in 1968 but now he decided to resist, and on 19 June refused to celebrate the traditional Te Deum in commemoration of the 'liberation' of Bilbao.[111, 112]

Galicia and Asturias also became centres of conflict. The Galician bishops stated that although they were opposed to the use of churches for political ends, they well understood the cause.[113] Oviedo, Gijón and El Ferrol saw a good deal of working-class activity backed by priests, and Bishop Elías Yanes Alvarez, appointed Auxiliary of Oviedo in November 1970 at the age of 42, soon became associated with a dynamic younger element among the episcopate eager for reform and anxious to end the links with Francoism.

It was against this turbulent background that the vote on the Ley Sindical took place in Cortes. The reactionaries Cantero Cuadrado and Guerra Campos defended the Law, the former in his speech on the floor of the house and the latter in an article in *Ecclesia*. This aroused many letters to the editor most of which attacked Mgr. Guerra and defended the expressed opposition of the Bishops' Conference to the new Law.[114] When the vote came the three remaining bishops in Cortes – Cantero, Guerra and Almarcha – were conspicuous by their absence. The new Act was passed and became law on 16 February 1971. *Cuadernos para el diálogo,* now the organ of liberal lay Catholicism, condemned it as a retrograde step which failed to reflect the just aspirations of the workers.

The 1970 Burgos trial of 16 Basque nationalists aroused bitter exchanges between the bishops and the régime.[115] Among the accused were two priests, Fr. Julián Calzada Ugalde and Fr. Juan Echave Garitacelaya, later sentenced to 12 and 15 years respectively. A joint pastoral was issued by Bishop Cirarda and Bishop Argaya Goicoechea of San Sebastian denouncing the procedure of the trial and the indictment under the law of Banditry and Terrorism. The Ministry accused the bishops of prejudicing a *sub judice* hearing and insisted on the 'legitimate violence' of authority. The defence lawyers replied stating that it was the Ministry that was interfering with the course of justice. The Falangist Press weighed in with bitter attacks on the bishops.[116] It was now common for Francoists to bring the charge of temporalism against ecclesiastics who 'interfered in politics'. The hypocrisy of the Franco régime is surely apparent here. No charges of 'interference' had been levelled when hundreds of bishops and clergy had preached Francoism from the pulpit during the years following the Civil War. Among clerics thus accused was the Abbot of Montserrat, Dom Cassia Just. He replied in an interview with *Le Monde* that it was the duty of all Catholics to

71

speak against injustice. The Church could not associate itself with a régime which executed men (including Catholics) for the simple 'crime' of opposing Franco.[117]

1971-75 – The Church and the Current Crisis

The change in attitude within the episcopate can, to a certain extent, be explained by the fact that most of the pro-régime element were of the older generation. As they died, their posts were inevitably filled by a 'post-conciliar' cleric. A major crisis occurred with the death of Mgr. Morcillo, leaving vacant the See of Madrid-Alcalá in June 1971. The Vatican stepped in quickly and appointed an Apostolic Administrator, in accordance with the Concordat. It was clearly realized that the seat of power was now in Madrid rather than in Toledo. The Administrator appointed was no less a person than the Primate himself, the now Cardinal Enrique y Tarancón. Cardinal Tarancón was soon confirmed as Archbishop of Madrid and the new Primate was Mgr. González Martín moved from Barcelona after a long popular campaign for his transfer. He was replaced by the Catalan Mgr. Narcis Jubany Arnau, Bishop of Gerona, who had supported the movement for free trade unions in 1969.[118] Archbishop Jubany was soon to be made a Cardinal and later made some outspoken statements against police brutality even going so far as to categorize the régime as one of 'institutionalized violence'.[119] Jubany's normal moderation lent great weight to this assertion. The diplomatic Enrique y Tarancón dissociated himself from Cardinal Jubany's opinions.

The liberal element were now in the ascendancy. One of their principal vehicles was the National Commission of Justice and Peace set up by the Vatican to examine social conditions. Its President was Bishop of Huelva, Mgr. González Moralejo, champion of the port workers and sailors who formed a high proportion of the population of his diocese. The Justice and Peace Commission's report of 1 January 1971, 'Every Man is My Brother', represents one of the most significant documents of the progressive clergy and laity. It was published to celebrate the fourth World Day of Peace and contains 22 clauses. Clause 5 referred to the death of the Pacifist Bertrand Russell (an atheist), Clause 7 attacked exploitation and class warfare, Clause 8 lamented the increasing role of ultrarightist groups of terrorists, Clause 10 defended the rights of ethnic and linguistic minorities. The whole document was couched in a moderate tone, but it still aroused great hostility from the conservative forces.[120]

The ultrarightist element referred to were the 'Guerrilleros de Cristo Rey' (Warriors of Christ the King) led by Mariano Sanchez

72

Covisa and supported by the faction controlling the magazine *Fuerza Nueva* under the leadership of Blas Piñar Lopez. [121] The Guerrilleros were responsible for many outrages. On 25 October 1871 they destroyed 24 Picasso canvasses at the Theo gallery in Madrid. Moreover, they had no compunction in inflicting physical violence on priests. As early as 19 December 1969 they caused a riot outside the Palace of Justice in Madrid demanding harsh penalties for the priest Fr. Mariano Gamo who had spoken out against the State of Emergency. This led to a statement from the office of the Archbishop of Madrid, then the right wing Mgr. Morcillo, denouncing the Guerrilleros. [122] Fr. Gamo was sentenced to three years' imprisonment. In Barcelona the Jesuit Fr. Bolado was beaten up. The Guerrilleros, self-proclaimed champions of traditional integrist Catholic teaching, seemed unperturbed by the prospect of the automatic excommunication which follows assaults upon the clergy.

In July 1970 the Bishop of Avila, Mgr. Maximino Romero de Lema, was threatened by the Guerrilleros following the announcement that an International Congress of progressive clergy was to be held in that city. Bishop Romero withdrew authorization for the Conference. Archbishop Morcillo also refused to allow the Conference to be held in his diocese, stating that the authorities would be called in to deal with the situation if his wishes were not observed. Foreign organizers of the Conference issued a statement critical of the Spanish régime and supporting the stand being made by liberal Spanish Catholics. [123]

However, it was not only meetings of progressive clergy that were discouraged. The organization of conservative priests (*Hermandad Sacerdotal Española*) held a Conference in Zaragoza in the diocese of Archbishop Cantero. The Permanent Commission of the Spanish Bishops' Conference refused to give official authorization to the Assembly. The Vatican agreed and the papal blessing was withheld. [124]

On 13 September 1971 Cardinal Enrique y Tarancón inaugurated the first Joint Assembly (*Asamblea Conjunta*) of bishops and priests, a type of assembly accepted by Vatican II but previously declared heretical. [125] The Communiqué issued at the end of the Assembly contained 56 Clauses. [126] They add up to a scathing indictment of Francoism, and the document goes on to advocate that the Church should sever all relations with the Franco régime, that the Concordat should be drastically revised and that the Bishops should resign their seats in Cortes. It laments the previous association of the Church with the ruling class and demands the right of the clergy to express themselves freely on political matters.

Even more sensational than the Communiqué were the resolutions passed by the Assembly. A resolution opposing the Bishops' seats in Cortes was passed by 170 votes to 56. This was hardly surprising given the climate in the Church at the time, but another resolution put before the Assembly must surely rank as historically among the most striking events to rock the Spanish Church since the Civil War. The motion was worded as follows: '*We recognize humbly and we ask forgiveness because we were not able in due time to be true ministers of reconciliation in the heart of our people divided by a war among brothers.*' [127] This was a reference to the Civil War in which the Church had, of course, overwhelmingly sided with the insurgents against a democratically elected Republic. The Resolution, in fact, was a repudiation of the Church's role in the 'Cruzada'. The result of the vote was as follows:

137	... For	10	... Abstentions
78	... Against	19	... Iuxta Modum (qualified support for Resolution)

A two-thirds majority required for policy decision, was not quite obtained, but there was a clear overall majority in favour. This meant that a second vote was taken with an Amendment inserted into the Resolution on the instigation of the Iuxta Modum voters. The Amendment substituted the words '*not always able*' for '*not able in due time*'. [128] Voting on the amended Resolutions was:

123 ... For; 113 ... Against; 10 ... Abstentions

Clearly, some delegates had shifted their ground, probably because of the extremely controversial nature of the issue. The second vote revealed the clear division into two opposing factions. However, it was the first vote that caused the most stir and the fact that such a Resolution was even discussed was bound to have a profound effect. Indeed, the repercussions still continue.

The Falangist press bitterly attacked the Assembly, as did *Iglesia-Mundo*, the organ of the right wing of the hierarchy. However, *Ecclesia* and *Vida Nueva* supported it. [129] A prestigious voice was added to the liberal cause, that of Mgr. José Pont y Gol, Bishop of Castellón, and soon to be elevated to the Archbishopric of Tarragona. He stated that the Assembly had been doctrinally correct according to the teachings of Vatican II. The Assembly Communiqué did, in fact, quote extensively from *Gaudium et Spes*.

Opus Dei, still dominant in government and with a powerful voice in the media, allied themselves with the conservative bishops in a conspiracy to discredit the Joint Assembly. The Opus-controlled Europa Press published a document authorized by the Vatican

Congregation of the Clergy, whose Prefect was the conservative American, Cardinal Wright. The document criticized the political role of the Spanish episcopate and their 'erroneous' theology, particularly regarding the validity of the Joint Assembly. Bishop Guerra Campos welcomed the letter stating that it had the backing of the Vatican. Cardinal Tarancón hurried to Rome to confer with the Pope and with Secretary of State Cardinal Villot, and succeeded in obtaining a statement from the latter to the effect that His Holiness had not authorized the Wright document which did not represent the views of the Papacy. Paul VI restated his confidence in the Tarancón line. Thus, not only was Cardinal Wright made to appear foolish, but the Opus stratagem was exposed. The Spanish liberals went so far as to demand the resignation of Cardinal Wright from the Curia. This was asking too much, but soon afterwards Bishop Guerra lost the Secretaryship of the Permanent Commission of the Bishops' Conference. He was replaced by the progressive Bishop Yanes Alvarez. Cardinal Enrique himself was re-elected President, a post he held since the death of Archbishop Morcillo. [130] The more conservative group now looked to Archbishop González Martín for leadership. The Primate, soon to receive the cardinal's hat, virtually the automatic prerogative of an Archbishop of Toledo, accepted a seat on Franco's Council of State, despite his claim to stand for the disestablishment of the Church. The liberals were dismayed, and such were their protests that the Archbishop threatened to resign from his position on the Bishops' Conference. [131] As for Bishop Guerra, he was soon transferred from Madrid to the obscure See of Cuenca, though he did maintain his vital access to the television studios.

In 1972 there occurred another cause célèbre which was to attract great publicity abroad. This was the arrest on 24 June 1972 of ten men in a Church at Pozuelo (Madrid) accused of illegal assembly. Among them was a worker-priest Fr. Francisco García Salve. This case (No. 1001) was not to be heard until December 1973, on the very day on which Admiral Carrero Blanco was murdered. Fr. García Salve hoped to include among his defence witnesses Cardinal Enrique y Tarancón, Mgr. Echarrén Ysturiz, Auxiliary Bishop of Madrid, and the Jesuit General Fr. Arrupe. However, the authorities forbade their appearance. [132] Fr. García Salve was sentenced to 19 years' imprisonment (later reduced on appeal). [133]

The position of the Bishops' Conference with regard to Church–State relations was made clear in a document published in January 1973, following a delay of two months. The drafting committee had the now inevitable liberal bias, and included Díaz Merchán, Cirarda, Gonzalez Moralejo and the increasingly powerful Yanes Alvarez. The 5,000 word text was put to the Plenary Conference and carried by 59 votes to 20, with 4 abstentions – a clear two-thirds majority. The document, entitled 'The Church and the Political Community', advocated independence of Church and State, the end of Franco's right to nominate bishops, abrogation of the Church's fiscal and other benefits and withdrawal of bishops from Cortes. It also stated that the hierarchy alone had the right to state the Church's view on political matters, not 'groups who usurp in the name of the Church' – a thinly-veiled reference to Opus Dei. The new declaration was attacked by Fr. Venancio Marcos in *Fuerza Nueva*, while *Iglesia-Mundo* denounced its lack of clarity and drew attention to the high (sic) number of votes against. The document was defended by *ABC, Ya* and *Vida Nueva*, although attention was drawn to the obvious fact that the bishops were divided. [134]

The rightist elements among the laity resorted more and more to desperate violence. The 'Warriors of Christ the King' assaulted six priests including the HOAC counsellor Fr. Eliseo Ruiz de Cortazar in Madrid, and caused an affray at Portugalete (Bilbao) following a 'leftist' sermon by Fr. Román Landera, who was later beaten by three policemen. Bishop Antonio Añoveros, now moved from Cádiz to Bilbao, solemnly excommunicated the policemen in accordance with canon law. [135] On May Day 1973, a secret policeman was murdered in Madrid. The Guerrilleros demanded that Cardinal Tarancón be shot as the person responsible for the killing. [136]

Many bishops were now rightly or wrongly associated with the political left. Even the Papal Nuncio Mgr. Dadaglio became involved, following his granting of asylum to 111 priests and workers sympathetic to ETA. [137] The culmination was, of course, the murder of Carrero Blanco. A truce was inevitable following this. The new Prime Minister, Arias Navarro, spoke of the 'undeniable conflict of recent years' but hoped for a 'new understanding' with the Church. [138]

Attempts were also made to improve relations with the Vatican. On 28 January 1974 His Holiness not only received a delegation of 40 Spanish bishops, but also one from the Spanish government. The meetings took place during the celebrations marking the canonization of the nineteenth century Spanish nun, Sister Teresa Jornet Ibara. The government delegation, under Agriculture Minister Tomás Allende García-Baxter, were greeted as 'worthy representatives of a nation whose virtues and noble sentiments we recognize'. [139]

However, the 'Añoveros affair' soon brought back the atmosphere of crisis. The famous homily by Bishop Antonio Añoveros of Bilbao, advocating cultural freedom for the Basque people, enraged the right who had accused ETA of the Carrero murder. On 27 February 1974 the Bishop and his Vicar General, Mgr. José Angel Ubieta López, were placed under house arrest – not a new experience for the latter.[140] Bishop Añoveros was to be expelled from Spain. An aeroplane was made ready. Unfortunately, the Bishop refused to cooperate; he could only leave his See by direct order of the Pope, he stated. He would have to be thrown out forcibly, and excommunication awaited any Catholic who laid hands upon an anointed priest. The authorities hesitated. Nuncio Dadaglio flew to Rome, and the Executive Committee of the Bishops' Conference went into hurried discussion. Support for Añoveros came from all over Spain, even from Archbishop Cantero. The ACNP also expressed their solidarity with the Bishop of Bilbao.[141] The official statement of support from the Episcopal Conference came on 9 March. Its moderate text – said to be the work of Cardinal Jubany – did much to cool the situation, but the whole affair, which attracted worldwide publicity, was a humiliation for Arias Navarro and showed that the Concordat had now come to mean very little indeed.

Meanwhile, negotiations continued in the search to find a compromise formula for a new Concordat with the Vatican. Secretary Casaroli and Foreign Minister Pedro Cortina Maurí were assisted in their deliberations by Nuncio Dadaglio. However, in November 1974 deadlock ensued and the Nuncio hastened to Rome for further consultations.

The liberal hierarchy were now becoming more vocal after the uneasy truce which followed the death of Carrero Blanco. Bishop Argaya Goicoechea of San Sebastian issued a pastoral denouncing the house arrest of Fr. Félix Vergara. The Bishop urged 'freedom of the pulpit' for all clergy and demanded the release of Fr. Vergara who had been arrested for preaching three sermons deemed 'politically offensive' by the authorities.[142] Añoveros also returned to the fray with a demand for a total amnesty for all political detainees. He was supported by a massive sit-in at a Bilbao church by relatives of prisoners. The Basque national hymn was sung at Sunday Masses and hunger strikes began in jails throughout Spain.

In September 1974 a statement was issued by the Social Apostolate Committee of the Bishops' Conference criticizing various aspects of government policy including the lack of freedom of association, unequal distribution of wealth, the poor social security system and the run-down of Spanish agriculture.[143] This statement was followed on 25 November by the long-awaited XXI Episcopal Conference. The Conference had taken for its theme the seemingly innocuous 'Evangelization and Sacraments' and spent much time discussing the impoverished state of the clergy. In his opening

77

address Cardinal Tarancón alluded to the turmoil of polemic in Spain. The Assembly elected five bishops to draft a policy document to be published some months later. Apart from Cardinal Primate Gonzalez Martín, all were liberals – González Moralejo of Huelva and the Auxiliary Bishops Yanes Alvarez, Montero Moreno and Setién Alberro. The Conference Communiqué issued on 30 November must, therefore, be seen as an interim statement. Its text was agreed by 64 votes to 6, with one abstention.[144] The document appeared softer in tone than previous utterances. It represents 'Taranconism' at its most subtle, combining demands for civil rights and institutional reform with condemnation of violence as the means to political change. It also asked for a gesture of clemency by the authorities towards political prisoners. The attitudes associated with Cardinal Tarancón now typified the Spanish Church in the eyes of foreign Catholics. This was made clear at the Synod of Bishops held at Rome in October and November 1974. The Cardinal addressed the bishops of the world in speeches insisting on the duty of the Church to aid oppressed peoples. He was supported in this line by Cardinal Jubany and Bishop Dorado Soto of Cádiz-Ceuta. Cardinal González Martín inevitably adopted a more conservative tone. He stressed the decline in moral standards and called for more emphasis on the Magisterium of the Church. So it was that the Spanish representatives at the Synod reflected the divided nature of the Spanish Church, the liberal voice being the stronger.[145]

The conservatives still kept a grip on the broadcasting media. Guerra Campos still remained 'television bishop'. The right also showed strength when Archbishop Cantero Cuadrado was supported by the other bishops of the Archdiocese of Zaragoza when he threatened to excommunicate the parish priest of Fabara, Fr. Wilberto Delso, for backing peasants dispossessed without proper compensation to create a new reservoir. Liberal priests who sided with Fr. Delso refused to celebrate Mass and finally 33 priests in all were threatened with excommunication.[146] Archbishop Cantero stated that the cause of the quarrel was a fundamental disagreement regarding the role of the Church in temporal matters.

Meanwhile, of course, Opus Dei had disappeared from government.[147] Many ACNP members were moving left and Ruiz-Giménez told the *Tablet* that he considered that Catholicism and Socialism were certainly compatible. Surely the most spectacular of all defectors from the Francoist camp was Calvo Serer himself who was forced into exile following the controversy surrounding the suppression of his newspaper *Madrid*.[148]

Another anti-régime gesture from the Church has been the nomination of the Catalan priest Lluis Maria Xirinacs for the Nobel

Peace Prize.[149] Among the organizations sponsoring the nomination were Pax Christi and Pax Romana, led in Spain by Ruiz-Giménez. This gesture follows similar actions such as the award of the Pax Christi Pope John Memorial Peace Prize first to Dom Helder Camara, socialist Bishop of Recife, Brazil, and later to José Luis Beunza, first Catholic to be jailed in Spain for conscientious objection to military service.[150] These gestures of support for opponents of the régime cannot but anger the authorities who are desperately trying to propagate their own 'liberal' image. Cardinal Enrique y Tarancón was opposed in the 1975 presidential elections of the Bishops' Conference by the Primate Cardinal González Martín. The result, a foregone conclusion, was a victory for Tarancon by 52 votes to 20.[151]

On 20 April 1975, after two long years, appeared the Bishops' declaration on 'Reconciliation in Church and Society'. This 9,000 word document was entitled 'Collective Letter', the first time that term had been used since the notorious statement of 1937. Collectivity was difficult because of deep divisions and compromise was, therefore, unavoidable. The liberal majority gave way on many points in order to achieve greater consensus. Even so, 11 conservatives still voted against the final text. While on the one hand there is a muted restatement of demands for free trade unions and basic civil rights, there is no call for a break with the régime. Also, while advocating religious tolerance, the document reaffirms traditionalist attitudes regarding the unique authenticity of the Roman Magisterium. What is explicit is the emphasis on the necessity to set Spain on a new path of reconciliation, finally putting an end to postwar enmities.[152]

The Current Situation

Despite the feeble tone of the Collective Letter, whether reconciliation between Church and State is possible now seems extremely debatable. There is no doubt that that the majority of the bishops, let alone the lower clergy, have moved into an attitude of hostility towards continued links with Francoism.[153] Confrontations with the régime continue. In March 1975 an Assembly of bishops, priests and laity was banned at Vallecas, a working-class district of Madrid. It was organized by Auxiliary Bishop Mgr. Alberto Iniesta Jiménez and was to be chaired by Cardinal Tarancón. The Interior Ministry stated that the ban had been made necessary by the 'infiltration of extreme leftist elements'.[154] As a result of the ban, many priests struck and no Mass was said in 30 Madrid churches, including 22 in Vallecas.

79

The suspension of the Vallecas Assembly had repercussions elsewhere. Priests struck in Pamplona, receiving the guarded support of Archbishop Méndez Asensio, and another socio-pastoral congress, due to be held in Las Palmas under the tutelage of Bishop Infantes Florido, was banned by the authorities on the grounds that the high percentage of laity expected to attend would render the meeting an 'illegal assembly'. This led to a bitter confrontation between the liberal Bishop and the Civil Governor of the Canary Islands, Enrique Martínez-Cañabate. Rightist extremists physically attacked nuns delivering copies of the episcopal bulletin, and feelings ran high enough for the Press to report the possible excommunication of the Governor.[155]

However, it was yet again in the Basque provinces of Guipúzcoa and Vizcaya that the clergy found themselves embroiled in controversy. The State of Emergency declared by the government in these provinces led to the arrest of many priests suspected of collusion with ETA. Fr. Eustacio Erquicia, Fr. Felix Iraurgui, Fr. Tomín Arteche and others were tortured and beaten by police during 'interrogation'.[156] The attitude of Bishops Argaya Goicoechea and Añoveros appeared somewhat equivocal. Bishop Añoveros drove to Madrid to consult with Nuncio Dadaglio before issuing a statement denouncing 'violence on both sides'.[157] This reaction by their one-time hero filled many younger clergy with dismay. A number of them appealed for support to Rome, and a strongly anti-régime sermon was read in some Basque churches on 8 June.[158] The sermon criticized the Bishops' weakness and spoke of the reign of terror imposed in the Basque country by the police and by the police-infiltrated 'Warriors of Christ the King', whose activities had now reached a new pitch of violence. The sermon stated that this 'blasphemous' group had made at least forty attacks on persons and property during the period. A thorough search was launched for the authors of the sermon and 16 more priests were arrested.[159]

The Permanent Commission of the Bishops' Conference issued an official statement. It followed the conciliatory line adopted by Añoveros but also spoke of the denial of civil rights which had been the cause of the troubles.[160] A news blackout had been imposed by the régime but in spite of this news got through of the only unequivocal attack on the government emanating from a prestigious ecclesiastical source at this time. This was a statement on 26 May by the Justice and Peace Commission. It called for an end to indiscriminate police action and demanded that the authorities condemn street violence by 'uncontrolled right wing extremists'.[161] o what extent the 'Guerrilleros' were 'uncontrolled' was debatable. There were rumours that they were under direct police command.

Conclusion

It is clear that the Spanish Church has its eyes set on the post-Franco era. Some commentators regard clerical opposition to the régime as mere opportunism.[162] They forecast that the Church will return to a reactionary role following the downfall of the Francoist system.[163] Whatever happens in the future, it is beyond doubt that the Church has made a major contribution towards the current disarray of the administration. Its statements, often backed with action, have been a constant source of harassment to the pseudo-liberalism of Arias Navarro's 'apertura' policy. The Church played a prominent part in exposing the fatuousness of this policy finally abandoned by the Prime Minister in his speech to the Cortes on 24 June 1975 in which he declared the intention of returning to a more overtly reactionary position. It remains to be seen whether this speech is more than just another example of the out-moded rhetoric of a moribund system. It is certain that the Church has long realized that the days of the 'Crusade' are over and is looking elsewhere for guarantees of survival. Spain has become secularized and the Church of the future will have to play a far less dominant role in Spanish life, a role more akin to that played by sister Churches abroad. The evidence seems to indicate that the Church in Spain has, at last, become reconciled to the modern world.

4

The Economic Policy of Francoism: An Interpretation

JOAN ESTEBAN

One of the achievements of which Franco's régime is most proud is the spectacular growth of the Spanish economy, starting from a *per capita* income of $200 in 1940 to $2,200 in 1974 (Bank of Bilbao estimate). There are factors like tourism, foreign investment, remittances from emigrant workers, etc. which have obviously contributed to this economic growth,[1] but the point we shall concentrate upon is whether or not Spain's political system has contributed to the achievement of this economic success.[2]

The régime's representatives argue that economic growth has been the result of both the government's determination to industrialize the country and its efficiency in the general management of the economy. Furthermore, they affirm that *per capita* income would have been even higher if the Western nations had not boycotted Spain up until the early fifties. Therefore, they conclude, Francoism has been a necessary condition for Spanish economic growth.[3] But, as we shall see, in the first place, the régime did not show any clear determination to industrialize the country until the mid-fifties and, in the second, its efficiency is highly questionable.

Another well known argument is that the régime's political institutions, by repressing the working class and keeping real wages extremely low, have allowed a high level of accumulation and hence rapid industrial growth.[4] And this has been so, it is concluded, because the régime is a class-dictatorship, i.e. the dictatorship of the bourgeoisie. But this is too crude an approach which leaves most of the relevant questions unanswered. We know that real wages in the early fifties were still 50 per cent below the prewar level, so the fact that the labour force has been highly exploited throughout the period is undeniable; but this evidence, as it stands, is not very

82

helpful for an understanding of the nature of the régime.

On the one hand, the 'non-working-class' is composed of a number of different classes and fractions with different, and often conflicting, interests; and it is clear that Franco's régime could not and did not satisfy all these interests at the same time. There is no economic policy that can fulfil this requirement. Therefore, an analysis of the economic policies followed by the régime may shed light on the different alliances undertaken by the régime, and therefore on the nature of its support. The precise links between the 'bourgeoisie' and the dictatorship have not yet been established. The practical non-existence of a party, the secondary role played by the Cortes, the non-involvement of many industrialists with the official 'trade-unions' and the limited role actually played by these 'unions' in policy-making, cast serious doubts on the existence of a stable, organic, systematic link between those social forces and the régime, lobbying by various interests taking place in an unsystematic, informal and personal way.[5] Finally, it is quite clear that the crucial decisions have always been personally taken by Franco himself; how different interests made themselves known and how they were weighed before a decision was taken is something that is still unknown.[6]

Another approach to the relationship between Spanish political institutions and economic achievements has been the analysis of whether or not these political institutions have limited the choice and implementation of economic policies.[7] It is then argued that not only has the range of policy objectives and available tools been at least as wide as any other European country, but policy-makers — and hence the whole political environment — have shown even more flexibility than elsewhere. But such an analysis, though valuable in some respects, fails to grasp the very nature of the régime. First of all, it does not pay any attention to the social forces underlying the different policy options. Secondly, the formal structure of this analysis sometimes suggests misleading answers. Particularly, it fails to understand that the same economic tools do not serve the same purpose in a dictatorship as they do, for instance, in a liberal democracy. There is still a question of degree, since after all the number of available instruments is quite limited, and we shall have to distinguish between different régimes by the intensity and the purposes of their use.

Summarizing we find that, for different reasons, it is generally agreed that Francoist political institutions have played an active role in the achievement of Spain's economic success. The reason has been, according to some authors, that the régime, as a 'dictatorship of the bourgeoisie', has always followed the policies which have

83

better served the interests of the 'bourgeoisie'; and according to others, that because of its fully pragmatic approach to economic policy decisions the régime has been able to undertake the most effective *ad hoc* economic policies for growth.

Contrary to these interpretations we shall attempt to prove the following points. In the first place, that the set of economic as well as social and political institutions created before 1942 were not *ad hoc* policies, but the expression of the will to implement a particular socio-economic system, very close to contemporary Italian fascism. Secondly, that the initial socio-economic system revealed itself to be unstable. (On the one hand, it created contradictions among different factions of the bourgeoisie – especially between agriculturalists and the big banks on the one hand and industrialists on the other – and it generated a high exploitation of the working class so that, in spite of fear and political repression, strikes and massive demonstrations started as early as 1951. On the other hand, the change in the international political situation after the fall of fascism showed that there was no room for an openly fascist régime in Europe.) Thirdly, that changes in the system of economic policy have been an attempt to ensure the political survival of the régime, menaced by the development of these contradictions. (Those changes have provoked a complete transformation of Spain's economic and social structure which in turn have developed new contradictions.) Finally, that throughout these thirty-five years the régime has been giving up many features of its original economic system though only a few of its political system. Nowadays it certainly resembles western European economies in most respects. But nevertheless, the interests of both the working class and a good fraction of industrialists and bankers seem now to coincide in the need for democratic liberties, which cannot be met by Franco's dictatorship, with which trade unions and political freedom are incompatible.

We shall divide our study into four periods. The first period, 1939-42, covers the building of the new socio-economic system. The second, 1942-51, shows its ineffectiveness and the factors which led to a major change. The third period, 1951-59, corresponds to the first attempt at economic liberalization and its failure. And the last period, 1959-74, deals with the second and more complete economic liberalization and the recent process of rapid economic growth.

The Beginning of the New Régime, 1939-42

If the Spanish economic system during this period had to be described with a single word, the most accurate would probably be fascism. It has been pointed out that far from being the expression of a deliberate aim to create a fascist socio-economic system, the economic policy in this period was the result of the *ad hoc* measures necessary to cope with the problems of postwar reconstruction and foreign trade disruption, first due to the Second World War and later to the international boycott until the end of the decade.[8] Furthermore, the kind of economic tools used in Spain during the forties and partly in the fifties did not differ too much from interventionism and protectionism in Europe during the war and postwar recovery.[9]

Against these interpretations, an attempt will be made to show that the set of institutions, aims and tools of economic policy corresponding to the early forties was remarkably close to contemporary Italian fascism.[10] Some of the declared aims started changing in 1942, some of the tools and institutions lasted until the late forties, some until the late fifties and some are still in force now, such as the basic corporative institution, the official 'vertical' syndicates.[11]

The most characteristic elements of the official ideology were: totalitarianism, anti-liberalism, subordination of the economy to political ends, preference for agriculture and rural values as against industry and urban values, and the persistent emphasis on the new way of life, the New State, the National Revolution.

As soon as Franco took power, in October 1936, it became clear that the régime was totalitarian. In his first speech as *Caudillo* he declared: 'Spain will be organized from a broad totalitarian approach by means of all national institutions guaranteeing its totality, unity and continuity'.[12] Furthermore, this principle became a guideline for economic policy and the creation of the Servicio Nacional del Trigo was justified as being the 'only totalitarian solution' to the problem of wheat.[13]

Anti-liberalism was also another major element of the régime's ideology, which inspired to a great extent its interventionist policies. Franco himself stated that 'our victory constitutes . . . the triumph of economic principles opposed to the old liberal theories . . .'[14] Furthermore, he was confident that with the victory of the Axis 'the liberal–capitalist system will disappear forever'.[15]

The subordination of the economy to political ends was the natural implication of the new totalitarian state, and indeed it was a common feature of contemporary fascism elsewhere. The preamble of the Fuero del Trabajo, for instance, states that 'the National State, as the totalitarian instrument at the service of the Fatherland, and syndical integrity, as a reaction against liberal capitalism and marxist materialism, undertakes the task of accomplishing – with a militarily constructive and gravely religious attitude – the pending revolution which has to give back to all Spaniards, once and for all, Fatherland, Bread and Justice. In order to succeed in this task we come before the nation with the intention of putting wealth at the service of the Spanish people, subordinating the economy to its policy.'[16] And the preamble of the Law creating the Instituto Nacional de Industria – which would channel the state's industrialization effort – justifies INI's task as a major help for 'the acceleration of our resurgence we need if the programmes which our historical destiny demands have to be fulfilled.' [17]

There is much evidence to indicate the Franco régime's preference for agriculture and rural values as against industry and urban values. This was a common feature of fascist ideologies, and it was fully developed not only in the Falange's own declarations but even in the text of some Bills and in official textbooks. [18] For instance, in 'La Nueva España Agraria', published by the government publishing house, it was stated that 'the true people, the most numerous, the most long-suffering, the most hard-working, the most peaceful, were from the very beginning on the side of the National Movement . . ., in contrast, the marxist revolution found its support among the well paid workers of the towns . . .' – and then continues – 'we shall transform Spain into a country of small farmers'.[19] But this attitude was only reflecting Franco's own point of view, partly grounded in the absence of support among the working class and in the cool attitude of some industrialists to the nationalist uprising.[20] This state of affairs is explicitly recognized in the preamble of a Decree in 1936 where it is stated: 'It has come to our knowledge that there are in our territory a good number of industries whose local managers appear to be indifferent about the cause of Spain under the pretext of the lack of communication with their board of directors.'[21] In fact, the country suffered a process of reruralization and the percentage of agricultural population stood above the prewar levels until the mid-fifties.[22]

Finally, throughout the first few years we find the widespread use of words such as revolution, the new totalitarian state, the new man, the new order, etc. . . . which seem to be the common phraseology in all fascist régimes.[23] During this early period this emphasis on novelty was applied in the most surprising fields. For instance, in the Decree regulating the maximum number of courses citizens were allowed to eat and their content, the legislator justified the measure arguing that the new way of life should obviously apply to diet, thereby reflecting the principles of the revolution.[24]

We shall now analyse how this ideology materialized in institutions and economic policy measures. The close parallel between some francoist institutions – the INI and the SNT – and the corresponding ones in Italian fascism has already been emphasized, but this similarity occurs in many other relevant cases. According to the contemporary Italian economist Amantia, 'Corporatism is nothing other than the economic side of Fascism' [25] and its basic characteristics are respect for private ownership and individual initiative and intervention in the economy through syndicates and corporations. [26] It is obvious that the first two characteristics were met by the Spanish régime. Let us, therefore, examine the other two in some detail.

The Fuero del Trabajo was Franco's corporatist manifesto, in which the main guidelines of the future socio-economic system were laid down. [27] This legal document not only bears strong resemblances to the Italian Carta del Lavoro [28] and the Portuguese Estatutu do Travalho Nacional [29] but it even goes one step further, [30] the main differences being:

> In Spain the whole industrial and services labour force is compulsorily organized in 'vertical' syndicates [XIII.2], whereas in Italy and Portugal workers were free to join the trade unions. Only members of the party were entitled to be appointed as syndicate officers [XIII.4], but this was not explicitly required in Italy or Portugal. Both employers and workers are organized in the same 'unified' syndicate, whereas in Italy and Portugal employers and workers were organized in different bodies. Furthermore, in these countries wages were settled by collective bargaining – under the 'tutelage' of the State through the corporations – but in Spain collective bargaining was not allowed until 1958, wages being fixed by the State.

The principles embodied in the Fuero del Trabajo concerning labour organization were later implemented by the Law of Syndical Organization. [31] But the main functions of National Syndicates were not only to maintain a tight control of the working class, but also 'to propose to the Government the necessary regulations for the discipline and encouragement of production, the storage and distribution of output, as well as the regulation of prices in the different stages of the productive process: to dictate the rules and undertake the measures leading to those ends.' [32] It is therefore clear that 'vertical' syndicates were designed to play a key role in Franco's socio-economic system.

J. Mª. de Areilza, Director General de Industria, states in this respect that 'autarchy and syndicalization constitute the two pillars on which the new Spanish economic policy is to settle . . . systematic criticism of policies of restriction and self-sufficiency or of the purpose of achieving a syndical and organic structure for the Spanish economy constitutes an attack on the independence and freedom of Spain and support for the perpetuation of social anarchy and class struggle among us' and then he warns – 'To those objecting to National Syndicalism or Autarchy, on the basis of nostalgia for the old economic or political liberalism, we shall not make any concession, because they have understood nothing of what has happened in Spain.' [33] It has been argued that interference of the 'vertical' syndicates in economic activity was in fact the legacy of war-economy organization and hence did not constitute a deliberate attempt at corporatist organization. Contrary to this point of view – if the previous evidence is not conclusive enough – it will be useful to point out that the process of 'syndicalization' of the economy started as early as 1937, even before the Fuero del Trabajo. The first sectors in which compulsory syndicalization was declared were only remotely related to the war economy: [34] production of tins for canned food; production of soap; production of paper and cardboard; and cotton textiles. Furthermore, when, shortly after the Fuero del Trabajo, the 'Commissions for the Regulation of Production' were created, [35] the preamble made clear its temporary character, because the final step was the full organization of the entire economy in syndicates which 'with full representation, efficacy and responsibility will intervene in the problems of production, proposing the solutions.'

It is well known that some of the principles laid down in the Fuero del Trabajo or other manifestos had still not been fully implemented by 1943, when military developments in the Second World War showed that the 'new order' was not to be established in Europe. Moreover, the process of implementation was taking place at a slow rate. These facts have given rise to the argument that the régime was not fascist, but an étatist right-wing dictatorship, [36] phraseology in speeches and manifestos as well as some of the political and economic measures being the result of the need for compromise with the more radical Falange. But, on the one hand, the Falange's relatively small capacity for mass mobilization hardly justifies this 'compromise', if it existed at all, while on the other hand, it has to be kept in mind that 'slow and gradual elaboration of its own theory of the State has been a characteristic of all totalitarian régimes . . . Because they are entirely different from the democratic States, totalitarian states, with the exception of Portugal, lack the key legal unit, a constitution . . . In the new Spain the theory of the State is being built up slowly and fragmentarily. This might well be a consequence of the abnormal circumstances the Fatherland is going through, but it fits very well with the ideological position of the government with regard to the political nature of the régime that is being built up.' [37]

In summary, it may be concluded that evidence on the régime's ideology and on the nature of its major economic institutions strongly suggests a close correspondence with Italian fascism.

Another important element of the régime's economic policy was autarchy. It has been suggested, wrongly, I think,[38] that autarchy was the crucial feature for the characterization of the régime's economic policy,[39] and indeed this issue has become the centre of controversies about the nature of the régime.[40] But autarchy was not new on the Spanish scene. Economic policy throughout the twentieth century has been seen as a long process towards autarchy,[41] so that autarchy after the civil war was no more than another step forward in the same direction.[42] Francoist representatives never denied in this earlier period that an attempt to develop autarchy further was being made;[43] moreover they claimed that the new autarchy was clearly different from the old protectionism.[44] The main difference was that the régime's autarchy was taken as a means to achieve political and economic independence both as an expression of nationalism and as the necessary pre-condition for a war economy.[45] Furthermore, it is undeniable that whatever the ultimate intentions had been, the principle of autarchy was taken as a major guideline for economic policy.[46]

It can be seen, then, that the main aims and central institutions of the economic policy followed by the régime in its first stage had a great number of points in common with contemporary Italian economic policy. But this is not to deny that some of the planned institutions were never fully realized and that the day-to-day working of the economy was not as 'vertically' controlled as a reading of the legislation might suggest. Specifically, the dream of a powerful autarchic economy was replaced by the less ambitious striving for simple economic survival; the leading role of the 'vertical' syndicates in policy-making was reduced to distributing raw material quotas among firms; the INI almost ceased promoting any new state industry.

Stagnation and Crisis: 1942-51

There were a number of factors which precluded the fulfilment of the original economic policy design. First of all, the Francoist side contained from the beginning of the Civil War vast sectors of the bourgeoisie and middle classes – especially among industrialists and the urban middle classes – which though closer to the Nationalists than to the more leftist Republicans, were reluctant to accept Falangist political predominance and the kind of policies advocated by the Falange. However, these lukewarm bourgeois groups did not start playing a significant role until the mid-forties, after the fall of fascism in Europe. Secondly, this change in the political prospects of fascism forced Francoism to give power to authoritarian, right-wing, Catholic – but not fascist – politicians in order to create a new political face for the régime. But this political group did not feel strongly committed to the old policy design and was more open to the suggestions put forward by industrialists, which though favourable to protectionism and to a tight control of the working class, did not support intensive state interventionism. Finally, intervention was so intense,[47] and the bureaucracy so inefficient and unprepared to cope with the difficulties of such state control,[48] that in order to avoid a complete economic breakdown, economic policy makers preferred not to develop intervention any further and even to tolerate the regular breaking of the law in the economic sphere.[49]

The day-to-day problems characterizing this period were the fight against starvation, a high level of exploitation of the working class and a permanent economic stagnation (with two major production crises, in 1945 and 1949, when total production fell to almost half the prewar levels).

'The forties have, as far as agriculture is concerned, one single objective: to avoid starvation.'[50] From a situation of abundance of food in the beginning of the civil war, the nationalist side became short of stocks as the urban areas fell into their hands. What was then seen as the transitory effect of the war, was to become a permanent threat until the early fifties.[51] The agricultural policy throughout this period was oriented towards autarchy. On the one hand, the production of exportable agricultural products, olives and oranges, was severely limited and on the other attention was concentrated on the achievement of self-sufficiency in cereals. High prices were guaranteed for cereals and some other agricultural products,[52] the SNT and the Comisaria General de Abastecimientos y Transportes being responsible for the full commercialization of the output. The result was that producers shifted from intervened to non-intervened production and channelled a good part of production through the black market.[53] Ration books started being issued in May 1939 and were not abolished until 1952.

Despite the oft-repeated argument that the industrialization of the country had always been one of the régime's primary objectives, the evidence suggests that the government did not make any major attempt at rapid industrialization until the early fifties. Firstly, the system of official prices tended to favour agriculture relative to industrial production. Secondly, the state, through the INI, did not promote any new industry during this period. Thirdly, state intervention, the quota system of supply of raw materials and the black market, although allowing for extra-high profits for some, were hardly the best conditions for industrial growth. In fact, industrial activity did not grow until 1946 and after the first ten years industrial output had only increased at an average rate of 1 per cent per annum. That a serious attempt at industrialization was not made until 1951 has been implicitly recognized even by some representatives of the régime. J.Mᵃ. de Areilza in 1953, emphasizing the distinct features of the new industrial policy started in 1951, pointed out that 'only a complete mutation of the official doctrine of the Spanish ruling minorities could open the way to a national determination to industrialize the country, currently accepted nowadays as a natural premise.' [54]

Autarchy and intervention had two major effects on Spanish industry. On the one hand, import – substituting light industry developed at the expense of basic industry, reducing the average industrial productivity because of the use of low quality raw materials, inadequate equipment and rudimentary industrial processes. [55] On the other hand, this period shows a tendency towards monopoly in almost all industrial sectors. New entries being virtually impossible, [56] the greater power of large firms for obtaining bigger quotas and/or import licences, on the one hand, and their better position for obtaining credits from both official and private banks, on the other, largely account for this process. [57]

The level of exploitation of the working class was extremely high up until 1953. Real wages in urban areas were until 1945 around 25 per cent of prewar wages, [58] and from 1945 to 1953 around 50 per cent. [59] The régime did not try to conceal the extreme inequality that resulted from the Nationalists' victory; Franco himself stated that 'our Crusade has been the only war in which the rich became richer. And this has been so because those goods and material wealth that were undervalued and jeopardized . . . have been overvalued by the end of the war.' [60] But which sectors of Spanish society benefited from this exploitation? Did this surplus result in a high accumulation of capital?

'There is a large surplus of funds in the country . . . and most of this accumulation of new money is undoubtedly in the hands of industrialists, merchants, contractors, intermediaries and large farmers.' [61] E. Fuentes and J. Plaza, although recognizing that in general 'private owners had been doing fairly well', [62] point out that landowners had particularly benefited from the régime during this period. [63] A new bureaucracy emerged connected with the political apparatus and, taking advantage of their control over import licences, raw material quotas etc. started businesses of their own. Finally, the big banks have to be considered as one of the major beneficiaries of Franco's régime. [64] Any new entry into the banking

91

business was virtually forbidden[65] and the big bank manager–directors were members by law of the Consejo Superior Bancario, which was the body designed to make recommendations about monetary and financial policy.[66] The big banks consolidated their positions and absorbed or controlled most of the small banks.[67] Moreover, their privileged position allowed the big banks to penetrate and control most of the Spanish big firms.[68]

It has been argued that the high exploitation of the working class allowed for the accumulation of an outstanding volume of surplus, which would later materialize in the mid-fifties in the form of capital investment in industry.[69] The basis for this claim seems to have been the fact that during the first fourteen years (1940-53), in which the real wages were extremely low, the average proportion of net domestic capital formation to the national income was only 9 per cent, whereas during the next fourteen years (1954-67), in which the real wages were higher, the average rate was 18.7 per cent.[70] This claim is highly questionable in many respects. On the one hand, the nature of this time lag between creation of surplus and capital investment is extremely obscure. On the other hand, the evidence suggests that a major part of the profits during this first period were spent in luxury consumption, real estate development and circulating capital.[71] Finally, it is not difficult to explain the high rate of investment during the second period without having recourse to this pretended time lag, e.g. foreign investment, greater thriftiness in the capitalist class (because of the existence of a greater number of investment opportunities), etc.

The State played the major role in capital formation during the forties (public investment stood at around 40 per cent of total investment), financing its investment partly by tax revenue and partly by issuing enormous amounts of public debt. The taxation system was – and still is – very regressive. Direct taxes represented about 40 per cent of total tax revenue, of which the highest was the one taxing labour income, personal income tax representing about 1.8 per cent only of total tax revenue.[72] Public debt issued until 1957 was automatically rediscountable in the Banco de España. Banks and saving banks as well as some state controlled institutions (Instituto Nacional de Previsión, Mutualidades Laborales, etc.) were legally compelled to devote a given proportion of their resources to the purchase of public debt. But because of its discountability, this debt could be immediately turned into cash, leaving the control of money supply in the hands of the private banks. Therefore, public investment was actually financed through 'forced' savings mostly drawn from working class wage-earners, by means of the inflation created by the public sector.

Summarizing, we find that by 1950 the results achieved after twelve years of the régime's economic policy were: (a) real income per head in 1950 was still below the prewar level; (b) agricultural output was below even the immediate postwar levels; (c) autarchy, interventionism and the black market provoked an evident misallocation of resources, reducing average productivity in most economic activities; and (d) in spite of the high level of exploitation of the working class the rate of accumulation of productive capital was very low.

The Régime has claimed that the stagnation in this period was due to war destruction and to isolation forced by the Second World War first and the economic blockade later. Although both facts certainly affected the Spanish economy they cannot bear the full responsibility for the economic stagnation. First of all, war damage was grossly exaggerated[73] and mostly affected the communications system and very little industrial capital.[74] But, in any case, the régime has recognized that reconstruction was completed by 1945,[75] so that war damage cannot be considered as a satisfactory explanation for stagnation during the second half of the forties. Secondly, although limited foreign trade was one of the causes of stagnation, it is necessary to emphasize that this isolation was a deliberate aim of Francoist economic policy,[76] that the blockade on the one hand was the consequence of the political choices made by the régime and on the other it was not very tight,[77] and finally that policy-makers misused to a large extent the import capability of the country.[78]

Free Market and Industrialization: 1951-59

The previous section has shown that the system of economic policy created by the régime soon revealed itself unable to solve the most basic economic problems and became an obstacle to economic growth. But, although the failure of the Francoist economic policy was clear for some,[79] the régime remained reluctant to bring about any substantial change in the prevailing guidelines until 1951. The 1951 change constitutes a clear case in which the political and economic institutions created by the régime, not only delayed the introduction of the economic programme that was to be the first serious attempt at growth, but also contributed later to its failure. Therefore, it appears that, on the one hand, Francoist institutions were not as flexible and open as has been suggested by some[80] and, on the other, that the régime did not have a neat and explicit alliance with any of the different fractions of the bourgeoisie, so that when

93

the time for undeferable decisions came the new policies were ambiguous and never fully carried out. Furthermore, though internal pressure groups played a significant role in bringing this change about,[81] US pressure accounts to a large extent for the introduction of the new attitudes in Spanish economic policy,[82] in addition to the increasing social unrest.

The change in economic policy introduced in 1951 deserves close analysis not only for the nature of the measures introduced, but because of the change in the underlying economic ideology. Roughly speaking, this new ideology corresponds to the capitalist liberalism widespread in contemporary western Europe and mainly promoted by the US, and was in open contradiction with the ideas held before.

The main elements of the new ideology in Spanish economic policy can be summarized as follows: (a) orthodoxy in the management of the public sector;[83] (b) open economy as opposed to autarchy;[84] (c) free market as opposed to interventionism;[85] and (d) private initiative as opposed to étatism.[86]

The restoration of the free market was in fact the main target of the 1951 programme of economic policy, and other policies can be understood as means to achieve it.[87] The only way to avoid economic chaos with the lifting of market interventions was to secure an abundant supply of all goods. In the short run imports were to be used to balance the market, financed by Spanish reserves of foreign currency and credits received from the US. In the long run, there was the presumption that industrial output would rapidly increase once the bottle-necks – shortages in raw materials and energy – were cleared up either by increased domestic production or by further imports. The INI was to start a new programme of public investment, now with the purpose of filling the activities not sufficiently covered by the private sector. Regarding agriculture, the new economic policy gave up the old pretension of achieving self-sufficiency in the short run by differential guaranteed prices, letting agricultural prices drop in relation to industrial prices[88] and promoting mechanization and irrigation systems instead.[89] The public sector was supposed to behave in an orthodox way, not introducing inflation in the system. Wages and salaries would be frozen at first, to let them rise later as domestic supply increased as a result of the new situation.[90]

The attention of policy makers switched from traditional agriculture to industry. The programme achieved some remarkable results in its initial steps.[91] The black market almost disappeared; the necessary imports were lower than expected; the retail price index went down and stablized later until 1954; industry started expanding. By 1953-54, most of the prewar macroeconomic levels were finally attained, e.g. income *per capita*, agricultural output, distribution of labour force, etc.[92]

Nevertheless, the full programme had not been completed by then – and never was; a good number of controls were not lifted; the public sector did not stop its chronic deficit, and the final result was a state of affairs that M. de Torres called 'semi-normality'.[93]

The eventual success of the programme depended on a number of presumptions.[94] First of all, the behaviour of the public sector had to be non-inflationary or even deflationary. Secondly, imports could not be very elastic with respect to the activity level, but exports should be,[95] so that with no major deficit in the balance of payments and stable prices the foreign exchange rate was not going to be affected by the programme. Finally, there was the belief that the increased supply and reduced prices for foodstuffs would divert part of private demand to manufactured goods so that demand could meet industrial supply at a new and higher level.

The first symptoms of failure appeared in 1953 with an excess production in some industrial sectors – especially in textiles. On the one hand, as we have seen, the success was partly based on the presumption that consumers would behave with respect to foodstuffs as if they were inferior goods – diverting part of their income to demand for manufactures, but real income for most of the population was so low and underconsumption so extreme that private demand for manufactured goods rose much less than was expected. On the other hand, higher imports of raw materials and intermediate goods primarily stimulated the consumption goods industry – expanded by the previous import substitution policies – with two negative effects, the extra pressure from the supply side on the market for final goods and the further distortion of an abnormal industrial structure with an atrophied basic industry.[96]

In order to overcome the excess supply, labour incomes were increased by Decree in 1954 and no further effort to restrain inflationary pressures was made.[97] The immediate result was a rapid inflationary process that lasted until 1959. Wages were increased again in 1956 (twice) overall by 50 per cent and inflation worsened. On the other hand, imports turned out to be much higher and exports much lower than expected.[98] Deficits in the balance of payments and inflation adversely affected the foreign exchange rate – which had improved in the early fifties – inducing capital to be illegally taken out of the country.

What started looking like a well coordinated programme became a free-for-all, in which the ministerial departments boycotted each other.[99] In particular, the Ministry of the Treasury never closely followed the programme[100] and the Ministry of Labour, by imposing

95

the 1956 wage increases, crushed the plan. By 1957 rapid industrial growth had been achieved, but inflation was higher than ever before, and foreign reserves were in the red. [101]

In February 1957 a new government took office, including some liberal technocrats linked with the Opus Dei, [102] with the clear determination to introduce complete economic liberalization. But, in spite of the existing economic chaos and the lack of any alternative economic policy, it took them more than two years to break the final resistance presented by different forces of the régime – and Franco himself – reluctant for a major change in the system. In July 1959 the Stabilization Plan was approved.

Stabilization and Growth: 1959-74

Much attention has been devoted to this stabilization plan and it has been seen as the crucial turning point in the Spanish economy since the Civil War. From 1960 onwards Spain has had a high and steady rate of growth, inflation has been kept within tolerable limits and the balance of payments has improved, especially in the seventies; and this is quite enough to permit one to speak of this last period as the golden age of Francoism. This evident success has been attributed to the new approach to economic policy introduced by the Opus Dei technocrats with the past being labelled simply as the 'period of autarchy and interventionism.' [103]

But, in fact, the economic ideology underlying these measures of economic policy does not differ very much from the one which lead to the change in 1951. Furthermore, most of the aims and some of the tools used in the 1959 plan were just logical conclusions of what had been started eight years before.

In order to understand this new attempt at liberalization it is necessary to take into account the particular circumstances present at the end of the fifties, which can be summarized in the following points:

a) the economic situation was desperate. Inflation rose to 11 per cent both in 1957 and in 1958; by June 1959 it was already 5.5 per cent, and foreign reserves were in the red again. [104] Moreover, since 1956 social unrest started spreading throughout the country. [105]

b) the previous experience made it clear that an ambiguous policy could not succeed in bringing about the substantial change the economy needed. Furthermore, there was no alternative but to pursue liberalization further. [106]

c) the process of international economic integration, the French stabilization plan and the Treaty of Rome created the impression that this was one of the last chances to join Europe. [107]

d) the call for economic liberalization gained a wider base of support – possibly because of the process of urbanization and industrialization that took place during the fifties – so that the new government was able to take action with a greater determination. [108]

e) at that time, policy-makers were aware of the precise political implications which the economic liberalization had. That is, it was assumed that the final and definite rejection of the old fascist economic policy would force a parallel process of transformation in the political institutions towards higher political liberalization. [109]

The measures undertaken by the government in 1959 contain two distinct but well connected plans; on the one hand, the stabilization plan designed to stop inflationary pressures and to restore equilibrium in the balance of payments, and on the other, the New Economic Order intended to bring about a more complete liberalization of the economy.

The Stabilization Plan consisted of the standard measures that the IMF recommended to many countries in this period and constituted a clear success. Prices stabilized for the next four years and foreign reserves rose until 1964. [110]

The Government's plans for economic reform were expressed in the 'Memorandum' sent to the IMF and the OECE and included actions directed towards the 'normalization' of the Spanish economy, that is, the creation of an institutional environment in line with western European economies in all respects but the labour market. [111] Some of these measures were implemented in July 1959 [112] and the rest during the next five years. [113] The overall result was a noticeable change in the institutional environment, although the most serious structural changes had not been undertaken. [114]

One of the major concerns of the new policy-makers was the coordination of economic policies. The first step in this direction was the creation of the OCYPE, Oficina de Coordinación y Programación Económica, with the task of coordinating public investment into a unified plan. Soon after the stablization programme the Government expressed its desire for wider coordination by creating the Comisaria del Plan de Desarrollo in 1962 and in order to get fresh ideas for the long-term objectives in economic policy it called an experts commission of the World Bank. The Report insisted on the recommendations for extending liberalization further, for introducing more rationality in public investment project selection, for greater orthodoxy in the public sector and for implementing a number of structural reforms. [115]

In December 1963 the first Plan of Economic and Social Development for the period 1964-67 was approved. Its conception was entirely inspired by French Plans and consisted of a set of macroeconomic forecasts, a compulsory plan for public investment and other major macroeconomic measures and a set of

97

recommendations to the private sector.[116]

The period covered by the first Plan was characterized by the sharp lack of coordination between short-term and long-term policies. The relative price stability which the country enjoyed until 1963 was shaken by inflation during 1964, which led to mild stabilization measures in November 1964. This started a period of 'stop–go' policies, with stabilizing measures being introduced in April 1965 and October 1966, which led to the devaluation of the peseta and a tougher stabilization programme in November 1967.[117]

During the first Plan the GNP grew at an average rate of 6.4 per cent per annum, but the average rate of inflation was 8.62 per cent and after the first year the Balance of Payments ran into deficit, with a loss of $400 million in foreign reserves during the last three years. The problem was not only the lack of coordination between short-term and long-term economic policies,[118] but the inability of the public sector to fulfil its own commitments. The public investment in some sectors did not reach 50 per cent of the planned figure.[119] In general, it has been said that the Spanish economy grew 'in spite of the plan' and the pretended efficiency of the Opus Dei technocrats has been widely questioned.[120]

After the 1967 devaluation the first Plan was 'extended' *sine diae* and it was not until February 1969 that the second Plan was published. This second Plan did not present any novelty with respect to the first plan, except for the above mentioned alarm signals and some slightly more modest objectives in terms of growth rates.[121] But the lack of coordination between short-run and long-run economic policies continued; the alarm signals rang but nobody listened to them, and policy-makers again preferred isolated and sharp stoppages to continuous and smooth policies.

During the second Plan the GNP grew at an average annual rate of 6 per cent, again well above the planned rate, 4 per cent; inflation, at an average annual rate of 5.25 per cent, did not represent such an important threat as it did during the previous period; and the balance of payments improved, especially in 1970 and 1971, with an overall increase in foreign reserves of $2,100 million.

The third Plan, 1972-75, approved in due course, has not presented new factual novelties. The most relevant change has been the emphasis on qualitative, as well as on quantitative, objectives, introducing consideration about quality of life, environment, and so on. The GNP has grown very fast (1972 – 7.8%, 1973 – 7.9% and 1974 – 4%), together with high inflation (1972 – 8.3%, 1973 – 11.5% and 1974 – 20%) and high surpluses in the balance of payments until 1974 (by the end of 1973 the volume of foreign reserves was $6,799 million).[122]

At this stage one may wonder why the Spanish economy performed so well, achieving such high rates of growth. This chapter does not try to give a complete answer to this question, but only to point out that one of the major causes has been the European boom during the sixties and early seventies, with its effects on the Spanish economy.

It has been because of this European boom that tourism revenue and emigrant workers' remittances have risen so rapidly. In 1973, for instance, Spain obtained $2,386 million in tourism and $1,718 million in remittances, in addition to $852 million in foreign investment. This important inflow of foreign currency has allowed the country to import at very high rates, overcoming a deficit of $2,939 millions in the balance of trade.[123] Furthermore, the European boom has provoked a substantial increase in exports (in 1973 exports were 9 times higher than in 1959) and a remarkable change in their structure,[124] which illustrates the extent to which the Spanish economy has been transformed.

Until the end of the sixties it was a commonly held belief that Spanish economic growth had an unavoidable upper limit given by its import capacity.[125] The mistrust in the long-term stability of tourism revenue and the conviction that the autarchic origins of Spanish industrialization would make industry incapable of exporting and filling the gap in the balance of trade, were the basis for a pessimistic view of the future.[126] But the high rates of investment throughout this period have drastically transformed Spanish industry,[127] changing the traditional pattern. If we consider the two sub periods 1959-66 and 1966-73, we find that while in the first imports grew 1.7 times faster than exports, in the second the trend reversed and exports grew 1.4 times faster than imports.

Spain is now an industrialized and urbanized country,[128] and this process of growth has developed new contradictions within the régime. First of all, we have to emphasize the increasing militancy of the working class, which has developed its own representative organizations. In response to this fact a good part of the industrialists seem to have changed their position towards the official 'vertical' syndicates, advocating a more flexible labour market (free trade unions but no State intervention in employment policy). Secondly, there is the question of the EEC. The idea that in the long run there was no alternative to joining the Common Market started spreading in Spain as soon as the Community was created.[129] Although many factions of the bourgeoisie were initially reluctant to make a rapid approach to the EEC, this attitude had changed by the late sixties and seventies. The reason might have been the economic growth and the change in the economic trend by

99

1966-67 which we have already mentioned. It is an idea now shared by most Spaniards that the basic prerequsite for being admitted into the Common Market is the change in the political system, and the pressures for political liberalization are becoming stronger and more apparent.[130] The key question at the present is whether or not the régime will be able to meet these demands.

Part II   The People

5

The Peasantry and the Franco Régime

EDUARDO SEVILLA–GUZMAN

1. Introduction[1]

The government which came to power in 1939 was destined to develop a political system which would witness the change of Spain from a pre-industrial society to a 'modern' one. From the 1936 rising to date, the system of domination established by the right-wing alliance has clearly had a class nature. Large sectors of the population have been and are still being exploited for the benefit of a narrow segment of society. Thus, in the past two decades there has been considerable economic growth in Spain which has been brought about mainly at the expense of the peasantry and the working class. While there has been spectacular economic growth, the ruling class, and those sectors which have enjoyed the exclusive benefit of that growth have cynically described it as 'social and economic development' for the whole country. Although in recent years the privileged sectors have widened noticeably, a large majority of the population is still oppressed and the gaps between the social classes are in many respects becoming wider.

This chapter is mainly an attempt to analyse one of the subordinate social sectors in question: the peasantry. However, to understand the peasantry it is necessary to focus on those social forces which have monopolized all power and authority throughout the period examined. Hence although the nature of the Spanish political system as such cannot be analysed here, nevertheless, some elements of it must be taken into account.

Thus before analysing the impact that Franco's régime has had in the Spanish countryside during the 35 years of its existence, it is necessary to define two key concepts, namely that of 'peasantry' and that of 'Francoism', as they will be used in this chapter.

The peasantry is taken here to be made up of family units of both consumption and production, whose social and economic organization rests on the agricultural exploitation of the land, regardless of the different modes of land tenure. Accordingly, we focus on the peasantry as a unit of sociological observation within which different social groups coexist. The nature of each group derives from the relations of production generated in the different types of agricultural enterprises. Thus, tenants, sharecroppers, and small landowners are very different social groups in many senses, but nevertheless all of them are peasants in the above sense. This working definition for this essay also includes as peasants the landless labourers, in spite of some doubts expressed by scholars with little first-hand contact with the rural world especially in present day so-called developing countries. In general, not only do such labourers work the land as wage labourers, but so do their families. Indeed, they function as family units of agricultural labour and have similar culture and economic organization to the other peasant groups, and even have the same links with the land in the sense that they reject the legitimacy of the landlord's ownership.

As analysed here, the most important characteristic of the peasantry is its asymmetric relationship with society as a whole. In this sense, the term peasantry implies a dependence imposed by the unequal distribution of power. From this perspective, the peasantry is to the agricultural sector what the working class is to the industrial sector. They are the largest, lowest, and the most intensely oppresed segments of society both in the cities and in the countryside. Both are the proletarians of society.

The term Francoism should not be taken to suggest that the régime is based on the accumulation of power and authority in the hands of General Franco. This term defines here the régime itself and the legal and moral bases on which it rests. Thus, sociologically, Francoism must be understood as an entire political system of class domination through which the landowning, the industrialist and the financial sectors exercise direct control of the state apparatus supported by military power. [2]

Having made the preceding definitions, it is now possible to proceed to an examination of the relationship between the peasantry and the Francoist régime. Three coherent periods, of approximately twelve years each, may be discerned. The limits of these periods are not absolute but they are far from arbitrary. Each one of them represents a distinct model of the peasantry and the interplay of social forces which have established its dependence. Each period or model is the result of one or more changing elements in the previous one. They are as follows:

1. 1939–51. Agrarian Fascism. It is characterized by the following elements: The ideology of 'peasant sovereignty'; internal colonization; a repressive system of agricultural labour and the beginning of class domination by the large landowners. Forced transfer of capital from land to industry and to the ruling class.
2. 1952-63. Stability of the coexistence between latifundia and minifundia estates. Characterized by the struggle between the fascist ideology of the peasantry and the need for capitalist industralization and accumulation.
3. 1963-75. Incipient agrarian neo-capitalism based on a new anti-peasant ideology. In this period the criterion of the maximization of profitability is the only one which really matters. The goal is the modernization of rural society by means of the 'de-peasantization' of the Spanish countryside.

2. Agrarian Fascism (1939-51)

It is not proposed to enter here into the discussion about whether Francoism is or is not 'fascism'. Nevertheless, there can be little doubt about the fascist character of the earlier years of Franco's régime.[3] There were certain features within agrarian society which closely resembled the fascist archetype. This was in part due to the fact that the main condition which permitted the change from pre-industrial to the modern world in Spain in a 'capitalistic and reactionary' way was the establishment of a 'reactionary coalition'. This was the rough operative alliance between 'influential sectors of the landed upper classes and the emerging commercial and manufacturing interests',[4] which rested within a narrow segment of the Spanish bourgeoisie.

Naturally, the Franco régime was committed to the maintenance of the rural social structure which had been threatened by the Republic. Among the small-holders of the North, this was relatively easy – since agrarian reform had hardly threatened them and their social and religious conservatism, fired by CEDA propaganda, had inclined them to support in varying degrees the 1936 military rising. In the South it was a different story. Republican social legislation and a tentative agrarian reform had raised the expectations of the great mass of landless labourers. This was expressed in a growing militance, strikes, etc. The newly installed régime now faced the problem of maintaining precisely the system whose injustices had provoked such militance.

This involved the creation of a series of institutions on which to base a new 'repressive system of agricultural labour'.[5] By direct and indirect means, the mass of rural labourers were compelled to work the soil under the most brutal conditions. The main objective of government agrarian policy was to maintain the dependence of the labourers on the large land-owners who controlled the labour market. The methods used were not dissimilar to those employed in Fascist Italy and Nazi Germany.[6] The labourers were deprived of the right to organize in unions; they had no guarantee of obtaining work, they had no right to strike. It was easy therefore for the owners to bring wages down.

In the period 1939-51 the most direct method employed in the creation of such a system was physical violence and intimidation. Already during the civil war itself, the nationalist capture of country towns had been followed by savage reprisals against those labourers who had shown leftist sympathies or even independence of spirit before the war. Moreover, many peasants occupied and farmed the large estates collectively during the war. Often they introduced major technical improvements but naturally when these areas fell to the nationalists, a brutal revenge was taken for the 'violation of the sacred right of property'.[7] The period of reprisals had run its course by 1943. By then the landless peasants had been forced to accept the repressive system of agricultural labour thereby imposed. For some years thereafter, large estates enjoyed the protection of both the Civil Guard and their own armed watchmen in constant vigilance against the pilfering of hungry peasants who did not even earn subsistence wages since they formed a labour reserve able to work only when the owners needed them and without any palliatives of a social security type.

The mechanism used to maintain this situation was the rural variant of the corporative vertical syndicates – the fraternities of labradores and ganaderos. They were based on the principle that both labourers and landowners had identical 'fraternal interests'. Latifundistas, small-holders, tenant-farmers, sharecroppers and day labourers were all represented by a single organization whose name revealed its social alignment (labrador = ploughman, but has come to mean a man of landed substance; ganadero; stock breeder). This was confirmed by the systematic reduction of agricultural wages between 1940 and 1951. In real terms, they fell by 40 per cent and the Hermandades as the new form of peasant association did nothing to stop this process.[8]

The consequent harshness of conditions was reflected in a growing migration to urban areas, where living standards were themselves brutally austere. The authorities tried to prevent migration (and therefore keep a large body of surplus labour available in the countryside) by imposing a system of passes and safe-conducts for travelling. In order to obtain a pass, the peasant had to produce evidence of good conduct from his local landowner and the local authorities often including the parish priest.[9] Nevertheless, it is possible to calculate that more than 800,000 migrated to the towns in the 1940s, in the main, day-labourers.[10] An anti-urban ideology was used by the régime to put a brake on this. In opposition to the city as 'the source of decadence, disorder and "marxism", a fierce propaganda praised the countryside as the ideal form of social peace, decency and traditional values'.[11]

This ideology might be defined as an *ideology of peasant sovereignty*.[12] It contained an idealized expression of the relations of production in agriculture and was an integral part of the Francoist political formula presented to the peasantry. Exalting the peasantry, this ideology presented agriculture not as mere economic activity but rather as a superior form of existence, which safeguarded the essence of 'the Spain's' ethnic and national virtues. According to it, there are no different classes within the peasantry; all peasants have the same social and economic interests, which are those of the nation at large. It is a native Spanish version of fascist *volksgemeinschaft* with roots in Carlist populism. Its intrinsic paternalism has been present in all the agricultural institutions created by the Franco régime until the late fifties.[13]

In fact, the ideological glorification of the peasantry was directed not to the landless labourer, but to the peasant with land. The proclaimed desire to create a nation of small-holders was never carried out, but it was none the less sincere. As one régime ideologue put it 'a country which is able to create a numerous class of land owning peasantry is a country insured against social disturbances, because the peasant landowner is above all interested in stability'.[14] To this it might be added that a phraseology of rural idealization was a natural corollary to the attack on urban marxism.

The practical realization of this ideology of 'peasant sovereignty' was to be found in the process known as 'internal colonization'. Colonization was a useful demagogic ploy which seemed to imply a readiness to attack the problem of the large estates. But as in Italy and Germany, it never went much beyond the level of rhetoric. Nevertheless, internal colonization was a prime objective of the Franco régime. The *Instituto Nacional de Colonización* (Institute for National Land Settlement)[15] was founded within six months of the ending of the civil war, in October 1939. Its declared aim was to create thousands of family plots (*huertas familiares*) as the basis of a new Spain.

According to the author's estimates only 23,000 such settlements were created between 1939-51 – a figure which represents only 0.2 per cent of the total number of landless peasants – and the decline thereafter was dramatic. See table 1.

105

Table 1. Evolution of new 'colonos' settled by the Instituto Nacional de Colonizacion from 1939 to 1970.

Years	Number of 'colonos' (in thous.)	Index (%)	Decrease per decade
1939-50	22.9	100.0	–
1951-60	19.8	86.8	–13.4
1961-70	9.9	43.3	–50.0

Sources: Estimates based on reports of the Instituto Nacional de Colonización, published annually by the Ministry of Agriculture, years 1966, 1968, 1970, 1971.

Pascual Carrión, *La reforma agraria de la Segunda República y la situación actual de la agricultura española* (Barcelona, 1973), p. 261.

Ramón Tamames, *Introducción a la economía española* (Madrid, 1972), p. 75.

Notes: 1. Since 1971 the INC has been integrated as a branch of the new Instituto Nacional de Reforma y Desarrollo Agrario (INRYDA).
2. The several publications of the Ministry of Agriculture and the studies made to date which use them, give different figures. See, for example, the contradiction between Jose López de Sebastian, *Política Agraria en España 1920-1970* (Madrid, 1970), p. 303 and Tamames' work, where both use official figures. I have used for my estimate more coherent figures.

In fact, in accordance with information supplied by the INC to the World Bank for its survey of the Spanish Economy, only 2,000 such settlements per annum were created between 1955 and 1965.[16] Since 1962, the number of new peasants who have received land from the INC had barely exceeded 1,000 per annum.[17]

The policy of colonization highlights the discrepancy between a pro-peasant ideology and the reality of Francoist objectives. Even more telling in this respect are the INC's technical activities regarding the improvement of the agricultural infra-structure in the areas where the colonization was to have taken place, i.e. the large estates. Such activities as programmes of irrigation,[18] the electrification of farms and villages, and the actual purchase of estates began in the second half of the 1940s.[19]

Ostensibly, the objective was to increase agricultural production to alleviate both urban and rural hunger; that the objective was not achieved may be attributed to technical inefficiency and lack of economic resources, but above all it reflects the real interests in whose favour agrarian policy was directed. The extent to which the régime owed its existence to the landed oligarchy could be seen in the absolute commitment to the concept of the sacred right of

106

property. Indeed, the INC devoted more effort to administering the return to their owners of estates expropriated under the Republic than to examining the question of the latifundio problem. Naturally, an institution which inaugurated its activities by expelling the peasantry from the land was unlikely to show great dynamism in the creation of thousands of family plots for landless peasants. [20]

Internal colonization should be seen as an aspect of the fascistic tendencies of Francoist agrarian policy; as a product of its fascist ideology. This is not to say, of course, that directly or indirectly, the traditional landed oligarchy, were not able to exploit the policy of internal colonization for their own interests.

Although, the policy of Internal Colonization was theoretically linked to an irrigation programme, the connection was not established at first. The early settlements of the INC were on unirrigated land which stayed so. [21] Owners of large estates saw a threat in this, fearing that their unirrigated estates would be liable to expropriation. In fact, they need not have feared since sheer economic inefficiency brought this policy to a halt, once it was recognized that to divide an unirrigated *cortijo* into plots was economic nonsense.

Moreover, during these early years Internal Colonization was extremely slow. The 'economic interests of the nation' had to be respected as well as the 'legitimate right of property', so 'the social problem of the land' had to be compatible with these two. [22]

It was at the end of the forties that the INC law on *Colonización y distribución de la propiedad de las zonas regables* (colonization and distribution of land in irrigated regions) was proclaimed. This was without doubt the most important law of the INC. It was this law which finally linked up the previously separate policies of internal colonization (promoted by the government) and the irrigation programmes (sponsored on the whole by individuals – though with some government loans). Thus from then on all the irrigation schemes came under direct control of State in the areas declared to be of high national interest for irrigation' under that law. Nevertheless, only a small part of this new irrigated land was actually colonized. It was only the so-called 'superfluous land' (*tierras en exceso*) – a minute portion of each vast estate – which was given to the peasants. These lands were divided into plots between 5 and 10 hectares. The peasants remained tenants of the State until they paid the price fixed for the land plus interest. Thus, the peasants settled would eventually get the ownership of the land, but only after a period of about twenty years of making payments. [23]

Most of the land continued to be held by the previous landlords, especially latifundistas, who benefited from the great improvements

107

in irrigation, with only minimal economic responsibility for their installation and upkeep. On the other hand, the plight of the settled peasants who had to pay a substantial rent for a long time to own his land and compete with the large owners in the market was desperate.[24]

A far more direct version of the way in which the large landowners used the set of privileges offered by the régime to their own advantage and at the expense of the smaller peasantry is provided by an examination of the role of price policy and of the Servicio Nacional del Trigo (SNT) (National Wheat Board).

It is commonly believed that the SNT was created to support the small-holders.[25] Indeed, Franco himself implied that this was the case in his 1938 New Year speech.[26]

Yet, in fact, the SNT, far from benefitting the small-holders in the wheat-growing sector, can be seen to have pursued the interests of the large land-owners.

Paradoxically, the large landowners derived great profit precisely by not selling their produce to the SNT. In the 1940s, a large proportion of wheat production was sold through the black-market at prices higher than those fixed by the SNT. Those peasants in whose interest the SNT had theoretically been created had not the means – transport, warehouse facilities, etc. – to allow them to play the black market. Their produce was requisitioned at artificially fixed prices.[27] Nothing more clearly illustrates the social selectivity of the 'years of hunger'.

Leaving aside this illegal exploitation by the wealthier owners of the conditions created by the SNT, there also existed legal methods which benefited the larger as opposed to the smaller owners. For instance, a clause in the wheat regulation law allowed those owners who had their own storage facilities to store wheat therein. Clearly benefitting only the large owners, this allowed them to sell their produce outside the control of the SNT.

3. Stability and Change (1952-64): Industrialization versus Ideology of Peasant Sovereignty

In the fifties, Spanish agriculture underwent a major qualitative change. The new course set by the economic policy meant the concentration of efforts on industrial activities and the 'starting point of a large scale industrialization process'. This general shift in economic policy, however, had no impact on agriculture. Thus, in the countryside, protectionist interventionism continued to be very widespread and the characteristics of the period, whose features led us previously to label it as 'agrarian fascism' remained valid in essence.[28]

During the early fifties, the ideology of 'peasant sovereignty' continued to embrace all the measures carried out by the government. Thus, ambitious settlement schemes (colonización) in Badajoz (1952) and Jaen (1953) [29] and the 'Concentración Parcelaria' (1953) – gathering of scattered plots into one single holding – began. It is in the latter, as we shall see further on, that there was still a strong tendency towards the glorification of the peasantry, with the intention of using what the government believed to be a deeply rooted conservatism, in order to ensure the continued existence of the social system of inequalities. [30] However, the requirements of industrialization within the productive forces and the production relations of a capitalistic character which had been already chosen to inspire the Spanish economic development were openly against the creation of a strong peasantry. Such a contradiction was clearly perceived by the falangist minister who, at that time, directed agrarian policy. A thorough analysis of the content of his public speeches allows one to detect a clear change in his lines of political thought. Thus one can see that there was a complete volte-face on his part if one considers his initial speech, in which he declared that the Spanish countryside by itself is capable of creating the greatness of Spain, openly condemning migration and then his pragmatic declaration in 1955 whereby aid is offered to the peasantry by the Ministry of Agriculture to look for jobs for their sons in the 'sister industry'. [31] However, such a recognition was only rhetorical. The existing contradiction between industrialization on the one hand and support of peasantry on the other hand, within a political system accepting capitalist development from a despotic régime was to remain during the entire fifties.

Another example of this contradiction is the setting up of a new public body: the Agrarian Extension Service (1956). It had a clear paternalistic character its aim being to evangelize the countryside, through its apostles – the agrarian extension agents.

In this period (1952-64) the overall economic policy of Spain meant a clear acceptance of the modes of capitalist production and a clear break with the period of autarchy, in order to move towards a situation of dependence on outside forces. The industrial liberalization policy allowed for imports of raw materials and thus for the expansion of industry. This policy of relative capitalist rationality – though it was not free of contradiction either as far as the whole economy is concerned – did not apply to agriculture which remained stagnant. The non intervention of the public powers in the private sector continued. The private sector did not invest in the countryside mainly because of the way in which the land was owned. In effect, the lack of economic means in the North with its structure of very small farms and the apathy and lack of concern for managerial efficiency in the South because of the fairly large profits produced by the farming estates, meant that private investment in agriculture was practically non existent.

In the period analysed here – 1952-64 – the proportion of national income invested in agriculture hardly increased. Accordingly, agriculture was far from getting benefits in proportion to its own contribution to the national wealth. [32] As far as the agrarian sector is concerned the technocratic pragmatism of the general economic policy (during the pre-stabilization period: 1957-59) brought about by the Opus Dei when they appeared on the scene had no success. This was simply further evidence of the existing contradiction between an agrarian policy still inspired by the ideology of 'peasant sovereignty' and an economic development characterized by capitalist productive forces and relations of production. Such a contradiction was accentuated during the Stablization Plan. In the late years of this period (1952-64) Cirilo Cánovas, the Minister of Agriculture, proclaiming total support for the message of Onésimo Redondo, a fascist agrarian leader who died in the Civil War, said 'It is necessary to consider the fact that the strictly economic aspects of the agrarian sector are suffering and are undergoing a definite change in order to adapt themselves to its new circumstances imposed by new international conditions . . . The countryside is no longer just a reserve of human values.' [33]

Yet, in spite of such statements, the agrarian policy in the years between 1952 and 1964 continued to be anchored to the 'romantic view' of keeping the peasant population in the countryside, of artificial support to small agricultural holding and 'modest and yet profitable family plots', which was clearly in contradiction with the socio-economic reality. [34] In fact, the process of industrialization was bringing about profound and chaotic changes in the rural social structure. The large scale exodus of the landless peasantry from the countryside and the ensuing terrible social toll were totally ignored by the pragmatic supporters of rapid industrialization – at all costs.

On the 18 December 1952, the Minister of Agriculture (Rafael Cavestany y de Anduaga) established the bases of the organism which would reveal the contradiction which has already been noted between the ideology of peasant sovereignty and the development of the capitalistic form of production: the Servicio Nacional de Concentración Parcelaria (SNCP).

A proposal was presented to the Cortes (an unrepresentative legislative body), its aim being to put on end to the fragmentation of land by a campaign of concentration of plots. Among the inconveniences attributed to this fragmentation, besides economic

110

and technical reasons, others enumerated by the Minister of Agriculture were 'the loss of the intensity of family life', and 'the loss, the most important and irreparable of the *agrarian spirit,* such that the peasant on seeing so little land, so divided, so difficult and *impossible* to dominate and *to love,* so little his, that he *ends up by abandoning it without any nostalgia and joins the suburban population from which he very rarely returns and in which he generally falls into a life of misery without ideals'.*[35]

In very few speeches are the main ideas of the ideology of peasant sovereignty so clearly expressed: The poorer social sectors of the peasantry with land are identified with 'the true peasantry'. The Spanish peasant is classified as 'probably, the most noble and worthy of help among those that populate the globe'.

But the really important thing in this speech is the explicit way which the subjugating function of this ideology is revealed. According to the Minister, the peasantry rises politically only 'when the ruling classes fail'. He then expresses the need of the régime to 'cover the dangerous split' which the peasantry can create, thereby avoiding another explosion of revolutionary independence like that of 1936: 'Before the picture of the victorious revolutions and its consequent devastation; before the sad proletarian procession dragging its chains of slavery, let us place the opposite, the picture of the peasant standing over his land with a house in the background, with his children playing at the door and over all of this a modest but divine crucifix as the goal of all the ways of the spirit and to which our faith and our ambition as Spaniards carries us.'[36]

Although the concentration of land was conceived free from the class nature of the INC which stemmed from the Civil War, it is still obvious that there was a latent function which clearly did pursue the class interests of Franco's régime within the ideological wrappings of 'peasant sovereignty'.

The results of the activities of the SCP show a marked bias in favour of areas which supported the Francoist side in the Spanish Civil War. The plot amalgamation that there was, centred almost exclusively in Castile, while Asturias and Galicia had a far more acute problem of plot fragmentation. This can only be explained in terms of 'spoils of war'[37] given the widespread participation of Castillian small-holders in the Francoist war effort. In the main, the Galician and Asturian peasant reaction to the military rising had been decidedly cool.[38] Moreover, after the war, the peasantry in both areas supported a guerrilla movement against the régime.

It is deplorable that these efforts can only affect a small number of people in the villages where the amalgamation occurs. In the five provinces (all are Castilian) which in the period considered showed

111

a higher proportion of amalgamated area, there are a small number of large or medium-sized farms which account for between 40 and 50 per cent of the whole area. More than 40 per cent of the farms in those five provinces were less than 5 hectares – a quantity which, in the dryness of Castile is clearly insufficient to maintain a peasant family unit with or without fragmentation. This means that only a minority of farmers benefited sufficiently from amalgamation to subsist and these are the few owners of large land-holdings and the rich peasants. A large majority of peasants continue with insufficient land to maintain a peasant family unit after having their land amalgamated.

But what leads us to see elements of 'residual fascism' in *Concentración Parcelaria* is not its entanglement with the ideology of the peasant sovereignty, which was at the end of this period (1952-64) to lose its folkloric aspects of bucolic idealization and ethnic exaltation, but the underlying class function that arose directly from its political conception. This allows us to classify the policy of land amalgamation as a new screen which distracted attention from the *latifundio* problem.

For, despite the growing emphasis on modernization, it was to be a modernization which would leave untouched the fundamental problem of the large estates, the *latifundios*. Increasing emigration tended to mask the extent to which the problem still existed. The Francoist system maintained the traditional system of local class domination intrinsic in the existence of huge estates.[39]

The class domination of the large estates is one of the several elements which led us to define the period 1939-51 as a period of Agrarian Fascism. It has remained, however, unlike the other elements, a constant fact in the period analysed here, and has even reinforced itself.

The privileged situation of the large estates derives not only from their position in the relations of production – supported by the 'repressive system of agricultural labour force' – but also, and above all, from the agricultural policies carried out by the government.

During this period (1952-64), the colonization policy, closely linked with irrigation programmes, meant a reinforcement of the large estates. This was brought about by the capitalization of the land (in the form of irrigation)[40] with which the government assiduously wooed the latifundistas. Added to these give-away concessions, the latifundistas were granted the possibility of obtaining a cheap labour force from the newly settled peasants.

The price policy of offering strong protection to a considerable number of crops on the large estates, such as beetroot, cotton, olives, etc. assures them of an enormous surplus.[41] Within this policy,

112

wheat continues to play an essential role. The protection of wheat during this period (which in fact still exists) meant that the government bought at much higher prices than those current on the international market. This policy permitted the large estates to continue a strong accumulation process through the generation of differential rents.

Furthermore a large number of latifundistas took advantage of this so-called 'protection of the wheat-growing peasants' to produce on their irrigated land which in many cases was obtained with the help of the state, wheat which was to be later bought by the SNT. In fact, from 1951 to 1962 there was an increase in the amount of irrigated land dedicated to the production of wheat. The increase was larger than 45,000 hectares from which more than 27 per cent was found in only three provinces, Badajoz, Cordova and Seville. It was precisely in these three provinces that there existed a larger concentration of land ownership. Without doubt the open support, with all its social and political significance, of the price policy of the large estates constituted a strong obstacle against agricultural development.[42] This was also the key element for the maintenance of the system of 'latifundio–minifundio' coexistence.

In addition, the fiscal policy, 'which while it tries above all to avoid fiscal pressure, which might prove itself to be excessive as regards the economic capacities of the small land owners, grants at the same time especially favourable conditions to the large land owners'.[43]

Together with this, one must consider the existence of a credit system, which discriminates against agriculture.[44] Such discrimination, in spite of the lack of research into this, seems to be not only of a sectional character but also of a social one. What little credit there is available in agriculture rarely finds its way into the hands of those who really need it. In fact, the evidence compiled by Jose Manuel Naredo allows us to affirm that the greater benefits of this credit policy are obtained by the large estates.[45]

4. Modernization as De-Peasantization (1965-75): Towards Agrarian Neocapitalism

There is a wealth of economic and sociological works which have come out in Spain in the last five years on the *crisis of traditional agriculture*. In spite of the obvious quality of some of them they generally suffer from a lack of political approach.[46] In other words, they analyse what happens in agriculture or in Spanish rural society but without taking into account the underlying values of the agrarian policies of the government.

113

Thus, the concept of the crisis of traditional agriculture has become so popular that it could even be affirmed that it has been incorporated as an element of the ideology of agrarian industrialism, which constitutes a key component of the present régime's general ideology.[47]

Francoism through its Agrarian Policy presents such a crisis as inevitable in the necessary process of adaptation and change from a traditional and backward society to a progressive and modern one.

There indeed exists an agrarian crisis in the long-period variations of economic activity in Spain and it probably started in the early fifties, when the crisis started as a consequence of mass-migration. It is certain also that the crisis went hand in hand with a radical transformation being brought about in the social organization of the Spanish peasantry.

If the peasantry is considered as 'a historical entity within the broader framework of society yet with a structure, consistency and momentum of its own: emerging, representing at some stage the prevailing mode of social organization, disintegration, re-emerging at times',[48] the crisis of a traditional agriculture in Spain could be interpreted as one of the historical stages of the disintegration of such a social entity.

Accordingly, we define de-peasantization as the process of change which takes place in the socio-economic organization of the peasantry as a result of the political imposition of material relations of production through which the disintegration of the peasant society is brought about. Thus, the changing attitude of the Spanish régime towards the peasantry – from its exaltation to a virtual assault on it – has been dictated by the specific needs of capitalistic industrial development in that country.

Different policies were always linked to large landowners' interests, though in specific cases such policies also supported some sectors of the peasantry with land. In this way in the previous two periods considered here (1939-51 and 1952-1964) a large amount of the incomes generated in agriculture has contributed substantially to the financing of the industrialization process in numerous different ways.[49]

In the period studied here (1965-75), the social tensions originated by the industrialization process were even officially supported. In effect, the first Economic and Social Development Plan (1er. plan de desarrollo económico y social) (1964-67) laid down the norms within which 'Agricultural Policy was to be orientated towards a transference of the working population from the countryside to other sectors'.[50] This did not constitute the active support of the conflicts and tension created by migration. Given that

114

such migration was inevitable under such conditions, what is deplorable is that no measures were taken to mitigate the social cost which was involved in the rural exodus.

After the second half of the sixties the 'ideology of peasant sovereignty' was entirely buried. However, with this the instrumentalization of the peasantry did not finish. New anti-peasant ideologies arose to justify the sacrifice of thousands of peasants, in order to obtain progress and economic development. What is not made clear in these ideologies is why this type of progress was necessary and who were the social sectors who were going to enjoy the benefits of that economic growth. It is hardly surprising then that the social tensions which originated in the route towards industrialism chosen by the government of Franco's Spain had their most significant repercussions on the peasantry. 'Moving people instead of moving capital' was the key element of that policy. Lack of employment opportunities in the countryside forced people to take the decision to migrate.

Government policy of encouraging migration meant the acceptance of an 'economicista' criterion of efficiency, which ignored other possible more equitable alternatives. The true nature of this policy was masked by ideological justifications perpetrated by the political formula of Franco's régime. It was claimed that this policy was directed towards the overall socio-economic development of the country. The corner-stone of this ideological justification is based on the assumption that in the historical processes of development in all countries, the stage of *laissez-faire* is an historical need during the formative period of modern industrial capitalism. [51]

With regard to agriculture, the 'desarrollista' ideology is based on the assumption that agriculture, for its own development, must reflect the course taken by industry. It is in this way that the 'ideology of Agrarian industrialism' comes into being.

According to the ideology of Agrarian Industrialism the social costs brought about by emigration; the new resulting dependent relations of the peasantry (due to hegemonic forms introduced by agrarian capitalism); the imposition of a system of urban values and, in general, the de-peasantization pocess, are all imperative for the welfare of society as a whole.

By the term *ideology of Agrarian Industrialism* we understand: 'the ideal expression of the dominant material relationships' [52] presented to the peasantry – and the public at large – by the Francoist political formula. The key element of these ideological constructions of reality is the presentation of agriculture in its necessary evolution simply as a branch of industry. And since the latter is fully dominated by capital, the former must ineluctably follow the same schemes as

115

those of industry in order to achieve development. Agriculture thus becomes just an economic activity and nothing else. The conception of agriculture as something tied to a way of life due to a peasant culture with a character of its own, (the ideology of peasant sovereignty) now goes against historical progress.

On 6 June 1972 Alberto Ballarín Marcial, director of the YRIDA (Institute for Agrarian Reform and Development)[53] presented 'a rallying-cry for the countryside: it is necessary to industrialize and urbanizo it'.[54] Rural villages were to be 'raised' to the category of agro-towns. This objective was expressed in its most extreme form by a gathering of the régime's agrarian experts. 'The new agriculture, with the entrepreneurs to the fore as organizers of the progress' must be based upon 'totally mechanized lands extending maybe even to the climate'. The tasks ascribed to the new peasant entrepreneur will be 'the production of cheap goods for the rest of the country, in a context of universal competitivity'. All this requires that 'two thirds of the people who live in the countryside change their activities and therefore that they should be provided as soon as possible with the opportunity to start organizing themselves for the new life'.[55]

Furthermore, this ideology goes beyond political spheres and reaches academic circles. Thus, Amando de Miguel, one of he best-known Spanish sociologists, even stated that 'the agriculture of the future must be a chemical–biological industry' and that it required 'the almost total extinction of family farms; this process having already taken place in some other industries',[56] as that of rationalizing the process of destruction of the peasantry. In effect, such an ideology is based on the presupposition that historical development processes are similar sequentially and taxonomically. Therefore to reach the situation of developed nations any country must ineluctably go through the same stages which these nations have gone through. The USA is generally considered to be the prototype of this kind of development. Thus, formation of large agrarian capitalist farms becomes necessary, which in turn implies a previous depeasantization of the countryside in the American style. Thus, a re-channelling of resources, of both capital and labour, from agriculture to the other sectors is achieved at the cost of great human misery and social disorganization. Acceptance of such an ideology means not only an ignorance of the human costs and social disorganization implied by its use for wide segments of the population, but also that accumulation of industrial and urban political power grows increasingly, which deprives the peasantry of any sort of defence.

All this does not mean, of course, that the development process does not bring about a channelling of resources, both capital and labour, from agriculture to the other sectors. What is not so obvious is why such a process should require the annihilation of the peasantry. It has been proved, so far, that agriculture must follow the same patterns as industry. From the existence in the past, and currently too, of bottlenecks in Spanish agriculture preventing a faster development, one cannot conclude that agriculture could not have been incorporated into the development process through democratic forms of vertical and horizontal integration applied to the peasantry. Faster does not mean better, and this remains true especially as far as economic development is concerned.

The rural exodus which started to spread in the early sixties to the lower middle sectors of the peasantry (small landowners, tenants and sharecroppers) has reached enormous proportions since the second half of that decade.

The coexistence of latifundist and peasant modes of production has now practically ceased. The market's law is imposed on both of them. The 'latifundistas' have the opportunity of becoming big capitalist entrepreneurs. The State has provided them with all sorts of facilities to capitalize their estates. Nevertheless, in general, this has not happened. This is mainly because these facilities were inserted in the wider context of strong governmental protectionism. This ensured them high profits without any need for them to take the possible risks involved in modernizing their estates. Hence the traditional crop cultivation system remained practically unchanged.

On the other hand, peasants with land began to realize that the protection offered by the price policy no longer provided them with a minimum satisfactory income. The only solution, apart from that of migration, would be a possible integration both horizontally and vertically. This would require a democratic context which didn't – and still does not – exist.

A massive emigration has been the response of the peasantry to this situation. The intended 'transfer of population' has in fact been achieved by the policy makers of the Francoist regime. Thus, in the first six years of the period considered here, that is from 1964 to 1970, there was a decline of the agrarian labour force amounting to nearly half a million people. This means a decrease of 11.5 per cent of the existing agricultural labour force in only six years. Of such a decrease 83.7 per cent corresponds to the peasantry, and from that more than 50 per cent refers to peasants with land. And yet the peasantry is not the social sector, within the active agricultural population, which is most affected by the 'long-period crisis'. However, such a decline in the labour force only reflects a partial view of the huge migratory process which is taking place in the countryside. A very conservative estimate of the rural–urban net migration suggests that in all the provinces with the exception of the provincial capitals the loss of population – in terms of net migration – during the first half of the sixties was as much as a million people.[57]

The biggest indices of migration both in absolute and in relative terms (per 1,000 people) are in Andalusia, La Mancha, Estremadura and Old Castille where the prevalent pattern for increase is larger.

What is worth stressing here is that the enormous rural–urban geographic mobility, supported and, to a large extent, induced by the government took its toll not only on the migrant peasants forced off the land, but on the social system as a whole.

In order to maintain this subjection of peasant interests to those of industry it became necessary to evolve an ideological framework to support this. Thus, a picture of urban life as superior and more rational than the peasant way of life began to be constantly protected by the political system through the mass media which they controlled.[58]

However there were other factors, apart from the régime's propaganda, which influenced migration. Lack of local autonomy and a very low level of social, cultural and health facilities were a strong deterrent as regards the social development of rural communities.[59] Thus the gap between urban and rural areas is becoming wider. In other words the traditional concentration of wealth, culture and power in the cities is now acquiring extreme forms.

There is no doubt that migration is one of the necessary demands of the industrialization process. However, what affects rural areas is not emigration itself but the intensity, the rhythm and the way in which it takes place.

In Spain several traits of the Francoist régime have severely constrained the natural evolution of peasant institutions. There has been a complete lack of freedom in rural society to organize any social, political or cultural association at a community level, unless they were under government control. Hence the vertical control of the peasant classes by pseudo-trade unions (*Hermandades de Labradores y Ganaderos*) depending directly on the government. The cooperativist movement is compulsorily integrated to such 'trade-unions' (*Sindicatos*). Any kind of local authority is directly elected by the government; lack of representation is therefore absolute. Together with these institutions for general control there exists a despotic and arbitrary control by the para-military Civil Guard in every rural community.

All these factors together with the agricultural and development policies have in fact acted as structuring agents of rural society. In other words, the political system itself largely generates and maintains the patterns of inequality, subordination, supraordination and social mobility. This is true for the whole of society but these features are more accentuated in Spanish peasant society.

Thus, migration in the present context, cannot just be regarded as the result of the relative position of city and countryside. Nor can it merely be considered as a factor responsible for the crisis of traditional agriculture. Migration is above all an agent of social homogenization in cultural terms, which is political and socially desirable in Spain.[60] From this viewpoint definitive emigration can be regarded as perhaps the most important of the elements provoking what we have defined as the de-peasantization process.

Among other possible elements we will consider two:

1. The new modes of proletarization of the peasantry, and
2. The forms of peasant dependence of the market.

Both must be considered as new patterns of class domination that Agrarian capitalism introduced in the peasant societies. There thus took place a *proletarization of the peasantry*[61] *with land*. That is to say a process through which the peasant family unit gradually lost the traditional forms of work in its volume of family economic activity. In this way new modes of dependence and subordination appeared.

Amongst others, three different forms of new economic activities could be pointed out:

(*a*) Seasonal migration abroad

(*b*) New forms of auxiliary industrial activities in peasant families

(*c*) Loss of the possession of the means of production.

(*a*) *Seasonal migration abroad*. Almost half a million peasants had to emigrate to France to work in agricultural jobs such as grape harvesting, strawberry picking, etc. during the five first years of the sixties. The following four years – from 1965 to 1969 – the figures increased to five hundred and eighty thousand peasants. Most of those moved from their rural communities in the South of Spain – mainly La Mancha and Andalusia.

'Seasonal migration to France in order to do agricultural jobs has meant an annual contribution of workers to France, superior to that represented by permanent migration, in absolute figures, mostly during the last twenty years'.[62]

But what is more relevant as regards seasonal migration is that a large part of migrant peasants are themselves small landholders who need to increase the insufficient incomes of their farms with the seasonal wages obtained by working as labourers in France. Accordingly, while a part of the peasant family labour force emigrate temporarily, the rest of the family remain in the rural

119

communities working their own land.

Thus, (b) *new forms of auxiliary industrial activities* in peasant families appear all over the country. In more industrialized areas these are more or less similar to what is known as part-time agriculture in European countries. Nevertheless, in many rural areas where the peasantry with land predominates, non-agricultural auxiliary activities constitute a new phenomenon which to some extent could be judged as an open exploitation of the peasantry. Thus, many agricultural processing and craft industries use auxiliary peasant family labour whose market price is lower – old people, women and children – in economic conditions clearly inferior to those which to be found in the labour market.[63] These forms of 'part-time agriculture' are qualitatively different to those which peasant family units traditionally made for the local market of their communities. They create new multi-directional forms of subjection of the peasantry which loses its basic family farm multi-functional unit of social organization, and which remains in the hands of new powerful outsiders.

Lack of free trade unions where peasant industrial workers are able to defend their interests increases this dependence and worsens the situation.

Finally, we shall consider as another form of peasant proletarization (c) *the loss of the means of production* as a consequence of the increase of the importance of working capital as against land capital. Urban concentration and the subsequent new consumption patterns accompaning the industrialization process changed largely the structure of demand. This change provoked a strong capitalistic expansion regarding agricultural means of production industries. This happens when long-period economic crisis pushes a large sector of the small holding peasantry into a hopeless situation. Thus, new agricultural industries came to offer a possible solution to those sectors of the peasantry by re-organizing the productive structure of their farms.

Accordingly, a large number of national and international companies introduce new and more sophisticated technology and offer peasants contracts to produce exclusively for them. A situation soon arises in which the peasant's working capital belongs in fact almost completely to these agricultural enterprises. Land and labour are the only peasant contribution. These dynamic firms diffuse industrial production methods; they offer credit facilities up to dangerous levels; they manage to control the first stages of production (incubation, multiplication); they busy themselves with the slaughtering of animals and the whole commercialization process.[64] In this way peasants working under the capitalistic

120

clientele relationship of agricultural industries are in a certain sense new peasant labourers with land under a new kind of lord: agrarian capitalism.

The dominance of this new capitalistic structure of production is practically complete in the livestock sector as far as the supply of the means of production is concerned. However, this phenomenon is spreading more and more to the rest of the agrarian sub-sectors. Accordingly this mode of proletarization of the peasantry starts to be a predominant pattern in the peasant societies that have a majority of peasants with land.

The last factor of de-peasantization considered here is intimately connected with the proletarization by the loss of means of production already studied. It will be called Peasant dependence on the market situation which means that if the harvest yield is low, a fair price for the products does not pay for the costs of production. On the other hand, if the harvest is good, prices diminish very rapidly and peasants have to sell their produce at a price which is also below the production costs. In either case the peasant finds himself plunged into a situation of accumulated debts which make it almost impossible for him to emerge from his desperate plight.

Some crops traditionally enjoying strong state support are no longer economically viable and the peasants, therefore, are forced to cease cultivating them as that support is at present insufficient, though this is not the case for the big landowners, unwilling to take risks – due to the existence of economies of scale.[65]

The peasantry is subject to a strong policy of production specialization which forces it to reduce its traditional crop and production diversification system directed both to self-consumption and to the local market.

The small peasant is faced, then, with the need to adapt his holdings to the new situation. In so doing he basically depends on one single crop, supported by the administration through short-run measures. Moreover, such a productive specialization forces him to introduce new technological advances which are presented to him as market requirements appreciably increasing the costs of production. Thus the more specialized the peasant in a single type of production or crop cultivation, the more dependent he becomes on two major factors conditioning his farms' profitability. Namely, (a) new technological advances which exert a strong impact both quantitative and qualitative upon production costs and (b) the need to accept contracts with companies of vertical integration for the marketing of his agricultural products.[66]

The peasant then stands caught between agrarian industries which supply essential goods (feed-stuffs, fertilizer, etc.) and others

121

which buy up, process and market his goods. Links between these industries and the state administration and the corporative union structure leave the peasant virtually without defence.[67] However, in the last few years, the peasants have begun to evolve a desperate reply. The peasants face the Administration, through illegal strikes known as 'the milk war', the 'peach-war',[68] the 'sugar beet war'[69] and so on. The 'milk war' for instance has gone on intermittently since 1971, when for eleven days most milk producers in Santander – a province with a large amount of peasantry with land and small holdings – refused to deliver milk at the 'Centrales lecheras' (Central dairies). It was in February and March 1974, however, that the 'milk war' reached its climax. Milk peasants asked for an increase in the price of milk claiming that the production costs were higher than their sale prices. This was recognized as being true, even by several prominent public officials (Cf. *Las Provincias,* Valencia 25-11-1974). Yet both the administration and the 'Centrales lecheras' refused these demands for higher prices. For more than three weeks, livestock-producing peasants of almost all the areas in the Basque Country, Cantabric area, Navarre and Catalonia stopped delivering milk. In the meantime the administration authorized imports of French milk at a higher price than that officially established in Spain. The Civil Guard had to protect the lorries passing the Spanish border from France and some milk peasants were gaoled when they tried themselves to sell milk at the market. The result of all this was the slaughtering of thousands of milking cows by the peasantry. According to a report from a Research Institution dependent on the 'Diputación Provincial of Gerona' 20 per cent of the total number of livestock were sacrificed.[70] They sometimes prefer to lose a certain amount of their production rather than to continue losing money. At times the administration's response is that of importing the same kind of agricultural goods at a much higher price than that demanded by the peasants as remunerative. These government actions were carried out in an atmosphere of absolute selfconfidence in its own strength, although it had to be backed very often by the Civil Guard and by the Political Police.[71]

The reason for such conflicts is the policy of the encouragement of productive specialization (fruits, dairies, etc.) carried on by the government since the second half of the sixties. The products on which this specialization takes place are strongly dependent on both the national and international market within the ideological framework of agrarian industrialism.

At the present, agricultural wars have a latent character in almost all agricultural products (wine, sugar beet, almond, pepper, most fruits, potato and so on) and livestock (dairies, chicken, pig, lamb, calf). These so-called 'wars' represent, to our understanding, clear symptoms that the peasantry is acquiring an increasing awareness of the repercussions of the depeasantization process.

Economic crises, and the uselessness of 'peasant wars' to solve them, even when they obtain the demanded increases in prices for agricultural products, are factors which cause the peasantry to become conscious of being exploited. They realize that any rise in agricultural prices which they manage to obtain is actually for the benefit of the agrarian industries' financial interests (which very often play the role of provocation).

However, the fact is that although they are aware that they are exploited by the agrarian financial interests, it still remains for them to be able to actually identify these concretely. What is concrete for them is the process of depeasantization – the disintegration of the social fabric of their tradition communities – which they are undergoing.

Whether they will be able to identify the causes of this process which is afflicting them, only the future will tell.

A Conclusion

The mode of domination established in Spain in 1939 was largely based on the complete control of the working classes and the peasantry by a state apparatus which was at the service of the victorious right-wing coalition. The success of this mode of domination was largely due to the political formula evolved by the specific Spanish version of modern despotism. During the early stages ('agrarian fascist phase') this success was based on a 'repressive system of agricultural labour' combined with physical violence and political terror. Simultaneously the ideology of 'peasant sovereignty' – a key component of the general ideology of the régime – helped to change the situation from the use of physical violence to more subtle modes of persuasion and the establishment of a widespread consensus – restricted land-settlement, family plots, land amalgamation, etc. All those operations were oriented towards the erection of a smokescreen to hide the chief agricultural problem of Spain: the *latifundio* as a local system of class domination. The peasantry's reaction under the circumstances has been a class reaction: rural exodus. In the forties we still saw 'war migration' of landless peasants to the towns. This incipient stream became a rural exodus in the fifties, largely caused by rapid industrialization. It was under the mode of capitalist development chosen by Francoism – foreign dependence, tourism, labour migration abroad, etc. – that the peasantry became an 'awkward class'. New ideological rationalization appeared in order to explain the 'depeasantization' that ensued, in open contradiction with the former official 'pro-peasant' ideology. It has been at this juncture that the traditional forms of class domination – the latifundio system – was re-cast in harmony with the new patterns of power and privilege which have emerged in contemporary industrial Spain. This adjustment has, of course, strengthened the latifundio system. Given that the Franco régime originated in response to a threat to the latifundio system, that is hardly surprising.

6

The Anti-Francoist Opposition: The Long March To Unity

PAUL PRESTON

The study of the anti-Franco opposition presents several problems. Not the least of them is the obvious difficulty of obtaining information about beleagured clandestine groups in the interior and exiles scattered throughout Latin America and Eastern Europe.[1] To this must be added the bewildering profusion of opposition groupings. The various parties existing before the Civil War – liberal democrats, Socialists, Communists, Trotskyists and anarchists, with their regional and ideological sub-divisions – were transferred wholesale into exile in 1939. Under the pressures of absence from Spain, splits occurred which often did not correspond to splits in the interior. Even in the 1950s when a new and indigenous opposition began to emerge, it was soon subject to a similarly kaleidoscopic process. Clandestinity and constant police persecution made the elaboration of consistent, meaningful policies and the establishment of stable leadership in the interior virtually impossible.

A greater difficulty is that of defining which groups constitute significant, as opposed to merely self-proclaimed, opposition. It is hard to include the interminable wranglings of the exiled Republicans in Mexico, for instance, among major threats to the stability of Francoism, although it has suited the régime's propagandists to do so.[2] Equally, there are individuals widely considered to be of the opposition whose contribution to the régime is far more positive than negative. Figures like Manuel Fraga, for example, represent a loyal dissent which aims more at altering the make-up of a given cabinet than at fundamentally changing the structure of the régime. Nevertheless, this kind of 'creative discord' has been denominated 'semi-opposition', although it hardly goes beyond the tactical manoeuvres of potential ministers or *ministrables*.[3] These same figures should rather be considered as a fake or pseudo-opposition, since they play a major part in making the régime appear tolerant and pluralistic when it clearly is not.[4]

Since the régime exists for the benefit of certain social and economic classes, the pursuit of their interests involves the exclusion from power of other sectors. The groups which support the régime, benefit from it and occasionally participate in power are various. Inevitably, there have at times been limited tactical debates among them or even a relatively combative jockeying for position within the élite. Obvious examples are the power struggle between the Falange and the Opus Dei and the manoeuvring by the Christian Democrat group *Tácito* in early 1975 for an evolution of the Franco régime as a prerequisite of its own survival.[5] The relations between these groups can only be considered meaningfully as opposition on those rare occasions when they constitute a serious threat to the régime. Hence, the activities of the extreme right[6] will not be considered here since their seeming discrepancies with the régime derive from a fervent desire to strengthen it.

There are, of course, groups such as the guerrilleros of the 1940s, the ETA terrorists of the 1970s or clandestine Communist cadres at anytime since 1939, whose oppositionism is not in doubt. The problem concerns border-line cases. The Christian Democrats of Gil Robles or Ruiz-Giménez may well be prepared to see the Francoist system reformed within strict limits, but it is unlikely that they would actively try to overthrow it. Equally, the Social Democratic Union of the ex-Falangist, Dionisio Ridruejo could well have been seen as a sharp critic of the régime but not as a threat to it.[7] Indeed, the degree of toleration afforded such groups in recent years, or to dissident monarchists in the 1940s, could well be a useful indicator if not an absolute criterion of definition. The régime has never shrunk from the use of the most violent methods against the militants of groups which it sees as a substantial menace to its existence. Communists, Socialists, anarchists, and workers' leaders, irrespective of political affiliation, have been the victims of imprisonment, torture and execution from 1939 to the present day. The fact that 'left-wing' Falangists, Christian Democrats and even some Socialists have not always received the same treatment indicates many things: a certain loyalty to ex-francoists, an awareness of world opinion, but above all a perceptive sense of the real innocuousness of such groups.[8]

This tolerated or 'alegal' opposition could be excluded from a survey of the opposition on the evidence that it is tolerated because it constitutes no danger to the régime. Another reason is its high degree of potential assimilability into the régime bureaucracy.[9] Yet, even excluding the alegal opposition, there remain problems of

126

definition. One commentator has suggested a classification according to readiness to undergo arrest, torture and so on. [10] Another has advocated division according to the kind of society with which a group proposed to replace Francoism. [11] Since any such analysis would be based on statements made with little relation to reality, the classification would be of little value. A more sensible proposal is that which would divide the opposition into 'revolutionaries' who wish to overthrow the régime and are prepared to use violence to do so, and 'reformists' who prefer evolutionary change. [12]

The Franco régime, however, has not made such sophisticated distinctions. It has dealt violently with all those who have constituted a serious threat to its existence, although with different degrees of ferocity. Whether the threat has come from Basque activists, Catholic labour leaders or even from pacifists like the celebrated *encartelado*, Gonzalo Arias, [13] the régime has not hesitated to strike hard and fast. Thus, without wishing to devalue the present debate on the definition of the anti-Franco opposition, it would be superfluous to enter it here. [14] This is a study of the organised political opposition which has tried to overthrow, or seriously resist the untrammelled exercise of power by, the Franco régime. It follows the régime itself in deciding which groups are worthy of attention.

There remains the temporal factor. It is obvious that the aspirations and difficulties of opposition have changed from the dour years of the all-pervading state terror to the years of the economic boom, when the regime was confident enough to relax the repression somewhat. The battle for survival of the Republican stragglers after the Civil War is very different from the activities of the prosperous lawyers and intellectuals who currently consider themselves to be at the forefront of the struggle. [15] It is therefore proposed to indicate the evolution of the anti-Franco opposition by dividing the period under consideration into four main parts – 1939-51; 1951-62; 1962-73; 1973 to the present. The periods are not water-tight compartments, but they do have a certain character, underlined by the symbolic dates which divide them.

The first period is characterized by the fact that the Civil War, despite the defeat of 1939 and the exile, continued until 1951. Opposition was conceived in terms of overturning the victory of the Nationalists. Militants looked for leadership to the old Republican cadres. Guerrilla activities were carried out as they had been in the Nationalist zone during the war. The period is considered closed by the symbolic withdrawal of the Communist armed groups in 1951. The recognition that the war was definitely lost led to a period of lethargy and demoralization. The 1950s were marked by a decline in the importance of the exiled Republican leadership and the slow emergence of a new internal opposition which, with the exception of the Communist Party (PCE), did not correspond to prewar divisions. The close of the period is taken as 1962 for two reasons. First, the strikes of that year altered the way in which the entire opposition viewed its task. Secondly, it was the year of the symbolic meeting of internal and exiled opposition at the Congress of Munich. The third period is marked by divisions and polemics arising out of the changed economic situation. Prosperity and continuing extreme unbalance in the distribution of wealth gave rise to debate between a European-style new left and more backward-looking leaders. The corresponding fragmentation hit the entire left but no one group more than the Communist Party. The process was only reversed by the death of Carrero Blanco in December 1973 at the hands of ETA militants. New perspectives were opened, the régime was left in its present crisis and all opposition groups began to put preparations for the immediate future before theoretical speculation.

Despite these vicissitudes of the opposition, there is a high degree of continuity. Two major patterns may be discerned, in broad terms, as on the one hand, the desire of forces to the right of the PCE to exclude it from the future, and, on the other hand, the desire of the Communists to by-pass the leaders of other opposition groups and take over their rank-and-file from above. Several attempts at creating organizations to unite the opposition but exclude the PCE have been made: the *Junta Española de Liberación* of 1944, the *Unión de Fuerzas Democráticas* of 1961 and most recently the so-called *Conferencia Democrática* of 1974. This reflects an under-current of anti-communism among these groups. Only in part a result of régime propaganda, it is a hang-over from the Communists' actions during the Civil War and also a reflection of the fact that the liberal opposition has always looked outside Spain for a solution to its problems and has therefore assumed that anti-communism was a pre-requisite of help from the USA or the Western European democracies.

Communist attempts to take over the opposition by pseudo-unificatory fronts have hardly differed. A central junta, usually in exile, is made up of Communists and other liberal figures. Regional and local juntas are then set up, consisting of Communists and prominent local liberal individuals or members of the groups which have joined the central junta. Since only the PCE has a well-organized national net-work and a well-produced clandestine press, these juntas are effectively PCE-dominated.[16] Prominent examples of theoretically wide local fronts nationally coordinated by the PCE have been the *Junta Suprema de Unión Nacional* of 1943 and the *Junta Democrática* of 1974.

Beyond these two general patterns, other tendencies have been consistent heroism and sacrifice at the rank-and-file level which has been regularly squandered by the narrow egoism and fragmentation of the leadership, especially in exile. The key-note, then, has been division and failure until the recent moves towards unity.

1939-51

It is remarkable that there was any opposition to Franco at all. The left had been militarily defeated in a bloody three year war. Half a million of the survivors went into exile. [17] Many could not, and were subjected to the political terror imposed on the zones captured by the Nationalists. [18] Thus, the onus of active opposition fell on the exiles. It was, moreover, natural that the defeated Republicans should look to the political leaders of the 1930s and that their first objective should be the re-establishment of the Republic. In fact, the exiled rank-and-file could do little. Those in Latin America were neutralized by distance. Others nearer Spain could have found themselves forced into the French Foreign Legion, German labour brigades or concentration camps. The need to learn new languages and find work in a hostile environment meant that most exiles had little time to devote to Spain. Activists were as likely to be fighting in the French resistance or British forces as thinking about Spain. [19]

Yet the greatest single factor contributing to the failure of the exiled opposition was the persistence of Civil War ideological divisions. The history of the exile is one of continuing fragmentation and quick-silver coalitions. The existing divisions of the Republican left were widened by geographical diffusion after 1939 and by embittered recriminations over the reasons for defeat. The most serious discord was to be between the Communists and the remaining groups, and to a lesser extent between pro- and anti-Communists within each group. This was particularly true of the Socialist party, the PSOE. [20] The Socialist movement had been divided even before the war and if now the theoretical issues had changed, the personal animosities remained to be exacerbated by recriminations over collaboration with the Communists. Socialists both inside and outside Spain were divided on this question, which effectively condemned the party to impotence. A minority favoured continued collaboration with the Communists (PCE) while the majority looked to the Allies for deliverance. The bitterness and sterility of the Socialist division might perhaps be illustrated by the sordid wranglings over the use to be made of funds which the exiles had taken out of Spain. [21]

The divisions in the once-powerful anarchist movement were hardly less bitter. The old CNT, FAI and FJL were united on 25 February 1939 into the *Movimiento Libertario Español,* which was rapidly dispersed by war-time circumstances with individual groups reconstituting spontaneously wherever they could.[22] These problems apart, the anarchists were already passing through a grave spiritual crisis as a result of their contact with the realities of political power during the Civil War.[23] Throughout the 1930s, the CNT had been divided into purists and those prepared to co-operate with other groups: divisions only accentuated by the war. They came to a head in 1943 when a report by Juan M. Molina (Juanel) and Felipe Alaiz called for the MLE to join the various Republican groups in the struggle to re-establish the Republic. By September 1943, the consequent split was so severe that there were two plenums each claiming to be the exclusive representative of the MLE.[24] The division was extremely complex, but broadly many exiled leaders in France adopted a purist position while a majority of militants in the interior believed that the Civil War was not over and a wide anti-fascist front was necessary.[25] Many of the South American exiles either favoured collaboration with other Republicans or else believed that since those inside were the front-line, they should decide.[26] The MLE in France was bitterly divided, with the purists under Federica Montseny and Germinal Esgleas opposed only by a group led by Juanel and his son-in-law, Ramón Alvarez (Ramonín).

The fact that the MLE in France fell into the hands of the Montseny faction was to have serious repercussions in the interior. Its growing bureaucracy insisted on the control of all activities, both syndical and military, which made the movement more open to Francoist infiltrators. Moreover, a desire for legal existence inside France saw the central apparatus in Toulouse refuse help for the anarchist resistance inside Spain.[27] In the mid-forties, the CNT had rebuilt an impressive underground union system with thousands of dues-paying members. However, the failure to divide syndical and military activities perhaps contributed to the union structure being smashed by the police in reprisals for the activities of the resistance. Deprived of aid from outside, the MLE tended towards atrophy and little was done to renew cadres or modernize ideas.[28]

Even the Communists did not escape unscathed from the spiritual hang-over of the Civil War. Certain leaders have claimed that they wanted a serious examination of the PCE's role in the Republican defeat. On the grounds that this would cause scandal and demoralization among the militants, the debate was cut off before it got under way. It was deemed necessary in Moscow that the Comintern should be cleared of any responsibility and that La

130

Pasionaria should be exonerated since she was being groomed by the Russians to take over the party leadership.[29] This process assured the PCE's loyalty to Moscow but left great reserves of bitterness among the senior cadres. Moreover, the consequent commitment to Stalinist methods robbed the party of flexibility in the difficult years to follow.

Slavish adherence to Moscow quickly caused difficulties with the interior. Given that the leadership had fled at the end of the war, this was inevitable. The Communists left behind had ended the war alone and so they determined to fight on alone. Their activities were limited to keeping their cells alive, attempts to help prisoners, distribute propaganda and occasional attacks on Falangists. In the absence of the Central Committee, Heriberto Quiñones from the Canary Islands emerged as leader. He claimed that only those in the interior could run the party. Before the clash with Moscow developed, he was captured, tortured and executed and the police smashed the interior's apparatus. Nevertheless, the Central Committee continued to denounce the crime of *Quiñonismo,* i.e. ignoring the Russian-based leadership.[30] Similar clashes continued. In 1945, the PCE had Gabriel León Trilla executed. In 1947, the then leader in the interior, Jesús Monzón, was denounced for Titoism which, like *Quiñonismo,* simply meant too much independence.[31] It could only have been demoralizing for the militants in Spain to see their comrades and leaders denounced as traitors and provocateurs, as agents of the Gestapo and of American imperialism, by leaders in exile.[32]

Stalinist methods also damaged the PCE's relations with other groups who were generally referred to as traitors. Early attempts at unity were based on the premise that the rank-and-file of other groups should abandon their leaders and join the Communists. Things only changed with the entry of the USSR into the World War. While most Republicans followed the fate of the Allies with the keenest interest, the Communists, in the light of the Nazi-Soviet pact, had execrated it as an imperialist squabble. Now the PCE began to enthuse about a wide anti-fascist front, to be called the *Unión Nacional.* The Communist press's turn-about in now proclaiming the war to be just and liberating merely emphasized the PCE's rigid dependence on Moscow. Ostensibly the reasoning behind 'national union' was that if Catholics and atheists, capitalists and proletarians, were fighting Hitler elsewhere, then the struggle against Spanish fascism could be undertaken by a broad front of groups which had fought on opposite sides in the Civil War. This was the project's weakness: it was a sound projection of Soviet needs but ignored the sufferings that the Spanish left had undergone at the

131

hands of those with whom Moscow now recommended friendship. The PCE readiness to join hands with their own executioners could only discredit the party, although in many respects it was a sound notion and one which was to form the basis of PCE policy to this day. In fact, when Quiñones refused to follow the new line and was denounced as an enemy of the people, it hardly inspired confidence in the Communists as allies.[33] National Union was accepted by a few individuals from other groups but was rejected by their organizations. A real union never existed. There were many regional and local juntas set up inside Spain but they were always Communist dominated. Neither the PSOE, the CNT nor the Republican parties were even consulted about the proposal.[34]

These groups were in any case developing their own projects for union. These were to suffer from two weaknesses: their determined anti-Communism and their faith in the Allies. In November 1943, the Socialists and a variety of Spanish and Catalan liberal Republican groups joined together in Mexico to found the *Junta Española de Liberación*. In August 1944, after the liberation of France, sections of the same groups together with the CNT met in Toulouse and founded a parallel JEL. This was the prelude to a depressing polemic between the *Unión Nacional* and the JEL. The JEL saw its task as the preparation of the way for the entry of the Allied armies into Spain.[35] It was a long time before the non-Communist opposition was to realize that their insistence on their democratic credentials could never be as attractive to the Western powers as Franco's unflinching authoritarianism particularly as the Allies were conscious of the cost of trying to dislodge Franco.

Along similar lines, but of inestimably greater importance, was the creation in the interior in October 1944 of the *Alianza Nacional de Fuerzas Democráticas*.[36] Made up of a wide front of Republicans, Socialists, and anarchists, the ANFD was the most significant move towards the unification of anti-Francoist forces until 1974. It represented a spontaneous attempt to overcome the continuous bickering of the exiles and to take advantage of Franco's impending isolation. Nevertheless, the ANFD needed help from outside and so, in September 1945, when the Republican government in exile under José Giral was constituted, the ANFD recognized it and became its instrument within Spain. This meant that when the government failed, it brought the ANFD down with it. However, at the time, the link with the government seemed the obvious move to make.

Having fought Hitler and Mussolini in Spain, most Republicans saw the World War as a natural continuation of their own struggle. For that reason, over 20,000 Spaniards died during the Second World War fighting against the Axis. It was widely and understandably assumed that when the Axis was defeated, the Allies would finish their task by turning against Franco. That this did not happen is hardly surprising. Nevertheless, the incompetence of the exiled leadership did not improve matters. Giral's government was not formed until the Allies were already war-weary and the Cold War was on the horizon. If a responsible Republican government had been formed in 1941 or 1942 when the Allies were desperate for aid and Franco strongly committed to the Axis, it is conceivable that such a government might have been recognized and perhaps subsequently installed in Madrid.[37] As it was, in 1945 the aim of the Giral government was to get recognition as a prelude to intervention and the re-establishment of the Second Republic. To both the British and Americans, in their growing anti-Communism, this seemed mere sectarianism and likely to provoke a new Civil War.[38]

Leaving aside the lack of Allied sympathy, the government in exile did not handle the situation well. There was certainly a failure of will.[39] One exiled government after another stuck to the notion of re-establishing the Republic when it was clear that the only hope of securing Allied aid was to create a government of concentration, which was also what many in the interior wanted.[40]

Of course, there were those who preferred to take up arms rather than wait for the Allies. So much so, in fact, that a case might be made for dating the end of the Spanish Civil War in 1951. Until then, the most serious opposition to the Franco régime was of a military nature. At the same time, the methods used against it were also military and general domestic policy in Spain closely resembled the Civil War repression carried out by the Nationalist rearguard. During the war, many Republicans cut off from their own lines by the advancing Nationalists took to the hills rather than surrender. These *huídos* or stragglers formed the basis of the guerrilla opposition. They represented a wide cross-section of Republican groups.[41]

The guerrilla was virtually the only possible response to the Nationalist repression. In a major effort to destroy the cadres of the Popular Front parties, of the trade unions and of the liberal intelligentsia, the Francoists executed probably as many as 200,000 people,[42] and imprisoned double that number.[43] The choice was between capitulation or resistance, although few had the latter possibility. Nevertheless, there were soon significant numbers of guerrilleros in the hills. Their struggle was mainly defensive; the first objective survival.[44] It was one way to avoid death or imprisonment; the others were exile or hiding.[45] However, acts of sabotage were carried out and large numbers of troops kept occupied. It has even been argued that they played a major part in preventing Franco

133

joining the war alongside his Axis allies.[46] In these early years, the most positive result of the guerrilla was probably in maintaining the morale of the cowed population.[47]

A significant change took place in 1944. In the autumn of that year, many of the Spanish maquisards who had played such a prominent role in the French resistance began to drift to the Spanish border. At about this time, Communist militants inside Spain appealed for help. Leaving aside the exaggerations of both Francoist and Communist propaganda, it appears that the PCE were to have some prominence in the organization of the guerrilla, since although the rank-and-file were indiscriminately Socialists, anarchists and Communists, the PSOE was relying on the Allies and the MLE irretrievably divided. The request for an invasion was agreed to by the PCE delegation in France and took place in October 1944 in the Valley of Aran in the Pyrennees. Snowbound most of the year and sparcely populated by shepherds and wood-cutters, it was no place to pick up support. The invasion seems to have been improvised and euphoric, overlooking the obvious point that a conventional military incursion was playing into the hands of Franco's numerous and well-equipped army. Moreover, it came at a time of low morale in the interior and few people were even aware that it had happened. Accounts vary, but it is clear that before a frontal clash could take place, the up and coming PCE leader, Santiago Carrillo, arranged a retreat.[48]

After the failure of the invasion, a steady stream of guerrilleros entered Spain with arms and supplies to join up with the existing *huídos*. By default of the anarchist and Socialist leadership, the Communists emerged as the coordinators, sending in hardened militants trained in the French resistance and the Ukrainian guerrilla.[49] The idea launched by the PCE at a plenum held in Toulouse on 5 December 1945 was for the guerrilla to be the catalyst of a wider popular struggle to take advantage of the seeming international hostility to the régime. Civil Guards were attacked, trains blown up, power lines brought down. At first the reaction of the peasantry seems to have been passively favourable especially when the guerrilleros accepted requests for specific actions such as the burning of municipal archives to prevent the collection of taxes. However, the guerrilleros drew their model from the French resistance rather than more traditional guerrilla struggles. They considered themselves as the vanguard of an eventual army of invasion and so were not over-preoccupied by the need to strike roots among the peasantry.[50]

In the long-term, then, the guerrilla was doomed to failure. The 1940s were years of great hunger in Spain. And after three years of

Civil War and several more of state terror, most people were too busy simply surviving to support the wide uprising which was the objective of the guerrilla. The régime was already on a war-footing and strong enough to evacuate entire areas where the guerrilleros established support, as happened in Malaga. The strongest guerrilla group was in the Levante-Aragón, which, according to General Lister, pinned down 40,000 troops. Yet even if villages were liberated for a few days, the Civil Guard would sooner or later re-appear and take reprisals. Given the impossibility of establishing safe zones, the peasantry began gradually to reject the guerrilleros, particularly after the régime started to use fake guerrillero groups as agents provocateurs. These counter-guerrilleros saturated a given area with terror to discredit the authentic ones and demoralize the peasantry. By the end of the 1940s, the guerrilleros were being driven to steal in order to survive.[51]

Figures vary both for the number of guerrilleros involved in the struggle and for the number of actions carried out by them. 15,000 men seems to be a reasonable approximation. It is difficult to calculate the number of actions, but they were probably not less than 10,000.[52] Under the circumstances, this was a remarkable success at a time when fear had been made a way of life. The majority of committed anti-fascist cadres were dead, imprisoned or in exile. The population was demoralised. In town and country, informers abounded. Curfews and a system of safe-conducts were in force. Many released from jail were seriously ill or else demoralized by the fear of being arrested again. Hunger and the virtual impossibility of getting work diminished the combative capacity of the Republicans. Conditions in working-class districts were staggering: people in rags searched for scraps, many lived in caves, there were no medical services.[53]

Thus, by 1948 it became clear that the hoped-for rising would not take place. With troops stationed *en masse* along the French frontier, it was becoming increasingly difficult to get supplies in. Moreover, both Communists and anarchists were beginning to doubt the wisdom of doing so.[54] At this stage, Stalin apparently suggested to a PCE delegation that the guerrilla be dropped and an effort made to infiltrate the vertical syndicates. In October 1948, a joint meeting of the PCE Politburo and the Catalan party (PSUC) executive met some guerrilla leaders to confirm the decision. To an extent, the guerrilleros were among the first victims of the Cold War since Stalin wished to avoid revolutionary upheavals in Western Europe. Yet the Communists seemed to have some difficulty in implementing the decision, although in view of the drift of international politics it was probably a wise one. The evacuation, in the form of a long forced march, began finally in November 1950, just as the Korean War was getting under way, and did not end until well in 1951. [55]

There was also an urban guerrilla movement which went on until the late 1950s and in which the Communists were not the most prominent. In Madrid, a hero of the French resistance, Cristino García, led the Communist-inspired guerrilla group of central Spain. Their activities consisted of bank raids and attacks on Falangist head-quarters but led to such massive arrests that they had to be seen as counter-productive. [56] The same was ultimately true of the much more important urban guerrilla of Barcelona, carried out by activists of the CNT. Groups such as *Talión* and *Los Maños* and individuals like Francisco Sabaté and José Luis Facerías took part in bank and factory robberies, assaults on informers and torturers and even attempts to free prisoners. Many of their acts were carried out with imagination and courage, but even when they were successful, they were usually followed by massive reprisals on the Barcelona working class in general. It is difficult to believe that urban guerrilla actions could have boosted working-class morale sufficiently to make up for the losses they provoked. [57] Moreover, the chances of extending actions to a point where they might merge with mass discontent were considerably reduced by the obstacles created by the MLE leadership in France, whose ranks were riddled with informers. [58]

Given the ultimate failure of both the rural and urban guerrillas, the only other chance remaining to the opposition lay with the government in exile. In March 1946, Britain, France and the USA issued a tripartite note calling on the Spanish people to remove Franco by pacific means and to create a government of transition which could call elections. This clearly showed that Allied aid depended on a broad, non-sectarian front including at least the Monarchists from among the Francoist forces. Monarchists had, in anticipation of Allied action, already been in touch with the ANFD. The rank-and-file favoured a government of concentration and both the British and American embassies were pushing for it. Yet Giral rejected overtures which might have cleared the way for a plebiscite in Spain. The exiled government's excessive optimism regarding the re-establishment of the Republic was to destroy the opposition's best chance, flimsy though it was, of overthrowing Franco. Giral's government showed no interest in establishing contact with the ANFD. When contact was made, the ANFD representative, Juan García Durán, was ignored when he pointed out the error of insisting on the exclusive legitimacy of the Republic. By supporting the government instead of going ahead with negotiations with the Monarchists, the ANFD chose certain as against only probable impotence.[59]

When the failure of Giral became apparent, he was replaced by the Socialist, Rodolfo Llopis, who tried to reach agreement with the Monarchists. Perhaps because of the inclusion of a Communist, Uribe, in the government, or simply because they now felt stronger, the Monarchists rejected the government's offer and stated that they would deal with the PSOE alone. In July 1947, only five months after its formation, the Socialists left the government. There was little reason to suppose that much would come of a deal with the *Confederación de Fuerzas Monárquicas* now that Allied interest was cooling. Having financed Franco's war effort, it is more likely that the Monarchists were just trying to make him see that their loyalty could not be taken for granted. The British ambassador commented, 'I have never known so many professed monarchists who didn't really want a king'.[60] Significantly, the pretender, Don Juan, never broke off relations with Franco. He never took any part in negotiations with non-régime forces and was therefore always in a position to disavow them, as in fact he did regarding the agreements reached between summer 1947 and autumn 1948.[61] Franco played off the Monarchists with great skill. When they finally made the Pact of St Jean de Luz with the Socialists in the late summer of 1948, Franco had already made a deal with Don Juan on the yacht *Azor*. The Socialists had been taken in by an elaborate exercise in duplicity, but they virtually had no choice, since collaboration was the pre-requisite of the Allied aid they so anxiously wanted.[62]

The negotiations had come to nothing and simply exposed the weakness of the anti-Franco opposition. The government in exile had been revealed as an obsolete anachronism, abandoned by all groups except those Republicans who still dreamed of a return to 1931. The Socialists were demoralized and discredited by the negotiations on which they had staked so much. The CNT was riven by internal dissent and decimated by police round-ups. The Communists were going through a similar experience, with militants being wiped out in the interior while Stalinist denunciations flew around among the exiled leaders. The moment when Franco might have been overthrown with Allied help had definitely passed. Already being lionized as the 'sentinel of the West' in the Cold War atmosphere, Franco had less to worry about in 1951 than at any time since the end of the Civil War. An immense task of re-building faced the opposition.

1951-62

Not only was the old Republican leadership discredited by the failures of the 1940s, but the opposition also faced a further problem in that the Cold War atmosphere was widening the gaps between the Communist party and the other groups. Accordingly, the early fifties were marked by lethargy and demoralization. Yet just at the lowest ebb, there were signs of the emergence of a totally new opposition. 1951 was significant not only for the withdrawal of the guerrilleros but also for a major strike in Barcelona. Whether or not it was great foresight on Stalin's part, the Communists had already started switching their efforts to agitation among the working class. This had hardly been viable in the years of the repression when the working class had suffered a massive military defeat and its best leaders were either dead, exiled or imprisoned. Since then a new generation of workers had arisen. The poor conditions under which they worked were already forging a growing self-awareness. This was something still very tentative and hardly at all political, but it was an omen of things to come.

In this sense, the Barcelona strike was the beginning of a new epoch. It was one of the first spontaneous and combative appearances of the masses under the Franco régime, more important even than the strikes which had taken place in the Basque country in the 1940s. The Communists have tried to claim the Barcelona strike as their own on the grounds that Gregorio López Raimundo, a Catalan Communist leader, was imprisoned in Barcelona at the time.[63] In fact, the events in Barcelona, and the strikes in Madrid and Asturias which soon followed them, reflected a changing economic situation as much as Communist influence. A major push for growth began in 1951. The first result of massive investment was inflation without corresponding wage increases. This forced workers to increase drastically their work hours simply to stay at subsistence level.[64] In consequence, the opposition to the dictatorship began to widen.

Working-class dissent was badly organized, sporadic and economic in motivation. Nevertheless, it heralded the appearance of progressive Catholic workers' groups, which were eventually to form an important section of the new opposition. However, the most apparent signs of renewal were in the Communist party, which began to re-build its cells as militants began to drift out of prison. The PCE lacked the theoretical sophistication to analyse the new stage through which Spain was passing. It failed to see that economic development was possible and that large sectors of the population might be tied to the régime by it. The PCE leaders chose to believe that the Francoists were a minute clique exploiting the rest of the country and that to overthrow the clique, it was simply necessary to unite the rest of the country against it. This was over-optimistic to an extreme. It was little more than an extension of the notion of *Unión Nacional*. But it did imply a major insight: a wide front would be needed to overthrow the dictatorship and to secure that front, there could be no going back to the Republic. The Communists failed to realize how long the road to that front was to be, but they were considerably in advance of other groups in seeing its necessity.

The PCE remained the dominant force in the opposition but these tactical re-adjustments were not easily executed. To attract other groups, the party began to re-construct its image and become a moderate element, postponing indefinitely its interest in social revolution and limiting its objectives to the overthrow of the Franco régime. The new line was elaborated with one eye on the Soviet wish to avoid revolution in Europe and consequently suffered from two grave weaknesses. At the height of the Cold War, this new moderation inspired those it was intended to attract rather less than they were repelled by the Moscow link. Francoist propaganda had identified the PCE with anarchy and disorder, and large numbers of the middle classes without being active Francoists saw the Communists as a dreadful enemy. At the same time, the party's real supporters were somewhat demoralized by the overtures to their erstwhile enemies. Those who protested were treated to all the rigours of Stalinist inner-party discipline.[65]

The new bid for unity of the opposition was preceded in true PCE style by a denunciation of those groups which had not so far thrown in their lot with the party. Then at the V party congress held in Prague in November 1954, the Central Committee report, presented by La Pasionaria, was a fierce attack on other groups.[66] The death of Stalin and the XX Congress of the CPSU combined to limit the asperities of the PCE's style and the new policy, to be known as national reconciliation, was elaborated. It called for a wide national anti-Francoist front on the grounds that it was time to forget the Civil War and adjust to the present situation within Spain. It was based on the belief, erroneous but plausible in view of the appalling social conditions then current, that the Francoist clique was taking Spain to imminent ruin. Accordingly, all those whose interests were thereby threatened could be united against this narrow oligarchy once Civil War divisions were forgotten. This recognition that the workers' struggle could be merged with the discontent of the more liberal bourgeoisie was the strength of the new policy, which was ratified at the 1956 plenum. Putting it into practice was a different matter.[67]

The policy of national reconciliation was, in fact, premature, although superficially events were to confirm the new PCE line. In the first place, 1956 had seen the start of major student troubles and the passing to the opposition of significant ex-Francoists like the Falangist poet, Dionisio Ridruejo. Then in 1957, there was a considerable strike wave which started in Barcelona and soon spread to Asturias and the Basque country. The Communists were quick to claim credit and to assume that the strikes were evidence of working class endorsement of their policy. Pointing out that Socialists, anarchists, Catholics and unaffiliated liberals had been involved, the PCE eagerly announced its readiness to make pacts and alliances with them.[68] Ignoring the extent to which the strikes had been a purely spontaneous reaction to harsh conditions, the Communist party called for a day of national reconciliation on 5 May 1958 and a national pacific strike for 18 June 1959. Both were failures. Individual Socialists and militants of the newly founded *Frente de Liberación Popular* took part, but the PSOE officially condemned the initiative. In its optimistic eagerness to clinch deals with other social sectors, the party was trying to use the working class for show-mobilizations to prove its own attractiveness as an ally. This involved considerable self-deception about the current level of worker politicization and about the party's influence. It was an approach which could only undermine the PCE's credibility.[69]

Elsewhere the search for unit continued but in a way which was even less in tune with the times than the Communist policy of total national reconciliation. In the early fifties, for instance, moves in Mexico to ally the CNT and the PSOE were disavowed by the leaders in France. The same combination of misplaced moral intransigence and petty jealousies which so demoralized the militants inside Spain continued to keep the exiles divided against themselves. In the case of the CNT, this reflected the continuing split between the French-based 'purist' bureaucracy and the 'collaborationists' in Spain and Latin America. In that of the PSOE, it represented the desperate attempt of an atrophying leadership to re-assert itself over a dying movement, whose membership had reputedly sunk to only 3,000. The increasingly narrow attitude of the PSOE was one of the main reasons for lack of recruitment. Moreover, the PSOE was becoming a party of old men, for there were no middle cadres since the Socialist youth movement had passed to the PCE in 1936. The backward-looking and egoistical approach of the Socialists was revealed in the August 1952 Congress of the PSOE held in Toulouse. A decision was made to inform those in the interior that they could make agreements with other groups only for the most specific, short-term, objectives.[70]

Many Socialists in the interior were more aware of the realities of the situation. Realizing that the PSOE was in no position to maintain exclusivist positions, they pushed for agreement with other groups. In 1956, one of them, Professor Enrique Tierno Galván, leader of a growing number of Socialists in the universities, produced a document on the possible transition to another regime. Amongst other possibilities, the document suggested that if those in the interior did not cooperate with liberal monarchists for the implantation of a democratic monarchy, then Franco might well establish a reactionary monarchy. The reaction of the PSOE and of the exile in general revealed just how out of touch they were. The document was denounced as treachery to Republican legitimacy. As if Tierno were the arbiter of Spain's future, the PSOE, the CNT and other Republicans met in Paris in February 1957 to define their position and to insist that the régime to follow Franco be neither monarchy nor republic until the issue was decided by a plesbiscite. [71]

The Paris agreements came to nothing. However, the interior Socialists continued their pressure on the PSOE for cooperation with other groups including the Communists. The VII Congress of the PSOE, held in August 1958, refused to go so far, but did declare the need for a national anti-Francoist committee, excluding the PCE. The wishes of the interior delegation were ignored and an attempt to join the party by some university Socialists was rejected. [72] The leadership continued in its quest for an anti-Communist unity and in June 1961, there was founded the *Unión de Fuerzas Democráticas,* a doomed attempt to revive the old ANFD. The irrelevance of such initiatives was underlined by constant police attacks on the PSOE in the interior. [73] The opposition was just in no position to be sectarian.

Yet the Socialists continued to think more in terms of agreement with the Monarchists than with the Communists. This was a vain hope, since as American support for Franco increased, the Monarchists were fading as an opposition force. At most, Don Juan was playing a waiting game. His son, Juan Carlos was being educated in Spain. Thus, when in January 1955, Franco intimated that his successor would have to be completely identified with the *Movimiento,* the pretender swiftly declared that the Monarchy had always agreed with the 'spirit of the *Movimiento*', although he was later, in his ambiguous fashion, to reproach the Caudillo for the lack of liberty in Spain. In 1957, an industrialist, Joaquín Satrústegui, founded a slightly more militant Monarchist organization, *Unión Española.* Despite being more clearly opposed to the régime, *Unión Española* merely exposed the limits of the Monarchist opposition. In January 1959, the lawyers, generals, industrialists and financiers of *Unión Española* gathered to hear Satrústegui demand freedom of association, the right to strike, an independent judiciary and the 'authentic representation of the people'. The régime was hardly bothered, fining the participants – a marked contrast with the fate that Communists, Socialists or anarchists might have expected. Yet Don Juan was annoyed and so met Franco to discuss the future in April 1960. If the Monarchists could not rely on their King, how could the rest of the opposition rely on them? The régime had every reason to be grateful to the Monarchists for their role in keeping the opposition divided.[74]

The reality of day-to-day opposition in Spain was very different from the theoretical squabbles of the exile or the fine banquets of the Monarchists. The distribution of pamphlets and newspapers, the maintenance of morale, were immense tasks given the strength of the forces of repression. No sooner were committees set-up or newspapers established than they would fall in police round-ups. The Communists were the favourite target, but the Socialists also lost six entire executive committees in the interior and the anarchists suffered equally.[75] The worst arrests were usually as reprisals for the actions of the anarchists trying to establish a full-scale urban guerrilla in Barcelona. Men like Sabaté and Facerías hoped to build up an effective infra-structure for action groups, but deprived of help from the MLE bureaucracy, they had to resort to robberies to finance their press and propaganda activities. This made it easy for the regime to denounce them as gangsters.[76]

Nevertheless, despite the difficulties, the opposition was growing. An entire generation which had not fought in the Civil War was now reaching maturity. Their political discontent was not connected with the issues of the war and was entirely related to the existing social order. One of the most important steps in the growth of this new opposition was Dionisio Ridruejo's break with Francoism to establish a social-democratic alternative. He was an important reference point for others since the normal Francoist smears of self-seeker or assassin of priests could hardly be applied to him.[77] Amongst other groups which emerged in the 1950s, perhaps the most significant in terms of financial support and potential middle class support was the three-pronged Christian Democrat movement. The left was formed by the social Catholic, Manuel Jiménez-Fernández, who founded the Christian Democratic Left in 1956. In the centre was the ex-Minister of Education, Joaquín Ruiz-Giménez, whose aim has been evolutionary change, to which end he has sponsored critical journals like *Cuadernos Para El Diálogo* (founded 1963). To the right of both of them is José María Gil Robles, the leader of the CEDA during the Republic. He and his group were interested in sufficient change to avoid the possibility of a revolutionary explosion.[78]

These conservative options found little echo among many of the

142

radical students formed in the university struggles of the mid-fifties. National reconciliation seemed to them a denial of class realities and anyway the bourgeoisie did not appear to be accepting the PCE overture. At the same time, they had serious doubts about the PCE's Civil War record. Thus, they were looking for a non-orthodox-Communist revolutionary alternative. Out of these sentiments was born the progressive Catholic and Castroist *Frente de Liberación Popular*. Much influenced by Cuba, the FLP pinned its hopes on the revolutionary action of the workers and peasants and, indeed, was to overreach itself by an optimistic all-or-nothing line in the massive strikes which broke out in 1962. Organized on a federal basis, called FOC in Cataluña and ESBA in the Basque country, the FLP aimed to unite all groups dedicated to national liberation by armed action. However, except in Cataluña, the FLP never got much working class support. Moreover, the FLP, as a revolutionary alternative, was subjected to the corresponding treatment by the police and was systematically smashed by wide arrests.[79]

The growing importance of the internal opposition in relation to the exile was symbolized by the meeting in June 1962 of 80 interior and 38 exile figures at the fourth Congress of the European Movement in Munich. Representatives of Satrústegui's *Unión Española*, Gil Robles, Ridruejo, the Christian Democratic Left and other non-Communist groups met exiled Socialists and Basque and Catalan nationalists. Ostentatiously excluding the PCE, the brains behind the operation, Salvador de Madariaga, got all to approve a common declaration on the conditions that the EEC should demand for Spanish entry. These were: a representative elected government, the guarantee of basic human rights, the recognition of national minorities, syndical liberties and the right to strike. In fact, Munich was little more than the culmination of the Socialist–Monarchist alliance and, as such, was not of great significance. Ridruejo felt that the most important thing was to have the right coming out against Franco. The FLP condemned Munich as a manoeuvre to secure evolution in Spain without fundamental change.[80]

Nevertheless, Munich showed how things were changing in the opposition. Probably the events which persuaded the various right-wing groups there to defy the régime were the series of strikes which swept across Spain in 1962. Beginning in Asturias, they soon spread to the Basque country, Cataluña and Madrid despite a massive turn-out by the forces of order. Starting in April, the strikes went on for two months and effectively ended in victory for the workers. The Communists were convinced that the national strike had started. In fact, like most other groups, they failed to realize to what extent the strikes were economic in motivation. They also did not see that the working-class victory was more the result of the economic development which was under way than of retreat by the Francoists.[81] Nevertheless, 1962 was a turning-point both because of the mass mobilization of the working class, limited though its aims were, and because it heralded a strengthened régime. As the opposition gradually came to terms with the fact that economic disaster was not imminent, it also had to face a major tactical re-think.

1962-73

The strike wave of 1962 indicated a qualitative change in the economic circumstances of the régime. The fascistic or extreme authoritarian forms of Francoism were increasingly seen by the ruling classes in Spain to have served their purpose. At the same time, the economic surge consequent on the capital accumulation of the early years of Francoism and on foreign investment coincided with the gradual recuperation of the working class. Thus there began a move towards a gradual opening-up of the system. Along with a move to economic *laissez faire,* there were indications of slightly more flexibility regarding strikes and censorship. Of course, repression against the left opposition continued unabated as the torture, trial and execution of Julián Grimau in April 1963 was to show.[82] However, the regime began to show increasing toleration for the milder forms of Christian Democrat and Social Democrat opposition. This somewhat divided the anti-Francoist forces since it re-kindled hopes of reform from within the system. In fact, 'liberalization' went some way to neutralizing certain groups, since the growing freedom to write and travel created subtle ties of dependence on the government. Moreover, it diverted attention from basic issues of how to overthrow the régime, as well as weakening their credibility among those further to the left.[83]

This was certainly the case with the various Christian Democrat groups. Because of conditions of clandestinity and the extremely unbalanced distribution of wealth in Spain, Christian Democrat groups have, with the increasing encouragement of the Church, become more radical than, for instance, the Italian Democrazia Cristiana under Fanfani. Nevertheless, the Christian Democrats have always been ready to listen to promises of liberalization from the régime. Gil Robles has advocated an opening of the political structure as a prerequisite of the containment of popular discontent. The advocate of a Gaullist-style neocapitalist alternative, Gil Robles, believes that if a strong Christian Democrat movement is not established, in time, then after Franco will come the deluge – i.e.

144

communism.[84] Jiménez-Fernández's Christian Democratic Left was considerably more liberal without in any way being a threat to the régime. Far more significant was the growing group around Joaquín Ruiz-Giménez. He was hardly committed to a break with the system but he had followers like Pedro Altares who advocated close links with Socialists. Throughout the sixties, Ruiz-Giménez acted as lawyer for working class leaders on trial and this did much to radicalize his thought, as did even more the publication of the encyclical *Pacem in Terris*.[85] The velvet glove treatment accorded them by the régime makes it difficult to see the Christian Democrats as strictly in the opposition. Nevertheless, Ruiz-Giménez has spoken for a large number of intellectuals and middle class forces. During the 1960s, as the opposition came gradually to terms with the implications of economic development, they also began to realize that significant change without the collaboration of the Christian Democrats would be difficult.

In a developed Spain, a democratic Socialist movement was also likely to be of great importance. The PSOE played no significant part in the opposition in the sixties, but it was undergoing changes of great importance for the future. Under the heavy hand of Llopis's exiled bureaucracy, the movement was in steady decline with the exception of Asturias, the Basque country and the University Socialist Group. Efforts from the interior to re-vitalize the PSOE programme were skilfully deflected by packed committees. By the end of the decade, the exiles were out of touch with conditions inside Spain. In January 1968, Professor Tierno Galván and some of his followers formed the Socialist Party of the Interior. Of little numerical importance, the PSI, as it was known, was crucial for the re-birth of Spanish Socialism. In the first instance, it disturbed the exiles sufficiently to impel them to concede a superficial autonomy to the interior militants at the XI Congress of the PSOE, held in August 1970. This was considered insufficient and a group of older leaders under Arsenio Gimeno together with non-Tiernista PSOE militants from inside Spain prepared the XII PSOE Congress for August 1972. To the chagrin of Llopis, delegates from Spain and from the emigrant workers overthrew his leadership and decided that the PSOE executive committee should be led from within the interior. This left both Tierno and Llopis isolated, and when Llopis tried to fight back at a mini-congress in December 1972, Tiernistas were present. They had backed the wrong horse, since the Socialist International decided to recognize the rejuvenated PSOE and not the PSI.[86] At the time, these events seemed of little consequence, but after 1973 they were to assume some significance.

Despite these hopeful developments within the Socialist

movement, the 1960s were a particularly disappointing period for the opposition, particularly after the hopes raised by the 1962 strikes. The failures were the same as ever – fragmentation and incorrect analysis of the situation. The most marked example of this was the opposition's inability to put up a united front during the December 1966 referendum mounted by the régime to convince the world that Spain was totally behind Franco.[87] However, the greatest difficulties arose from the need to adjust to the new economic conditions and no group suffered more from this than the Communists.

The PCE, believing Spain to be ruled by a narrow oligarchy which had taken Spain to economic disaster and anxious to unite the country against it through 'national reconciliation', saw the 1962 strikes as a confirmation of its analysis. The party's secretary-general, Santiago Carrillo claimed that 'what in other countries might have been just another more or less serious labour conflict gravely undermined the entire régime in Spain, revealing its impotence and senility and shaking society to its very foundations' and that the strikes were 'a call to build a national front uniting all anti-Franco classes and sections of society'.[88] Throughout the 1960s and despite overwhelming evidence of economic development, the official party line changed little. It was persistently assumed that the régime was on the edge of a disaster and the working class about to make the national general strike which overthrow it.[89]

Given the exploitation to which the Spanish working class was subject and the acute shortages of housing and schools, the PCE analysis was understandable. Even groups like the FLP, which disagreed with the Communist desire for alliance with the bourgeoisie, were equally convinced that economic development, foreign capitalization and the integration of the workers were unlikely. However, a process of economic expansion was under way which was to change the nature of working-class discontent and consolidate the tendency towards *obrerismo,* or straight non-political wage claims. The tourist boom and the export of labour was to solve some of the worst structural problems of the Spanish economy and began to render incorrect the PCE prediction of impending doom. Yet the PCE continued to act on that premise and squandered much of its influence in the working-class movement on that account. The Workers' Commissions were damaged by calls for street demonstrations as shows of strength, which simply facilitated repression. Equally Communist prestige was lost by dramatic appeals for 'days of national action' which were ignored, as on 27 October 1967 and 14 May 1968.[90]

It was largely as a result of the debates provoked by this basic misinterpretation of the situation that the PCE suffered a series of grave internal crises. These led to the expulsion of the party's most sophisticated theorist, Fernando Claudín, in 1964, the schism of the young Maoists in 1967 and the departure of the hard-line Stalinists under General Lister in 1969-70. The reasons for all three splits were different, but they all shared a protest against the lack of inner-party democracy and against the uncritical reformist line of Santiago Carrillo.[91] The response of the central committee was to refuse internal debate, expel the offenders and then claim that the numbers involved were negligible.[92] Nevertheless, the party went through a crisis in the sixties from which it is only now recovering.

In intellectual terms at least, the expulsion of Claudín was the most serious loss. Claudín had been disturbed for some time by the evident dichotomy between the PCE's optimistic predictions about the régime's weakness and the strength and willingness of the working class to overthrow it and the real situation in the country. The key issue in his disillusion was the failure of the party to analyse the 1962 strikes in the light of the economic boom and not as the confirmation of party predictions. Another major issue in the debate between Claudín and Carrillo was over the level of development reached by Spanish capitalism. Carrillo's position, based on the premise that Spain had the same structural problems as in 1931 – fragmented industry, semi-feudal agriculture, was that a bourgeois democratic revolution would therefore be necessary before socialism could be achieved in Spain. Claudín, on the other hand, argued that the economy had reached a high stage of state-dominated monopoly capitalism and was therefore at a level of economic socialization which made it ripe for a direct transition to socialism, although the political and social conditions which might allow such a transition were far off. Carrillo believed that a democratic revolution would remove the reactionary ruling clique and the obstacles to the destruction of feudalism. It followed that bourgeois allies would be easy to find. However, Claudín pointed out that the economic necessity had passed for a democratic revolution, since Spain had developed on the Prussian model.

Carrillo was convinced that Spain was on the verge of catastrophe, and that the bourgeoisie would eagerly join the working class in overthrowing the régime. That none of this came to pass is because, as Claudín showed, neocapitalism was well on the road to expansion and the bourgeoisie thus had no motive to overthrow the system. In fact, Carrillo had confused a crisis of the régime, deriving from the obsolescence of fascist forms of domination, with a wider crisis of Spanish capitalism. Yet there was benefit to be gained from the situation, since many bourgeois sectors shared with the working class a desire for political liberalization. Carrillo's search for compromise with the bourgeoisie did make sense, but not his extreme over-optimism and his readiness to commit the PCE to a lower historical stage than the one which Spain had already reached. Claudín agreed with Carrillo that the party must push for a pacific road to socialism. However, while opting for alliance with the bourgeoisie, Claudín warned of the need for awareness of the great limits of that alliance. Given Spain's integration into international capitalism, it was the only option open, but the party must try to avoid playing the game of the haute bourgeoisie. [93]

The discrepancies were theoretical and, in part, over style, but Carrillo did not admit criticism. Claudín was excluded from meetings and a smear campaign was carried out against him without the chance to reply. For denying the imminent collapse of Francoism and emphasizing the high level of capitalist development in Spain, Claudín was accused of defeatism and revisionism. To justify the expulsion which was already being prepared, party cells were merely informed that it was necessary to condemn the erroneous theses of some party leaders attacking the official party line and endangering party unity. The majority group of the central committee organized a 'referendum' among the rank-and-file whose terms called for unconditional adherence to the position of the secretary-general as against that of Claudín and his fellow dissenter, Federico Sánchez (pseudonym of the novelist Jorge Semprún). So accustomed was the party to a lack of inner democracy that in all Cataluña only two militants asked to read the erroneous theses before condemning them. Thereafter, the VII Congress of the PCE was held in secret to minimize the repercussions of the expulsion. [94]

Carrillo was eventually to admit that Claudín's analysis had been correct and that his only error was 'to have been right too soon'. [95] However, throughout the 1960s, he persisted in the same theoretical line which had been criticized by Claudín. At times, his overtures to the bourgeoisie were so exaggerated as to damage his credibility, especially among his own militants. He declared in 1965 that 'the Communist Party less than anyone today believes in making the communist revolution in Spain'. By 1970, he was declaring that to finish with Franco, the PCE was 'ready to pact with the devil'. [96] This caused considerable discomfort to both young leftists and old Stalinists in the party. Offers were made to the Church and the Army which, while unlikely to convince either bishops or generals, could only disillusion militants. This led to fierce criticism. [97]

The all-embracing search for alliances clearly ran up against the harsh reality of class contradictions. And those members of the bourgeoisie who did seek change were doing so to assure their own

148

future. Effectively the representatives of the Army, the Church and the haute bourgeoisie would only ally with the PCE when it could offer guarantees to keep the working class in check. Increasingly, many in the party began to feel that Carrillo was either harbouring vain illusions or prepared to play such a guarantor's role.[98] The first visible sign of this crisis was the schism of the pro-Chinese youth who wanted the party to adopt a frankly revolutionary line of armed action against the regime. In 1967, there was a major division in the Catalan party, the PSUC, when a group called *Unidad* left as protest at what was denounced as Carrillo's revisionism. At the same time, some Madrid students left the party in the hope of creating a genuine bolshevik alternative. Thereafter, there was a complex proliferation of Maoist and Trotskyist fractions, of which the most significant were probably the PCE-ML (Marxista–Leninista), the PCE-Internacional, Bandera Roja and the Liga Comunista. Their ideological differences were often minimal and at other times oscillated alarmingly. In the case of the PCE-Internacional and the PCE-ML, they were to lead to attacks on militants from other groups who disagreed with them.[99] The existence of these myriad fractions did considerable harm to the Communist movement and to the opposition as a whole. Often gaining control of the workers in individual factories, they then wasted their energies in useless show actions.[100]

More serious in their consequences, were the actions of those who developed their Maoism into a strategy of sporadic violence against the régime. The results of these actions were largely negative insofar as they confirmed for many of the middle classes the régime's denunciation of communism as violent and anarchic. Public opinion in general did not follow the doctrinal twists and turns of these groups and simply saw them as communists. Violent actions against the régime also led to indiscriminate reprisals. The most notorious of the activist groups grew out of the PCE-ML. Known as FRAP, the *Frente Revolucionario Anti-fascista y Patriota,* it aimed at creating a wide front of groups dedicated to the violent overthrow of Francoism.[101] The front hardly went beyond the PCE-ML and its student group FUDE. Moreover, its militants, having been prominent in the student struggle, were easy prey for the police. The most significant FRAP action was the killing of a secret policeman on May Day 1973. Even the FRAP's own bulletin admitted that it provoked a tremendous wave of arrests and torture of leftists not connected with the incident.[102] It also led to the establishment of a hard-line cabinet under Admiral Carrero Blanco.

Even more serious for the PCE than the schism of the Maoists, or at least so it seemed at the time, was the departure of the Stalinists under Enrique Lister. The immediate occasion of the division was the Soviet invasion of Czechoslovakia in 1968. Since the PCE was publicly committed to democratic socialism, it had to protest in order to maintain its credibility. On 21 August, La Pasionaria expressed the PCE's disapproval to the Kremlin. In September, a plenum of the PCE central committee voted 66 to 5 to condemn the invasion. However, two leaders, Agustín Gómez and Eduardo García, continued to campaign against the party line and were expelled. It appears that the Russians were encouraging them to do so in order to pressure the PCE into reversing its decision. The battle was then taken up by Lister, who made a bitter personal attack on Carrillo for Stalinist crimes of which it is difficult to believe that Carrillo was any more guilty than Lister himself. Carrillo was also accused of anti-sovietism, nationalism and anti-marxism. The Russians made their position clear by a growing rapprochement with the Franco government, allowing the export of Polish coal to Spain during the Asturian miners' strike of December 1970. Prevented from presenting their views to the party, Lister and a considerable number of followers were driven to leave the party and form a rival PCE. The seriousness of the schism was only diminished when the PCE-Lister also became subject to internal divisions. Lister formed another party, known as the *Partido Comunista Obrero Español* (PCOE). Carrillo had kept the central apparatus of the party and therefore had won the day. The Russians were gradually to realize this and to come to terms with the PCE. [103]

Nevertheless, by the end of the sixties and the early seventies, the opposition seemed more fragmented than ever. The PSOE and the PCE were divided and the CNT was hardly better off. An attempt had been made to re-unite the MLE in 1961 but the old 'purist' bureaucracy did everything possible to sabotage it. However, out of the initiative there came an attempt to return to the activist anarchism of earlier days. Throughout 1963, the anarchist *Consejo Ibérico de Liberación* placed bombs in *Iberia* aircraft in an effort to put tourists off going to Spain. The CNT leadership, the PSOE and the PCE condemned this as useless provocation. In 1966, the *Primero de Mayo* group was founded and began a series of strategic kidnappings, like that of the ecclesiastical counsellor at the Spanish embassy to the Vatican. *1.º de Mayo* was part of a movement of revulsion within the MLE against the bureaucratic paralyzation of the official leaders. The most constructive move in this direction was the foundation of the lively journal *Frente Libertario* which advocated the reunification and revitalization of the CNT. Encouraged by *Frente Libertario*, many new young anarchist groups began to emerge inside Spain. In 1972, there appeared another group devoted to

150

revolutionary activism, the *Movimiento Ibérico de Liberación*. MIL began a series of robberies which culminated in the capture, and later execution, of Salvador Puig Antich. [104]

The activities of groups like *1.º de mayo* and MIL did little to alter the fact that there was little future for anarchism in Spain. In fact, in 1973, the future looked bleak all round for the opposition. Each group was divided and overall unity still seemed far off. Strikes were increasing in importance, but the road to a general strike was extremely slow. [105] To make matters worse, the FRAP's killing of a policeman had been instrumental in the formation of the Carrero Blanco government of June 1973. Constituted to prepare a holding operation to cover the transition from Franco to Juan Carlos, it was a cabinet which not only augured a return to 1940s-style Francoism but which had every indication of longevity. [106] Yet the pessimistic perspectives facing the opposition were dramatically changed in December 1973. The assassination of Carrero Blanco by a commando of ETA reopened a series of options which seemed to have been closed only six months before.

1973-75

The immediate reaction of the Spanish left to the death of Carrero was understandably one of fear of indiscriminate reprisals. However, the mood changed when it became clear that the moderate General Díez-Alegría had forestalled an ultra-rightist coup. Relief gave way to optimism when Carrero's successor, Carlos Arias-Navarro, made promises of liberalization. Those on the right of the opposition felt that the promises heralded evolution from within; those on the extreme left rejected them out of hand. However, for those committed to a peaceful road to democracy and to socialism, the mere fact that the government should feel the necessity to make such promises was seen as a promising sign. Both Communists and Socialists began to feel that the moment had arrived to make a serious effort for unity. If there were those within the régime anxious to change it, then there were clearly even more outside anxious to remove it. The situation had changed sufficiently to underline dramatically the relevance of the PCE policy of the pact for liberty. [107]

The first half of 1974 passed in a mood of hopeful cooperation on the moderate left. The feeling that Carrero's death had imposed new options was reinforced by events abroad. The Italian divorce referendum, the French presidential elections and the Portuguese revolution were watched in Spain with intense interest. All these events polarized the situation and did much to politicize Spain by

151

proxy. The fall of Caetano, the defeat of Fanfani, the near victory of Mitterand and later the collapse of the Greek colonels convinced the left that their time was near and many on the right that change must be given before it was taken. With possible success nearer than ever before, disputes about the distant future were replaced by a more pragmatic approach to the immediate task of removing the Franco régime.

The events in Portugal were crucial in bringing this about. By seeming to destroy the régime's paternalistic theses that certain countries were not ready for pluralist democracy and that all institutional change was necessarily violent, those events generated considerable optimism in Spain. Above all, it was encouraging to see an army and a people united. [108] All over Spain, there was a growing movement in favour of what was known as 'the democratic break'. Already democratic round tables and juntas had begun to spring up spontaneously throughout the country in 1973, rather on the model of the *Asamblea de Cataluña* which had emerged in 1971. [109] This process now accelerated and the Communists were among the first to attempt to systematize it. In April 1974, the PCE decided that the Portuguese situation so closely corresponded to its own predictions for the end of Francoism, that the time was ripe for an initiative. The Communists considered that Caetano had fallen under pressure from something that resembled the 'Pact for Liberty' – an alliance of workers, the army and 'the most dynamic and liberal sectors of capitalism'. The Secretary General proclaimed the need to make alliances like those already emerging and condemned sectarian attitudes. [110]

Already in September 1973, the executive committee of the PCE had sought authorization from the central committee to establish contacts with representatives of neocapitalist groups anxious for dialogue with the party. Contacts made in 1973 were intensified after the death of Carrero. According to Santiago Carrillo, these groups were convinced that the official vertical syndicates were incapable of preventing strikes. Moreover, they were unhappy with a political situation which forced workers to attack the régime by the only method open to them – more strikes. [111] That such groups were preoccupied about the future and willing to cooperate in bringing democracy to Spain was clearly indicated by meetings held by notable figures of the Madrid and Barcelona bourgeoisie during 1974, such as that held in the home of Joaquín Garrigues-Walker in Aravaca. As legal adviser to many important corporations, Garrigues was an accurate barometer of 'liberal capitalist' opinion. That figures like him were interested in political change gave substance to Carrillo's claims.

Naturally, as Claudín had long since pointed out, these sectors sought an integrated working class in a bourgeois democracy and would only pact with the Communists in return for promises to control the workers.[112] Carrillo recognized that it was a question of securing a pacific transition from one kind of outmoded bourgeois régime to another more advanced one. The circumstances of the fall of Salvador Allende in Chile and of the successes of the Italian Communist Party have confirmed Carrillo in his conviction of the need for a wide alliance, an historical compromise or a pact for liberty. Thus, he states that 'it is necessary to have the courage to explain to the workers that it is better to pay a surplus value to the bourgeoisie than to risk creating a situation which could turn against them'. To many on the left, this is taking compromise too far. Nevertheless, if the party can avoid tying its hands for the future, the policy of alliances is arguably the most realistic way of securing the first objective on the road to socialism, the removal of the dictatorship and the establishment of democratic liberties.[113]

The Communists were not alone in thinking that success was possible if unity could be achieved. The other main group in the push for change has been the rejuvenated PSOE. No longer the radical workers' party of the 1930s, it is now more directed towards the liberal middle classes. The renovation begun at the August 1972 Toulouse Congress was consolidated in October 1974 at Suresnes. This coincided with a genuine surge of popularity amongst those who were impressed by the Portuguese events and were anxious for major change in Spain, but were not prepared to join the PCE. The PSOE found that in addition to its traditional prestige, it had become fashionable. In the changes envisaged by Carrillo's allies, the dynamic and liberal capitalists, there would clearly be a considerable future for a moderate social democrat party.[114]

During the summer of 1974, Communists, Socialists and other groups involved in the creation of the regional democratic *mesas* were negotiating a national framework when Franco fell seriously ill. Perhaps to galvanize those who were dragging their feet or to pre-empt anyone else dominating the proceedings, Santiago Carrillo, along with the exiled Opus Dei theorist Rafael Calvo Serer, announced the foundation of the *Junta Democrática* in Paris simultaneously with a similar announcement in Madrid on 30 July 1974. The Junta's manifesto called for a provisional government, amnesty for *all* political offences, trade union liberties, the right to strike, free press and media, an independent judiciary, the separation of Church and State, elections, and entry into the EEC. The declaration implied that a wide spectrum of forces was involved in the Junta, although apart from the PCE, the only evident members were Calvo Serer in an individual capacity, Professor Tierno's PSI, now renamed *Partido Socialista Popular,* and the Carlists.[115]

Soon after the precipitate announcement of the Junta, it became clear that neither the PSOE nor the Christian Democrats were involved. The PSOE declared that, while belonging to the various regional *mesas,* it had nothing to do with the Junta.[116] The *mesa democrática* of Madrid, made up of militants of the PCE, the PSOE, Tierno's PSP and some Carlists, announced that it agreed with some points in the Junta's manifesto but not all and that it was not connected with the Junta.[117] It seemed that by the manner of its founding, the *Junta Democrática* had virtually guaranteed the non-cooperation of the PSOE.

The extreme left also condemned the Junta, which was hardly surprising given the manifesto's effective denial of the realities of the class struggle.[118] The PCE-ML, committed to the violent line of the FRAP, denounced Santiago Carrillo for playing the oligarchy's 'continuist' game. The Trotskyist *Movimiento Comunista Español* also condemned what it described as a sell-out to the haute bourgeoisie.[119] Perhaps the most serious criticisms came from the internal left opposition of the PCE itself. This was a group of militants, mainly in Madrid and Valencia, who had constituted an internal pressure group after the VIII party congress had shown the impossibility of internal debate within the party. Remaining anonymous to avoid expulsion, the *Opi,* as it was known, devoted itself to coherent marxist criticisms of the aberrations of the official party line. The internal left opposition claimed that Carrillo's role in the Junta constituted a major concession to the *aperturistas* within the regime and was undertaking a de-marxistization of the PCE to fulfil the banks' conditions for cooperation with the Junta.[120] There was only one argument against these theoretically sound analyses – that realism demanded such compromises. It makes more sense for the PCE to aim at the possible target of establishing a régime of democratic liberties than the impossible one of overthrowing Spanish capitalism.

Unless agreement is reached between the Junta and the Socialists, however, even the minimum target could be virtually impossible. Having participated in the early negotiations for the creation of the Junta, the PSOE, always super-sensitive to real or imagined threats of Communist hegemony, was taken aback by the PCE's jumping the gun in July 1974. Moreover, the PSOE claimed that it was in agreement with only part of the Junta manifesto, considering that it conceded insufficient regional autonomy and went too far in extending amnesty to the repressive forces of the regime. Above all, the PSOE held aloof from the Junta because the PCE seems to have made total acceptance of the manifesto the minimum condition for entry. Arguing that the Junta was little more than a collection of individuals in which the only nationally organized force was the PCE, the PSOE felt that to enter the Junta would be to accept Communist dominance. The Socialists claim that they are prepared to negotiate on equal terms for the creation of an operative alliance. [121] In the meanwhile, the PSOE has been in contact with the liberal Christian Democrat groups around Ruiz-Giménez and with Ridruejo's Social Democratic Union. These contacts led in the spring of 1975 to the foundation of the Platform of Democratic Convergence. Partly on the initiative of Ruiz-Giménez, the Platform has been negotiating with the Junta.

There is then a major movement towards unity on the Spanish left. There are groups like FRAP and ETA who continue their battle against the régime. FRAP has undertaken the somewhat enormous task of over-throwing both the régime and American imperialism. As a preliminary step, a minor wave of indiscriminate violence against the police has been launched last summer. [122] Given the unevenness of the struggle against the régime, and the impossibility of such tactics being successful, the only achievement of FRAP is to make things more difficult for those who aim at the establishment of democratic liberties. Other left marxist groups have increasingly come to accept this. *Bandera Roja* re-entered the Communist flock in early 1975. Then the PCE-I, transformed into the currently booming *Partido del Trabajo de España,* announced its entry into the *Junta Democrática.* [123] Even more remarkable has been the incorporation into the Platform of the Trotskyist *Organización Revolucionaria de Trabajadores.* If this process of concentration continues and agreement can be secured between the Junta and the Platform, there is some chance of the Spanish opposition reaching the long sought unity which appears to be the minimum pre-requisite of the success it seeks. The demise of Franco and the coming of Juan Carlos do not greatly alter the task faced by the opposition. Nevertheless, the new situation is fraught with opportunity and risk. The gratuitous brutality of the recent executions did much to cement opposition solidarity. As repression intensifies to cover the transition to Juan Carlos and the ultra-right becomes more frantically violent in its attempts to frighten the left, that solidarity is increasingly necessary. The main threat to it is the degree of democratization permitted by Juan Carlos. However, it seems probable that to split the opposition, the new King would have to offer a level of freedom which would itself change the nature of the regime. If he does that, the opposition would divide naturally within a new political pluralism. If he does

155

not, the regime without the charisma of Franco is unlikely to be able to withstand the sort of pressure the opposition would bring to bear. After thirty six years of Francoist persecution, it is unlikely that the opposition would not take the chance offered it now by the transitional stage faced by the regime.

7

The Working Class under the Franco Régime

SHEELAGH ELLWOOD

Introduction

It is the aim of this chapter to look at the Spanish working class as participant in a dynamic process; to examine the evolution of working-class conditions and consciousness in response to the changing circumstances of the Franco period, at national and international levels; to trace, in particular, the nature, form and significance of working-class dissent in a context of economic development, limited social change and political rigidity. [1]

There are a number of things which the study does not pretend nor intend to be, among which: a chronological history of strikes; a detailed historical analysis of the particular groups, parties, unions or movements which claim or claimed to represent the working class; an evaluation of particular strategies employed by working-class militants in specific phases of their struggle. Least of all does it claim to be exhaustive or definitive.

In painting, with broad strokes as it were, the picture of the development of the working class, the Franco era has been divided into three periods, two of which are divided again into two sub-periods each. All divisions of this nature are, to a certain extent, artificial, though not necessarily arbitrary. Points have been chosen at which there seemed to be a distinct change already discernible or emergent in the working class, or in the régime, or sometimes both at once without any definite cause and effect relationship being immediately visible. Where the change, in direction or nature, was some time in being effected, no one particular year is given as the cut-off point. Again – and this is of the very essence of the Franco régime – change in one sector was not always, or not immediately, accompanied by changes in all sectors, so that the periods distinguished overlap to some extent. It is hoped that this will give some intimation of the continuity of the processes under examination.

Finally, whilst the theme of the study is the working class and this will be its specific focus, the working class must be seen, on the one hand, as one part of an historical process and, on the other, as one part of a social, economic and political whole; it must always be remembered that isolation is merely for purposes of analysis.

1. 1939-59

In class terms, and putting it very briefly indeed, the Civil War was the answer to a question posed in the course of the Republic to the industrial and financial bourgeoisie, together with the traditional land-owning oligarchy: would it be possible to maintain the status quo in social and political terms, whilst at the same time instigating something of a 'great leap forward' into a modern capitalist economy, within the framework of the Republic? Would it be possible to find some authoritarian means of controlling and exploiting the economic horse-power of Spain – the working classes – via the right-wing, fascistic CEDA[2] or 'Falange Española y de las JONS'[3] for example; or would it be necessary to have recourse to the ultimate force, the Army? The beginning of the answer was 18 July 1936.[4]

It was, however, no more than the beginning. The Civil War was only the first phase in the process of subjugation of the working class necessary for the subsequent development of a capitalist society in the mould of the 'more advanced' European neighbours.

But the process was slow. The economic miracle could not be achieved on the morrow of a war which had reduced the country to social, political and economic ruins.

The two decades following the war saw the gradual transition from economic autarchy to the beginnings of development:[5] from political isolation to reinsertion into the world concert of nations; from government by repression and fear to the first signs of 'liberalization'. The period also saw, particularly in the latter half, vast social changes which were closely inter-linked and the product of the basic historical changes outlined above: migration, emigration, urbanization, industrialization. In sum, a transformation of the social structure; and of social and economic, but not political, relations.

Gradually, the working class began to acquire consciousness of the new national and international configuration and of its own position therein. New forms of conflict began to emerge, made possible by objective changes in labour relations, even if, at this stage, they were essentially motivated by the workers' subjective perception of their situation.

(a) 1939-50

This was the period of economic autarchy, of the fight for mere survival; of stagnation. Politically, it was a continuation of the war: repression, elimination of dissidents, control from above.[6]

For the working class, economic and political factors were all one; they were the nuances of the one overriding characteristic of the period: exploitation. Exploitation based on massive and brutal repression and control, by and for the economically dominant class – the financial and industrial bourgeoisie – whose interests were protected and bolstered by tariff barriers against foreign competition and by State mobilization of resources (e.g. INI and the Banco de España).[7]

The most important of the resources mobilized by the State was labour. This was effected by the Syndical Organization,[8] a procrustean system imposed on workers and employers, with origins in the corporativist ideology of the prewar fascist organizations, 'Falange Española' and the 'Juntas de Ofensiva Nacional Sindicalista'.

The Statutes of the single party created in 1937 by the amalgamation of 'Falange Española y de las JONS' with the Carlist organization 'Comunión Tradicionalista',[9] recognized that body as the basis and inspiration of the new Spanish State.[10] With regard to labour, 'FET y de las JONS' would 'create and maintain the Syndical Organizations appropriate to the organization of Labour and Production and to the distribution of goods'.[11]

Direction of this Organization would rest with one man and the Organization would reflect the structure of the Movimiento itself: 'The National Direction of the Syndicates will be conferred on a single militant and their internal organization will be graduated as a vertical hierarchy, after the manner of a creative, just and ordered Army.'[12]

Section XIII of the 1938 Declaration of the Labour Charter (Fuero del Trabajo) gave specific form to the general principles enunciated in the Statutes of the Movimiento. The nine principles it laid down anent the Syndical Organization remained unchanged until the Organic Law of the State in 1967 modified the wording slightly.[13] 1. The State Nationalsyndicalist organization rests on the principles of unity, totality and hierarchy. (The 1967 modification removed the words 'Nationalsyndicalist' and 'unity, totality,

159

hierarchy', replacing them with the concept of the 'syndical organization'.) 2. All economic factors will be incorporated, according to their particular branch of productive activity, into vertical Syndicates Membership will be obligatory. (The 'vertical' concept was also removed in 1967; the Syndicates were henceforth to be composed of associations of employers, technicians and workers on an egalitarian basis.) 3. The SO is a public corporation under State direction. 4. The hierarchy will necessarily be staffed by Falange militants (this qualification requirement was dropped in 1967). 5. The Syndicate is the instrument of State economic policy with power to intervene in the organization, inspection and fulfilment of labour. 6. The Syndicate has the power to initiate, maintain or finance various organizations and services connected with production. 7. Offices will be set up to find employment for the worker in accordance with his aptitude and merit. 8. The Syndicates must provide the State with the data necessary for the elaboration of production statistics. 9. The Syndical Law will decide how extant economic and professional organizations will be incorporated into the new system.

The Decree of 21 April 1938 disposed that all Syndical activities would be carried on under the auspices of the Ministry of Syndical Organization and Activities, created in January of that year. In accordance with this Decree, employers and employees hitherto belonging to the Falangist organizations ('Centrales de Empresas Nacional-Sindicalistas' and 'Centrales Obreras Nacional-Sindicalistas' respectively, both created in 1934) and to those professional organizations not declared illegal, for example the Catholic 'Confederación Nacional de Sindicatos Católicos Obreros' (the UGT and CNT were declared illegal by a decree of 13 September 1936), were incorporated on a provincial basis into unitary syndical centres.[14]

The January 1940 Law of Syndical Unity formalized the provisions of the Labour Charter, giving legal status to the unity imposed by it. All participants in the productive process were henceforth considered de facto members of the 'national-syndicalist community' (with the exception of public employees, domestic service employees and members of the liberal professions).[15] The fact that the employers had not suffered a major repression left them in a stronger position than the workers[16], in a system which proposed to eliminate the class shuffle by the forcible fusion of the classes[17].

The organization comprises two kinds of syndical entity: the National-Syndicalist Centres (Centrales Nacional-Sindicalistas) and the National Syndicates (Sindicatos Nacionales); each operates within a given territory at national, provincial and local levels and both are responsible to the National Direction of Syndicates (Delegacion Nacional de Sindicatos)[18]. The incumbent of the latter position is also a government Minister and in this way the Syndical Organization is directly linked to the State. The SO also has representatives in the Cortes. The Centrales and the Delegación Nacional constitute the command or political line ('línea de mando'); the Syndicates constitute the representative line ('línea representativa'). The holders of positions in the former are appointed by the government, whilst, as mentioned above, all participants in economic activity are automatically members of the latter. The Syndicate is characterized by a hierarchical internal structure in the same way as the Organization as a whole. It is divided into two sections, the social (or workers') and the economic (or employers'). Only the lowest positions in the hierarchy are filled by direct election of representatives, other positions being filled either by indirect election or appointment by the Movimiento via the Delegación Nacional. Official sources maintain that the two sections co-exist in relative peace and independence, but other sources, according to the ILO report – and this is confirmed by an examination of worker demands in conflict situations – maintain that the workers feel themselves in a position of inferiority vis-à-vis the employers, that they are not truly represented in the Syndicates.

This has been the case from the beginning of the Syndicates' history. Writing of 1945, Barba Hernández, then Civil Governor of Barcelona, shows at once the workers' disaffection from the obligatory system and one of the reasons for their attitude: 'The workers still collect secretly among themselves for International Red Aid, and there are those who still have membership cards for the prohibited groups: Syndicalists of the CNT, Communists and Socialists.'[19] Disturbances would be avoided 'if the working class found itself to be represented in its own organisms. That the working masses do not always find themselves represented in their Syndicates is obvious.'[20]

Such, then, was the form and nature of the structure created to organize and control the labour force.

The workers were either hostile or indifferent to it, for it was alien to the Spanish labour tradition and erected on the grave of their own spontaneous, truly representative, autonomous organizations. However, if they did not enthusiastically espouse the new doctrine, they had not the means nor the opportunity to react. In the immediate postwar years, too, they had not the will to resist. Their leaders had been shot, imprisoned or exiled and the old organizations largely liquidated with them. They were demoralized by their defeat and physically weakened by living at subsistence

161

level. The constant threat of physical reprisals was a further deterrent long after the war was over. [21]

And yet, towards the end of the forties, there were signs that worker resistance had not been completely crushed. In 1947, there were protests – motivated by economic desperation – from Madrid engineering workers, Catalan textile workers and in some Guipuzcoa factories. On May Day, a general strike occurred in Bilbao, initiated in the 'Euskalduna' factory in which some 50,000 workers were involved. It was put down by the intervention of armed police and the Civil Guard after ten days of arrests, searches and some 14,000 dismissals. It was a failure but it was an important event, for it was the first manifestation of a collective response to repression and exploitation, a clear rejection of the Syndical Organization and a demonstration to the régime that the combination of social and economic discontent with political grievances (the strike was organized by the 'Basque Resistance Council') could produce an opposition of considerable force. [22]

(b) 1950-59

The beginning of the end of autarchy was foreseen in the end of the Second World War and in the heightening of East–West tension in 1947/48. This new international configuration, coupled with the clear impossibility of maintaining a policy of economic self-sufficiency indefinitely, raised hopes among the Spanish financial and industrial bourgeoisie of re-integration with the allied powers and re-insertion into the world market economy. [23] The new era which began to dawn in the fifties revealed not only the inability of the economic structure to cope with the American and European challenge; but also that some concomitant political changes would be necessary, if only to make the régime more acceptable to the controllers of the Washington purse strings.

In 1947, a law was promulgated providing for the establishment of Works Committees (Jurados de Empresa), ostensibly affording a measure of participation and true representation to the workers in matters of conditions, social security, job classification etc. In practice, the law was not implemented until 1953.

The Falange was fading into the background, but still maintained the Syndical Organization as its domain. The régime was prepared to change its form, even its principles and ideology when circumstances required it, but not its essential content, not the mainstays of its continued existence. [24]

The 'noviazgo' contracted with the USA in 1951 with the start of large-scale loans led to the Pact of Madrid of 1953 (which has, like most marriages of convenience, been something of a mixed blessing to both parties). This two-fold military and economic agreement represented the formalization of Spain's re-integration into the international capitalist system,[25] ending the isolation imposed by Spain's exclusion from the Marshall Plan for postwar European reconstruction. Development and modernization of economic structures on competitive lines was now of paramount importance; a kind of 'dictatorship of development' was beginning to appear.

Also essential was a change in labour relations; a new approach which was and, equally important, which could be seen by foreign observers to be, more modern, more flexible, more 'acceptable' was required. 1953 was a key year in this sense too.

After a six year delay, legislation was passed which made it possible for the 'Jurado de Empresa' decree to be implemented.[26] In providing for the election to Works Committees of worker representatives to act on behalf of the plant work force in consultations with management on such issues as basic wage rates, conditions, job status, production levels and technical modifications, this laid the foundations for further devolutionary legislation in the late fifties and marked the beginning of a policy of 'integration' with regard to the working class, in response to the realization that development could not be mounted on a system of overt social, economic and political repression. In fact, at least until 1958, it was little more than window dressing, for control was still firmly in the hands of employers, Sindical Organization and State. It was change without difference; a minimal attempt by the régime to relieve the strains imposed on the original structure which did not fundamentally alter the positions established in 1939.[27]

The upsurge in industrial development had as its social counterparts three major effects: urbanization, large-scale internal migration, the creation of an ever-expanding proletariat.

Cities which had previously been commercial or, as in the case of Madrid, administrative and governmental centres, now became industrial centres as well, whilst traditionally industrial areas – Barcelona, Bilbao, Valencia – experienced rapid growth in population, extension and activities. For the working class, city life frequently meant living in over-crowded, under-serviced, jerry-built workers' suburbs – veritable ghettos which furnished land speculators and construction firms with quick returns and kept the lower classes cheaply housed well away from fashionable upper-class districts. What was not realized at the time was that it also created the basis for suburb-based organizations – the Suburban Workers' Commissions (Comisiones Obreras de Barrio) for example, or the Residents' Unions (Unidades Vecinales de

163

Absorción) instituted by the Sindical Organization – whose activities might easily be linked to those of factory-based action groups, given their identity of interests, claims and membership.[28]

The industrializing towns drew their new population from the depressed rural areas, particularly from Andalucia and Extremadura. These areas suffered seriously in the fifties from the predominantly industry-oriented economic policy which tended to attract private capital away from investment in rural areas and to divert public money into industrial rather than agricultural concerns; from the failure of government to effect serious agrarian reform, particularly of land distribution; and from the combination of high cost of manufactured inputs with low returns for agricultural produce. Sheer economic necessity forced surplus rural labour, impoverished peasants and, eventually, small shopkeepers into the new industrial centres, where they formed the bulk of a new and expanding class of wage earning industrial and service employees.[29]

The rapid expansion of the urban proletariat involved a number of factors. On the one hand, the all important pool of labour was kept well stocked, which in turn meant that wages could be kept down, organic capital investment relatively low, output high and, therefore, profits also high. In 1940, the maximum average daily wage of an agricultural labourer was 10.37 pesetas; that of a metal worker 13.66 pts. By 1954, these figures were 22.01 pts and 25.30 pts respectively, i.e. an increase of approximately 100 per cent. Yet, in the same period, the cost of living rose by 240 per cent. Between 1939 and 1959, industrial prices rose by 676.8 per cent and production by 200 per cent, permitting a high rate of capital accumulation at the expense of labour.[30] For the working class, the effects of low wages, exploitative conditions of work, social and economic dependence are exacerbated by the continual arrival of reinforcements for the army of surplus labour and competitors for scarce social and economic necessities like housing. There is a tendency for intra-class antagonism to flare up, often along native/immigrant lines.[31] The immigrant workers are prone, at least temporarily, to be coopted by the system, since they are both grateful for and unwilling to risk the improved circumstances it offers them.[32]

These factors, together with the generally low level of political consciousness undoubtedly contributed to the nature of worker protest in the early fifties: sporadic, disorganized, economic in motivation and quickly resolved by minimal concessions and/or physical repression.[33]

Nevertheless, there were signs of a potential politicization of conflict beginning to appear in the new generation of shop stewards ('enlaces') and works councillors ('jurados de empresa') amongst

164

students and teaching staff (which culminated in the 1956 University crisis) and in Catholic circles, particularly the 'Hermandad Obrera de Acción Católica' (HOAC) and its youth organization 'Juventud Obrera Católica' (JOC), which played an important role in the radicalization and organization of young workers, in support of strikes, demonstrations and distribution of propaganda, in publicizing the workers' cause and in souring Church–State relations.[34]

The mid-fifties saw an attempt to push ahead with industrial development on the basis of loans from international agencies like the Ex-Im Bank and IMF, aid from the US under the terms of the 1953 pact and the earnings of exports. In fact, the average price per ton of exports fell, whilst that of imports increased; dollar reserves fell from $94 million in 1955 to $10 million in 1957; the US refused to grant more than $650 million over a period of five years, whereas Spain was demanding $200 million per annum indefinitely as a minimum; and by 1957 the overall budget deficit was 16 billion pesetas.[35]

The resultant continual rise in the cost of living, together with low industrial wages provoked strikes in 1956 in Pamplona which spread to Barcelona, the Basque country, the Asturias and Valencia demanding a guaranteed minimum wage of 75 pts per day.[36] The protests did have some effect, for the government introduced a minimum wage policy ('Salario Mínimo Interprofesional Garantizado') according to which, different minimum wages were established for different regions. The highest was Madrid at 36 pts; this was not raised to 60 pts until 1963, still 15 pts below the 1957 Pamplona demand.[37]

Of much greater importance was the Collective Contracts Law passed in the following year (The law was passed in April, 1958; and Syndical norms pertaining to its application were passed on 23 July 1958).[38] Its immediate significance lay in the fact that it reversed the centralizing tendency of labour legislation adopted in 1938 and confirmed by a Law of 1942, which placed the regulation of labour conditions and salaries under the jurisdiction of the Ministry of Labour. A further Decree of 1948 prohibited the conclusion of informal agreements between workers and employers (whether or not they were negotiated within the Syndicate), though this measure was revoked in 1956. The 1958 legislation had three main aims:

1. To simplify, by largely eliminating, the complicated network of Ministry regulations and, at the same time, to institutionalize the system of informal negotiations at plant level.
2. To facilitate the modernization and rationalization of industry, giving employers greater freedom in the fixing of wages and conditions,

thereby enabling them to link wage increases to increases in productivity via technical modifications to the plant structure or production processes.

3. To provide a channel for worker participation and expression, thereby avoiding conflict situations detrimental to the enterprise.

The legislation, whilst apparently devolving a considerable amount of power to the producers, nevertheless maintains the negotiating process within the Syndical structure (except in the case of intra-factory negotiations) and always subject to its guidance. The terms of the contract are considered obligatory minima, i.e. improvements to wages, conditions, etc. can be made according to laws, regulations or agreements reached at factory level over and above the conditions stipulated by Collective Contract. The terms of the Contract may not adversely affect management's power of direction or discipline nor the state of the national economy.

Collective Contracts are negotiated by the Syndical representatives of workers and employers and may be of varying scope, covering:

1. A group of employees within an enterprise or those of one branch of a single enterprise.

2. All the workers of one enterprise.

3. A group of enterprises with common characteristics, on a local, regional or provincial basis.

4. A group of enterprises covered by the same Ministry regulation, on a local, regional, provincial or interprovincial basis.

The initiation of negotiations, composition of the negotiating 'commissions' and actual negotiating process are all closely supervised by the Syndical Organization. Finally, the Contract agreed upon is necessarily subject to approval by the General Directorate of Labour (Dirección General del Trabajo).

Should no agreement be reached by negotiation, the labour authorities are empowered to impose an obligatory regulation (Norma de Obligación Cumplida), workers having no legal right to strike in this situation. An NOC can also be imposed should one of the parties fail to participate in negotiations, or if it is proved that the party which initiated negotiations has been subject to fraud or intimidation by the other.

From 1958, the use of the collective bargaining procedure virtually replaced the former system of Ministry regulations: in the period at present under consideration (i.e. up to 1960) the number of contracts concluded rose from 7 in 1958 to 368 in 1960. [39]

The aim of linking collective bargaining to productivity via wage settlements and technical modifications was realized in the course of the following years. By 1963, 81.5 per cent of the year's collective contracts included clauses regarding the control or stimulation of productivity,[40] whilst a report of the Syndical Organization states

> Collective contracting at factory level has permitted, in the metallurgical, chemical, construction and other industries, the restructuring of numerous industrial entities with the result of sensational improvements in the productivity indices of labour. Unfortunately, the increase in retail costs which compose the family budget have not enabled full advantage to be taken of those improvements in benefit of the standard of living of the workers . . . [41]

The new system proved, however, to have unexpected consequences in so far as it provided a new platform and channel for worker protest; a legal arena for direct confrontation with the ruling class; and the indirect creator of aspirations whose satisfaction was then denied by the same system. The observation of Gino Germani is relevant in this context:

> If one . . . generates in large numbers of people an aspiration for higher standards of living, but does not provide sufficient jobs to achieve the realization of these hopes, discontent generated by the disparity between aspirations and opportunity may set in motion revolutionary forces. [42]

In the Spanish case, it is not only a lack of jobs but of basic liberties which will provide the motive force.

The conflict which arose in the late fifties, however, was not yet of revolutionary proportions though the strikes of January 1958 involving 15,000 workers in the Asturias mining region provoked the suspension of certain sections of the 'Fuero de los Españoles' and there were disturbances throughout the rest of the country – in Barcelona, in the Basque country, Madrid, Zaragoza and Valencia. [43] The Collective Bargaining procedure proved capable of absorbing and channelling nascent conflict. Strikes in protest against rampant inflation were met with concessionary pay/productivity deals; prices chased wages and wages prices in the inevitable spiral. [44]

An important, though as yet embryonic, movement made its first appearance during the 1958 strikes: the Workers' Commissions (Comisiones Obreras). At this stage, they were no more than spontaneous committees of workers set up on an ad hoc basis in individual factories and in response to a specific conflict situation. The Commission dissolved itself on resolution of the conflict. [45] The Workers' Commissions did not become more organized, widespread and permanent until the sixties, but the principles on which they were based were being evolved in the intervening period; for this reason a résumé of those principles will be presented here. [46]

The movement is not motivated by 'exclusivism or factionalism'; no 'one section of the tendencies now attempting to represent the workers and their struggle should take predominance' and 'the highest spirit of service to the workers' movement' is of primary consideration:

1. The official syndicates are rejected because they deny the reality of a difference of interests between workers and employers.

2. The struggle for the right to associate is of prime importance.

3. Unity, independence and liberty are also crucial to the movement.

4. The movement must not be dependent upon a political party, although there is room for 'political parties which are identified with the aspirations and interests of the working class'.

5. The workers must recognize their status and position as an exploited group, from which they must emancipate themselves. Organizational independence in this matter does not preclude 'joint actions with other social groups for the achievement of coinciding aims'.

6. The 'effective instrument' of the movement will be a federation of labour, whose principles will be freely and democratically decided upon by Assemblies of workers in each place of work.

7. All the democratic freedoms are a sine qua non of a labour movement and all tendencies within the movement must be respected. The Assemblies of unions must contrive to avoid control by particularly strong or well-organized groups, at the same time respecting the groups which represent the majority.

8. 'We hope that some day we will have at our disposal instruments of the law of the land which guarantee the possibility of our coming under the auspices of a united federation of labour according to the will of the workers, freely and spontaneously expressed.'

9. All militants of the workers' movement must collaborate in the propagation of ideas, in the constitution of negotiating and discussion teams, in the coordination of the efforts of all those involved in the workers' struggle.

10. The key to success in the achievement of 'traditional and present-day objectives' is unity.

The economic crisis of the end of the period culminated in the Stabilization Plan of 1959. For the working class, this meant wage freezes; the suppression of overtime, which, according to the Vice Secretary of Social Organization of the SO, reduced workers' wages by an average of 23 per cent;[47] redundancies stemming from the contraction of markets, credit facilities and investment; greater subjection to the dictates of government and employers; and a feeling of impotence in that situation. Even where collective bargaining was possible, the workers found that their position was very much weakened because of the crisis. 1959 saw the beginning of large-scale emigration, enforced by the internal situation and encouraged by the government as a means of alleviating it. [48]

By the end of the 1950s, then, the economic and social scene had changed considerably from what it was at the beginning of the decade. Control was still the keynote, but with development now as the motive and 'integration' as the form. The overall effect of working class exploitation for the maintenance of the ruling class had not changed, but the composition of both had: a financial and industrial capitalist élite, backed up by a rising technocracy, had superceded the old land-owning and Church oligarchy in the corridors of power (though this is not by any means to say that these classes had entirely lost influence therein); whilst the dominated class was no longer a large, dependent peasantry and, to a lesser extent, an embryonic urban working class, but an organized, mass scale, dependent proletariat constantly replenished by marginalized rural elements.

2. 1957/8/9-69

This was the period of real 'take-off'; the period when the dictatorship of development which replaced that of selfsufficiency in the early fifties began to bear fruit, to make itself really felt. It was a period of rapid social and economic change, but within the same basic political structure. As Maravall puts it, it was characterized by changes in the façade based on belief in the régime as a modernizing, technocratic agency, politically legitimated by economic achievements. [49]

(a) 1957-61/3

The architects of the 1959 Stabilization Plan were the technocratic politicians who began to replace the Falange bureaucrats in the key governmental positions from the mid-fifties onwards, particularly after 1957. Usually identified as 'the Opus Dei technocrats', [50] the representatives of the new monopoly capitalism were pro-Europe and pro-liberalization. The austerity measures of the Stabilization Plan and the orientation of the Development Plan, the effects of which were unevenly spread throughout the society, suggested that they were no more pro-working class than their predecessors.

The Collective Bargaining legislation was also essentially the work of the 'liberalizers' and as much a weapon in political in-fighting as part of a socio-economic strategy. For it dealt a blow to Falangist power at all levels. In transferring the negotiating process to plant level, an attempt was made to de-politicize it and maintain it within economic bounds over which the Falange had no control; on the other hand, where stalemate was reached (as was frequently the case because of the fundamental contradiction between workers' and employers' interests) and recourse was had to the higher levels of the Syndical Organization, what soon became apparent was the unrepresentative character of the workers' representatives, the ineffectuality, inefficiency and inadaptability of the Organization in and to the new context. In these circumstances, workers and employers preferred to bypass Sindicatos, where their cases met with long delays and an eventual solution satisfactory to both sides was far from guaranteed, and revert, in effect, back to intervention by the Ministry of Labour in the form of compulsory arbitration awards (Normas de Obligación Cumplida). The unintended result of this state of affairs was that it gave the workers the opportunity to politicize their struggle, in that it gave them the initiative in provoking a direct workers–State confrontation.

The main axis of tension, then, with the scene set for technically rational development, was the ambiguous nature of the development framework. On the one hand, the employers, organizers and governors, wanting to use and coopt the workers via a strategy of limited concessions; on the other, the workers, increasingly aware of the strategy and of the double-edged sword constituted by taking the opportunities it afford them. They might be able to achieve certain immediate gains – higher wages, minimum guarantees, social security provisions and so on; it might even be possible to work towards changing the system from within; and at least it was an opportunity to publicize workers claims. At the same time, however, there was always the risk that representatives would be coopted by the official body; that concessions would satisfy virtually pauperized workers; and that militants could be easily identified and eliminated. This central problem of whether or not to cooperate with the system has been a continual bone of contention within the working-class movement and has probably been the main cause of disunity which can only weaken it vis-à-vis State and employers.

Towards 1960, this problem was only beginning to be part of an awakening and expanding working class consciousness which manifested itself in sporadic strikes and a proliferation of organizations – all illegal though not necessarily clandestine – which attempted to offer a means of organized expression to the workers and, at the same time, to be an alternative to the Communist Party. It was felt, particularly after the aborted General Strike called in 1959, that the Communist Party strategy of infiltration of the official Sindical structures was tantamount to cooperation with the system and that the tactic of the general strike was inapplicable to the contemporary situation. Hence the creation of a number of new groups: 'Alianza Sindical' in 1959-60, from the remains of the exiled

170

CNT and UGT, plus the Basque group, 'Solidaridad de Trabajadores Vascos'; this in turn gave rise to 'Alianza Sindical Obrera' (ASO) in 1962, comprising UGT and CNT dissidents, 'Solidaridad de Obreros Cristianos de Cataluña', STV elements (from 1965 onwards) and support from the international engineers group, 'Federación Internacional de Trabajadores Metalúrigcos'. Left wing Catholics established 'Acción Sindical de Trabajadores' in support of the Comisiones Obreras, which came to the fore after 1962, and another Socialist-Christian group emerged, the 'Unión Sindical Obrera', ultimately amalgamating with ASO in 1965. In reply, the Spanish Communist Party attempted to organize a united, militant, sindicalist front – the 'Opposicion Sindical Obrera'. [51] Clearly, however, all these groups were operating against enormous odds; apart from anything else, the basic technical requirements for organization – leaflets by the thousand, newspapers, buildings, money – were not present. [52]

In spite of the difficulties, or perhaps because of them, the years 1961-63 were important in the field of labour relations in particular and for the socio-economic and political context in general. [53]

The labour conflicts which broke out in those years were the result of development: the increasing monopolization, concentration and private appropriation of wealth and power by the employing classes on the one hand; on the other, the massification of the production processes, the socialization of impoverishment and the alienation of an expanding proletariat.

The 1962 strikes in the Asturias mining area and in Catalonia, Andalucia and the Basque country were essentially a spontaneous, apolitical reaction to the immediate effects of this contradictory situation. The catalyst was the Collective Bargaining system, through which employer intransigence and complicity with the official Trade Unions made clear the true position of the workers. The latter were not demanding power at factory or Sindical level, nor the overthrow of the régime; they were seeking immediate settlement for economic claims. [54] The Asturias strikes, which caused the government to declare a State of Exception in the area, were defensive in nature. The coal industry was in decline; wages were low; the infrastructure was antique; imported coal was cheaper and of better quality; other forms of energy were highly competitive. The proposed rationalization of the sector – via shut-downs, lay-offs, mergers and so on – was to be carried out at the expense of the workers in benefit of the owners. Indeed, in some areas it was suggested that the employers deliberately provoked a strike in order to provide 'legitimate' cause for dismissals.

The miners did make some gains as a result of their action in respect of production bonuses, piece rates, basic wages, the problems of silicosis sufferers and so on. More important in the long term were the effect on worker consciousness of direct confrontation; the demonstration that concerted, united action was more successful than endless dialogue; the experience of struggle and the realization of the crucial need for solidarity and organization; the emergence of the Asturias as a revolutionary vanguard whose example could be emulated in other areas and other economic sectors; the creation of the first 'Comisiones Obreras' on anything like a coordinated, permanent, organized basis – again an example which would spread in subsequent years.[55]

The official Sindical Organization attempted to cut the ground from under the feet of the workers' movement; Solís, the Minister Secretary General of the Movement made grandiose promises of free, truly representative sindical elections in 1963 and the Consejos de Administración Law (providing for committees of workers and employers to share organization and decision-making at plant level) was promulgated. Once the Asturias situation was temporarily pacified (though the usual recourse to armed force did not deter the miners from launching another massive wave of protest in 1963), a new government was installed which was a mixture of liberals like López Rodó and Fraga Iribarne, and strong men like Alonso Vega (in the Ministry of the Interior – nerve centre of the control and repression apparatus) and General Muñoz Grandes (in the newly-created vice-presidency of the government).

Neocapitalist economic development, slow and limited liberalization, order and repression – these were the three major axes along which the new government was to move towards integration into Europe. The First Development Plan, elaborated under the direction of López Rodó during 1962-63 for putting into operation at the beginning of 1964, was the blue print to be followed. It was to organize and modernize all sectors of the economy, eliminating uneconomical enterprises, bolstering weak but essential sectors like the steel industry, and facilitating the expansion of the dynamic sectors; all this motivated by the desire to achieve an increase and a more just distribution of the national income, particularly in pro of the 'disfavoured' sectors of society.[56]

(b) 1964-69

The second half of the sixties saw the technocrats in government making unstinted efforts to present Spain as a dynamic, industrializing, modern society – an attractive proposition for foreign investors, with the advantages to capital of political stability, cheap labour and a developing internal market. Foreign capital

172

needed no second bidding; but while investment was important, even more so was the amount of profit extracted. For the working class, the net outflow of capital meant that it had been turned into an 'international' proletariat, repressed by the national forces of order for the benefit of foreign employers. ('Proletariat' is not used here in the conventional Marxist sense.)

Emigration continued and increased as a result of the low wages, high prices, lack of opportunities syndrome which made life in Spain impossible for the Spanish worker. Not that they wanted to go; there was simply no alternative. The government encouraged, even assisted, this export of labour, for it relieved the pressure on urban services in cities whose building programme could not keep pace with the influx of migrant workers; removed what otherwise might turn into a volatile mass of discontented, desperate opponents; and provided a substantial source of income in the form of remitted earnings. If the idea occurred that, by allowing workers to see and experience less authoritative forms of government, better standards of living, the freedom for workers to express themselves, trouble might be being laid up for the future, it was evidently considered that the advantages outweighed the disadvantages. It was probably hoped, too, that material improvements would concert the working class into the consumer allies of the employers, pre-empting the former's revolutionary potential. [57]

The superficial manifestations of the liberalizing policy continued in, for example, the 1966 Press Law, which did indeed go a long way towards freeing the Press from the stultifying effects of strict censorship, but nevertheless allowed no journalist to operate outside the 'rules of the game'; and the revision of Article 222 of the Penal Code, which recognized 'professionally' but not 'politically' motivated strikes (until this date all strikes were illegal, irrespective of motivation).

Meanwhile, the reverse side of development was keenly felt by the working classes in an escalation of the effects referred to in the previous section: redundancy, poverty, insecurity, inadequate social services of all kinds, lack of basic necessities, over-crowding, repression and so on. This in an atmosphere of general prosperity and with such concepts as 'progress', 'Europeanization', 'integration', 'welfare', 'participation' and the like raised to the level of shibboleth.

With the contradictory nature of the claim and the reality on full view to those who were also most aware of the mechanisms involved in producing that situation, there was a rapid and important rise in the level of consciousness of the working class. Largely under the auspices of the 'Comisiones Obreras', the initiative for active protest

173

passed from the traditional sectors and areas (Catalonian textiles, Asturian mining and steel) to the dynamic spheres (Madrid engineering and construction; Barcelona car manufacturing). As a result, action became political to a much greater extent. The protagonists were in a relatively strong position because of their real ability to threaten key sectors of the economy and because their social and economic situation was relatively good (though not in the construction industry, certainly) they were able to pass quickly from the purely economic level – which might serve as the initial motivation for action – to a political level, demanding truly representative unions, freedom of association and speech, the right to strike and so on.

The 1964 Councils of Workers (Consejos de Trabajadores) and Councils of Employers (Consejos de Empresarios) [58] were a last-ditch attempt to institutionalize the conflict, totally rejected by the workers. The degree to which the workers rejected the Sindical Organization as a whole is reflected in the increase in the number of 'Norma de Obligación Cumplida' arbitration awards made during the sixties:

In 1963, 63,051 workers were organized according to compulsory arbitration. By 1965, this figure had risen to 438,288. In 1966 alone, 79 per cent of all steel and metal industry workers and 58 per cent of all miners had Ministry-awarded contracts. [59]

Some analysts of the situation were of the opinion, however, that the Sindical Organization was indispensable as a generalized context of conflict, since the struggle was not against individual employers but against the exploitative relationship inherent in capitalism. Besides, with the increasing tendency to separate ownership and management functions under the conditions of a modern capitalist system, together with the increase in the number of international corporations operating in Spain, it was often impossible to locate the employer or the owner, since the functions of these were dispersed throughout the enterprise, throughout the world.

There is not space here to discuss the pros and cons of this argument but it is one side of what was certainly an important question in workers' circles in the sixties and which is still relevant in the seventies, a question touched on in a previous section: infiltration of the Sindical structure or complete rejection of it? And in the event of the former, for what purpose – transformation and adaptation to real worker' needs or destruction? The crisis suffered by the workers organizations in the latter half of the sixties was largely centred on this polemic. [60]

The strikes, protests, go-slows and works to rule of the late sixties were too numerous to recount in detail; and it must be remembered that these were the 'highlights' of a continual, nation wide situation of intransigence, delays in reaching agreement in negotiations, intense feelings of antagonism, tension and frustration on both sides etc. The strike of the Madrid engineering workers, breaking out intermittently for four years between 1964 and 1967 was typical in so far as it expressed the discontents and manifested the potential for conflict of a wide range of economic and geographical areas. It was a pioneer and therefore of particular importance for a number of reasons:

It revealed to the workers that it was possible to confront police, Syndicates, legal institutions and government and not only survive, but actually achieve some of the ends of the action: the 20 per cent pay increase demanded by the workers at the beginning of 1964 was granted in September; deliberations for a new contract were begun in November; the employers were forced to abandon their refusal to negotiate before 1965; the workers' cause received wide publicity.

It showed the value of solidarity, unity and persistence: in January 1964 and April 1965 there was combined action with construction workers and the students respectively.

It was the testing ground for a new tactic – the mass public demonstration, which in turn brought police brutality onto the streets, a factor of some importance in a city in which foreign diplomats and press correspondents are present.

It revealed the essentially anti-working-class nature of bourgeois opposition groups. The reticence and inaction of Christian and social democrats showed their reluctance to transcend class differences by joining forces with the spontaneous, popular movement in an action of generalized political opposition.

Most importantly, it was the birth-place of the Madrid Workers' Commissions and the final blow to the Syndical Organization's attempts to contain nation-wide, latent conflict.

The two latter developments were simultaneous, for it was at the Madrid headquarters of the Sindicato del Metal that the meetings took place between Syndical officials and an assembly of workers' representatives from which the officials were obliged to concede the immediate election of a Commission which would support the workers representatives in the official syndical structure.[61] Faced with gatherings of workers several thousands strong, the Syndicates had to agree to the holding of weekly meetings of the Commission, which came to assume the form of general assemblies of considerable size.

These meetings were prohibited after three months and the old situation of delay / intransigence / minimal concessions /

demonstrations/repression was returned to. Unlike previous occasions, however, the Commission did not dissolve, but went on, in semi-clandestinity to perform vital tasks of organization, unification, leadership and education at shop floor level, ultimately achieving coordination on provincial and even national scales. [62]

In spite of police persecution, arrests and the circulation to factories of blacklists of activist workers, the Commissions achieved considerable development in the mid-sixties, thanks mainly to the direction of the Spanish Communist Party (PCE) and a militant Catholic group, Accion Sindical de Trabajadores (AST) which ultimately became laicized, radicalized and transformed into the Organizacion Revolucionaria de Trabajadores (ORT). [63] In recent years (since c. 1967) there has been considerable division within the Comisiones generally over the question of Communist domination and the ideology of that party within the Comisiones. The Communists are accused of 'reformism' and of wanting to use the working class movement as part of a manoeuvre to effect an alliance with middle-class democrats and 'the non-monopolistic bourgeoisie'. [64] The marxist-leninist elements of the movement and the AST became particularly hostile to the Communists; internal divisions which contradicted the movement's aim for a united working class.

In 1966, however, the Commissions were at the height of their activity and the massive participation in the Syndical elections of that year was the implementation of the Communist tactic of infiltrating the official structure and then coordinating work on two levels – open, legal, official and clandestine, illegal, informal. A danger quickly became apparent in the wave of strikes and partial stoppages which affected many parts of the country and many sectors of the economy in 1966 (e.g. transport and engineering in Barcelona, light engineering in Madrid, Seville and Pamplona, banking in Catalonia); because of their participation in the elections, the workers' leaders were easily identified, isolated and dealt with. Some were dismissed from their Syndical posts (revealing the fragility of the 'guarantees' protecting the worker incumbents of syndical positions); [65] some were also sacked from their jobs; some were arrested – Julián Ariza, Manuel Otones, Marcelino Camacho, for example, 'los dirigentes de más prestigio'. [66] ('the most prestigious leaders'.)

Of the many strikes which took place, the most famous was that in the Echevarri engineering works in Bilbao. [67] For 163 days the workers sustained a strike in protest against wage reductions occasioned by the restriction of State credit to the firm. After the Civil Guard had broken up an occupation of the plant, the management imposed a lockout, laying off 564 strikers and dismissing 15. At the ensuing trial, with the workers demanding reinstatement of all workers, Ruiz-Giménez for the defence maintained that it was a professional strike and therefore legal under the terms of the revised Article 222 of the Penal Code. The prosecution maintained that it was a political strike and, therefore, illegal. The court decided in favour of the management, judging that the 564 suspensions were in order and that compensation was not payable to the workers.[68]

1967 was another year of strikes and demonstrations which were becoming increasingly radicalized and widespread, but at no point reaching general strike proportions. A State of Exception was declared in April; there were lock-outs, court cases and suspensions throughout the country; the 'Comisiones Obreras' were formally declared illegal; a massive demonstration in October in Madrid ended with clashes between police and demonstrators, and several arrests, including three Bilbao priests. The year ended with the suspension of the Development Plan and a wage freeze to cope with its total failure to prevent control or alleviate the inflationary spiral.[69]

Whilst in 1968 more arrests were made of Comisión leaders and Minister Solís urged the workers to abandon the Comisiones in favour of the legal channels for the pursuit of their claims and defence of their interests,[70] certain self styled 'progressive' employers and politicians were advocating recognition of the clandestine organizations as a reality in labour relations; Ruiz-Giménez, for example, a Christian Democrat politician and Durán Farell, manager of 'Catalán de Gas' and 'Maquinista Terrestre y Marítima'.[71] There were even secret meetings between Sindicato officials and Comisiones leaders (followed by arrests and dismissals). The aim was to smother the vital force of an authentic, spontaneous workers movement by institutionalizing it and absorbing it into the system.

1969, the year of the 'MATESA' scandal, was also notwithstanding a year of political and and economic recovery. It was not so for long. The processes set in motion in the sphere of labour throughout the decade were irreversible and a fresh wave of disputes, strikes and confrontations was the response of workers being asked yet again to tighten their belts and toe the line in order to maintain the economic, social and political dominance of a visibly corrupt élite.

1969, the year of the thirtieth anniversary of the end of the war, ended with the declaration of yet another State of Exception.

3. 1970-

The State of Exception declared in 1969 was the climax of the crisis which had been building up throughout the sixties.

Development based on borrowed money and exploitation of the national working class proved to be development based on borrowed time, for the artificial social and political stability which was its context became increasingly difficult to maintain throughout the period. This was the message of the 1967-69 strike wave.

The progress, social and economic, promoted by the ruling classes had also created a number of unintended problems in that it placed the working classes in a series of new contradictory circumstances.

They had been given the means for certain economic improvement, but it was hedged round with limitations and provisos which nullified its potential effect. Although the discrepancies in data given by various agencies make one hesitate to quote any of them, what they all seem to indicate is that throughout the fifties and sixties, whilst cost of living and productivity rose, real wages did not keep pace and the proportion of the national income assigned to labour actually went down. [72]

They had been promised the means for legal protest and attempts to improve, or at least defend, the working-class position, but proposals on paper were often not accompanied by provision for their implementation in reality. [73]

They had been offered the image, aspirations and some of the structures of a modern, democratic, European Society but these were without the corresponding political content and economic base.

They had been given the desire to participate, but it was nipped in the bud whenever such participation threatened to disregard or exceed the framework laid down by government.

The mixture could not fail to be explosive. Yet the régime could and did survive the threat posed by the workers, students, intellectuals and discontented lower middle-class service employees because, in the final analysis, the 'liberal' elements relied on coercion and physical repression in the same way that the old style fascists had done.

The seventies have already given ample proof of this fact in spite of the continuing 'integrationist', 'reconciliationist', 'liberalizing' and 'aperturist' demagogy.

The pattern is monotonously repetitive: a breakdown in collective bargaining talks; deadlock; closure, suspensions, dismissals; a hard line taken by both sides; the forces of law and order called in to force a return to work. And since there is no dialogue with truncheons and pistols, a return to work *is* forced, with the initial demands unattended to. In this way, the extraordinary circumstances of 1969 have become the norm in the seventies.

Evidence is not hard to find.[74]

In the Madrid Metro strike of 1970, the workers returned to their posts under threat of army intervention, following a three month dispute over wages and fulfilment of the collective contract. In Seville 5,000 construction workers were involved in a five month wrangle with employers which ended with the award of a Ministry NOC (March–July 1970). Three workers were shot dead in Granada (July 1970), also following a dispute over the collective contract between construction workers and employers. Two workers were shot in Erandio following a demonstration against atmospheric pollution and one in October 1971 during a strike at the Barcelona SEAT plant, which was the climax of four years of conflict provoked by organization of draconian authoritarianism. In all, since 1969, there have been ten deaths in the course of labour protests.

Even where no deaths occurred, repression was brutal, either by arrests or suspensions, dismissals, lock out etc. Such was the reaction of management to disputes at the 'Maquinista Terrestre y Marítima' factory in Barcelona, 1970-71 (whose manager, it will be remembered, Durán Farell, had in 1968 advocated dialogue with the 'Comisiones Obreras'); in the Madrid and Barcelona construction sector, 1971; and in the 'Citroen' plant at Vigo, 1971-72.[75]

The 'manifesto' presented by a group of Catalan entrepreneurs to the Provincial Delegate of the Barcelona Engineering Sindicate in 1971, expressing their anxiety over recent unrest and setting out their recommendations, encapsulates the attitude of Spanish employers at that time. Inter alia they wrote:

> The employers feel it their duty to convince our government that it must act with greater energy, in order to avoid the creation *outside the enterprise* of politically motivated conflict situations which, once established within the enterprise, are disguised as labour conflicts and presented with considerable skill. Justified dismissals, especially in these cases which concern us, must always be WITHOUT COMPENSATION, since otherwise there arises the professionalization of social conflict and compensation. *More aggressive political and economic action is an absolute necessity in order to guarantee freedom of entrepreneurial action, complete socio-economic peace and the confident hope that the future of this country will be stable but vigorous.*[76]

The new Trade Union Unity Act of 1971 was ostensibly an attempt to put into practice some of the opportunities theoretically offered by the 1967 13th Declaration of the Labour Charter (Fuero del Trabajo) with regard to the formation of Professional

179

Associations within the Syndicate.[77] It was potentially the culmination of a process begun by the 1967 Organic Law of the State and the aforementioned Declaration of the Labour Charter whereby the Syndical Organization would, via the creation of free and representative professional associations of employers, technicians and workers become a system of participation and representation rather than organization and control.

If such was the aim of the 1967 legislation, it has not been realized by the 1971 Syndical Law, for whilst it does provide for the creation, by employers, technicians and workers of 'syndical associations for the defence of their particular interests, as determined by economic activity or professional speciality . . .' such associations are closely bound to the Syndical Organization, each being part of the organic structure of the appropriate Syndicate and therefore subject to its jurisdiction; and whilst it recognizes, in the separation of categories, differences of interests, it allows only for the defence of those interests, not for the taking of initiative in a participatory or representative role. Furthermore, of the four types of association recognized – the syndical section at factory level, associations, unions and 'agroupments' (federations of associations at provincial and national level), and Councils (of workers and employers, set up in 1964) – the most important given the increasing tendency to negotiate collective contracts at factory level, the factory Syndical Section, has not been provided with the regulations necessary for the implementation of the law. Similarly the organization of the other entities proposed has also been delayed in the Syndical 'pipe line'.

The Sindical Organization must surely feel itself threatened by the increased politicization of labour disputes; increased radicalization of worker attitudes; increased demonstrations of solidarity from peripheral sectors of the economy; increased support for extra-Sindicate workers' groups from representatives of the Church – and that not only from the lower echelons (see, for example, the crisis over the pronouncements made by Mgr. Añoveros in support of the workers, in 1974). The sheer numerical increase in the number of disputes and the number of workers involved must alone give the SO pause. Consequently, the Sindical elections of 1975 were first postponed for it was widely feared within the Organization that the representatives of the clandestine workers' organizations would sweep the boards. And they did.

As far as the last eighteen months–two years are concerned, it is difficult at such short range to do more than simply recount the events; even more difficult is it to predict their effects in the future.

Of great importance for the Spanish working class is likely to be the employment situation in those European countries which have become the destination of emigrants – Germany, France and Belgium in particular. The German government, for example, gave assurances in 1974 that Spanish workers under contract to German employers would not be made redundant as a result of that country's unemployment crisis. Nevertheless unemployment amongst immigrants has been greater than amongst nationals since Minister of Labour, Walter Arendt ordered that preference be given to the latter when filling vacant positions.[78]

One must consider, too, not only those who may return but also those who will not now be able to leave, in a sense 'doubling' the surplus of Spanish labour. It remains to be seen whether those who do return might act as an organizing, catalyzing force in the national working-class movement in the light of their experience abroad.

If a reversal of the migratory pattern occurs,[79] its effect on the labour market is likely to be exacerbated by other results of the world economic recession: reduction in the tourist trade (obviously of greatest immediate importance to tertiary sector employees in Spanish holiday resorts, but having repercussions throughout the country and society as a whole); crisis in industry, rising prices, falling real wages, unemployment and so on. In addition, this externally-imposed crisis comes on top of the ever-latent internal crisis which the régime has consistently repressed but never resolved.

The signs are that, world crisis or no, the Spanish working class will give no quarter and that it is late in the day for such palliatives as the release of the '1001 Trial' prisoners.[80] That one act is counterbalanced by others, too numerous to recount in detail, of a contrary nature: the arrest and trial of priests speaking and acting in favour of the workers, usually sanctioned with fines well beyond the financial resources of the lower clergy and consequently replaced by prison terms;[81] the police invasions of Church meetings in workers' districts and the prohibition of Church-organized assemblies there;[82] the arrest and trial of workers staging strikes, demonstrations or sit-ins[83] in protest against the failure of management, Syndicates and government to meet what are by now traditional demands: freedom of association and organization, of press and speech; true worker representation; freedom from intimidation, dismissal or other reprisal: the right to strike.

Recently, a Bilbao industrialist's house was blown up following a long and bitter dispute at the 'Firestone' tyre plant in that city.[84] It is likely that this kind of incident will be repeated with increasing frequency as long as employers and government continue to deny and/or disregard the demands of the working class.

The Syndical Organization is no longer efficient in its role as intermediary between State and workers, preventing direct confrontation, exercising control, communicating government requirements, channeling worker activity.

The relationship between these forces is no longer linear and hierarchical as originally intended, it is triangular; three distinct but interdependent points linked by lines which are increasingly antagonistic. It remains to be seen whether the régime will continue to be able to resist the pressures arising from this three-cornered confrontation or whether the collapse of one of the forces will occasion change, permitting the emergence of new forces, new structures, new relationships.

8

Power, Freedom and Social Change in the Spanish University, 1939-75

SALVADOR GINER

I

This chapter represents an attempt to understand and analyse one aspect of contemporary Spanish culture: its system of higher education from 1939 until 1975. It examines the relationships which have obtained during that period between the political structure of domination established in the country in 1939, the important social transformations which occurred in Spanish society, and the people directly involved in higher education – students, teachers and researchers. Their sociological explanation has been attempted with the help of four historical models, each one possessing a logic of its own in the development of its conflict patterns, and each leading to the next.

I would like to think that the periods into which the study of higher education under Francoism has been divided here are not arbitrary. In elaborating a model for each period I have overlooked minor fluctuations and secondary exceptions, and chosen key historical dates to delimit each in time, but I am sure that they are neither watertight nor altogether satisfactory. They are as follows:

1. The 'Fascist' University, 1939-54, characterized by the partly successful attempt at building a fascist system of higher education.
2. The 'reactionary' university, 1955-66, characterized by an open struggle for republican legality and by the defeat of fascist institutions.
3. The university of 'antidemocratic expansionism', 1965-71. [1]
4. The 'crisis' university, 1971-75. [2]

II Towards a Fascist University (1939-54)

As far as the universities and other institutions of higher learning and education were concerned, the drive towards fascism went far enough to mark out a distinct period of their history. As elsewhere in Europe, this was characterized by the common pattern of terror, paralysis of creativity and a very grave regression (rather than mere stagnation) in the cultural life of the country. Two factors made this possible: the first contributory element was the presence, dating from before the outbreak of the Civil War, of militant fascist groups within the University. The SEU (*Sindicato Español Universitario*) was a fascist-syndicalist group created in 1933, soon after the foundation of its mother-organization, the Falange.[4] It appeared as the fascist alternative to the chief students' union, the FUE (*Federación Universitaria Española*) which was staunchly republican, and soon began a policy of violence against it. As the Falangists themselves now recognize, 'at the zenith (of the pre-Civil War anti-Republican) struggle, the Falange lived almost exclusively upon the structure of its University cadres'.[5] This was so, amongst other reasons, because the limited number of Falange militants at that time, coupled with the national ambitions of the party, put the greatest pressure on its (relatively) numerous student members not to struggle in the restricted area of university politics alone. With their para-military training and organization, SEU militants were able to join in the uprising in a most efficient manner. They soon began to man and, to a large extent, control the propaganda, radio and press apparatus to the right-wing forces. They never, however, forgot their university connection.[6] A very high mortality rate in combat, the aura of being, supposedly, the rising youthful force of the 'New State', their claim to be the intellectual élite of the régime, as well as certain external events, such as the spectacular expansion of the Axis from 1939 to 1941, apparently gave this Falangist group a unique claim and opportunity to 'conquer' the university – to use an expression dear to its members.[7] The opportunity for creating a fascist university was also enhanced by a second factor: the large-scale emigration of the republican intelligentsia, which deprived it of its most creative and valuable members. Furthermore, the new régime had launched a witch-hunt or purge – officially known under the euphemism of *depuración* – against those supposedly sinister free-thinkers, members of an international masonic conspiracy, whose sole aim had allegedly been and still remained the destruction of 'eternal Spain'. The seriousness of this policy was demonstrated by the ensuing terror during the postwar years and by the provisions of such legal decrees as the notorious Law for the Repression of Communism and Free-Masonry. Under these circumstances it appeared that the Falange would easily have a free rein in the university, from which so many of its early members originated. Veterans crammed the reopened classrooms and received privileged

184

treatment in examinations. Student delegates of the SEU – since 1940 the sole permitted student political organization – appeared in the Falange uniform, as did other members of the party. Later, the 1943 University Law[8] established that even the Rector of each University must be a member of the Falange and that every teacher must swear allegiance to the régime. An atmosphere of triumphant fascism seemed to impregnate universities, and it appeared as if a thorough 'fascistization' of higher education was at hand.

Yet the new régime was the result of an alliance of cooperating but distinct right-wing forces. As in most of the other complex institutions of the post-Civil War, universities largely reflected the general power structure. Politically they were subject to two forms of control: the Falange controlled the student body, while Catholics of extreme traditionalist orientation predominated amongst the staff. The latter often belonged to the *propagandistas* or ACNP Catholic association, an interest group which benefitted from the victory in a spectacular way. (About 80 university chairs were still held by the ACNP in 1974 apart from countless other influential posts in the administration.)[9] These factions shared out amongst themselves the academic spoils of a war whose devastating effects upon Spanish culture cannot be overemphasized. For one thing chairs were taken over by the incompetent in an unprecedented manner. It should be noted that the republican intelligentsia had managed to achieve, over approximately forty years preceding the outbreak of the war, a notable degree of competence in science, philosophy and in some of the social sciences. No wonder that the memory of 'republican' achievements, has never ceased to play an active role in contemporary Spanish university life. Even under the new conditions and with very rare exceptions, Falangists were not in a position to compete for posts of responsibility on the staff: they had too short a history to possess a senior generation of militants who could be defined as scholars, scientists or intellectuals to fill the staffing gap. University Falangists almost immediately realized the extreme danger that this represented for their future, especially as they sensed that their national party chiefs were already compromising with conservative forces of the winning side – the military, the landowners, the Church. At a national assembly of the SEU[10] in 1940 they still felt strongly enough to publicly denounce 'anachronistic military dictatorship', in the words of the comrade who opened the congress,[11] and to threaten those who 'wanted to destroy and undermine their pending revolution'. At the same meeting, Joaquín Ruiz Giménez – who was to become minister of education years later – defended several fascist postulates, some of which, using his own terms, can be summarized as follows:

1. The Spanish University was to be thoroughly committed to Catholicism and to Falangism. 'The purest dogmatic orthodoxy' and Falangist beliefs were to be enforced.

2. Each university was to completely control any 'cultural movement' that would take place within its orbit. Its authoritarian tutelage would extend from the humblest primary school to the highest cultural organizations in the territorial area allocated to it.

3. Chairs would be filled by the traditional system of *concours* (*oposición*) but the 'moral and political purity of professors and teachers will be strictly controlled by the Falange'. [12]

The years that followed, however, saw an erosion of some of these principles. The military dictatorship, of course, was far from unaware of the Falangist threat to its monopoly of commanding power. It was for this reason that, in an early attempt at neutralization, some of the most vocal and militant SEU members of 1939 and 1940 were conveniently 'bureaucratized' and given 'harmless' posts, sinecures and privileges. A number of them were even to become mimisters in later years. [13] It is worth noting that this erosion of 'revolutionary' Falangism took place without liberalization. One of the most important agents of the process of its decline was the militarization of the student body. This occurred in two different ways. Firstly, the creation of a *Milicia Universitaria* flattered the students by giving them the opportunity to carry out their military service in an 'élite corps', while it isolated them from the *classes dangereuses*. [14] Secondly, a campaign of anti-Soviet propaganda was aimed at recruiting the most active, militant students for the Division which was to leave for the Russian front on the Nazi side. About two thousand students joined it, [15] and among them were many of the most revolutionary and idealist Falangists, already disillusioned with the 'pending Falangist revolution' in their country. As one Falangist writer has implied, by fighting on the Eastern Front, their revolutionary elan was conveniently spent, [16] especially as many never came back. Yet some of those who returned became the first protagonists – and victims – of an act of student violence against the régime, a bomb attack on one prominent general. As a reprisal a SEU member was executed, and acts of this type against the militaristic, non-Falangist power elite were never repeated.

Throughout this first period of student life, and especially after 1942, the SEU leadership began to accept the régime with all its consequences. That meant that they were prepared both to act as a 'campus police' and to organize whatever demonstrations of solidarity with the régime or of hostility to certain foreign powers the government deemed opportune. Nothing else seemed to remain of the brief moment of elation after victory, except perhaps for the Falangist control over some cultural activities – whose quality always left much to be desired. In 1945 the defeat of the Axis meant the complete domestication of the SEU: subservient officers were nominated and, following the new government line, much emphasis began to be placed upon the religious element in life. 'Too much science' – the then Minister of Education, Ibáñez Martín, explained – 'does not bring you near the Supreme Being.' [18] There were some feeble reactions against these policies throughout the period, but they originated solely from the SEU rank and file. (Although the republican FUE was clandestinely reorganized in Madrid in 1946, and lasted until 1950, [19] it was ineffective and succumbed to repression.) Thus in 1956, the year that marks the first watershed between the phases demarcated here, Falangist SEU militants were still clamouring for 'agrarian reform', 'Falangist revolution', etc. By that time, though, politically minded non-Falangist students were already working under cover of the SEU, or taking part in its 'actions' and demontrations in order to redirect them to other targets. The 1951 general strike in Barcelona had already been joined by such students, and the 1954 mass demonstrations in Madrid, officially staged against England and demanding the reversion of Gibraltar also turned – after violent police charges – into a demonstration against the government. The purges that the government inflicted upon the SEU further debilitated its militant cadres. Henceforth it only attracted some opportunists, and soon even these began to discard it as futile.

This period had seen the rise and fall of a Falangist University, the maintenance of a backward-looking structure of higher learning, and a university which had reached its lowest point in modern history: over-bureaucratized, corrupt, legalistic, unexpanding, rigid and, worst of all, dogmatic and poor. Furthermore, the government had set up in 1939 the *Consejo Superior de Investigaciones Científicas* (CSIC) or Higher Council for Scientific Research, a continuation of a body founded by the Republic which absorbed the small funds earmarked for research in the national research budget, leaving nothing to the universities. It may be of interest to mention that one of the *Consejo*'s chief aims was to 're-establish the Christian and basic unity of the sciences, destroyed in the Seventeenth Century', [20] and that its first president (from 1939 to 1966) José María Albareda, was a rising personality of what then appeared as a little-known Catholic 'sect', the Opus Dei. Its overall control was – during its first times – in the hands of the ACNP, the reactionary Catholic organization mentioned above. [21]

Even if Francoism represented an attempt at economic

187

modernization,[23] it was a modernization which nevertheless was fatally divorced from educational reform. Strengthened by a rabid anti-intellectualism – secular learning being associated with republicanism – the new government entirely neglected the university during its first crucial years. Not only did universities and higher schools of technology undergo the immense regression just described but they became considerably impoverished materially. The slow reconstruction – in the form of an architectural mixture of 'Castilian imperial' and 'Mussolinean' styles – of the University City in Madrid, through whose campus the front-line had run during the endless siege of the city – epitomizes the situation.

Another example is the abolition of the prestigious Autonomous University of Barcelona as part of the policy of cultural genocide against Catalonia carried out by the government.[24] During the period 1939-54 only one new faculty was open, and that was the Faculty of Economics and Political Science, in Madrid, in 1943, which, together with the Institute of Political Studies, was entrusted with the indoctrination of the students in the ideology of economic autarchy and in the specific Spanish brand of the fascist doctrine.

III The 'reactionary' university (1955-65)

After 1951 Spanish universities began to admit students who, born during the brief Republican period, could hardly remember the war. Their parents had no doubt countless times given them the stern advice not 'to meddle in politics' – a pattern of socialization not unknown in pre-Civil War Spain, but now emphasized by a majority of families. These students had undergone schooling during the years of doctrinaire militancy and utter poverty, the forties and early fifties. It was only in 1952 that the per capita income of the average Spaniard slightly exceeded that of the last year of peace – 1935 – after remaining well below that mark from 1940 to 1950.[25] For this reason, they saw themselves, like their counterparts in the other Mediterranean societies, as a very fortunate stratum. More than ever the university system seemed unchangeable: the twelve state universities, with their rigid systems of faculties and chairs, their incredibly underpaid non-professorial staff, their networks of influences for passing exams or, indeed, obtaining a chair, seemed immutable. The higher technical schools also seemed invulnerable and impervious to change: *numerus clausus* made entry very difficult; but a degree from, say, the *Escuela de Caminos,* opened the way to considerable social prominence. Indeed, after the decline in Falangist activism, the parasitical bureaucratization of the SEU,

188

and the growth in Church influence from 1945 onwards, the University was viewed by the livelier and more aware students as a stale, *ancien régime* affair, under the veneer of a nineteenth-century Napoleonic reform and of the fascist rhetoric still used by the régime. (It is in this strictly allegorical sense that the concept of an *ancien régime* university is used here; it will also help to convey the feeling of disgust and shame that overcame the student political and cultural élites of that generation when they realized the increasing gap between their country and the new world emerging elsewhere in Europe at the time.)

The student population remained fairly static through this period. There were 64,281 university students by 1957 (as against 33,623 registered during the first full academic year under republican auspices – 1932-33), but then numbers remained stationary until 1963-64. On the other hand, students entering higher education in the early fifties followed the same vocational patterns as their predecessors: greater numbers went into law and medecine; law reached an all-time high in 1953; girls and nuns flocked to philosophy and letters; pure science faculties were half deserted; pharmacy was sought after by those whose parents already owned a pharmacy, thus aspiring to the secure life of the monopolistic shopkeeper: the examples could be multiplied. Basically, the majority of students came from the traditional strata that could afford to give their children an education, almost invariably sending them to the nearest university. In spite of some growth of *colegios mayores* (students' residences), family ties and dependence continued to be kept throughout the period – as they are still today, though to a increasingly lesser extent.

Yet, these were the students who first 'politicized' Spanish universities after the 1939 debacle; they challenged the SEU authority, gained some freedom for themselves, publicly manifested their democratic and republican beliefs, and utterly rejected the 'eternal and imperial Spain' whose scions they were supposed to be. Their success was, in practical terms, far from complete: the régime was too strong and their own numbers too small. Above all, the predominant political attitudes in society were not in their favour. (This point often tends to be over-looked by left-wing critics of the régime, who overemphasize repression and police action: these were all too efficient but, in addition, the necessary desire to challenge the authorities during this period was lacking at least in the middle and upper classes whence the students came.) As for the social origins of the students' leaders of this first generation of revolt there is evidence that most of them were the children of middle-class professional families formerly committed to republican tendencies, often of

189

intellectual background (in Madrid) or of Catalanist tendencies (Barcelona).[26]

Towards 1955, members of this generation were entering their second or third year in the university. Their first years as students had coincided with a period which – in the circumstances – may be described as particularly favourable for a *prise de conscience* of their situation. Apart from the decisive generational fact mentioned above – their lack of 'vested interests' in, or direct experience of, the Civil War – a number of humane catholic (or lukewarm Falangist) intellectuals had managed to occupy posts of responsibility in the Ministry of Education and in the universities. (This may have been allowed to happen by the Government in order to acquire greater international respectability. This policy, incidentally, was partly successful: in 1952 Spain was admitted by UNESCO as a member.) In 1951 Ruiz Giménez, who was drifting towards a tolerant form of catholicism and had shed his early totalitarianism, was appointed Minister of Education. Simultaneously, the Nazi-sounding ministerial Department of Propaganda was taken out of the Ministry of Education and transferred to the apparently less virulent Ministry of Information and Tourism. Antonio Tovar, a repentant Falangist (although not yet publicly so), a man of 'liberal' leanings, was nominated to the Rectorship of Salamanca, and Pedro Laín, a man of similar persuasion, Rector of Madrid University. The effects were soon felt. The University became the only relatively free arena of political discussion in the entire country. A slight – but qualitatively important – degree of liberalization was felt in the more sophisticated journals.[27] French Catholics, disciples of Maritain, began to meet regularly in San Sebastián with Spanish liberal Catholics. Even the theoretical organ of the régime, the *Revista de Estudios Políticos*, notorious in the past for its defence of the *caudillaje* (*Führerprinzip*) doctrine, began to open its pages to a less fascist political science and, soon, even to sociology.[28] Simultaneously, certain books and publications from abroad began to be occasionally available on request. Informal seminars were organized to study and discuss them and did not always meet on university premises.

The politicization of these student élites occurred very rapidly, as could be expected of a country whose polity presented the characteristics then prevalent in Spain. Thus, to give two examples, the commemoration of the death of the philosopher José Ortega, in 1955, in a joint public lecture organized by members of the Boscán literary seminar, led to its forcible dissolution; in November of the same year the preparation for a first National Conference of Young Writers in Madrid was stopped by the Government. The students involved in events such as these – even when they were not arrested or directly bothered by the police – began to give up all hope of being able to go along with the 'policy of the outstretched hand' then advocated by the 'liberal' Ministry. Frustration made them see that radicalization and political action were the only way out. By the winter of 1956 incidents against the SEU broke out in Barcelona; later outbursts in Madrid became more serious as some bloodshed combined with Falangist over-reaction led to a government crisis. The 'hawks' claimed that the active student opposition to the régime was the consequence of the 'soft' Ministers' policies. As a consequence, Ruiz Giménez resigned and Raimundo Fernández Cuesta (Minister of the régime's political organization, the *Movimiento Nacional*) was deposed. Finally, in May 1956, political trials against rebellious students began.[29]

All this, of course, further radicalized the students. By now, clandestine political parties and the first free organizations had appeared, such as the UDE (*Unión Democrática de Estudiantes*) in Madrid, gathering Christians and Socialists; the *Nueva Izquierda Universitaria*, a forerunner of the left-wing FLP (*Frente de Liberación Popular*) both in Madrid and Barcelona; MSC (*Moviment Socialista de Catalunya*) in Catalonia; and the Communist Party. Needless to say, the latter was systematically accused of plotting and inspiring everything that was happening in the universities. For this reason, it paid a heavy toll in casualties, but it also soon began to lose members in periodical internal crises due, above all, to the extreme conservatism of its central leadership, combined with their disregard of internal democracy. In this connection it is significant that in 1956, just after the first outbreak of the crisis between the government and the students, when temperatures were running highest against the régime, the exiled CP Central Committee ordered all its members to subscribe to an improbable policy of 'national reconciliation' between the victors of 1939 and the vanquished – the most active of whom were too busy avoiding prison and torture to seek reconciliation with anybody in power. The reasons for this incongruous policy of appeasement lie beyond the scope of this paper and must be sought in the general policies of Soviet Communism within three years of Stalin's death, but its consequences for the fate of communism in Spanish universities or, indeed, amongst contemporary Spanish intellectuals, are most relevant.[30] Both students and intellectuals have been leaving the CP ever since, either in intermittent waves or by a constant trickle of individual desertions, because of the inconsistency – as they saw it – between their own revolutionary interpretation of Spanish social reality and the party's conservative policy.[31]

It was against this general background that the first steps towards

191

the institutionalization of a democratic and independent organization were taken by the students. Until then we encounter only unofficial demonstrations or small clandestine parties and more or less ephemeral illegal 'students' unions'. But in 1957, in defiance of the SEU, the Barcelona students openly managed to hold the First Free Students' Assembly (surrounded and locked in by the police). Of course, the recently reshuffled government responded swiftly by repression and academic sanctions; but in the end it had to give in on some matters. As a result of the 1956 and 1957 events the SEU was reorganized (October 1958). For the first time it included representation, though only at its lowest levels, the *consejos de curso* and *cámaras sindicales*. And, inevitably, such democratic representation as was granted soon began to be used as an increasingly more threatening instrument for the struggle against the authorities. The 1957 victory set a pattern to be replicated in the years immediately following until, between 1962 and 1965, the SEU, fully eroded, became extinct as far as the majority of students was concerned.

Until 1965, however, the government clung tenaciously to the SEU as the (and its) only existing organization in higher education. Of course, after 1957 – and in spite of the good will of Falangist squads – it could not rely on it as a satisfactorily repressive weapon; thus police in often clumsy disguise made their appearance in classrooms to the bemused surprise of their 'fellow students'. In order to achieve a measure of success with the student, several experiments were tried, which all failed in political terms. While the TEU (*Teatro Español Universitario*) managed to create some fairly good theatre groups – who did their utmost to put on revolutionary plays – it is also true that the SUT (*Servicio Universitario del Trabajo*) – an organization through which students got jobs as miners, fishermen, peasants and industrial workers during the long vacation – was a dangerous experiment, which made many students politically sensitive, whilst others used it to 'spread the word' amongst the workers. After a crisis and a reorganization, the SUT experiment was hurriedly called off. [32] By 1960 and 1961, students' strikes aimed to prove that the SEU was useless and impotent, unless it became thoroughly representative. This the government could not grant, for the whole political structure of the state apparatus was based on 'vertical' unions, with officers nominated from above. If one union were to break away from this pattern, the others would try to follow suit. Faced with such dilemmas the government hesitated and bid for time. Meanwhile, an atmosphere of freedom – albeit limited to internal matters – was growing within the student bodies in the different universities: they were perhaps more busily engaged in political debates, cultural activities and seeking links and coordinating their actions with the outside world – especially during the vast 1962 strike waves in mining and industry – than they were in their struggle with the authorities and the government. This intense 'internal' activity mainly consisted in the formation and development of political parties as well as clandestine students' unions, some of which – like the Barcelona-based *Inter* – achieved a remarkable degree of efficiency, seriousness and harmony among the various parties competing for their control.[33] Thus, to the parties mentioned earlier and which stemmed from the 1957 crisis, others were now added such as the small but ideologically important *Union Democrática de Estudiantes* (in Madrid) which introduced Christian democracy in the student movement in 1962. Old and new parties in that city joined the *Federación Universitaria Democrática Española*, FUDE, a free illegal, non-party students' union, very much like the Barcelona *Inter*.

As the power of the clandestine unions rose, the idea of controlling the SEU began to wane. Yet in 1962 and 1963 free unions in many universities still thought it expedient to occupy as many posts as possible in the ailing SEU in order to complete its disintegration. By the autumn of 1964, in the course of an eventful 'Week of University Reform', originally planned as a series of cultural events in several universities, the crisis between the SEU and the students reached deadlock, and the period under consideration came to a close: the students and their free unions completely ignored the existence of the SEU. This opened the way of the serious disturbances which took place early in 1965, after the Madrid students had held another Free Assembly of Students – the fourth in Spain since 1957.

The huge and peaceful assembly of six thousand Madrid students on the University campus had found widespread and very active support amongst teachers and a number of professors. It was perhaps this unprecedented fact that prompted the police into rash and brutal action against the students and staff who marched through the campus in quiet and orderly manner to deliver a petition at the Chancellor's house. Police repression and academic sanctions included the expulsion or suspension of five professors.[35] Simultaneously, the government was bent on reaching some agreement with the students: during the months preceding this latest clash frantic attempts had been made to negotiate with the students' freely elected representatives – who by now ignored SEU officers as if they did not exist or belonged to the secret police. This contradictory policy triggered off further demonstrations, and a few more assemblies took place in the most provincial and isolated universities. Once thirteen out of Spain's fourteen university districts had officially and openly rejected the SEU, international recognition of the illegal unions was forthcoming. The French students' union, the national UNEF, for instance, not content with recognizing them as the only existing students' organizations in Spain, sent its president to take the chair at a free assembly in Barcelona. By the end of February, in cloak-and-dagger conditions, delegates from all over Spain managed to meet in the same town, helped by the whole union apparatus, which had been mobilized to mislead the police as to their meeting place and whereabouts. The Government gave in – that is, conceded as much as its nature could allow: the Decree of 5 April 1965 interred the SEU and created the Professional Students' Association, APE a vague name for a nebulous institution one of whose aims was to avoid conflict with the official 'vertical' union structure.

The students had already gained some victories in their struggle against the *ancien régime* University: moral reprobation of favouritism, academic incompetence and authoritarianism were widespread; the acceptance of representative, free unions was universal; strong demands for a democratization of student recruitment were constantly heard; a significant number of teachers – especially young ones who had been students and led the revolt in 1956 and 1957 – were also unambiguous in opposing the government. The students – as the socialist professor Enrique Tierno said in a celebrated article – had 'discovered complexity': in the postwar, semi-fascist years everything was black or white; one was either a fervent defender of 'eternal Spain' or her deadly enemy, deserving only moral – if not physical – extermination. [36] Now the young generation of students accepted political complexity – pluralism as well as the religious, cultural and national diversity of their country. This, in a sense, expressed a wish – though by no means a nostalgia – for a return to Republican conditions. In this, as in many other ways, the Spanish student disturbances and movements were different (some would say 'behind') similar forms of generational conflict which were then beginning to develop in other universities. Thus the Berkeley campus atmosphere in and after 1964 was totally alien to the Spaniards who, between 1955 and 1965, had been struggling for associational and academic freedoms and cultural progress of a kind unrelated to the millenarian and violent student gauchisme which was then appearing elsewhere. In contrast to these emerging movements – typical of more affluent societies – Spanish students had been struggling for 'classical' liberal goals: free unions, a modern educational system, the development of science and research, and free circulation of ideas. Concomitantly, they had often integrated themselves with political parties with a

194

long republican tradition, thus claiming a political legitimation for their actions which was linked with the kind of legitimation they desired for the general polity: this again contrasted with the isolated political units of young people which were already forming in other Western countries – such as the University of California rebels or the Dutch provos – and which took their stand precisely against such liberal traditions and conceptions of legitimacy.

Most of the institutional features of higher education after 1965 remained untouched however. The presence of the Francoist régime as a structuring factor in the overall system of social inequality of Spain has been decisive for the permanence, over the last phases of its existence, of many aspects of any *ancien régime* university, e.g. obscurantism, professorial feudalism (*caciquismo de cátedra*), black-listing . of staff and students, rigged *oposiciones*. But as demographic, economic, cultural and social class transformations began to gether momentum in the late sixties, a new pattern emerged in the world of higher education in which such elements had to combine with other, emerging trends.

IV Antidemocratic modernization (1965-71)

Social change accelerated in Spain during the sixties in an unprecedented manner: migrations, economic growth, large-scale foreign tourism, industrialization, urbanization, they all took spectacular strides which cannot be discussed here. Nor is this the place to come to grips with the interesting sociological problem of the successful way in which the Francoist system of domination managed to come to terms with such amounts of change over the years since 1959, when sweeping new economic orientations had to be adopted. Yet it is against this background that we must now look into a period of higher education in Spain which is far more complex than the preceding two. In order to get a clearer picture, I shall look first at some important quantitative and cultural transformations, then at the specific educational policies undertaken by the ruling élites, and finally at public criticism of such policies followed by an analysis of the new patterns of conflict generated by the situation.

1. Social transformations and cultural change
1965 represented more than one divide. The government, which by that time had already adopted the outward style of 'non-ideological', even 'apolitical' efficiency characteristic of the latter stages of the régime, still failed to give a thought to serious reform in higher education. Yet, secondary education statistics had been warning for a long time that the intake of higher education was bound to rocket in the coming years. Tables 1-3 clearly show the speed of this

growth, as well as the narrowing gap between Spain and other, significant countries.

To give an idea of the rate of growth of the number of students in higher education suffice it to say that, between 1960 and 1970, while

Table 1. Number of students registered in Spanish State Universities from the academic year 1957-58 to the academic year 1975.

Academic year	No. of students
1957-58	64,281
1958-59	62,985
1959-60	63,787
1960-61	62,105
1961-62	64,010
1962-63	69,377
1963-64	80,074
1964-65	85,148
1965-66	92,983
1966-67	105,370
1967-68	115,590
1968-69	134,945
1969-70	150,094
1975-76	383,000
	(estimated)

Source: Anuario Estadístico de España, 1967 Figures do not include students in Higher Schools of Technology. 1975 estimate, FOESSA'S Informe 1970, Madrid 1970, p. 963.

Table 2. Number of registered students in higher education per 100,000 inhabitants

Year	Students
1863	56
1914	157
1927	176
1932	153
1940	145
1950	195
1955	207
1960	253
1967	463
1970	638
1971	708

From A. de Miguel Manual de Estructura social de España, Madrid: Tecnos, 1974, pp. 476-7.

Table 3. Number of university students per 100,000 inhabitants.

	No. of students in years (*circa*):		
	1950	1960	1970
USA	1,574	1,998	3,698
USSR	597	1,109	1,849
Japan	377	684	1,472
Western Europe	303	487	849
Latin America	112	229	492
Spain	195	253	638

From A. de Miguel *op. cit.*, p. 474.

the population of Spain grew annually by a 0.97 per cent cumulative, the numbers of registered students[37] at the university level did so by a yearly cumulative 9.65 per cent.

It can thus be seen that the student population of Spain, having remained stagnant during the entire first half of the present century has lately entered into a boom of unprecedented proportions which does not parallel but, rather, surpasses, the rates of economic growth and industrialization prevalent in the sixties and seventies.[38]

Economic expansion soon had its effect upon the purchasing power of the lower middle classes who often could now afford to send their children to university, while, as a new and important phenomenon, many students themselves earned some money in a variety of jobs which saw them through their studies.

Meanwhile, during this period, the lower classes continued to be excluded from higher education, and this to a greater extent than elsewhere. By all accounts, class discrimination, or *clasismo*, is recognized in Spain as the worst of evils in higher education.[39] The particular ideology of the régime linked to the traditional Catholic notion of 'charity' though slightly undermined after 1959 created an insurmountable barrier to real social justice.

All the modernizing trends of the period – urbanization, neocapitalism, tourism, greater literacy, travel abroad – soon had serious effects on the outlook of youth. The numbers of students who, in spite of the nature of their early education, began to abandon Catholicism grew steadily. (What is interesting in this context is that indifference, rather than traditional anticlericalism was their new attitude. By the same token, many of those who remained in the Christian or Catholic camp became *cristianos progresistas*, that is committed, active left-wing christians). Secular and hedonistic attitudes made considerable inroads in the students'

197

mentality. Significantly, the numbers of students who preferred a good university education to merely being rich increased. As could be expected, regional differences remained strong, but the overall trend initiated during this period was towards a greater modernity of approach to every aspect of life, religion, sexual mores, social inequality, individual achievement, science. [40] By and large, then, it is necessary to conclude that the ideological victory of the régime in this field, while costly, has been ephemeral: the trends of cultural modernization of which the Republic had been an expression have come to the fore again, and have reached a point of no return.

The data in table 4 quite vividly reflect the changes in expectations and mentality and the new possibilities offered by the new social division of labour in Spain.

Table 4.

(A) *Number of students registered in several faculties*

Academic year	Faculty			
	Economics, politics and Commerce	Law	Medicine	Science
1957-58	4,082	17,847	16 592	10 397
1966-67	16,850	14,781	22 991	21 536
1969-70	20,347	18,270	30 318	31 307

(B) *Number of students registered in Higher Schools of Technology Architecture, Engineering, etc. in State and Private Institutions*

Academic year	No. registered	No. of degrees obtained in that year
1959-60	17,439	709
1966-67	36,038	1,312
1970-71	44,457	–

(C) *Number of students registered in Higher Schools of Fine Art*

Academic year	No. registered	No. of degrees obtained in that year
1957-58	9,138	421
1966-67	3,901	481

Source: Annuario Estadístico de España 1972

Given the growth in numbers over this period it is clear that one can hardly speak of modernization in some fields of study as pure science, where the influx of students just kept ahead of their overall

198

growth in numbers. But other data more than warrant such assumption. One of the most important and – for a Mediterranean society such as Spain – one of the most revealing is the drastic reduction in absolute and relative numbers of law students, to the advantage of economics and commerce. (Not surprisingly there is only one full Faculty of politics in the country.) Another factor of equal weight is the steady growth in the intake of women in the universities. During the first full academic year under the Republic only 6 per cent of the students were women; by 1966-67 the women had risen to 30 per cent of intake, and continued to rise slowly in the early seventies.

In sharp contrast with these encouraging trends there are many features in Spanish higher education which leave much to be desired. Hurried expansion has deteriorated the teacher–student ratio, endemic conflict tends to keep the university in an intermittent state of disruption, classroms are incredibly overcrowded, the standards of teaching and research have deteriorated in some areas (while improving in others, because of the arrival of new, more responsible and critical staff). The word invariably used in Spain to encompass all these problems which bedevil education is *masificación,* a notion which conveys the anonymous, impersonal, bureaucratic and distant treatment of the students under the new conditions.

2. The Government's Response to Change and the Educational Policies of the Opus Dei.
Until 1969 – the year that marked the highest political triumph of the Opus Dei organization – the Spanish Government had not tried to tackle the problems of higher education except by piecemeal and erratic reforms. However, the assumptions of some sociologists of education that there appears to be a high positive correlation between levels of secondary and higher education and intense economic growth or considerable economic development[41] seemed to obtain in Spain before that date. In 1960 – in spite of a decline in the per capita income from $362 in 1958 to $292, owing to financial austerity measures, the economy began to enter the phase of intense growth and development which has characterized it until the early seventies.[42] It was from the same year onwards that the percentage of the budget devoted to educational purposes began to rise, marking a definite change of attitude in the ruling elite towards these matters, as shown in table 5.

Moreover, in 1969, the ministries of Education and Finance announced a joint plan of educational development, to be financed by special taxation and loans from the private sector. This plan was connected with a White Book on Education published earlier in the

199

Table 5. Percentages of Spanish Governmental Budget devoted to education compared, in some years, with per capita income

Year	Percentage	Year	Percentage	Per capita income $
1925	6.04	1960	8.57	292
1930	5.36	1961	9.72	
1935	6.60	1962	9.65	382
1940	5.51	1963	8.92	
1945	4.79	1964	11.41	500
1950	7.86	1965	10.60	583
1955	8.22	1966	12.75	656
		1967	11.74	606
		1968	11.37	676
		1969	13.81	738
		1970	14.47	800
		1975	–	1,500 approx.

Source: for percentages – R. Tamames, *Estructura Económica de España,* Madrid, Guadiana, 1969, p. 721: for incomes – in 1969 US $ corresponding to Spanish 1958 pesetas, *Informe social,* 1968, Asociacion Católica de Dirigentes, Barcelona, 1969, p. 57. For 1969 and 1970 – *España Hoy,* Ministry of Information, Madrid, April 1970, no. 2, p. 78 and *Extebank* Sept. 1970, p. 2 (I $ = 70 pts in 1970).

year by the new Minister of Education, José Luis Villar Palasi. (Professor Villar had been appointed to the Ministry after the deterioration of student and university relations during the year 1967-68, and remained in it after the November 1969 reshuffle which had marked the greatest political victory of his faction, the Opus Dei.) The White Book openly recognized some of the anachronisms of Spain's system of education, the rigidity of the university structure, its neglect of scientific specialization, and even its evident painfully inegalitarian flaws. [43] Critics soon expressed·doubts as to whether the White Book's ambitious plans would ever be realized: on economic grounds alone the sums to be raised were fantastic for the Spanish economy, they said, implying also that they would be assigned to education only if greater political changes came about. Supposing that at least two-thirds of the educational expenses were to be financed by the State, they would represent, in the years to come, no less than 40 per cent of the budget, on the optimistic assumption that the budget would represent at least 15 per cent of the GNP. [44] The scope of such provisions can be appreciated if one considers that, in 1966, Spain was spending only 2.46 per cent of its national income on education – the smallest percentage in Europe. [45] As if to confirm these strictures, the joint plan of the Ministries of Education and Finance – which appeared months later – did not meet such requirements. Yet, it certainly allowed for some much-needed additional expansion in buildings, educational materials, increase in teachers' salaries and student scholarships, and further development of second universities to alleviate great overcrowding in the universities of the two great metropolises. The implementation of these plans has been erratic, and, in the last years subject to stop-and-go policies which are a direct reflection of the factional struggles going on at the top of the power structure. [46]

By and large, increased educational budgets, large fund-raising plans and their immediate effects in the improvement of higher education have accompanied the rise in power and influence of the Opus Dei more closely than the rise and fluctuations of the standard of living of the Spaniards. And, as already mentioned, real expansion has taken place since control over the government was assumed by the Opus. By 1968 other ruling groups and personalities had realized that higher education reform was inevitable. Paradoxically, the first reaction to this, aggravated by the fear that the Paris May events of 1968 would be repeated in Spain, was to launch a new wave of repression in the first months of 1969, when a national state of emergency was called. (The earlier Law of Banditry and Terrorism had conveniently been disinterred the year before to deal with Basque separatism and workers' unrest.) It soon became clear, though, that the mere recrudescence of police-state tactics could not solve the problem. It was at this juncture that the Opus acquired a decisive majority in the Government. Amongst the factors that made this possible one at least is relevant in the present context: the Opus had been claiming for a long time that it alone held the key to the solution of Spain's problems in every field, and especially in higher education, the 'key', of course, being modernization without democracy. (Not even the most dogmatic materialist could have put it more clearly than Sr López Rodó, a member of the Opus and Minister and Commissioner for the Economic Development Plan at the end of 1969: 'The government's number one objective is to reach a per capita income of $1,000; the rest, be it social or political, will in consequence be solved by itself, as a matter of course'.) [47] Even allowing for inflation, the country soon surpassed that mark and nothing was 'solved by itself'. If anything, conflicts kept growing worse in every sphere.

It is not possible to give here an account of the internal characteristic of the Opus Dei religious association, [48] nor to attempt a sociological explanation of why and how it arose in the framework of modern Spanish society. Suffice it to say that one of the decisive factors for its rise to power lies precisely in its attitudes to higher education. From its very beginnings, in pre-Republican Spain days, the Opus emphasized the importance of 'improving and Christianizing the world' through the occupation of 'posts of responsibility' in society by selected individuals. The obvious channel at the time seemed to be the university. As early as 1939 an Opus Dei man was chosen for the 'highest post of responsibility' in the CSIC, as we saw. Later on, studious members of the lay order obtained university chairs in spite of growing, though unpublicized, protests.[49] This was the Opus' chief activity in the area of education until 1947. After that date it began to spread in other directions, first in publishing by controlling the learned journal of the CSIC and founding a publishing house.[50] By 1949 the Opus had managed to establish the 'Studium Generale' of Navarre in Pamplona, a private institution of higher learning. It escaped no one that *studium generale* stood for university and, although private universities were not allowed by law in Spain, the Jesuits and the Augustines already had higher education centres in the country.[51] After some difficulties the Studium Generale became the fully-fledged private University of Navarre in 1962.

In view of later developments, it is doubtful that – as the otherwise acute critic of contemporary Spanish issues, Professor Aranguren, claimed – the Opus was 'withdrawing from the conquest of the state university', as it had already been defeated there.[52] Far from being defeated, the Opus' policy has consisted in a double strategy: the control of the official educational levers *and* the establishment of a flourishing private university, suming that this type of diversification would ensure future survival. Thus by the end of 1969 at least sixty full professors or *catedráticos* in the state universities could be identified as members or ex-members of the Opus. Also many of their chairs were amongst the most strategically important. The numbers of Opus lecturers at the time was presumably much greater.[53] Meanwhile, the Opus' influence in state universities grew uninterruptedly, often indirectly helped by political repression. Thus, when staff are expelled or suspended *en masse* (as in the Barcelona disturbances of 1966[54] or during the 1969 state of emergency) it is always the 'liberal' non-Opus intelligentsia that suffers. The democrats' own chances of occupying 'posts of responsibility' are thus further curtailed, their degree of alienation from their own institutions greatly heightened.

3. The rise of public criticism: its effects

Many passages in the White Book of 1968 and the General Bill for Education (*Ley General de Educación*, 1970) which followed it seem to echo several traditional attacks by the 'opposition' upon the structure of Spanish education. In fact both the White Book and the subsequent reform law appeared after a renewed wave of criticism which was made possible in the sixties by a precarious but sufficiently noticeable period of 'liberalization' in some specific areas of public opinion. Thus Professor Angel Latorre's thoughtfully critical *Universidad y Sociedad* (1964) was followed by other books and studies in the same vein – some of them incorporating belated recantations of Falangism.[55] The influential Christian left-wing *Cuadernos para el diálogo* published special issues devoted to educational problems in 1966 and 1969[56] and has continued its campaign for a more democratic university ever since. From around 1965 onwards some critics managed to express their unorthodox opinions in the dailies.[57] This latter trend continued and some writers, who excelled in the art of criticism within the often erratic rules of censorship, governmental fines and the Press Law.[58] It was also after 1965 that special book series specializing in educational matters began to appear and that some symposia were published coming from a camp definitely hostile to the régime.[59] Even the 'liberal' wing of the political class within the régime tried its hand at 'criticism' of sorts.[60] Opus Dei members, for their part, were quite silent, as they were themselves busy implementing the programme of reform, led by one of their members, the Minister of Education José Luis Villar Palasí. Even a criticism of education based on a critique of capitalism has joined the general expression of discontent, through the work of Ignacio Fernández de Castro. Finally, to complete this picture it should be mentioned that studies and reports were published on the history of Spanish higher education by distinguished republican exiles, such as Alberto Jiménez's *Historia de la Universidad Española* and Pere Bosch Gimpera *La Universitat i Catalunya*,[61] which blantatly showed the extension of the regression occurred with the triumph of the Francoist régime.

Quite revealing of the tenor of criticism expressed from these very different quarters is the fact that economic and budgetary considerations as well as sociological criteria loomed as large as purely ideological or humanistic critiques of the prevailing system. Some of the arguments expressed were old, such as the perennial complaint about the lack of research funds, or the demands for more academic freedom and freedom of opinion. Others were also familiar, though cast in a new form, such as pleas for the democratization of the university. Statistics were produced that

203

showed the overwhelmingly inegalitarian traits of Spanish higher education, accompanied by undisguised attacks on those policies which have aggravated class discrimination, such as the so-called Labour Universities. Grave deficiencies in the staff–student ratios were pointed out: one report in 1970 stated that 26,000 teachers were immediately needed instead of the actual 8,000.[62]

There appeared, in addition, a new body of literature on the specific problems of university life, for instance the low pay – often much less than a pittance – received by assistant lecturers and lecturers, or the absurd system of *oposiciones,* and the corruption of the method whereby a chair is obtained. (Not surprisingly, criticism of this last aspect remains weak to this date – while in theory it ought to be central. Perhaps this has something to do with the fact that many of the critics themselves are *catedráticos*).[63] Another specific problem which now attracts attention is the staggering number of drop-outs in higher education (more than 50 per cent in 1967); reports link this situation with the lack of scholarships and to the general weaknesses of primary and secondary education.[64] On the other hand, the government is directly blamed, for the brain drain which, in some fields, has reached sweeping proportions.[65] On the whole, though, it should be stressed that there have been serious limitations to criticism. Thus, *none* of the publications referred to have come to grips with issues of corruption, political favouritism, police repression, and ideological bias which are essential if what is required is a rational and systematic critique of higher education and research in Spain.

It is clear that since 1968 (with the appointment of José Luis Villar as Minister of Education and Science) important sections of the governing élites have come to accept reform as a necessity and even as desirable. The presence in several bramches of the administration of more competent men than in the past has also helped the authorities' effort to answer all these strictures from the 'opposition' with all the initiative for innovation the régime would allow. But the room for manoeuvre has been very limited, and that has been shown at the highest level, in stop-and-go and highly contradictory policies. Villar, the author of the 1970 General Education Bill, (aiming at 'technocratic' reform, expansion, efficiency, the opening of new universities – even at granting them a token degree of autonomy) was sacked in 1973, when the Opus influence at government level suffered a heavy set-back, and substituted by a hard-liner and simplistic man, Julio Rodríguez, whose preposterous efforts at radically changing the university calendar and high-handed ways soon earned him universal derision and unpopularity. The abrupt death of his protector, Admiral

Carrero (December 1973) preceded his replacement by Cruz Martínez Esteruelas. The latter has taken up the reform programme initiated by Villar, backed in cultural affairs by the serious efforts at liberalization of the censorship made by the minister for information, Pío Cabanillas. (So serious, that Cabanillas, in turn, was summarily dismissed in the autumn of 1974.) It is clear that Sr Martínez Esteruelas' is unable to follow a policy of true liberalization. Thus, next to significant efforts at reform such as the creation of an Open University in Spain in 1973 *Universidad Nacional de Educación a Distancia*,[66] and the Decree of Student Participation (October 1974) there is no sign that the Ministry opposes at all the political and police repression exercised upon university life since it became substantially alienated from the régime in the sixties. The harsh policies of the academic year 1974-75 have been a final confirmation of all this.

4. The diversification of the student world and its politics

The process of modernization of certain structural aspects of Spanish society was accelerated during the sixties. Likewise during that period and very markedly after 1965, the students began to acquire new sets of attitudes. Throughout the history of the régime their political stand of course varied geographically as well as by party, faction or ideology; yet when it came to the crunch, it was nearly always a question of 'them' – the authorities – and 'us'. This dichotomy simplified matters, and as long as the régime lasts will be a source of student unity. Yet, definitely, a diversification of strategies and interests, and a growth in complexity of the student movement has now set in, bringing the Spanish student life much closer to – though not making it identical with – student life elsewhere in the West.

To begin with, internal student solidarity has been broken in some areas by the professionalization of some graduates. Thus, hostility against private schools such as the Opus Dei University of Navarre or the Jesuit Faculty of Chemistry in Barcelona – whose graduates readily found jobs even without official titles – had already been strong. But it was the suppression of *numerus clausus* in the technological schools that triggered off professional strikes and protests – quickly labelled as 'reactionary' by other left-wing students. These protests by students who had managed to get admitted, often after great financial sacrifice by their families, into the *écoles d'élite* marked the beginning of a pattern – the strictly occupational protest – which is now almost as familiar in Spain as in several other industrialized countries. According to some left-wing critics of the situation, this 'professionalization' of protest became then stronger than the tendency 'that subordinates the problems of the University to the great political options'.[67] However, it would be wrong to infer – even if such an assumption were correct – that the future of student unrest will be increasingly restricted to the expression of occupational grievances. A politicization of occupationally-based conflict amongst students is a typical phenomenon of certain modern societies; in some countries, students with an insecure professional future have related their distress to the issues of the wider society as they saw them. It is clear though that the first phase in the diversification of the student movement consisted in its split into two trends, 'the political' or revolutionary one, and the 'professional interests' one, not always exempt from conservatism. In this new context, between 1965 and 1967, the 'professional associations' (APE), with which the government had tried to replace the SEU fell under the attack of the perennially rebellious student body. Simultaneously, a new, well-organized, free union was formed, the SDEU (*Sindicato Democrático de Estudiantes Universitarios*) with the explicit intention of creating a stable organization: the time of the improvised free assemblies had gone, the students proclaimed.[68]

During 1968 and 1969 the SDEU grew in prestige, efficiency and size, under conditions that would have broken its predecessors: special campus plain-clothes police, shock police patrols on the university premises, repeated suspensions of courses, expulsions of students, and arrests and trials before a special court, the *Tribunal de Orden Público*. Two facts are worth mentioning in this period: the intensity of SDEU activity and student unrest in the provincial universities which had been quiet until then, such as Santiago; and the heightened degree of solidarity of the staff with the students. This solidarity itself began to acquire new forms, often linked to events which were by then taking place beyond the Pyrenees. Thus, many 'liberal' professors and teachers accepted open 'critical trials' (*juicios críticos*) from their students and engaged in professional self-criticism. It must be stressed that these developments – soon forbidden by the rector in Madrid – went on in an atmosphere of civility which contrasted with similar exercises elsewhere; but then the situation was also different in Spain. The proclamation of the state of emergency in January 1969 ended all this.

It did not, however, end the further process of political diversification of the student body, that is, the multiplication of its active minorities. The first new element, predictably enough, was the emergence of *gauchiste* groups which soon and inevitably collided with the SDEU – temporarily destroying it as a national union – and with parties supporting traditional 'republican legitimacy'. The *gauchistes* – of either Maoist, Trotskyist, or anarchist extraction – began to pose problems not altogether dissimilar to those created in less dictatorial contexts. However, left-wing FLP members or FLP sympathizers continued to carry weight, in spite of the FLP's endemic crises and eventual demise and so did, of course, the CP. Yet the CP has remained under attack from the left to this day because of its already mentioned conservatism, and as a result has suffered the same loss of prestige amongst wide sectors of the politizised student body as in other European countries.[69] Yet the Communist Party has managed to maintain a high level of recruitment and has been highly skilled in the control of student representative bodies. Likewise, it has managed to exert some fascination for other organizations, such as *Bandera Roja* (influential in the early seventies, first split and then diluted into the CP in 1974) whose policies have been as much geared against the common enemy as oriented towards the CP. Further politization has meant the revival of traditional social democratic parties (PSOE) in the universities as well as new ones such as socialist parties in the Catalan Countries with an independentist slant, such as the PSAN, *Partit Socialista d'Alliberament Nacional*. In the Basque country the existence of guerilla activities by the ETA – itself not entirely unconnected with the student world, especially in its political and cultural branches – has created a situation entirely different from that prevalent in Valencia and Barcelona.

Common cause with the workers, which had been an ideal since 1955 finally became a reality in 1962. Yet, be it because of fairly effective police action or because of serious workers' distrust of the students as children of the privileged, durable contact and common action have tended to be limited to small groups of intensely active students. This, once again, may look like a situation not unfamiliar in, say, London or Berlin; however, it can be asserted that because of both the dictatorship and the still relatively 'backward' socio-economic structure of the country, the alliance between the students' and the workers' own clandestine organizations is anything but utopian in Spain as, for instance, the Madrid May Day demonstrations of 1968 clearly showed. Acts and declarations of mutual solidarity have become normal even since.

V Higher Education in Crisis (1971-75)

Generational change, political immobilism, an uneven pattern of economic growth, and considerable changes in the culture and mentality of the younger people and the new staff, all combined to create a situation of permanent active dissent in the late sixties. The publication of the Educational Reform Bill and the physical expansion and multiplication of Universities (23 state-run by 1975 in contrast with the traditional 12 of the forties and fifties) could have been a welcome development had it not been accompanied by other, rather sordid, 'reforms' such as the introduction in 1968 of the hated *policía universitaria,* or campus police, on a permanent basis. This, coupled with the constant threats (or actual policies) of further toughness by the government has brought much university life to a state of permanent disorder.[70] It would be inappropriate to record here the countless periods during which institutions in higher education have been closed down by the authorities. By 1971 the situation became endemic and the government's options in front of the perennial *problema universitario* were very limited. The 'hawks' were of the opinion that the only solution was to encapsulate the university world, as it were, and isolate the rest of the society from its contagion. (The layout of some campuses, by the way, seems to respond to this attitude; and the single gate and the enclosures which surround the autonomous University at Madrid have certainly been built on strategic principles.) By contrast, the more intelligent members of the ruling élites realized, from the start, that such policies were self-defeating in a society which was by now too modern to allow itself the luxury of separating its students from the outer world. The October 1975 decree of student participation partly responded to these structural needs of the new society as seen by the more liberal wing of the power élite. Yet, it excluded any of the basic political freedoms enjoyed by student unions in other European countries and was declared to be of a provisional character. Besides, as a student delegate pointed out at the time, there has always been student representation (referring to the SDEU) and *de facto* negotiation between authorities and students through their 'illegal' representatives. Thus the 1974 participation decree only recognized an already existing situation.[71]

Circa 1971, then, a new pattern or period began to emerge. It was a period which, to put in a nutshell, could be defined as that phase in the history of the Francoist university in which the pace of official reform could in no way catch up with the pace of internal change in higher education. In the remaining section of this chapter I shall try to point out some of the additional characteristics which are important in order to comprehend what has happened and how critical the situation really has become during the last few years of the régime.

(1) The new culture of the universities
The students of 1956 and 1957 were practically alone in an

208

atmosphere of silent antagonism and vocal disapproval by their fearful middle-class parents at home. Although some of them discovered marxism, existentialism and other theories and ideologies, those who did so were a small minority. Such 'alternative' ideologies, by contrast, penetrated the Spanish campuses like a great, unofficial flood in the sixties. By that time, also, younger members of staff – some of them ex-student dissidents – were spreading these 'alternative' outlooks, which by the early seventies were firmly established on the campuses. Analytic philosophy, marxology, modern sociology, linguistics, symbolic logic, socialist economics, to mention only a few trends in the humanities and the social sciences, have made important inroads in the world of higher learning. Outstanding academic journals such as *Teorema* and *Arguments* (Valencia) *Sistema* (Madrid) *Papers* and *Recerques* (Barcelona), fully testify to this claim. Similarly, annual meeting such as the *Conferencia Nacional de Filósofos Jóvenes* and the influential Summer University in Prada (in French-administered Catalonia) are examples of significant extra-mural activities which were not precisely foreseen by the Ministry of Education. [72]

This sketchy picture would not be complete without reference to the great importance marxism (in all its varieties) has acquired among the student population. The demise of *cristianismo progresista,* so important in the sixties, was followed by a great interest in psychoanalysis (still alive) and marxism and revolutionary thought generally. Francoism, by singling out marxism as *the* enemy ideology to what 'eternal Spain' meant and the régime was, has had no small influence in the vast success of marxism as an ideology among students and an important sector of the younger staff. How deep and how serious this marxism is, is another matter which would now be premature to discuss.

(2) The new staff
When, in 1965, several full professors overtly took the side of the student democratic movement it could have looked as if finally the much-purged and controlled members of staff were beginning to join it. But that did not occur. There were, from then on, more and more 'liberal' professors and lecturers but their behaviour tended to be very timid. The *oposición* system for obtaining chairs, which demands subservience and obedience for years before a chair is ever won, old habits and economic reasons in a still not all-too-rich society, help explain the shyness and undemocratic behaviour of the professorial staff – let alone other obvious factors such as their frequent membership of the ACPN or the Opus, which need not be discussed again. The fact is, though, that the spectacular expansion of higher

209

education and its needs together with generational change have created a new layer of staff (*agregados* and *adjuntos*) of non-professorial status (*profesores no numerarios,* or PNNs) with a different mentality, a more demanding attitude towards scholarship, much more politically committed, and very much aware of their own rights. The rise to prominence of the PNNs cannot easily be exaggerated. They have organized themselves in free assemblies and unions throughout the country, and through their contacts in the world of journalism, the professions and the university itself they have practically become the spearhead of the reform movement. Thus, the presence and activity of the PNNs has considerably changed the traditional picture in every conceivable way. PNN staff often enjoy greater prestige than old-fashioned and authoritarian full professors, they often produce scholarship and research which puts to shame that of the establishment and, above all, they are a serious and grave nuisance to a government élite which is unwilling and frightened of change.

Now, I do not want to convey a rosy picture of the new generation of teachers, for indeed there are serious flaws in the situation. For one thing, in the fields of scientific research the brain drain is of enormous proportions and the amount of frustration and waste that has gone on since 1939 to this day cannot be easily described. Then, the attractions of subservient and sycophantic behaviour and endless intrigue at the expense of honest teaching and good research are still very great and many are those who succomb to their temptations. Finally, the authorities have not been entirely idle *vis-à-vis* the troublesome PNN staff: in 1972 each one of them received a threatening letter forbidding him or her to attend staff assemblies under menace of expulsion. Certificates of 'good conduct' and 'loyalty to the Francoist Movement' have also been demanded. Mass expulsions and suspensions of PNNs, countless non-renewal of contracts, the systematic denial of tenure, and actual expulsions are everyday occurrences which now often elicit a vigorous response among staff and their students. The university has ceased to be tame. In this, the PNNs – and other related groups such as medical interns in Faculties of Medicine – have shown a kind of behaviour which is similar to that of the Professional Colleges – the lawyers' Bar Association, the Colleges of Architects, the Engineering Association, the Journalists' Association – which have become since the early seventies, foci of democratization and often open challenge to the arbitrary and high-handed rule of the régime.

(3) The future of higher education in Spain
The university has thus escaped the tight control of the authorities in
210

several important senses – though by no means as regards funds and independence from police interference and the active meddling in its affairs of the 'special jurisdiction' of the Public Order courts. In spite of the latter, and under the circumstances, it is inevitable that the institutions of higher education and learning in Spain should become centres of political activity and agitation, for normal political life is even more thwarted outside their gates. Reforms carried out after 1971 (legislation of student representation, introduction of departmental structures alongside traditional chairs, larger grants for research and materials, etc.) may not have had any effect in neutralizing the universities: rising expectations, generational changes, new political ambitions, ideological change, and so many other factors come into play that nothing short of a fundamental change in the nature of the polity may put an end to this *impasse*. This is clear from the fact that the structural constraints suffered by the Francoist ministry of Education and Science are simply unsurmountable. Its head, Sr Martínez Esteruelas, after the usual promises of liberalization and about the introduction of a 'new look', acted with characteristic brutality when, in early February 1975, he closed down the four Faculties of the University of Valladolid for the rest of the academic year – as its members dared to strike in protest for the arbitrary detention of some colleagues. Even the alleged reform against *clasismo,* an essential part of the 'Villar reform' programme was later counterbalanced by what many see as an insidious renewal of the *numerus clausus* policy, under the misleading name of 'selectivity'.[73] The democratic challenge from the university goes on relentlessly, however. The General Assembly of staff and students at the Autonomous University of Barcelona (March 1975) in which civil rights, expulsion of the campus police, national minority rights and greater facilities for research and education were demanded might have been followed by the usual reaction, but points in the direction of an even greater divorce between the university, as a whole, and the régime. It is in the light of these developments that every observer will have to conclude that there is not much hope for higher education and science under the present régime.[74] It is obvious, however, that the centrality of the university in the structure of any modern society, together with the tradition of freedom and democratic struggle which has characterized key sectors of the academic world ever since the Civil War was lost, will assure that it plays a continued and decisive role in the building of a freer and more humane Spain.[75]

211

9

Basque Revolutionary
Separatism: ETA

JOHN LLEWELYN HOLLYMAN

The struggle of the Basque nation for its freedom has been most effectively led in the last fifteen years by the revolutionary movement known as ETA[1] which had the attention of the world's press when in 1970 the military tribunals held in Burgos brought them to trial. The sixteen men who were sentenced to terms of imprisonment of up to thirty years represented not only the vanguard of their own national movement, but the most spectacular form of opposition to the Francoist state. In 1970, ETA had been in existence for a decade asserting its rights against the state; it had been punished harshly for its early attempts at direct action, and Burgos marked the most publicized stage in the persistent struggle. It was, however, only to be expected that eventually the activities of ETA would be directed more against the centre of the Francoist political machine. And in fact, in December, 1973, the most dramatic and effective plan of direct action was carried out on the morning of 20 December when the official limousine bearing the President of the Government, Luis Carrero Blanco, from the church of San Francisco de Borja in the Calle Serrano, Madrid, where he had just heard mass, was blown up in the street, the force of the blast carrying the car above the level of the neighbouring buildings and over the roof of the church courtyard on to a balcony. Carrero Blanco's chauffeur and bodyguard died instantly and the Prime Minister died later in hospital. The commando group of ETA responsible for the assassination escaped without trace after successfully completing what was later revealed as 'Operación Ogro'.[2]

In a number of ways this act was uncharacteristic of ETA since it took place outside Euskadi, was directed at a politician rather than at local agents of state repression such as the Guardia Civil, and in subsequent explanations of its conception, appears to have stemmed from almost accidental information. Furthermore, the hooded men who at a press conference near Bordeaux on 28 December claimed responsibility for the operation were thought by some to have been decoys for the real killers, whom speculation singled out as anarchists, extreme Left revolutionaries, or connected with the defendants in the 'proceso 1001' of ten members of the Comisiones Obreras held in Madrid only a short time after the bomb-blast. The idea was even suggested of 'agents provocateurs' of the Right acting in an attempt to justify a purge of the opposition.[3] Though it is true that no less than four Spanish Prime Ministers have been assassinated, two of them by anarchists, Anarchist responsibility in this case was unlikely and speculation was based on an exaggerated past reputation.[4] Having claimed responsibility, ETA has proved beyond any doubt that its commandoes eliminated Carrero. But more important than this for all who are involved in opposition to Franco is that the act was done. It removed the Caudillo's successor, the right-hand man in his own image who was to carry on Francoism after Franco, and it sharpened the crisis within the ruling oligarchy. Having survived for so long, the inherent contradictions within the régime seemed to well up and threaten to overcome it, though externally matters seemed to pass without undue concern.[5] Having suffered a repression of both nationality and class, the Basque people had struck back in the name of freedom through ETA to re-assert the independent spirit of the ancient Basque nation, Euskadi, against the Franco régime.

The history of the Basque nation with its distinctive cultural and social identity is one that has survived the division and incorporation into the Spanish and French states in the eighteenth and nineteenth centuries. Throughout the last two hundred years the Basque provinces have all been distinguishable by the conservation of their language, which had defied classification, and the independence of their character, which is unwilling to submit to the narrow confines imposed by the governments of France and Spain. Like many of the secessionist movements in modern times that have failed to achieve their goals, there is a breadth of outlook that unwelcome impositions and outright oppression have been unable to eliminate.[6]

The nationalist movement, the PNV (Partido Nacionalista Vasco) was founded by Sabino de Arana in the last quarter of the nineteenth century and resembled closely the Carlist movement in everything except the exclusiveness of its uncompromisingly Basque nature.[7] Insisiting on the ethnic unity of the people of the Basque territories, Sabino clearly laid much importance on their language culture and religion as the basis of their awareness of nationality and met with hostility not only from the Spanish Socialist Party, the

PSOE, and its affiliated union, the UGT, to which many of the Basque working class belonged, but also from eminent Basques like Baroja and Unamuno, who described nationalism in Euskadi as an 'absurd racial virginity', influenced no doubt by the undoubtedly racial overtones of much of the PNV's philosophy.[8] But the PSOE went too far in its contemptuous dismissal of nationalism and failed to judge the susceptibilities of its Basque members. Even the Communist leader La Pasionaria believed that the Socialists were too far removed from Basque sympathy and with Astigarrabia she created the Partido Comunista Vasco, a subordinate northern branch of the PCE, as an identifiably Basque left-wing party. Sabino de Arana had recognized Basque nationality and had created the movement which exists today as the traditional vehicle of its expression, the PNV. What La Pasionaria recognized was that not only nationalist aspirations but also the need for social justice had to be met if any mass movement in Euskadi was to be successful. Then, as now, opposition to the capitalist system was axiomatic to the Basque worker, but Spanish (Castilian) centralist capitalism was doubly condemned. In discussing the early philosophical arguments within ETA the question arises over which instinct, that of class or nationality, is more important or natural, or whether it is true that the two are not mutually exclusive and that the error lies in being unable to accept the fact of national feeling despite the absence of a politically defined national entity.

What are the factors which make the Basque nation distinct and which have helped to solidify a social and cultural awareness into the nationalism which we know today? In the first place, the apparently paradoxical situation arising from the high income per capita pertaining in Vizcaya and Guipúzcoa allied to a feeling of resentment by these Basques that they are subsidizing the rest of the State, is singled out by one commentator as important.[9] Socially more progressive and culturally often more advanced than their equivalents in Castle and elsewhere, the Basques pay more taxes than their region receives in benefits from the central government. As an employer of migrant southern labour, together with Cataluña, the Basque country is obviously a vital part of the Spanish state's economic structure. But out of the purely economic facts emerge less tangible but probably more real issues which over the years turn the Basque mentality even more stubbornly against the central government and in support of their own national identity. There is the myth of the hard-working Basque being a materialist in the eyes of the non-Basque, and that of the Castilian as lazy and undeserving. There is the important fact of the local administrative machinery in the Basque country being run by non-Basques, the police system, the judiciary and the wide range of official local matters dealt with by people without a knowledge of the Basque language and almost certainly out of sympathy with even Basque cultural aspirations.

The evident superiority of the Basque country compared with large areas of Spain-and-Cataluña is seen by Jean-Paul Sartre as no argument against his view of Euskadi as having the relationship with Spain of a colony, for it is evident that it is the central government which benefits and therefore exploits its relationship with its rich northern territory.[10] Add to this the postwar vendetta against the language, the drafting into Euskadi of more and more non-Basques who dilute the cultural and linguistic foundations that have seen some revival in recent decades, and the Basque finds it easy to see himself persecuted because he is Basque and for no other apparent reason.

The most immediately evident fact which distinguishes the Basque is his language, and this vital point is closely linked to the political issue of nationalist aspirations that we shall examine in following the growth of ETA. In the industrial regions of the Basque country the frictions mentioned above are exacerbated by the high levels of political awareness among the people who in other parts of the peninsula are not yet at more than a superficial degree of politicization. The Cortes voting of 1971 for example produced a turn-out of only 33 per cent in Vizcaya and only 26 per cent in San Sebastián which is more an indication of active repudiation than of apathy since both areas demonstrate a high level of involvement in local affairs.[11]

At this point the language issue and the political awareness of the Basques may be seen as inter-linked. The independent school movement known as the 'ikastolas' now provides education in Basque for about 25,000 children who would otherwise be without any chance of an education in their own tongue during their most formative years. The banning of the language under the new Franco régime not only silenced the public cultural life of the Euskadi of the forties and fifties but ensured that the new generation would be unable to speak their language through the fear of their parents, who obviously spoke nothing but Spanish for the future 'good' of their children.

Immigration of Spanish-only speakers added to the heavy bias against Basque until the semi-clandestine movement of the 'ikastolas' (halls of teaching) began in private homes in the late fifties. As it grew, the state of the Spanish educational system and the attitude of the Basque clergy both aided the growth of the movement, since the former meant that a private educational institution could easily get off the ground and be aided by the local church as it grew. Any gathering of children in a church hall could be described as a catechism class. The authorities are aware of the movement and the reason for its existence; their tolerance has even extended to their providing in Guipúzcoa in 1973 no less than 300 state nursery schools providing the odd lesson of Basque but nothing in the language. This move has been greeted with suspicion as a sop to local feeling, and the new schools are finding it hard to provide teachers, who would prefer to accept less money and worse conditions in order to work in the 'ikastolas', now providing education up to the age of 14. On their part, and on the part of the parents, the decision to involve children in a Basque educational system that clearly distinguishes between 'our country' and Spain is more and more a political one. Much of the current running of the ikastolas is criticized for having diverged from its popular roots and conformed to the 'bourgeois' regulations of the Spanish education system. [12]

Of the 2 million 300 thousand Basques, today about $\frac{1}{2}$ million speak the language and are to be found in southern Euskadi. There is no doubt that amongst these people alone the link between the language and a political stance is becoming clearer. The Basque clergy, traditionally close to their people at grass roots level can be seen as made up of three groups; pro-Franco older clergy, a large group of moderates who support reforms such as the use of Basque in churches, and a highly radicalized group of young priests who have seen their group in prison, involved in sit-ins, demonstrations and active collaboration with the ETA. In March 1974, the storm over the pastoral letter of Mgr Añoveros, [13] Bishop of Bilbao, was ironic in that his original appointment was opposed by 196 priests who felt that their then bishop, Mgr Cirarda, was being replaced for his sympathetic pro-Basque views by a conservative outsider. The bishop of Pamplona in 1971 denounced the results of torture which he had seen, and therefore it is no longer certain that the hierarchy retain their conservative view. It is for this reason that one may now speak of the whole Basque church, despite evident internal disagreements, as another source of opposition to Franco from a nationalist standpoint.

Just as the Church has progressed in its social attitudes in Spain and above all in the Basque country, so the Catholic nationalists of the PNV have modified their centre-right views. They called a general strike in the Basque country in 1947 of about 100,000 workers, organized by their trade union wing. Despite their belief in the legitimacy of the Basque government of 1936 they have recognized the reality of contemporary life under Franco and are prepared to give financial aid to ETA with whom they maintain close links. There is a strong belief among them that after Franco they will again have a role to play in Basque politics; until then ETA serves to keep the message of nationalism clear in everyone's mind. ETA regards the PNV as being out of touch and too right-wing to be able to deal competently with any revolutionary working-class upheavals in the Basque country; for example, the reaction of the PNV leader, Jesús María de Leizaola, to Carrero Blanco's death, was initially one of disbelief that such an act could have been committed by any Basque.

In its origins, ETA is wedded to the ethos of action and violence as opposed to long-term political evolution and steady forward planning. It began as a society of Bilbao students who met in 1952 to crystallize their unformed yet deeply felt thoughts about their nation. A magazine emerged from their study groups and discussions, Called *Ekin* (Action) and as a result the group adopted the same name. These university students, (almost by definition middle class) had undergone the process of disillusionment with traditional nationalist thinking and organization in the face of the impotence of the Basque country against the Franco government.

Apart from the 1947 strike already mentioned and a further attempt at action in 1951 they saw the collapse of organized opposition. From 1952 to 1956, *Ekin* organized secret cells to inculcate the intellectual aims of their group and to solidify the basis of a secret Basque movement. From 1954 until 1957 the PNV and the *Ekin* crossed each other's paths with the PNV's youth group emerging as an area of common ground and dispute for loyalty. A compromise was reached when after demands from the PNV, *Ekin* was merged with the youth group, Euzko-Gastedi (EGI), into a joint youth organization. Such an alliance proved unsuccessful in view of the deep roots of incompatibility, and after a year the young men of *Ekin* were driven away by the image and the de facto attitude of a party of old men fossilized into out of date policies and outlook. Thus it was that in 1959 the first ETA (Euskadi Ta Askatasuna – Basque Homeland and Liberty) was formed. Until the break, *Ekin* had seen itself as a vaguely Christian Democratic movement, but the new ETA was nationalist, democratic and a-confessional, very much the home of young, flexible views as yet unconfirmed into set ideologies but with a clear idea of action and radical nationalism. Its propaganda sheets and pamphlets at this period such as *Zutik, Zabaldu, Zutik-Berriak* and their direct action – the placing of the Basque flag and wall daubing – caused little worry to the authorities, but then in 1960 both EGI and ETA members were arrested in Vizcaya and Guipúzcoa, traditionally the strongest areas of national awareness. The coincidence of the arrests of these two

217

groups' members is some indication both of the relatively restrained policy of ETA then and the eventual strength of the attraction for EGI of ETA, the former merging with the latter in 1972. From 1960 onwards, the development of ETA ideologically is reflected in the regularly held assemblies and the growth of acts of violence against property in the first instance and then individuals.

The first such act was the attempt to derail a train carrying Falangists to San Sebastián for the annual 18 July celebrations. The attempt is described by one anonymous leader as being arranged to ensure that as little damage to life as possible was caused; but not one of the trains passing the selected spot was derailed.[14] Nevertheless, the attempt was evident to the police who arrested over 100 people and began their use of torture for the first time against the ETA. Some of the detainees were found guilty and sentenced to periods of 15 and 20 years in prison, others escaped into exile while on parole and the organization suffered heavily because of the lack of coordination among its independent cadres from the top:

In May, 1962, therefore, the first Assembly was held north of the Pyrenees. It was evident at this Assembly that the youthful leadership of the new movement had almost unwittingly developed into a political group from beginnings which were culturally inspired in the broadest sense and which had therefore not felt the urgency to organize, establish a programme, or formulate a clear ideology. During the course of the Assembly, principles were established which were printed and distributed in the time-honoured underground fashion to the extent of 30,000 copies, a large distribution for a group so small in numbers. In these principles, ETA defined itself as a revolutionary Basque movement of national liberation with the objectives of both national liberation (the freedom of Euskadi from the domination of Spain) and social liberation (the entry into possession of their full social freedoms and responsibilities as citizens) for the Basques. The tone of the Assembly was predominantly that of the individual voice and its argument as against a concerted line on any abstract theory, but approval was expressed for the struggles of the anti-imperialists in Vietnam and Algeria and the position of Cuba where the anti-imperialism combined with the social revolution of Castro's programme provoked admiration.

Far as these places were geographically and socially from their own relatively advanced society, the pattern of exploitation was clearly discernible in all of them; the necessity to first become a nation before achieving internationalism was also an obvious corollary to their attitude. The second Assembly held in March 1963

218

set about the creation of international delegations of ETA in Europe and South America but six months later a further large scale series of arrests seriously disrupted lines of communication within the movement, particularly in Vizcaya. The organizing committee acted provisionally in consequence to establish permanent organizers, the restructuring of the zones of the movement, a massive campaign directed at the people through propaganda and a reaffirmation of the revolutionary principles established at the first Assembly. These provisional arrangements met with the approval of the third Assembly and formally adopted at their publication in a clandestine manifesto called 'Insurrection in Euskadi'. [15] Though the insitution of the full-time 'liberados' as area commanders was an effective move, the revolutionary war proposed in the pamphlet bore little relation to objective reality. It was during the period around the third Assembly that a vital growth of support was experienced from non-students in the Basque country – petty bourgeoisie and peasants who certainly constituted different social strata from the founding group and thereby demonstrated to a limited extent that ETA was a popular movement but by no means supported and guided by the working class. What this new support showed was that the old Ekin's break with the PNV was one caused by differences over the PNV's bourgeois conception of nationalism which was far from the rapidly evolving anti-imperialism and anti-capitalism of the new ETA. To some extent, this orientation was rationalized in a letter (the 'Carta a los intelectuales') issued by the fourth Assembly to all supporters which said in substance that the national and social problems of Euskadi (the class freedom of the peoples of a free Basque nation) were two abstractions out of the one reality: namely the development of capitalism in Euskadi. The only answer capable of solving that real problem was a single and equally realistic one that encapsulated the double problem. Such a solution required the recognition of a simple fact: that Euskadi was a nation and that its people could be mobilized to struggle against their oppressors. It was this reasoning which led ETA to declare its solidarity with other colonial nations and the parties which headed their drives to freedom, the Algerian FLN and Castro's Cuba. [16]

In a clandestine organization like ETA with its movements made difficult and its organization based on the small unit, constantly moving and dependent on sporadic financial and physical aid, the influence and importance of individuals becomes disproportionately great. Within ETA the leadership finds itself hampered by the Pyrenees that separate the repressive police actions of the Spanish state in Euskadi south from the relative freedom of Euskadi north. When forced into 'exile' in Euskadi north or in Belgium and other countries, individual leaders have tended not only to re-establish themselves after a period but also to initiate new ideological divergences from the internal leadership precisely because of their lack of contact with daily events in the anti-Franco struggle. Conversely, after arrests, forced flight and voluntary exile among an established leadership, new leaders emerge within Euskadi south who can diverge radically through inexperience, outside pressures or opportunism from the previously held line. This happened in the period before the fifth Assembly in 1966 when the influence of the Basque section of the FLP (Frente de Liberacion Popular) called ESBA, (Eusko Sozialisten Batasuna) which then tended to Trotskyism, had considerable influence on individual members of the internal leadership, then to be found in the hands of the Political office. Being in a position to propagate new political ideas, ESBA via the Political office soon commanded some power. When it was realized that the leadership faction was now considering postponing the national interests of Euskadi until the achievement of a socialist society, the grass roots and exiled leaders expelled them from ETA in December 1966 during the first session of the fifth Assembly.

This dispute had been preceded by a split from ETA led by Zumalde over excessive FLP influence and a lack of preparation for the projected development of activism, already becoming regular and successful. But the grass roots opposition to the Political office leadership is interpreted by commentators in different ways since at the centre of the split was the question of the degree of marxism and the nature of the socialism ETA members were aiming for.[17] Some describe the inner tensions leading the 'bourgeois' leadership to face the fact that a more radical socialist policy based on a rigorous examination of ideology was bound to come, and that they as bourgeoisie were the main stumbling block to the adherence of the working class.[18] Great emphasis is placed by these critics on the fact that since the origins of the modern ETA are bourgeois, sprung from the PNV and therefore tied irreversibly to their outworn attitudes and their class allegiance, it is inevitable that the leadership of ETA should not have understood the true nature of the struggle which they had begun. This view implies that ideology cannot adjust to the fundamental barrier of class origin and that proletarian strength is the only basis for the success of a revolutionary change; it gives no credit to the PNV as a bourgeois democratic paty in the traditional mould adhering to a legally granted Statute of autonomy and using the most obvious means open to it at the time to achieve its aims, as was the case also in Cataluña. It also ignores the fact that while a purely cultural upsurge in the Basque country might well have been prosecuted by the bourgeoisie, as a beginning to a national awakening it could parallel the course of events in Cataluña in the last century and grow into a popular political movement. Furthermore it crushes any hope that national feeling alone can be a stronger and more deeply rooted force to change the national status of Euskadi than a class solidarity that uses ideologies that historically have been often fundamentally modified to suit individual national circumstances. A further consideration must be added: ETA was loosely organised in its beginnings and therefore capable of pressure from many quarters. It started without a rigid ideology and therefore borrowed and adapted policies according to the pressure of events and the needs of its expanding membership – that is, the majority counsel seen in a democratic way.

We have already seen some of the pressures existing in the Basque country that have led to the formation of a nationalist feeling and the sectors of the population where support might be reasonably relied on to emerge for nationalism in general and ETA in particular. But what is difficult to assess is the extent to which ETA may be expected to rely on actual organizations in Euskadi and how far these organizations aid the movement. The clandestinity of the opposition means that figures and trends are even more difficult than usual to discern. Two organizations outside ETA and the PNV are specifically Basque in orientation while a third is Basque by geographical accident. This group is of course the Comisiones Obreras who were formed in Vizcaya and Navarra in about 1962 and suffered repression in 1964. While the CCOO in Navarra are still Communist dominated, in Vizcaya a Basquist element was introduced with the infiltration of ETA's Frente Obrero in 1967, until in 1968 the strikes in the Bilbao area can be definitely ascribed to the ETA's worker front (see below). The Vizcaya Comisiones are strongly influenced by the Basque interest. Of the other two organizations, the STV or ELA (Eusko Langillen Alkartasuna) and its influence are more difficult to assess since it is divided into a party and a union wing. The party wing, known as the MSE or Movimiento Socialista de Euskadi, is in favour of a broad patriotic front in Euskadi with the Basque working class being politically independent and ready to collaborate with the bourgeoisie. Such a front and the freedom envisaged is not possible without the collaboration of these two groups in the initial stages, but the working class is seen as continuing to aim for change in Euskadi towards a socialist democratic society. It stands for the immediate autonomy of Euskadi as a first step before any anti-Franco alliance with the Spanish democratic anti-Francoists. Real Basque power must be parallel with any democratic change in the Madrid power

221

structure. The union wing follows a line of provisional action within the pursuit of the national and social freedom of Euskadi. With the UGT and the CNT it is in the Alianza Sindical de Euskadi and a member of the International Free Trade Unions Organization. It is democratic in outlook and independent of all parties but committed to the cooperation of all patriotic forces in a Frente Vasco. But it makes it clear that it will not countenance the UGT or the CNT participating in a Frente Nacional Vasco and it is this factor which makes it exclusively Basque in its outlook. The third organization, the Comisión Obrera Provisional de Guipúzcoa (COPG) was a group which had as its primary aims the unity of the Basque workers to achieve Basque liberation and thereby their freedom from exploitation. In its declaration of principle it underlined the independence of the COPG from all other Comisiones outside Euskadi, its right to participate equally with other workers in the Peninsula in the struggle for freedom and the independent equality of its organization with all other similar movements. It also stated that anyone who sells his labour in Euskadi is a member of the Basque working class. Such is its stance that it rebuked the call of the Madrid CCOO in 1967 for a 'national' assembly, reiterating its own independence and equality with the *international* working classes comprised within the Iberian peninsula. It was disbanded late in 1967.

Such ideological variations have in common the insistence on the Basque homeland and freedom first, as a consequence of which class freedom is envisaged as developing within its newly gained democratic boundaries. For such a state of affairs to exist, Francoism must cease to exist, clearly. But if Francoism disappeared tomorrow, their question remains – what is the certainty that Basque aspirations would be listened to and acted on under a new style of government? [19] Only the Basque people making an independent decision can see to it that they are governed as they wish. Any movement using the vehicle of Basque nationalism to postulate different ends, however laudable, does not in the long term serve Basque interests, but those of the rest of Spain. The proof of this seems to lie in the fact that the one government of this century willing to concede even the minimum measure of autonomy did so only to secure its own survival, not that of the Basque people whom it distrusted for its close adherence to the Church, a deeply held belief among broad sectors of Basque society. On the whole therefore only a broad guess at the kind of support available to ETA can be made, but the general conclusion that can be reached is that support for a move that will bring independence for Euskadi will find favour. Active support is another matter that depends on the attitude felt towards violent direct action and the negative results of it in the shape of violent reprisal and the hardening of official attitudes towards an area that essentially needs time to consolidate and expand its cultural and social identity and achieve as a result a political awareness. So not only is there doubt over the support for violent action but also deep disagreement over the effects of such action. Inside ETA this split has shown itself too.

After the December 1966 meeting of the fifth Assembly, at which the 'españolista' line of class solidarity along socialist lines for the whole of the Spanish working class and not just Euskadi was put forward, a second session of the Assembly was held in March 1967 at which revolutionary principles of nationalism were reaffirmed, followed by a structural reform of the movement. The ideological results of the second session were that the view emerged of Euskadi suffering a unique double repression under Franco compared with other parts of the Peninsula. The Basque proletariat was seen as suffering at once a class and a national repression; ETA brings into relief the principles of proletarian internationalism and its application to the Spanish and Basque peoples. In this respect, therefore, ETA departs even further from the PNV's philosophical/idealist theories and its legalist/reformist tactics. It also departs from the 'españolista' left wing trend which is anti-Basque because it believes that concern for the nation is a bourgeois conception that ignores what it regards as the real issues of social and class injustice in Euskadi and everywhere else in the peninsula. In other words the existence of a Basque nation is not for them even a primary concern but the existence of an oppressed working class is.

The fifth Assembly proclaimed ETA a Basque socialist movement of national liberation, the notion was formulated of a Pueblo Trabajador Vasco and the insistence was made on the dual function contained within the single reality of the Basque worker – his exploitation as a worker and his oppression as a Basque, both carried out by the Spanish State. This defence of the worker of Basque country – irrespective of whether he be an immigrant or native – marks a significant break with previous Basque nationalist traditions, which tended to be extremely hostile towards the *Maketon*, as non-Basques were known. The notion of a Pueblo Trabajador Vasco is one conceived of by the Frente Político, one of four fronts into which ETA is divided.[20] Its function is to link together all political tendencies not of the Right into a Frente Nacional which eventually assumes overall leadership. The Frente Obrero is for the welding together of the working class and leading it into the national movement. The Frente Cultural works for the

223

struggle against the destruction of Basque culture by the Spanish State; and the Frente Militar has the role of breaking the backbone of the régime by armed violence and direct action designed to demonstrate its own superiority in its ability to combat large troop and police mobilization by guerrilla tactics and causing disruption through its attacks on targets of its own choosing. The whole operation is sustained by the proceeds of bank robberies, the extension of propaganda and the consolidation of support among the people. As mentioned above, while active involvement in ETA is a dangerous and important step to take, clearly passive support for activists is easily found and willingly given. One has only to remember the enormous counter-operations mounted by the Guardia Civil, its secret service branch and the BPS (the political police) all of which bring concrete results even if they are achieved on the basis of mass arrests and torture. Against such well organized forces wTA succeeds regularly and must depend on local help from house-holders, priests, church buildings and border villages, all of whom take great risks in taking fugitives from the régime into hiding. The case of the French Basques who recaptured the German consul Eugen Beihl after his escape from kidnapped confinement by the ETA in northern Euzkadi and who subsequently uttered not a word of the matter to the French is one example of their sympathy.

The trend of the thinking in ETA indicated by the proposals of the fifth Assembly not only alienated the 'españolistas' but also a group of some of the original founders who resigned complaining that ETA was becoming a monolithic movement led by Marxist Leninists. [21] They would have preferred it to continue its broader line in which their own brand of socialism could have co-existed with the Marxist-Lenininism of the majority. Such a split was small, but nevertheless caused fewer problems since its sympathy for nationalism first and foremost was never in doubt. Only its socialism varied from that of the majority. Meanwhile the expelled socialist group mentioned before called themselves ETA-Berri or the new ETA, then changed their name to Komunistak, and finally dropped any pretensions to Basquism and called themselves the Movimiento Comunista Español. [22] The leadership group which emerged as a result of the schisms described stood for revolutionary Marxism with a 'Guevarist' leaning as opposed to what it regarded as the reformism of the ETA-berri. The futility of ETA-berri's programme was proved with the clamp down on union activity and the introduction of wage-freeze policies by the régime at the time of the schism.

Critics of the fifth Assembly ideology and organization point out tht the ultimate goal of a Frente Nacional Vasco which gained credence soon after the assembly is a contradiction which attempts to cover the inherent weakness of an alliance between a proletarian base and a bourgeois political group at the head. Perhaps the fact is that in Euskadi class differences are less important than the issue common to all, that of national freedom. Perhaps the cynical view that in any case no racial link exists to unite all the people living in the Basque country is pre-empted by the fact that the fifth Assembly recognizes all who give their labour in Euskadi as Basque workers by definition and that insistence on the purity of the race died with Sabino de Arana. Certainly the Consejo Nacional of the Falange in early 1971 stated that in the Basque country the term 'españolista' has become a real handicap in terms of economic, cultural and social relations.[23]

The inter-related reasons for the divisions which make themselves apparent around the time of the fifth Assembly are therefore the issue of whether the fight for the working class should come before the fight for the Basque nation and whether the methods used in opposing the Spanish state should be direct and violent or traditional, long-term and peaceful. In respect of the latter, the view which the proponents of long-term methods put forward is that the nature of the direct action prepared to condone violence is counter-productive in that it creates very difficult conditions for any opposition group, brings intense and often indiscriminate repression of known suspects and brings the temperature of long distance confrontation to the boiling point of imprisonment and torture, spreading a mood of suspicion and mistrust. Furthermore violence is essentially individual in respect of those who use it, not participatory, and therefore useless in helping the opposition into solid unity. It is essentially individual in respect of those who are its victims, who as policemen, Civil Guards, customs officers or local officials feel their personal safety endangered. It therefore does not weaken the system but ensures that retaliation is massive, a hammer to crack a nut that causes little real damage. In Euskadi it has given rise to the existence of an organization dedicated solely to the safe conduct of those who find themselves the object of reprisal. This organization is the APV (Accion Patriótica Vasca) which raises its funds from every social class.[24] This readiness to support passively the actions of others as opposed to carrying out individualist action is one reason why opponents of activism and militarism feel that if a solid organization were established with an attractive and viable programme in which all strata of society, but particularly the Basque working classes, felt able to participate, then this would eventually achieve success. The division between the two wings of the IRA is very similar in this respect.

The particular example of the use of direct armed attacks on individuals (and the first cold-blooded attempt on life as opposed to incidental shooting incidents with the Guardia Civil) was the killing of the Chief of Police Melitón Manzanas in August 1968 as a direct response to the prior killing in June of a 23-year-old executive member of ETA, Javier Etxevarrieta. The state of emergency declared immediately after this killing in Guipúzcoa between August 1968 and March 1969 entailed a thousand arrests and many torturings and exiles. Spring 1969 saw the emergency lifted but the arrest of leading militants continued together with ambushes, killings and arrests on the part of the authorities.

So it was that in Burgos summary military tribunals were set up, designed to accommodate the wave of prisoners and suspects who were to be charged under the laws of national security and military subversion, leading to the best publicized trial, no. 31/69 at the end of 1970.[25] The total sum of the 1968/9 repression is estimated as about a thousand arrests with five hundred accused, 250 exiled from Euskadi and 250 sentenced to penalties of varying duration and harshness. But for the internal organization of ETA the most significant outcome of the period of repression and difficulty was the reaction it evoked from certain sections of the leadership, shocked by the damage done to the organization, the decimation of followers, the loss of momentum and direction and the apparent futility of activism. Prior to the period of activism and arrests in 1968/9 ETA had reached its most active role in Spain as the vanguard of the anti-Franco forces. The CCOO had suffered from repression in a similar way and their illegal but only semi-secret existence and their semi-official relations with firms and industry could not be maintained.[26] Furthermore the freezing of wages, decreed in 1967, and the 5.7 per cent upper limit on wage claims declared in 1968 meant that the 'jurados de empresa' lost what effectiveness they had, leaving the workers seething with indignation and left with only ETA as the expression of their anger. But with its pressing need to organize and rethink its policies and limitations, ETA was becoming plagued with factionalism by the autumn of 1969. Having seen the effectiveness of the strikes of early 1969 at Altos Hornos de Vizcaya, Babcock and Wilcox and La Naval in Bilbao, mostly organized by the PSOE through 'comités de empresa', the leadership faction, mainly composed of former area commanders hastily elevated to the leadership because of the exile and imprisonment of former leaders, began to see the need for extending its influence among the workers and a resolution was passed that ETA should call itself the Partido Comunista Vasco. At the same time it organized a campaign called Batasuna (Union) aimed at the PNV and the EGI with a view to eventually forming a Frente Nacional Vasco.

The difference between the Front demanded by this faction (eventually to be known as ETA Sexta – 6a – or the sixth Assembly) and that foreseen by the fifth Assemblyists (Quinta – 5a) is that while the 5a seeks alliance with the bourgeoisie and other non-proletarian sectors against the prime enemy of the oligarchy in a popular revolution that is essentially nationalist in its ultimate aims and aspirations, the 6a is prepared to consider tactical, short-term alliances with certain sectors of the bourgeoisie only on the basis that the final objective is the freedom of the working classes. They insist that this does not mean putting off the demands of nationalism until after socialism is achieved, but that this is inherent in the struggle for socialism. The former see a front with the bourgeoisie as an alliance to the end of achieving national freedom, the latter sees that alliance as succumbing to bourgeois ideology. The 6a faction received overtures from the PCE at this time, the latter no doubt attracted by the notion of a Front not far removed from its own Pacto por la Libertad being set up in an area where it had previously had little success. But having sent representatives to the Aberri Eguna,[27] the Basque national day, the membership rejected the leadership's dalliance with the Communists and the taking of the name Partido Comunista Vasco.

Bearing in mind this pre-Assembly range of ideas, the position of the tendencies within ETA at the time of the Assembly in July 1970 was that two of them moved to expel a third – what is now known as the militarist wing of ETA, opposed to the leftward swing of part of the leadership and adhering to the originally agreed programme as set out at the fifth Assembly. The 5a's support is largely among the activists of the Frente Militar, and the exiles in Euskadi north. Of mixed classes, this group feels that the views of those forced into exile is being ignored in favour of 'españolista' tendencies in the south. ETA 5a is regarded as nationalist, militarist and right wing by its opponents, but it sees itself as welding into a mass patriotic struggle all who fight oppression in Spain and France to form a Basque national government leading to a Basque Socialist State.

Splitting off in the opposite direction from ETA 5a is a section led by Escubi variously known as the Saioak group or as the 'Células Rojas'. When the activities of July 1970 broke out – the hold-ups and break-ins of banks and government finance buildings for the purpose of compensating the deaths of workers in the Granada strikes – the Células Rojas were certain that activism would continue inside ETA and their discontent came to a head. Seeing that the exile group was causing splits in the internal organization by its independent attitude it demanded their expulsion from the sixth Assembly called

227

by the Executive committee. After the expulsion of the 5a's representative Julen Madariaga, the 'Células Rojas' focussed discussion on the contents of the Executive's latest manifesto (the Carta a los Makos) written for the imprisoned militants in Burgos, and declared that talk of a Frente Nacional Vasco was a utopian ideal without basis in reality. It saw the manifesto as a petty bourgeois document wholly alien to their own conception of the aim of the movement namely the creation of an Iberian proletarian front. When the response was that such fundamental disagreements could not be displayed to the membership and the people as a whole, the Saioak group resigned from the sixth Assembly. It may be summed up as a group without much significance at the present but which acted as an ideological ginger group on the sixth Assembly, in a stream of pamphlets and articles that by their abstract nature only succeeded in removing it even further from the real appreciation of the facts of political life in Euskadi.

To sum up, while the activists of ETA 5a saw the future ETA as a resistance movement gathering together divergent classes into one front, the sixth Assembly saw it not as a front pure and simple but as a proletarian front within the mixture of classes of Euskadi as a whole. The Saioak group denies the fact that ETA can be a front at all because there exists not the slightest element of proletarian unity in ETA. As the majority group until about 1972 the adherents of the sixth Assembly followed a strictly Marxist-Leninist line and took the third International's view of multinational states interpreting this view dogmatically. It is for the voluntary union of the Spanish and Basque nations within an Iberian state. It says that while it is a bourgeois view to assert that the class struggle takes the form of a struggle for national freedom in Euskadi, it is perfectly acceptable to state that the proletarian struggle in Euskadi should take on and lead the struggle to obtain nationalist demands. All of these divergent tendencies were veiled at the time of the Burgos trial by the sense of unity engendered in the atmosphere of international observation and criticism of the régime.

The inevitably blurred movement of the variable tendencies within ETA must be seen also against the activities undertaken in Euskadi by the CCOO, Workers' Commissions, and the PCE, who, by the nature of the strikes and demonstrations organized from 1970 onwards seem to have been in the forefront of activities; nevertheless ETA's name was in the ascendant because of the publicity arising out of the Burgos trial. Within the movement the sixth Assembly view was shared by the leading cadres, but the bulk of the ordinary membership still adhered to the line of the 5a, that of the legitimacy of the fifth Assembly and of the men who carried out its policies and were imprisoned for it. This belief was upset somewhat by the publication of a letter from the imprisoned Burgos men addressed to the executive committee which appeared to support the policy of the 6a with regard to a FNV.[28] The declarations of the Burgos prisoners are worthy of a separate study, but in brief, their view is that activism has been overtaken by the success of its own results in activating the masses who should now be involved in a workers' front leading to future party of Basque workers. This letter marked a turning point in the political relationships within ETA for it forced the fifth Assemblyists to re-think their views on the kind of FNV they wanted and made them more clearly Marxist-Leninist while maintaining their particularly, but not exclusively, Basque demands.[29] They broke with the past and saw that the Burgos trial had generated much support internationally – in Spain and in the rest of the world – for their Basque patriotism in its fight against the régime. The Tupamaros and Black September movements further proved the effectiveness of activism but even more significant, the letter stressed that the national liberation/social revolution duality should never again be allowed to split what was a single struggle. The Basques must act with the Spanish people and the French people against their governments to create a popular democracy, not as the result of a petty-bourgeois right-wing FNV but from an FNV including all those in sympathy with the ultimate goal of a popular democracy. But perhaps more important was the clear unity of minority activism with mass action.

In November, 1971, the workers of Precicontrol went on strike and were eventually sacked for demanding higher wage rates. During the hunger strike of worker representatives, the secretary of Precicontrol's board of directors, Zabala, was kidnapped by ETA, his release made conditional upon the reinstatement of the sacked workers, payment for days lost by the stoppage, and an increase in wages. From this moment on, the role of activism in workers' mass action led to a vast increase in ETA's support from many more of the already highly politicized working force in the Basque country.[30]

In the course of 1971 ETA 6a suffered a further internal split; those who favoured the FNV among the leadership published in an internal magazine *Kemen* no. 6 a programme for the Front which listed as its aims:

  (i) The violent destruction of the state and the take-over of power by popular armed councils;
  (ii) The reunification of Euskadi through a Basque popular government based on the councils;
  (iii) The socialization of the wealth of the oligarchy;
  (iv) Freedom of political parties and trade unions;
  (v) The equality of the Basque and Castilian languages.

229

This programme, and its conception of its duty with regard to the State threw over nationalism for internationalism instead of seeing the latter as an inevitable adjunct of the former it implied the destruction of the whole of the Spanish state and its control by the forces of the proletariat. Such a programme alienated the other constituent groups of the proposed Front, the bourgeois PNV, its youth group and the Basques of Euskadi north.

Despite a further factional split from the 6a by an exile group calling itself the Bloque (protesting at the centralized bureaucracy of the leadership) the proponents of this new strategy called on the Burgos prisoners to go on hunger strike on the anniversary of their trial in order to arouse public sympathy and to politicize feeling in time for the newly proposed government arrangements for collective wage agreements in industry. The hunger strike ended in 60 days solitary confinement in punishment cells for the prisoners; its results led to very little positive benefit for the leadership whose theoretical position had evolved to that of the fourth International.[31] Indeed, this line so alienated the vast majority of the membership that ETA 5a regained ground that it had lost and took in former followers of the 6a as well as covering new ground and gaining new adherents in areas of Alava and Navarra. During the second session of the sixth Assembly this Trotskyite leadership was expelled in its entirety by the members who were clearly not as enamoured with Trotskyism as the executive and who were much impressed with the growth and prestige of ETA 5a. ETA 6a remains therefore as one more revolutionary group in Spain based on the proletariat and concerned with the ideological consequences of such a belief rather than with the Basques as such. The Trotskyite sixth Assembly is currently believed by such British fourth internationalists as *Red Weekly* to be still significant within the Basque movement, but the fact that it has lost any petty bourgeois support it had in its determination to proceed to the revolution without them is significant and reflected in the fact that in the wake of the seventh Assembly which they organized, they joined forces with the French-inspired Liga Comunista Revolucionaria.[32] ETA continues to exert considerable influence among the workers of the Basque country and while on the one hand it uses its violence against those who exert power with violence – the police and the Civil Guard deployed throughout the Basque country – with other parties and movements it supports the wave of strikes in the Basque country that have demonstrated labour's opposition to the régime since autumn 1974.

After the tangled overlapping of factions in ETA south of the Pyrenees, the northern Euskadi movement is much more clearly defined.[33] It is known as Enbata, and was begun in 1963, three years

230

after a magazine of that name was launched. It has been very much a weaker brother of ETA, insipid and almost entirely cultural in its beginnings. Having started out with only the vaguest of political ideologies, its philosophy started from the notion of federalism within France and within a united states of Europe. By 1969 the movement had become more active and radical and was geared primarily to the aid of refugees from south of the Pyrenees. Adopting a socialist policy in its congress of 1972, there is a more easily discernible European attitude in their thinking. Because of the social composition of the French Basque country which is entirely rural and underdeveloped the movement is less sound in its social philosophy than ETA 5a, but national liberation is seen as the first stage in social liberation corresponding to the popular revolution. Though the French authorities banned ETA outright in 1972 and tried to suppress the protection of refugees, their attitude has caused the exiles to make it clear to the local people that they still need their solidarity; this has been forthcoming and Spanish Basques still make use of the relative freedom of French territory when they invite the press to hear of their plans or exploits. Such was the case at Bayonne where both ETA 5a and Trotskyites have staged sit-ins and hunger strikes at the cathedral. In the first month of 1974 Enbata was proscribed by the French government along with other separatist movements in French territory, but each one, and Enbata not the least, is likely to be forced into more radical positions as a result.

This difference between the Basques of the north and the French Basques in the way they have organized and conceived their nationalism is interesting to examine because it helps to clarify the key factors of the problem in Euskadi south and the reasons for the development of ETA there. The absence of a violently oppressive régime in France has meant that unlike ETA, Enbata was born and still is an educated, strongly cultural movement that is aware of the cultural violence that has been inflicted by a notoriously centralized French government as much by neglect as by design on its outlying areas – the killing of the Breton language is a good example of this. Its primary concern, leading eventually to a political awareness is cultural, social, partly even utopian and romantic. This was never the case in the Spanish Basque country where the social composition of the area after the early years of the movement's leadership by Sabino de Arana meant that a more vigorous, strongly Catholic and clearly political party headed the nationalist feeling and organized it. The legacy of the PNV, although rejected for its irrelevance by the ETA provided the precedent for political nationalism that the French Basques did not have. The war and the destruction of

Guernika, the repression of the early years of the Franco régime and the continued oppression of legitimate national aspirations have all served to politicize an already socially responsive Basque nation. In the search for new and effective ideas after years of such oppression, it is not surprising that a young movement should have gradually been drawn towards violence via direct action and rejection of the State apparatus. The violence of the Franco régime was tangible and carefully used, whereas in France the violence was cultural and though more destructive in the long term, not capable of leading to reprisal. ETA was inevitable; but the question remains, does it serve a purpose, can it survive, is it good for the Basques as a whole? It has served and continues to serve a purpose in Spain as a means of drawing attention to the perennial problem of Basque nationalism, so easily forgotten. In the process, it helps to underline Franco's rule throughout Spain as oppressive and reactionary. ETA has inspired an admiration for its Robin Hood tactics and the way it has dealt directly with problems that normally would have taken years to resolve, a surgical solution that can only improve a malignant political situation.

Among the Basques, ETA is undoubtedly admired by those who have no financial indebtedness to Madrid as a demonstration of the vitality of their nation and their unwillingness to accept the second class status imposed by the Franco régime. Among the bourgeoisie there is vagueness over the ideology of ETA and though violence is often regretted, it is understood to be inevitable in view of the violence which provokes it. The involvement of Catholic priests in the movement has done much to persuade doubters that it is the only organization which understands what Basques want because it puts their nation first. Herein lies its strength. Despite the highly complex arguments over the relative prominence of nationalism and socialism in their ideology and programme, ETA 6a is closer to ETA 5a than it would wish to admit. For both branches, and especially the fifth Assembly, which now effectively means ETA to the outside world, the Basque nation must be the source and the goal of their activities. Any other priorities will produce splinter groups of the sort that is all too familiar within the opposition in Spain.

As 1975 came to an end, it was one of the last acts of the failing General Franco before his fatal illness and one of the first acts of Juan Carlos to concern themselves with the Basques. On September 27th, five militant anti-Francoists were shot, including three members of FRAP and two Basques accused of terrorism through ETA, Jose Garmendia and Angel Otaegui. As the infamous Burgos trials, so, five years later, mass arrests during a state of emergency had culminated in the 'trial' of ETA militants. Despite opposition to

232

the shootings from every quarter and worldwide disgust at the trial and its consequences, Franco persisted in imposing a unanimous cabinet decision and it became clear that this act was the last desperate attempt by an old man to regain his grip on modern Spain, regardless of outside opinion. In the wake of the firing squad, it was in November, with Franco being kept alive by respirators, kidney machines and a vast team of doctors that a glimpse of the possibilities of the future was permitted by the acting Head of State. The decree announced in the summer of 1975 that permitted the legal use of Spain's regional languages in a wider sphere of public and official life was made law. Despite its caution and its timidity, such a move was a clear attempt by Juan Carlos to calm the political ferment in Euskadi and consolidate his future by recognising, if only symbolically, the rights of the Catalans and Basques, who, whether revolutionary in their political methods or not, demand as a right that their language be afforded full status. Juan Carlos' action may well be interpreted by moderate Basque nationalists as hopeful for the future.

The PNV's belief at present, in common with many Spanish social democrats is not only that ETA's complement of active members is small, but that with any developments towards a democratic Spain after Franco they will become superfluous; violence probably will become less appealing with the passing on of the man who has used it so systematically against the Basques for years, but it is doubtful that the socialist unity and fervour apparent in the strikes that Euskadi regularly produces will cede to the middle class appeal of the PNV. ETA represents the spirit of a nation that any democratic government in Madrid will be bound to recognize if it is to succeed. To ignore Euskadi would be fatal.

10

The Catalan Question Since the Civil War

NORMAN L. JONES

To speak of nationalist movements in Spain in 1975 is to call to mind first and foremost the Basque Country and the violent activities of ETA during the last seven years. There has been no parallel to this spectacular development in Catalonia; yet it would be surprising if Catalan nationalism proved to be a spent force in the 1970s, precisely when the *franquista* régime would appear to be losing the will, or at least the confidence in its ability, to suppress opposition. For in spite of the internal social and ideological contradictions of the catalanists,[1] and the incompatibilities of their goals, the Catalan Question was, for forty years, one of the dominant issues in the political life of the Monarchy and Second Republic, as widely disparate sectors of Catalan society, ranging from traditionalist lawyers and conservative manufacturers to intellectual republicans and revolutionary labour organizations, repeatedly made tactical alliances, notably in 1907, 1917 and 1931, to press Madrid to grant a large measure of autonomy to the four North-Eastern provinces.

Until 1931 Madrid resisted the demands, not only from the natural reluctance of any government to divest itself of part of its powers, but also because it scented in administrative devolution the beginning of a process by which Catalan and Basque economic supremacy might eventually challenge the Castilian political hegemony in Spain. It opposed catalanism as a threat to national unity; as the economic egotism of a rich industrial region seeking to evade its responsibilities towards the backward agrarian provinces; and as the agitation of a small minority whom it chose to regard as unrepresentative of the mass of the inhabitants of Catalonia, and in particular of the immigrants from other parts of Spain who constituted one fifth of her population.[2] Nevertheless, none of the Spanish parties succeeded in winning support in Catalonia after the

'Tragic Week' of 1909; conservative constitutionalism, progressive republicanism, socialism and communism were all represented by quite separate Catalan counterparts (respectively *Lliga, Esquerra, Unió Socialista* and *Bloc Obrer i Camperol*) which reflected the divergences at all levels of society between Barcelona and Madrid. The interests of the bourgeois manufacturers of Catalonia conflicted with those of the landowners of Central and Southern Spain; the identification of the professional middle classes with Catalan language and culture was uncomprehended, when not derided, in the capital; the lower middle classes, sharing this sentimental nationalism, resented the dominance of 'Castilian' local functionaries and police; whilst the workers of Catalonia showed an overwhelming preference for the regionally-orientated anarchosyndicalist CNT rather than the Madrid-based UGT – a fact which compelled the small Catalan socialist and communist parties also to lead a separate existence from their Spanish equivalents. In short, catalanism was the expression of an economically and culturally dynamic region's impatience with the institutionalized centralism of a lethargic State.

Neither of the two regional administrations conceded to Catalonia before the Civil War was an unqualified success. The 'Mancomunitat' of 1914-25 was not a legislative body but merely a merger of the four provincial councils. A model of enlightened local government – for that time, and for Spain, at least – it was obliged to enter systematically into debt because the revenues it was supposed to receive were not allocated to it in full until 1921;[3] four years later it was swept away under the Dictatorship of Primo de Rivera. Not dissimilar was the lot of the 'Generalitat', the Catalan parliament and executive council set up under the Republic after the landslide result of the plebiscite of August 1931, when the Draft Autonomy Statute was approved by 80 per cent of the region's electorate. Transference of services to it was carried out with dilatoriness in 1933, and many were still pending when it became locked in conflict with the right-wing Central Government over areas of respective competence and its president, Companys, rashly led it into alliance with the socialists in their abortive rising of October 1934. Madrid suspended the Generalitat and imprisoned its president and councillors.

The experiments in Catalan self-government thus hardly had the opportunity to prove themselves during their limited operation;[4] what they did conclusively demonstrate was that restricted forms of Catalan autonomy were unlikely to work unless regional and national governments were of similar political complexion. It was not therefore surprising that, during the first chaotic months of the

Civil War, the reinstated government of the Generalitat seized for itself powers it had always coveted – over economic and fiscal affairs, education, justice, and even frontier control and military matters; nor that Negrín's government of the Republic took the first opportunity to recover these powers in May 1937, transferring its own seat from Valencia to the Catalan capital five months later. When Franco's troops occupied Barcelona on 26 January 1939, Catalan autonomy had been a dead letter for a year and a half.

The Repression of Catalonia (1939-43)

When Primo de Rivera 'solved' the Catalan Question in 1925 by suppressing the Mancomunitat, he was reported to remark: 'Regions? Out of the question. A quarter of a century's silence about regions, usually the mask of separatism . . . and Spain will have been freed from one of her gravest perils.' [5] Primo's solution, as in so many other areas of the new régime's programme, proved a precursor of Franco's policy; in 1938, with his armies already crossing the Segre into Catalonia, he declared that: 'Spain is being reorganized within a broad totalitarian concept . . . The character of each region will be respected, but without prejudice to national unity, which we desire to be complete, with a single language, Castilian, and a single personality, the Spanish one.' [6]

The repression in Catalonia was different from that in most of the rest of Spain by being directed not exclusively against the *rojos* – the working class *and* the Left – but against practically all sectors of society, against the Catalan people as a whole, who had to pay for their collective offence against 'national unity'. Rather than repression *in* Catalonia, it was the repression *of* Catalonia. This is not, of course, to pretend that the same means were employed against all; the workers' leaders and those who had held posts under the Generalitat naturally suffered most from physical violence to their persons. Although the nature of the final campaign in Catalonia and the proximity of the French frontier provided an escape route for half a million who chose exile, the prisons nonetheless filled, and overflowed into requisitioned warehouses, and the *Manchester Guardian* in July 1939 reported official statistics of three hundred executions each week in Barcelona. [7] Yet for the middle classes too, if in a less drastic way, Cambó's prophecy was realized: 'Things are going to be worse, in Catalonia, than in 1714.' [8]

For a few members of the highest echelons of the bourgeoisie, whose *españolismo* was vouched for by their past services to Primo de Rivera and their opposition to the Autonomy Statute, there were high positions in the new State. Eduardo Aunós (who had been

236

Cambó's private secretary before serving Primo as minister of Labour) led economic missions to Rome and Buenos Aires, was ambassador to Belgium, and in 1943 entered the cabinet as minister of Justice. Joaquín Bau, the Croesus of Tarragona, provincial leader of Primo's *Unión Patriótica* and member of his National Assembly, a bitter opponent of autonomy and, as a traditionalist, a *Bloque Nacional* deputy in the 1936 Cortes, became Industry minister in Franco's war cabinet, member of Falange's National Council, and ultimately president of the *Consejo de Estado*. Miguel Mateu y Pla, an immensely wealthy *españolista* industrialist, was appointed mayor of Barcelona in 1939.[9]

But these were exceptions. For the majority of the upper middle class, who had supported the *Lliga,* exclusion from power and indeed from any form of public office was the rule. Even the names of many could not be mentioned in the press during the 1940s. This applied to the party's leadership, which fled abroad in 1936: old Abadal, the chief of the *Lliga* group of members in the Cortes, Puig i Cadafalch and Duran i Ventosa, former president and vice-president of the Mancomunitat, and Coll i Rodés, ex-mayor of Barcelona. It included many of those who while in exile had contributed handsomely to the rebel cause (like Cambó himself, who did not obtain permission to return from Argentina until 1947, and died on the eve of departure). It even affected *lligueros* who had worked actively for Franco within National Spain, such as the industrialist Eusebi Bertrand i Serra, a founder-member of the party, who directed war reconstruction from San Sebastián until 1939, and Bertran i Musitu, another of the *Lliga's* founders, who organized Franco's intelligence network in France. The *Lliga* haute bourgeoisie had turned to Franco in their dismay at the social revolution in Republican Spain, and at the end of the war they recovered their decollectivized factories, their law practices, their fortunes and estates; but their original sin as catalanists generally made them ineligible for public life. The more distinguished gravitated towards what was eventually to become the monarchist 'tolerated opposition'; less privileged *lligueros* resigned themselves to the inevitable. A minority, who had continued loyally to serve the Republic, suffered imprisonment.[10]

It would not however be exact to suggest that the Catalan bourgeoisie was penalized heavily or without distinctions. Many accepted the fascist dictatorship eagerly, just as their fathers had welcomed General Martínez Anido's 'white terror' against the labour organizations in 1920. For in the postwar autarchic economy any product made in Spain was sure of a market, and the Catalan factories, antiquated and labour-intensive, again began to suck in a stream of immigrants from Southern Spain. Throughout the 1940s manufacturers paid starvation wages and usually made high profits; often the families benefiting most expressed their adherence to the régime with ostentatious *españolismo* and the deliberate abandon of the use of Catalan, even in the home.

At the same time, there was undoubtedly strong economic discrimination against Catalonia. Firstly, as Ridruejo recalled, in the 'countless applications made by Catalans to invest Catalan capital in the creation of new industries, which were given approval with the proviso "authorized for outside Catalonia" '; [11] the régime had decided to industrialize Madrid at the expense of Barcelona, thus creating an economic counterweight to Catalan influence, and this was achieved over the next fifteen years by the simple bureaucratic expedient of denying Catalans permits to build, obtain raw materials, import machinery, etc. Secondly, the régime obstructed the financial institutions of Catalonia. As is well known, the native Catalan banking system had succumbed long before the Civil War to the competition of the larger enterprises of Madrid and Bilbao; its demise was consummated in the collapse of the Banco de Barcelona (1920) and the Banco de Cataluña (1931). But Barcelona was still, before the war, the principal stock market in Spain, the official Bolsa de Barcelona co-existing with the older and more important Free Stock Market known as the *Borsí*. In 1940 the official Exchange was reopened, though with transactions limited to spot dealing only; but the *Borsí* was not permitted to renew trading, nor its brokers to participate in the official Exchange, a measure which effectively broke Barcelona as the major Spanish stock market. [12] As for the still surviving Catalan banks, they were rapidly swallowed up by the Madrid giants; in 1942 the Banco Hispano-Americano absorbed the Banco Urquijo Catalán; from 1947 to 1951 the Banco Central took over five Catalan banks, including the important Banca Arnús and Banca Marsans. A further share went to the Banco Español de Crédito, which between 1942 and 1950 digested no less than one dozen local Catalan banks. Ten years after the end of the war, the supply of credit to Catalan industries had for all practical purposes passed totally into the hands of Madrid. The interlocking directorships of the big Spanish banks were frequently held by ex-ministers of the régime and their relatives. The absorption of the Catalan banks does not constitute a clear case of discrimination against the region, since it simply prolonged a trend that had been apparent since 1920. Yet it is interesting that the bulk of the absorptions coincided with the period of strongest anti-Catalan measures, and that towards the end of the 1950s the trend reversed; significantly, too, the Banca March survived the forties unscathed in the personal control of the *franquista* March family as the fourth largest Catalan bank.[13]

With the exclusion from public life of former members of the Lliga and the other autonomist parties, the spoils of office in provincial and municipal administration fell to the small number of Catalan old-guard falangists (perhaps the best-known of whom was Fontana Tarrats, *jefe provincial* of Tarragona and original editor of *Destino*[14]), to former Lerrouxists, and to men from the old *Sindicatos Libres,* the 'yellow' union sponsored under Martínez Anido, who naturally took most places when the régime's own Syndical Organization was created in 1940. As in the rest of Spain, the thousands of minor public posts made vacant by the flight, imprisonment or dismissal of their former holders, were filled by *excombatientes* and *excautivos.* In distinction from the rest of Spain, however, the majority of the *excombatientes* were foreigners to the region who 'invaded Catalonia like an alien flood, behaving like conquistadors, and generally distinguishing themselves by their hatred for the Catalan language and culture.[15]

One striking case of mandatory decatalanization of functionaries was that of primary education. 'Purifying committees' investigated and purged all teachers. Those who had been directly connected with catalanism were dismissed out of hand, whilst – in the words of a circular signed by Pemán, the Burgos government's first education chief – 'those who, being professionally and morally irreproachable, have sympathized with the so-called nationalist parties . . . shall be transferred'. Transfer meant, of course, exile to posts in distant parts of Spain; to replace them, between April and August 1939, the National Service of Primary Education reported that 700 schoolteachers had been drafted to Catalonia from Castile and Extremadura. A prime qualification for their posts was their total ignorance of the regional language.[16]

Measures against the Catalan language had commenced even before Franco abrogated the Autonomy Statute in April 1938, as his troops crossed the Segre into Catalonia. Right-wing Catalan refugees in Burgos and Sevilla were vexed and fined for, as one sentence put it, 'showing a lack of patriotism by speaking in Catalan dialect in the dining room of the Itálica Hotel.'[17] Catalan was almost invariably referred to as a 'dialect' and, to quote one newspaper among many, 'too serious a game has been played with the dialects – which when all is said and done are merely warts that have grown on the language – for them to be heard sympathetically in National Spain.'[18] The use of Catalan was identified with separatism, and contempt and hatred for everything recognizably Catalan was a natural consequence of the falangist obsession with

239

national unity. Under the conditions of war propaganda it became paranoiac. Catalonia was the 'wanton daughter' who, 'rich and proud, rebelled against Mother Spain'. The falangist press invented an artificial anti-semitism: the region's inhabitants were repeatedly described as *judeo-catalanes,* and Companys (and Cambó and the leaders of the *Lliga*) were claimed to be secret Jews. [19]

Draconian punishment for Catalonia was demanded; the precedent of Sodom and Gomorrah was cited as fit fate for Barcelona, and there were serious suggestions that the region be made to revert to an agricultural livelihood, exacting war reparations from Catalonia by physically removing its industries to the rest of Spain. The mayor of Zaragoza officially requested the cession of the Catalan city of Tortosa to his province as 'Aragon's gateway to the sea'; *El Norte de Castilla* demanded the incorporation of the whole of Catalonia into Aragon; while maps in some school textbooks published in National Spain showed Lérida as an Aragonese province, a dismemberment on paper in which the Syndical Organization and the National Statistical Institute have since persisted. [20]

Barcelona was occupied by General Yagüe on 26 January 1939. The keynote of speeches made by military and falangist leaders in the succeeding days was not the 'Crusade' against communism but the crushing of separatism. There was little regard for tact. An extreme example was the delirious broadcast made over Barcelona radio by the fascist poet Giménez Caballero: 'You are listening to a Spaniard who loves you ... We Castilians, Spaniards of the heartlands – severe, dry, ardent, jealous, vehement, Donjuanesque – have always desired you with fire in our lips. Because you, Catalonia, belonged to us ...' [21]

For six months thereafter, until the end of July, Catalonia was subjected, under a special régime of occupation, to a campaign of unmitigated vandalism which essayed the total destruction of half a century's cultural labour. Before the war, over seven hundred books were published annually in Catalan; Barcelona alone had seven Catalan daily newspapers and two hundred other periodicals. After 1939 absolutely nothing, not even devotional literature, might be printed in Catalan. Publishers were obliged to hand over their stocks of Catalan books for pulping; bookshops and public libraries were similarly purged. Nor were private libraries neglected; there were Savonarolesque scenes as the collections of Pompeu Fabra and Rovira i Virgili were burned in the street. [22]

The Catalan language, which had held co-equal status with Castilian under the Autonomy Statute, was banned from any public use. Posters exhorted the population to 'Speak the language of the

Empire!' Orders threatened functionaries with instant dismissal if they spoke Catalan, even to old acquaintances or monoglot peasants. Catalan was prohibited in public and private schools, and every branch of Catalan studies – language, literature, law and history – eradicated from the university. The internationally prestigious *Institut d'Estudis Catalans* was converted into the *Instituto Español de Estudios Mediterráneos* and ceased publishing anything of value. Serrano Súñer was made its president.[23]

The cultural inquisition descended to petty details. Eight public monuments to Catalan personages, from Casanovas to Prat de la Riba, were demolished in Barcelona. The names of towns were castilianized. Scores of street names were changed, not merely obvious candidates with political significance, but ones named after medieval writers or modern artists (Bernat Metge, Gaudí); even the street dedicated to the Virgin of Nuria was renamed Virgin of Covadonga. The titles of all Catalan businesses were castilianized, and firms fined for using up stocks of invoices or bus tickets printed in Catalan. Much of the region's music was banned, and for a time even the dancing of the sardana.[24]

The Church, formerly an ardent upholder of Catalan culture, was not excepted from this forcible castilianization. The catalanist archbishop of Tarragona, Vidal i Barraquer, who had refused to sign the Collective Letter of the Spanish episcopacy in 1937, was not allowed to return to his see from exile in Switzerland, where he died in 1943. In March 1939 the Navarrese Díaz de Gomara, bishop of Cartagena, was appointed apostolic administrator of Barcelona and did everything in his power to eliminate Catalan from the churches of his diocese. The Catalan clergy, many of them with vivid memories of the anticlerical terror of the first months of the war, in general accepted the régime with a deep sense of gratitude, but the linguistic injunctions were frequently disobeyed and were a constant source of friction between parish priests and hierarchy. Díaz de Gomara was succeeded in 1942 by Modrego Casaus, an Aragonese nominated by Franco, and together with the like-minded Benjamín de Arriba at Tarragona, and the rabidly *franquista* Aurelio del Pino at Lérida, would unsuccessfully attempt to impose a universal *españolismo* on the Catalan Church for over twenty years.[25]

The Clandestine Opposition (1944-50)

The whole of Catalonia had been defeated. The régime established in 1939 was not simply anti-catalanist, but anti-catalan. With the 'exceptions' of Aunós and Gual Villalbi, no Catalan was to be a member of the Spanish government until 1965.

A portion of the bourgeoisie was happy, and prosperous, with the régime. The majority of the middle classes, whilst reluctantly accepting it as a lesser evil compared with proletarian revolution, were embittered by the extent of the cultural purge and continued to nourish catalanist sentiments. The working class suffered the rigours of repression and depression; cowed and hungry, broadly indifferent to the cultural question, it was forced into political apathy.

A Catalan opposition – active opposition – to the regime began to appear only in 1944, as Franco's Axis allies were defeated, and came from three sources: the exiles, the militant minority of the workers, and the intellectuals.

The formal opposition of the Catalan government in exile suffered a history which, in its internal dissensions and ultimate ineffectuality, was similar to that of the government of the Spanish Republic in exile. In 1939 Companys had dissolved the Generalitat and set up in Paris a *Consell Nacional de Catalunya* with five personally designated councillors, all of them moderates and intellectuals. [26] Its members were dispersed by the German invasion of France in 1940, and the Vichy regime complied with a Spanish request to extradite Companys, who was tried by summary court-martial and shot in Barcelona on October 15th. The *Consell Nacional* was then re-established in London by Carles Pi i Sunyer, former finance minister of the Generalitat, its four other members including Josep-Maria Batista i Roca – a former associate of Macià and history lecturer at Cambridge – and the celebrated surgeon Josep Trueta.

On the liberation of France Josep Irla, ex-president of the Catalan parliament, declared the Generalitat reconstituted, and attempted in 1945 to reorganise the *Consell Nacional,* the membership of which had been considerably increased and its policy reorientated by the incorporation of delegates from the Catalan diaspora in America, who were now urging a Federal Iberian Republic as the only solution to the Catalan problem. This was clearly inconvenient at a time when, in the euphoric aftermath of the San Francisco founding assembly of the United Nations Organisation and its veto on Spain's membership, all the Spanish exiles were trying to present a united front. Indeed, two Catalan representatives, Santaló and Nicolau d'Olwer (of *Esquerra* and *Acció Catalana*) had joined Giral's all-party Government of the Republic in Exile. Pi i Sunyer therefore dissolved the *Consell Nacional de Catalunya,* to noisy protests from the American Catalan federalists. [27] Santaló continued to serve under Giral's successor Llopis; but when the socialists abandoned him in September 1947, the only Catalan republican to remain in the collapsing Government in Exile was Salvador Quemades, who had left the *Esquerra* to join *Izquierda Republicana*.

More in theory than reality, the *Consell Nacional de Catalunya* had created a 'resistance movement', the *Front Nacional de Catalunya,* to operate inside the region. It could do little beyond disseminate small quantities of propaganda and hang Catalan flags in inaccessible places; it lost its leaders in police raids in 1943. [28] What remained of its organisation was subsumed in 1945 into the *Consell Nacional de la Democràcia Catalana,* a co-ordinating committee presided in Barcelona by the *Esquerra* ex-deputy and novelist Pous i Pagès, who had returned from exile to Spain at the age of seventy-two, ostensibly to a quiet retirement. The committee acted as a link between Catalan republicans, syndicalists and socialists (MSC[29]); it paid lip-service to Irla's Generalitat in Exile, [30] but insisted on its own independence to act (a promise for the future rather than present praxis) in Catalonia.

If less ineffectual than the Catalan republicans, the second source of opposition to the regime in Catalonia, that of the surviving militants of the two great proletarian movements, anarchist and communist, was also to be torn during the post-war decade between divergent strategies proposed by factions in their leadership abroad, until ultimately the issues at stake disappeared or were decided by the activists within Spain.

The Great Schism between 'purists' and 'collaborationists' in the Libertarian Movement (MLE) was essentially a refighting of the doctrinal battles of the past by leaders living in exile in France. The militants of the interior were faced with the more practical problems of avoiding arrest – fifteen successive CNT National Committees were detained by the *Brigada Social* between 1943 and 1953[31] – while rebuilding the syndical network. Once the regime gained confidence that the Allies would not intervene in Spain, it directed the full rigour of police operations to breaking up the clandestine CNT, which had achieved an appreciable reconstruction during 1944-46. In May 1947 over one hundred syndicalist leaders were arrested in Barcelona, including the entire CNT Regional Committee, which by now claimed over 20,000 paid-up members in Catalonia in fourteen industrial unions – metallurgical, textile, printing, etc.[32] In August twenty-seven activists recently arrived from France were arrested. In June 1948 the capture of the MLE delegate Blanco, together with all his lists of addresses, led to the identification and gradual elimination of practically all the Catalan CNT organizational cadres.

In the face of mounting police persecution the Catalan anarchists – and especially the Libertarian Youth Movement – stepped up their war of urban terrorism against the authorities. The preferred targets were the police themselves, banks (whose 'compulsory donations' were welcome to the chronically empty coffers of the CNT), and suspected informants within the movement. From 1947 to 1949 the streets of Barcelona were the scene of frequent shootings, explosions and hold-ups. The Catalan anarchists' strength lay in the cities; there was no activity by rurally-based guerrilla bands such as occurred in Andalusia. The trek across the Catalan mountains from France, source of arms and propaganda material, was in fact the most exposed part of the terrorists' operations, for the peasantry felt only slightly less hostile to them than to the Civil Guard. If at the beginning terrorist activity helped to maintain sympathizers' morale, it was not long in becoming both counterproductive – antagonizing the populace – and costly to its authors, the majority of whom were killed or captured by police and Civil Guard by 1949, and thereafter this genre of opposition was prolonged only by isolated survivors such as Facerías and Sabater. By then it was becoming clear that the way for the working class to make its protest felt was collective action, and not spectacular coups by individuals in whom idealism jostled with psychopathic tendencies.

The Catalan communist party, the PSUC, was not an offshoot of the *Partido Comunista de España* but a native Catalan creation formed five days after the outbreak of the Civil War by a merger of Comorera's *Unió Socialista de Catalunya* and Vidiella's smaller Catalan Federation of the Spanish socialist party (PSOE); it affiliated to the Komintern at its inception.[33] The PSUC always had a notably more Catalan complexion than the CNT: whereas the libertarians' principal newspaper *Solidaridad Obrera* was printed in Castilian, that of the PSUC, *Treball,* was in the regional language, and this continued to be the case in their postwar clandestine versions.[34]

The PSUC had been obliged to establish a joint Politburo with the Spanish Communist Party during the war in order to gain the latter's support against the anarchists; but in 1939 it insisted on maintaining a separate affiliation to the Komintern, and the small number of its leaders selected by the Russians to make the journey to exile in the Soviet Union found that they had to carry on a bitter fight in 1943 to prevent the PCE digesting the Catalan party. Comorera left Moscow after the first disagreements and lived in Mexico and Cuba until moving to France in 1945.

The communists at first held aloof from the ANFD (National Alliance of Democratic Forces), the resistance coordinating organization created inside Spain by the underground UGT and CNT. They preferred to promote their own UNE (Spanish National Union) 'open even to the Carlists and the CEDA', until the débâcle of its attempted invasion of the Pyrenean Vall d'Aran in October

1944 induced it, a little belatedly, to join the united Republican front and participate in Giral's government. Like the socialists and the anarchists, the communists withdrew from the government in Exile when it became manifestly irrelevant in the autumn of 1947. Like the anarchists, too, they saw the clandestine network they had laboriously constructed in Catalonia during 1944-46 broken up in 1947, and its militants (like Puig Pidemunt and Valverde) executed or imprisoned. In these years of frustration the quarrel between PSUC and PCE broke out again and in 1949 reached crisis point. Comorera was removed from his post of secretary general of the PSUC, accused with del Barrio of 'Titoism' [35]; his successors Moix and López Raimundo followed a more orthodox line in step with the PCE and Moscow.

Unlike most of the mountainous regions of Spain – the Cantabrians, Sierra de Gredos, Sierra Morena, Sistema Ibérico between Valencia and Aragon – Catalonia was not a threatre for communist guerrilla operations. An explanation is offered by 'Juan Gros', claimed to be one of the party's most experienced couriers across the Pyrenees, who states that when in 1948 the Spanish Politburo decided to run down guerrilla activity and conserve only the most reliable highland units, he was sent by Santiago Carrillo to reconnoitre the possibility of mounting an operational force in central Catalonia. After three months talking to the people – peasants, miners, textile workers – he says he returned to France disillusioned and reported to Santiago Carrillo: 'We have missed the boat ... The people we talked to were not keen on guerrillas ... They opened my eyes; if we start shooting we shall make more enemies than friends.' [36]

The account is not entirely plausible. Even if such a reconnoitring expedition really took place so late, the truth was probably that the communists were influenced by other considerations. The field of violent resistance in Catalonia had been pre-empted by their anarchist rivals, who had not been strikingly successful or popular. Better therefore to wait until the anarchists' urban terrorism spent its forces, and then present the communist party as the only properly organized, serious and disciplined movement, capable of undermining the régime rather than merely sniping at its minions. Furthermore, the quarrel between the PCE and the PSUC was at its height, and collaboration, and even good faith, between the sister parties might not be total. [37]

Both the CNT and the PSUC made conventional obeisance during the 1940s to the principle of Catalan autonomy, if only because their programmes formally committed them, initially, to a return to the Spain of 1936. The communist programme of 1945 included 'the recognition of the national personality of the peoples of Catalonia, the Basque Country and Galicia . . . within a democratic federation of the Spanish peoples.' [38] The resolutions adopted at the MLE Paris Congress in 1945, whilst generally antiparliamentary, bound the anarchists to 'defend the autonomist claims of the Iberian peoples, protect the autonomy statutes, and struggle against centralism.'[39]

For the anarchists and communists the Catalan question was nevertheless naturally subordinate to the broader Spanish situation of the class struggle. But in the background the first signs of a revival of traditional catalanism were reappearing amongst the intellectuals. The climate of universal repression of Catalan culture relaxed slightly as falangist influence waned after the fall of Serrano Súñer. A small token was the permission given in 1943 to Josep Cruzet, who had spent the war as a refugee in National Spain, to found Editorial Selecta and publish the first postwar books in Catalan – three reprints of nineteenth-century verse by Verdaguer. In 1946 a literary quarterly in Catalan *Ariel* was authorized, and a year later the review *Antologia* appeared; it included articles by Pous i Pagès (and Anthony Eden) and was promptly suspended. In 1947 Editorial Alpha was allowed to begin a series of Catalan works devoted mainly to the fine arts; and collections of new poetry – *Ossa Menor, Proa* – soon followed. This timid literary renaissance in Barcelona took place several years later than its equivalent in Madrid, where it had been fostered rather than impeded by the Falange; and, of course, all these publications were printed in minute editions.[40]

There were stirrings in the university of Barcelona also. Apart from a small monarchist nucleus, there was no open disconformity with the official falangist atmosphere until 1945, when some students celebrated the Allied victory by tearing down portraits of the Caudillo and painting *Visca Catalunya!* on walls. For three days thereafter a 'cheka' operated in the SEU headquarters as falangist students 'tried' and beat their fellows suspected of regionalist sympathies, identified as those associated with the 'Torres i Bages' Catalan-Catholic group which circulated a cyclostyled bulletin with translations of Maritain and other socially-conscious foreign Catholics. The Catalan-Catholic group continued to exist in the university in spite of falangist harassment, acquiring tenuous links with the clandestine opposition through such returned republican refugees as Pous i Pagès, Claudi Ametlla and Amadeu Hurtado. It exerted a formative influence on many of the future leaders of the Catalan Christian-Democrat movement (Benet, Canyellas, Pujol) and even socialists (Reventós). [41]

This intellectual catalanism had, however, little ideological coherence, nor any means of contact with the Catalan people. If the régime permitted some slight slackening of the censorship after the end of the Second World War, it was certainly not with the intention of rescuing Catalan language and culture, but in order to present a less totalitarian image abroad. To Madrid, 'Catalan' was still synonymous with 'anti-Spanish'; thus, while minor concessions were made to literary activity, there was no remission of the total prohibition of the use of Catalan in the mass media and education.

Abruptly, in 1947, something totally different occurred: a manifestation of popular catalanism sponsored by the Church, or more exactly by the monastery of Montserrat under its new abbot Aureli M Escarré. [42] The ceremony held on 27 April to celebrate the enthronement of the Black Virgin, patroness of Catalonia, had been carefully prepared during the previous year by a commission under Escarré and Josep Benet, which roused public interest by a series of parish meetings throughout the region. The response was nevertheless unforeseen by the authorities: over 100,000 Catalans of all classes congregated at the mountain in the first demonstration of regional sentiment since the Civil War. The régime correctly interpreted its significance; the hapless Civil Governor of Barcelona, Barba Hernández, was dismissed, for later that summer Franco himself was due to make his first visit to Catalonia since the war.

The Emergence of a Collective Opposition (1951-59)

The gesture at Montserrat could not be repeated, though vague popular catalanism found occasional legal refuges as the régime entered its second decade; in the *Germandats Obreres d'Acció Catòlica* (GOAC), built up by Guillem Rovirosa as the Catalan branch of the apostolic worker movement HOAC; in the *minyons de muntanya,* the scout movement protected by the Church but under constant attack from the falangist *Frente de Juventudes* [43]; and, not insignificant in a situation where every decision of this sort had political undertones, even in support for the 'Catalan' *Club de Fútbol de Barcelona* rather than the city's rival 'Spanish' team *Club Español de Fútbol.* [44]

Nevertheless, the chief characteristic of the opposition in Catalonia during this period was identical to that in all the other regions of Spain: the reappearance of collective action by the working class. In March 1951 Barcelona took the lead: a six-day boycott of public transport in protest against higher fares was observed with total solidarity and the increase was rescinded. [45] Inspired by this success, one week later the first general strike seen in postwar Spain began. All 300,000 workers in Barcelona came out, and many demonstrated in the centre of the city against the steep increase in the cost of living. Police opened fire, killing two and wounding twenty-five. Three thousand police reinforcements arrived by rail and destroyers disembarked troops in the port, and on the third day the workers were forced back to the factories. Thousands of arrests were made, and though the strikers gained the symbolic victory of the dismissal of the Civil Governor Baeza Alegría, the mayor, and the provincial head of the Syndical Organization, it was mitigated by Baeza's replacement by a notoriously 'hard' general, Acedo Colunga, a veteran of the repression in Asturias in 1934. The authorities claimed that communists had been responsible for the strike – the PSUC's leader in the interior, López Raimundo, was among those caught in police swoops – though it appears to have been rather a spontaneous popular reaction to the effect of inflation, and in the ad-hoc strike committees former CNT members undoubtedly predominated.[46]

The events in Barcelona were the start of a series of strikes and disorders that spread over Northern Spain during the spring of 1951 and contributed to the major governmental changes in the summer. The changes, the effect of which was primarily to redistribute ministerial power by the inclusion of monarchists and the reinforcement of the Catholics in the cabinet, served to encourage the rapprochement with the United States and the Vatican by implying that the régime might be about to evolve in a faintly Christian-Democrat direction. Part of this *suggestio falsi* was the holding of the XXXV International Eucharistic Congress in Barcelona in May 1952. Over half a million Spaniards attended, together with 30,000 foreigners, including 4,000 Americans led by the admiring Cardinal Spellman. The Congress was heavily politicized by the presence of Franco, who pronounced the public dedication of Spain to the Holy Sacrament, recalling the 'countless legion of martyrs and soldiers fallen for the faith in the recent Crusade'. The Canadian Monsignor Vachon reminded his hearers that fifteen years earlier Barcelona had been the centre of 'the most bloody religious persecution'.[47]

The Congress, presented in the Spanish press as a public act of contrition by Catalonia, provoked cynicism among the working class (who called it 'Dr Modrego's Olympiad'), and unease in progressive Catalan Catholic circles. One of the principal figures of the Catalan Left Christian-Democrat movement was the forty-eight-year-old engineer and medieval scholar Miquel Coll i Alentorn, leader of the prewar *Acció Catalana* Youth and now secretary of *Unió Democràtica de Catalunya,* which had continued a clandestine existence after the war and, during the fifties, had an influence on young Catalan

248

intellectuals similar to that which Giménez Fernández's *Izquierda Democrática Cristiana* had somewhat later in the universities of the rest of Spain. It rarely tried to make public impact. In 1952, on the occasion of the US Sixth Fleet's visit to Barcelona, American naval officers were showered with catalanist leaflets dropped from the topmost balcony of the Liceo opera house. As they were in English, police detained all Catalans who had held posts at British universities (Triadú, Sarsanedas, etc.) and also arrested Coll i Alentorn, suspected of having organized this incident and an earlier one at the funeral of Pous i Pagès, when a wreath was sent from the *Unió Democràtica* and a small demonstration occurred. The arrests were meant as a warning: no charges were brought for lack of evidence. Coll i Alentorn spent thirty days in prison on Acedo Colunga's personal order.[48]

If the régime's economic stagnation was causing increasing hardship to the working class, it was also hurting the industrialists of Catalonia. Exports of cotton textiles had suffered especially, dropping in 1951-55 to less than one third of the 1946-50 level. In 1954 a deputation including Güell, Gual Villalbi, Mateu i Pla (representing the manufacturers' *Fomento*), and the presidents of Barcelona's Chambers of Commerce, Industry and Agriculture, visited Acedo Colunga to set out a series of requests. They sought an end to bureaucratic restrictions on commerce, the abandoning of retroactive fiscal measures, the cessation of discrimination in power cuts (which since 1951 had affected Catalonia alone), and various public works projects long overdue – electrification of Catalan railways and improvements to the port of Barcelona. Above all, they asked for permission to publicize their demands. The government made certain concessions – it appointed the president of the Chamber of Commerce to the port's administrative board, and granted Mateu i Pla's plea for preferential status for private investments in INI – but equivocated over what was effectively the grande bourgeoisie's request for official sanction to act as a pressure group. In October 1955 the Catalan oligarchy continued its lobbying on the occasion of Franco's fourth visit to Catalonia, and was granted audience by the Caudillo at the castle of Perelada, the sumptuous property of Mateu i Pla. For the first time former leaders of the *Lliga* – Ventosa i Calvell and Bertran i Musitu – were allowed to be included in the deputation, which repeated the appeal for fiscal reform, liberalization of trade, and permission to import new machinery. Franco listened impassively; he limited himself to observing, in a speech on 5 October, that 'Catalonia is an important factor in the greatness of Spain'.[49]

In the spring of 1956 widespread cost-of-living strikes provoked by the accelerating Spanish economic crisis seriously affected Catalan factories. Wage increases were nullified by rapid inflation; a two-week boycott of Barcelona public transport was observed with a solidarity as great as that shown in 1951. Strikes continued; but the communist party did not realize in Catalonia the broad support from the working class that it had expected to follow from the disintegration and organisational disappearance of the CNT. This became particularly clear in 1958: the biggest factories in Barcelona – SwAT, ENASg, Hispano Olivetti, Farbra y Coats, La Maquinista – were closed for sixteen days by a strike for higher wages, but the one-day *political* general strike (the 'Day of National Reconciliation') called by the communist party in May was largely a failure. Even more decisively, the 'Pacific National Strike' announced for 18 June 1959, with a profusion of clandestine propaganda, was generally ignored in Barcelona. Both of these calls for short, massive political strikes were the consequence of the communists' adoption in 1956 of a new policy of National Reconciliation, based on the exiled Central Committee's analysis of the Spanish situation as one of imminent decomposition of the régime. In Catalonia, the PSUC set up a coordinating committee for the 1959 Pacific Strike with representatives of the *Moviment Socialista de Catalunya*, the *Unió Democràtica de Catalunya*, and the *Front Obrer de Catalunya* mthe Catalan counterpart of the Catholic-marxist FLP). It ended in total discord, with MSC, UDC and FOC accusing the communists of attempting to take over their organizations and withdrawing from the strike. [50]

The major Spanish crisis of 1956 precipitated a rapid politicization of the universities, taking its most visible form in the struggles to establish a democratic student union to replace the official SWU. The violent February riots in Madrid, which caused the removal of the progressive Ruiz Giménez from the ministry of Education, were echoed by disturbances in Barcelona. These continued and a year later, in the turbulent atmosphere following the city transport boycott, Barcelona took the lead by holding the first *Asamblea Libre de Estudiantes* in the university's main amphitheatre. Police drove out the six hundred participants with accustomed brutality, and academic sanctions later expelled some students permanently, whilst the majority lost the year's studies. To the extent that it is possible to distinguish ideological tendencies within a heteromorphic student revolt, two nuclei appear to have been influential. The more extreme, in its opposition to any compromise with capitalism (and therefore, after 1956, unattracted by the communist party), found its intellectual centre in the ostensibly literary *Seminario Boscán*, run for three years by the anthologist and critic Josep M. Castellet, who had been briefly

250

detained in 1956 as one of the organizers of the Congress of Young University Writers. A repentant ex-falangist, Castellet, together with the novelist Luis Goytisolo and the publisher Carles Barral, disseminated a revolutionary utopian socialism, with an anti-centralist orientation verging on catalanism. The larger nucleus in the university was explicitly catalanist, and was known by the initials CC (*Catòlics Catalans*). Originally a religious group with a spiritual approach to the Catalan question, its increasing preoccupation with social problems, especially those arising from the immigrant influx, soon attracted it into the orbit of the Christian-Democracy of Coll i Alentorn and opposition to the régime. The chief CC personality within the university was a dynamic medical student born in 1932, Jordi Pujol i Soley, who would shortly find himself at the centre of the explosion of catalanism in 1960.[51]

The situation in Catalonia had changed greatly by 1959. The region had emerged from the shadow of the Civil War, and once again was ripe for one of those periodic resurgences of nationalist sentiment in which the internal divisions of Catalonia were temporarily forgotten in an alliance against a central power in crisis. The gratitude felt by the bourgeoisie in the 1940s for being saved from proletarian revolution was now tempered by concern at being cut off from the European development boom, and resentful awareness that the State was deliberately channelling taxation and savings from Catalonia through the INI and banks into other regions, and especially into the industrialization of Madrid. The appointment of Gual Villalbi as minister without portfolio in February 1957 (the Barcelona press baptized him 'the minister for Catalonia') was soon seen to be an empty gesture. In the same month a confidential report by J. M. Marcet, the *franquista* mayor of Sabadell, told of the discouragement of the régime's supporters in Catalonia.[52] He spoke of the government's neglect to provide for housing, schools or hospitals in Catalonia; the state of roads and ports was deplorable; and the attitude of the national press was woundingly anti-Catalan. Above all,

> In the political appointments of the Spanish Administration one rarely comes across a Catalan; in the Syndical Organization Catalans have no place in the leadership at national level, not even in industries predominantly located in this region . . . There is a political problem in Catalonia, which can only be solved by a policy designed to eradicate the sensation of 'separatism from Madrid'.

The middle classes' gall at what they regarded as economic and political discrimination against Catalonia was exacerbated by the continuing cultural repression. True, nearly two hundred titles were

251

published annually in Catalan in the last years of the decade, but they were a symbolic concession to a minority and Madrid was still intent on reducing the language to the status of a *patois* by excluding it from the mass media and above all by forbidding the teaching of Catalan in public or private schools.[53] The *Institut d'Estudis Catalans*, which had been privately re-established by individual academics, led a precarious existence harassed by police.[54] The consequence of the régime's cultural anti-catalanism was that virtually the whole of the intelligentsia, and the opposition movements in the university, were *ipso facto* catalanist.

Within the Church the division subsisted between catalanist clergy and *españolista* hierarchy. At the latter's insistence, the Concordat of 1953, departing from usual Vatican practice, made no reference to safeguarding the rights of cultural minorities.[55] An extreme example of the *españolista* attitude was Dr Moll Salord, reported as saying that as long as he was bishop of Tortosa he would not authorise a single service in Catalan.[56] The torchbearer of the Catalan Church continued to be the monastery of Montserrat, which in October 1959 took advantage of ecclesiastical exemption from censorship to begin publication of the monthly *Serra d'Or*, wholly in Catalan. Initially distributed only by subscription, it soon reached a circulation of 12,000, devoting an ever larger proportion of its pages to contemporary social and political questions.

The most profound transformations to occur in Catalonia during the 1950s affected the working class. The first was political: the communists partially inherited the mantle of the CNT, though they failed to attain the clear pre-eminence in worker militancy that they achieved in other industrial areas of Spain, notably in Madrid. The second, and the more fundamental, was demographic: the influx of unskilled immigrants into Catalonia was running at unprecedented levels. Between 1940 and 1960 the population of Catalonia rose from 2,959,117 to 4,001,892. Of this increase nearly 70 per cent was due to immigration: 256,000 non-Catalans arrived in 1941-50, and 439,000 in 1951-60. The sources of immigration changed also; in 1932, when immigrants accounted for one fifth of the population of Catalonia, half of them had been born in neighbouring Valencia and Aragon (and many of the Valencians spoke Catalan), and only one eighth in Andalusia. By 1960, the Andalusians were over half the total (167,000 in the city of Barcelona alone). Immigrants were no longer concentrated only in Barcelona and its satellite towns; they constituted 18 per cent of the inhabitants of the three rural provinces of Tarragona, Gerona and Lérida. The immigrant birth-rate was high: in 1960 six out of every ten children born in Catalonia had at least one non-Catalan parent. Moreover, the influx was still accelerating. Of one thing there could be no doubt: these *nuevos catalanes* (less politely, *xarnegos* or *coreans*) would complicate the Catalan question.[57]

The Resurgence of Catalanism (1960-66)

A chain of events in 1960 marked the reappearance of a catalanist opposition movement with broad support from the middle class. They were set in motion by a celebrated scandal in the previous autumn when Luis de Galinsoga, editor since 1939 of the main Barcelona daily *La Vanguardia* (and author in 1956 of the adulatory biography of Franco *Centinela de Occidente*), entered a city church and, outraged to hear the sermon given in Catalan, interrupted and berated the priest before his congregation. A highly effective public boycott of the *Vanguardia* was organized by the CC group (Pujol, Benet, Canyellas); its circulation crumbled, advertising dropped drastically, and within two months, in February 1960, vainly appealing for support to the ministry of Information, Galinsoga was obliged to resign.[58] During these same months Acedo Colunga opened a polemic with Escarré, whom he accused of fomenting 'subversion' through his monastery's *minyons de muntanya* centre in Barcelona. The Civil Governor unsuccessfully tried to have Escarré removed from his abbacy.[59]

Shortly afterwards, in May 1960, Franco paid his sixth visit to Catalonia, conceived as a gesture of goodwill to the middle classes. He was accompanied by the entire government, and remained several weeks. The gifts he brought included a municipal charter to give Barcelona the same special administrative status as Madrid, authorization for the codification of Catalan civil law, and the demilitarization of the fortress of Montjuïc, grim symbol of Castilian domination overlooking the city, for conversion into a park and museum. Yet the most memorable feature of Franco's visit, and the one which vitiated the purpose of this *Operación Sonrisa*, was the episode at the Palau de la Música.[60] At the end of a concert attended by several ministers, a large part of the middle-class audience broke into singing the prohibited *Cant de la Senyera*, traditional concluding piece for Catalan choirs. The doors were locked and police arrived; some of those present, and the many Catalan intellectuals subsequently arrested for questioning, suffered gross ill-treatment at police headquarters. phe incident had evidently been prepared in advance, and leaflets with the words of the song had been surreptitiously distributed before the performance. The police chose to place responsibility on Pujol: he admitted organizing the *Vanguardia* boycott, but in spite of beatings he denied any part in the events at the Palau de la Música (which had nevertheless been the work of other members of CC). In protest against the treatment of those detained, Escarré refused to attend the official farewell to Franco. Pujol, who was making his début in the financial world as founder of the rapidly growing Banca Catalana, was sentenced in July to seven years' imprisonment, of which he served two and a half; he became overnight the hero and martyr of catalanism, his name painted on a hundred walls beside country roads. There were mass sit-ins by young Catalans in churches and vigils outside the episcopal palace of the unresponsive Modrego Casaus; these led to further police intervention and protests at the brutality employed from the College of Lawyers and from the two native Catalan bishops of Solsona and Vich. A collective letter was signed by four hundred prominent Catalans.

Within weeks Acedo Colunga was dismissed, but the catalanist ferment continued. In 1961 *Omnium Cultural* was founded in Barcelona, well endowed by various industrialists, as an association to foster Catalan cultural enterprises, and – in the opinion of Madrid – to promote catalanist agitation. It financed the *Institut d'Estudis Catalans;* it subsidized concerts of popular music (this was the period of the launching of the *nova cançó catalana,* the new-wave protest songs composed and performed by Espinás, Pi de la Serra, 'Raimon' and scores of others, which swept Catalan youth during the sixties); and it finally overstepped the invisible limits set by the régime when it organized a region-wide *Campanya de la Llengua Catalana,* involving the signature of petititions to the government requesting permission for the teaching of Catalan in schools and the publication of Catalan newspapers. The point was that the régime was willing to allow Catalan to be used in semi-intellectual cases, though it was already uneasy at the rapid flowering of Catalan culture in the early sixties and its appeal to students (the two landmarks of postwar Catalan literature, Espriu's *Pell de Brau* and Pere Quart's *Vacances Pagades,* both appeared in 1960). It was yet more worried by the success of the *nova cançó* and its popularity with youth of all classes.[61] It was positively alarmed by the *Campanya de la Llengua,* since the crux of the Catalan cultural problem has been the language's absence from the schools, the only means by which the immigrant wave might be assimilated. In September 1963 the government closed down *Omnium Cultural* and confiscated its files.

For Madrid – and not only for the ultra-right, but also for the inveterately centralist left – the agitation in Catalonia bore the mark of the old *bête noire*: the plutocracy exciting romantic nationalism for its own nefarious economic ends. But to many Catalans, this interpretation seemed an obstinate persistence in looking at their

254

society through the prism of 1917. If the Catalan bourgeoisie still lived handsomely at the expense of low-paid immigrant labour, it had evolved considerably since the days fifty (or twenty) years earlier when it had no social policy beyond blind faith in the Civil Guard and the *sometent*. It was more intelligent and more European; or at least its younger generation was. One example of the new leaders who began to represent the progressive sector of the Catalan middle class in the sixties was Antoni Canyellas Balcells, jeweller, lawyer, and intimate of Pujol. Nine years older than Pujol, he had helped pass members of the French resistance over the Pyrenees, and witnessed the clashes between falangists and catalanists in the postwar university. During the fifties he reguarly attended world congresses of the international Christian-Democrat movement, met the Kennedys, knew Schuman, Frei and Fanfani, and became an admirer of the Italian Left Christian-Democrats. Secretary of *Justitia et Pax* and of the Friends of the United Nations in Barcelona, in 1963 he launched a youth magazine in Catalan, *Oriflama,* which reached a circulation of 12,000 and mixed, in trendy format, features on modern music and rock-climbing with articles on worker control and enthusiastic accounts of nationalist movements . . . in Ireland or Africa. Such attempts to publicize the Christian-Democrat left (Canyellas insisted he wanted nothing to do with the right of Gil Robles)[62] naturally reached only a minority – the youngsters who read *Oriflama* were probably the children of the same parents who bought *Serra d'Or* – and they were inevitably reminiscent of the ideology of the ineffectual prewar *Acció Catalana,* which was crushed between the *Lliga* and the *Esquerra.* Circumstances were nevertheless very different from those applying under the Republic. There was no longer a conservative catalanist party to represent the bourgeoisie as the *Lliga* had. And the economic boom that began spectacularly to raise the general Spanish standard of living after 1964 was much more propitious than the depression of the thirties to a progressive Christian-Democrat solution and an understanding with the working class.

Through Josep Benet, Canyellas had strong links with Montserrat. In November 1963 Escarré again became the focus of attention through an interview given to *Le Monde,* in which he denoucned the Spanish State as oppressive and the Spanish Church as its accomplice, citing Catalonia as a clear case of ethnic discrimination. Six weeks later falangist incendiaries burnt out the monastery's *minyons* centre in Barcelona, and on the next day the first mass catalanist demonstration seen in the city since the war marched in protest to the Plaça de Catalunya. The minister of Information, Fraga Iribarne, mounted a press campaign against

Escarré, and diplomatic and hierarchic pressure was applied in Rome which finally resulted in Escarré being summoned to exile in Italy.[63] In 1964 Fraga made a totally unappreciated attempt to soothe regional feeling by erecting large hoardings in the centre of Barcelona to celebrate the régime's silver jubilee with the slogan 'Twenty-five years of peace' prominently displayed in Catalan.[64] This did not prevent another more traditional commemoration, that of 11 September, anniversary of the defence of Barcelona against the Spanish army of Philip V, being celebrated for the first time since the war by two thousand demonstrators at the site of the demolished monument to Casanovas.

The relationship between catalanism and radical movements in the Church and University was underlined by events in 1966. The demise of the SEU and its substitution by the scarcely less unrepresentative 'Professional Association of Students' offered little improvement to those who wanted to change the anachronistic structures of Spanish higher education. Although the CC movement had disintegrated, the student activists still made a religious house the venue for the constitutive assembly, on 9 March, of the Democratic Syndicate of University Students of Barcelona (SDEUB). The Capuchin Fathers' convent in Sarrià was besieged for two days by police who cut off food supplies and finally arrested all present. Their legal defence was organized by Benet; eventually twenty-seven students were expelled and sixty-eight university teachers were suspended from their posts for having participated. On 11 May over a hundred priests filed through the centre of Barcelona to present at police headquarters a letter protesting against the serious injuries inflicted on one of the students; before reaching the *jefatura* the procession was attacked by contingents of police whom astonished citizens saw chasing and beating the priests with their bâtons.

The majority of the region's clergy had catalanist sympathies, and the retirement of Modrego Casaus in 1966, after twenty-four years as bishop (later, archbishop) of Barcelona, brought general expectation that he would be succeeded by a Catalan. This hope was dashed, and the appointment of a Castilian, González Martín, provoked a violent campaign under the slogan *Volem bisbes catalans* (We want Catalan bishops) in which the episcopal chair in the cathedral was burned.[65]

The Contemporary Catalan Situation (1967-75)

Such episodes were however of little relevance to the working class. They could hardly be expected to be; for by now the great majority of the Catalan working class, and practically the totality of its unskilled and semi-skilled members, were recent immigrants. In the ten years after 1960, in spite of one of the lowest native birth-rates in Spain, the population of Catalonia rose from 4,001,892 to 5,184,813. During the decade the *net* migratory flow into Catalonia was 684,436. Between 1962 and 1965 alone, 341,720 non-Catalans settled in the province of Barcelona, and a further 43,397 in the other three Catalan provinces. In such enormous suburbs of Barcelona as Cornellà, Badalona, Hospitalet or Santa Coloma, hardly a word of Catalan could be heard, and the overwhelming tide now reached up to the small townships of the Pyrenees, where immigrants had hardly been seen previously. Catalanists naturally insisted that the fact that the immigrants spoke Castilian was far from meaning that they preferred Catalonia's affairs to be decided by a centralist government in Madrid. They quoted studies which showed that even in areas with densest immigrant population, one third of the newcomers had learned to speak Catalan within twenty-five years. [66] The ability to speak Catalan as a second language was not, however, the same as to share in the historical and cultural ambience from which the autonomist movement derived.

This was evident in the demands formulated by the Workers' Commissions which, somewhat later than in the rest of Spain and with GOAC and FOC leadership rather than that of communists, [67] sprang up in the major industries of Barcelona during the mid-sixties. They arose as the result of the legalisation in 1958 of collective bargaining at local or factory level, and organized the roughly biennial strikes which greeted the expiry of each major agreement with the immediate aim of improving the employers' wage offers. The Commissions, which were of course illegal since negotiations were supposed to take place exclusively within the Syndical Organization, also sent delegates to regional and national assemblies which issued communiqués with a more general political content. It is interesting to compare the communiqués issued in early 1968 by the Workers' Commissions of Vizcaya and of Catalonia. [68] Both express in nearly identical terms demands for increased minimum salary, an end to repressive measures against workers, respect for human rights, more State provision for education, and so forth. The Basques then go on to include a long section on the 'national' problem, with references to the historic reality of Euskadi and the need for a multi-national solution to allow the peoples of Spain to express their 'will for self-determination'. In contrast, the Catalan communiqué, signed by the Commissions of eighteen towns scattered throughout the four provinces, omits all mention of the Catalan national question; in fact, the corresponding

257

place in the document is occupied by a call for solidarity with Vietnam and the closure of US bases in Spain. It is only in the report of the Fifth National Assembly of the Commissions of all Spain, in 1969, that brief collective reference is made to 'the struggles waged by the peoples of Euskadi, Catalonia and Galicia for their national rights'.

The Metallurgical Workers' Commission of Barcelona in 1967 cautioned workers not to attend a further 11 September demonstration at the site of the monument to Casanovas, as risking confusing their objectives with those of the bourgeoisie. A similar message came from the FOC Political Committee in connection with the 11 September demonstration of 1968:

> We workers are aware that in Catalonia economic exploitation is linked to a national oppression characterised principally by the repression to which the Catalan language is subject . . . But we are aware too that the national question has a different meaning for the bourgeoisie and for us . . . For us, the national question is not above the class struggle but part of it. [69]

Commenting on these statements, the French Catholic-marxist periodical *Frères du Monde* remarked that the difference between the Catalan and the Basque national questions was that the Basque capitalists were fundamentally centralists and identified through Basque banking with Madrid; whereas the fragmentary structure of Catalan capitalism and the lack of a strong native bank were responsible for a confused situation in which both workers and employers coincidentally aspired to a form of autonomy.

The situation in Catalonia was indeed confused; and the confusion was compounded in September 1967, when the first direct elections of 102 members of the Cortes – two *procuradores pro familia* in each province – produced a fascinating result in Barcelona. One of the two 'official' candidates, Juan Samaranch, well known as president of the provincial *diputación,* of the *Español* football club, and of the Spanish Olympic Committee, was elected by 526,367 votes. His partner in the 'official' candidature, Colomer Marqués, received only 173,916 votes; and Balcells Gorrina, an Opus Dei challenger, 93,913. The man who was elected as Barcelona's second *procurador,* by 435,275 votes, was Eduardo Tarragona. Fifty-three per cent of the electorate had voted, and Tarragona did well in two apparently incompatible areas: the traditional catalanist towns of the interior (Vic, Manresa, Igualada); and the ring of immigrant towns surrounding Barcelona. [70]

Tarragona, who rather liked being called by his enemies 'the new Lerroux', was capable of meaning all things to all men. The son of a Leridan landowner-turned-industrialist, in 1936 as a member of the

258

CEDA Youth he had reported to a Civil Guard barracks on the night of 18 July, only to find that it had decided not to join the uprising. He crossed into National Spain, and was a sergeant at the war's end. The family business prospered, and Eduardo was for a time president of the sub-group of ball-bearings manufacturers within the Syndical Organization, conceiving an abiding contempt for its verbose and incompetent functionaries. He studied business management, frequently travelled to business congresses abroad, and after 1958 became a prolific contributor to newspapers and magazines. He wrote, and lectured, on economic and political topics, attacking the technocrats and the Development Plan, criticizing State bureaucracy, calling for businessmen to be granted a place in the Administration, and beating the drum of private enterprise.

This was music to the ears of the Catalan bourgeoisie, which was convinced that governmental centralism was responsible for the relative decline in Catalan economic importance and progress (Barcelona had just fallen to fifth place among Spanish provinces in terms of per capita income, and eighth place in industrial growth-rate[71]). The 'Barcelona school' of economists – Trias Fargas, Ros Hombravella, etc., – produced data to confirm the impression of discrimination against Catalonia. They showed that a Catalan surplus of 20,000 million pesetas on trade with the rest of Spain was turned into a balance of payments deficit by taxation, social security contributions, compulsory deposits by savings banks in public funds, and transferences by immigrants, little of which ever returned to Catalonia. They admitted the responsibility of a rich region to subsidize poorer ones, but claimed that the Catalan contribution was excessive and undermined reinvestment at home. Further, public spending on infrastructure in Catalonia compared badly with the rest of Spain: since 1940 the funds allotted to the *diputación* of Barcelona by the State had steadily diminished as a percentage of the total for all Spanish provinces, although its population had practically doubled. State expenditure per capita on education in Barcelona was only half of that provided to Burgos in rural Castile, in spite of the desperate need for schools in the suburbs as a consequence of immigration.[72] Madrid's neglect of Catalonia was, they claimed, apparent in every aspect of public works – in bad roads, unmodernized railways, an antiquated port of Barcelona, and even in the shameful water supply to the city.

Eduardo Tarragona's obvious appeal lay to the bourgeoisie, but his regenerationist programme included something for everyone. For the workers: he called for genuinely representative syndical elections (many of the shop stewards elected in 1966 had been disqualified by

259

the Syndical Organization), he denounced middle-class tax evasion, and urged slum clearance, cheap housing, and more schools and clinics in the suburbs. For the *franquistas*: he stressed his personal admiration for the Caudillo, and limited his disconformity with the régime to its bureaucratic inefficiency. For the catalanists: he used the vague but classic phrase 'recognition of the historic personality of Catalonia', translating this as the need for a minister for Catalonia resident in the region;[73] and he distributed a proportion of his propaganda in Catalan. But the main element in Tarragona's electoral success was perhaps the evident fear of him manifested by the régime's local representatives, who were unable to resist the temptation to use every time-honoured device to obstruct his campaign. They prevented him holding meetings in Barcelona until five days before the election; for a public meeting in Igualada he was allocated a school classroom seating thirty, while for another he was given a hall without chairs. In contrast, Samaranch and Colomer had all the resources of the *Movimiento* at their disposal.

The 1967 Barcelona election result showed that the marxist analysis of the Catalan situation was unappreciated by the mass of depoliticized or immigrant workers. They were ready to follow their militant élite along the beaten paths of industrial disputes; but in an economic boom which brought tangible increases in their standard of living, and under a régime that betrayed no diminution in self-confidence, talk of revolutionary class conflict made little impact on them. The analysis of *Frères du Monde* was irrelevant: the working class was not being subverted by the nationalists who demonstrated at the site of Casanovas' monument, but throwing itself into the arms of a Catalan variant of *franquismo*.

This became yet clearer in the second election of *procuradores* to the Cortes, held in September 1971. From 1967 to 1969 Tarragona had consolidated his reputation as a thorn in the side of the Administration. He inaugurated a weekly 'surgery' for constituents' complaints, an unheard-of innovation in Spain. He encouraged the creation of Residents' Associations in the outlying suburbs to protest about their lack of schools, lighting or sewerage. He maintained a nine-month campaign which finally obliged the government to bring subnormal children under the provisions of Social Security. He asked 159 formal question in the Cortes, none of which was properly answered by the minister responsible; he was one of the leading figures in the 'Wandering Cortes' meetings of progressive *procuradores* in 1968; he voted against approval of the State budgets (as unacceptable to any competent accountant), and against the designation of Juan Carlos as successor. Finally, in October 1969, after his request for permission to establish a 'Civic Union of

Catalonia' was rejected by the government, Tarragona did something utterly unprecedented: he resigned from the Cortes. [74]

Tarragona's campaign for re-election in September 1971 brought him an undoubted personal triumph. He presented himself, in a macaronic mixture of Castilian and Catalan, as 'the man who calls a spade a spade'. [75] Turn-out dropped from 53 per cent to 35 per cent of a disillusioned electorate. Samaranch's vote was halved, from 526,637 in 1967, to 273,495 in 1971. His 'official' companion Torras Trias received 234,014. [76] Yet Tarragona's share of the poll rose from 44 per cent to 56 per cent, with 389,159 votes; and again, he did strikingly well in the working-class areas of outer Barcelona.

The novel feature this time was the presence of an explicitly catalanist dual candidacy, not Christian-Democrat but Social-Democrat, represented by Joan Barenys Oriol and Xavier Casassas Miralles in Barcelona, as part of a *Coalició Democràtica de Catalunya* which also stood in Lérida and Tarragona. Barenys was a forty-one year old lawyer active in social work in the immigrant suburbs of Terrassa, where in 1967 his election to the town council with 75 per cent of the votes had been invalidated by the authorities. Casassas was a savings-bank manager and president of a district Residents' Association in Barcelona; he had twice been arrested, once at the age of fifteen for participating in the 1951 strike, and three years later for distributing clandestine publications. With minimal finance (they spent one and a half million pesetas on electoral propaganda, one sixth of Eduardo Tarragona's expenditure, and less than one twelfth of that officially admitted by Samaranch), they put forward a programme including democratic elections for town councils and all syndical posts, restoration of the Mancomunitat of the Catalan provinces, special attention to immigrants' problems, respect for basic human rights, fiscal reform, and Spanish entry into the European Economic Community. They met with even more obstruction than Tarragona: their propaganda was authorized for distribution four days before the election, in drastically censored form; they were unable to use the radio, as the other candidates did, during their campaign. In the event, they won a 12 per cent share of the vote (Barenys 83,084; Casassas 66,935). In Barenys' home territory of Terrassa he gained 31 per cent, only 8 per cent less than the victorious Tarragona, and in the industrial city of Manresa, with a strong team of canvassers, they actually headed the poll. Yet in suburban Barcelona their share dropped to 6 per cent, and in areas of dense immigrant population, like Cornellà, to 2 per cent. [77] This was to be expected, for 90 per cent of their propaganda had been printed in Catalan.

Undoubtedly, linguistic assimilation of immigrants still went on, but at a much slower rate than twenty years ago. In spite of the danger of confusing language and identification with the region, the ability to speak Catalan is still probably a good indicator of integration within the community. For obvious reasons no Spanish census has ever recorded data on the numbers of speakers of regional languages. We have nevertheless two guides to the linguistic situation in Catalonia. In 1965 Badia i Margarit, of the University of Barcelona, estimated from 3,450 replies to a postal questionnaire that 62 per cent of the city's inhabitants used Catalan as their first language; but for various reasons this figure is probably a considerable exaggeration.[78] The more methodical FOESSA survey of 1970, based on interviews with a representative cross-section of 605 housewives throughout rural, urban and metropolitan Catalonia, found that 77 per cent *could* speak Catalan, but only 54 per cent *preferred* Catalan as their first language (exactly 50 per cent of those interviewed turned out to be immigrants or children of immigrants). As one would expect, there were appreciable differences between rural areas (where 82 per cent preferred Catalan) and the metropolitan area (47 per cent); and between women with no education (24 per cent preferred Catalan) and those with secondary or higher studies (62 per cent). Nevertheless, practically all (97 per cent) said they would like their children to speak Catalan; 70 per cent wanted this 'very much'; and 87 per cent thought it 'necessary'. Between 52 per cent and 59 per cent said they would prefer newspapers, radio, television and cinema to be in Catalan.[79] In short, for 54 per cent of the women interviewed Catalan was the language they preferred to use in every aspect of their lives; a further 23 per cent were bilingual with a preference for Castilian; and 23 per cent were Castilian monoglots.

The *Coalició Democràtica de Catalunya* promised its supporters that it would increase its propaganda in Castilian in the 1975 election campaign. But with the best will, it is difficult to see it improving its support radically: if people will vote only for what appears to them to be viable – such as Tarragona's Catalan *franquismo* – and the *Coalició*'s proposals for genuine democracy have no prospect of implementation under the present régime, it scarcely matters which language it uses to distribute propaganda.

Catalanist incidents have continued unabated. 1967 saw a further *Català a l'escola* campaign for permission to teach the language in schools. In 1968 the emotional scenes at the funeral of Escarré found Eduardo Tarragona amongst the mourners. *Oriflama* and *Destino* suffered various sanctions. In 1969, after the ETA killing of a police inspector in Guipúzcoa and the proclamation of a state of exception, the authorities were uncompromising in their suppression of many

Catalan cultural activities. In December 1970 the tension caused by the passing of death sentences on ETA members at the Burgos trial was reflected in Catalonia by an illegal assembly of three hundred Catalan intellectuals, writers and artists at Montserrat, where the new abbot Cassià Just nurtured the tradition of Escarré. Civil Guards isolated the monastery for two days, threatening to storm it; heavy fines and other sanctions were applied to the participants. In 1971 and 1972 two small terrorist groups, MIL and FAC, respectively anarchist and separatist, tried consciously to emulate ETA and begin guerrilla operations in Catalonia; they attracted no support and police claimed to have broken them up by 1974.

In November 1971, possibly as an outcome of the meeting at Montserrat eleven months earlier, an *Assemblea de Catalunya* was set up, claiming to represent united Catalan opposition to the régime, of left and right. Its programme, the lowest common denominator of its component groups, is limited to three points: amnesty for political prisoners, guaranteed liberty of expression and association, and the provisional re-establishment of the Autonomy Statute of 1932. It is too early to speculate whether it can prove to be more than another ineffectual broad alliance front; at the moment, judging by the clandestine propaganda it distributes, and the identity of 113 members surprised by police in a raid on a Barcelona church in October 1973,[80] its 'breadth' would appear to be limited to the PSUC and sympathizers, with a certain number of well-known lawyers and academics of the nationalist left such as Solé Barberà and Jordi Carbonell, and ultra-radical priests like Xirinachs and Dou. The catalanist centre-left and centre-right have held aloof.

Catalanist culture flourishes in literature (700 titles annually), music, and the visual arts, in spite of occasional attacks on reputedly catalanist bookshops and publishers by ultra-right commandos. It is still excluded from the mass media, though the Opus-owned *Mundo Diario* has just begun to publish one of its pages in Catalan, and there are continual rumours of the appearance of a Catalan daily financed by Pujol, now vice-president of Banca Catalana, which controls a large holding in the *Correo Catalán,* and in February 1975 bought *Destino.* Spanish Television has introduced a monthly programme in Catalan ... broadcast at 5 p.m. on a weekday. Grudging permission has been given to run courses in written Catalan in a few schools ... after hours, with unpaid teachers, and pupils of all ages in a single group. In a not untypical case, in Cornellà, the town council responded in late 1974 to a survey which showed that 97 per cent of parents – mainly immigrants – wanted their children to learn Catalan, by organizing voluntary courses in local schools, with the cooperation of headmasters. A few days before they were due to begin, the inspector of schools for the area, a Castilian, intervened to prohibit the courses unless they were taught by teachers of his choosing, all of whom happened to be monoglot Castilians.[81]

The sudden liberalization in official tolerance of discussion of previously taboo topics during the second half of 1974 took Catalonia unawares. As late as December 1974 the only delicate matter exercising Barcelona city council was a proposal to re-erect the demolished monument to Dr Robert, a founder of the *Lliga,* which had been discovered in a warehouse. Unexpectedly, on 4 March 1975, a councillor, Soler Padró, presented an amendment to the city budget, to allocate 50 million pesetas to the promotion of Catalan language and culture, and requested in vain permission to speak in Catalan. The amendment was rejected by 18 votes to 9 (with Eduardo Tarragona, also a member, voting in favour). Immediately an unprecedented explosion of protest from every conceivable quarter shook the region; accounts of the furore filled the pages of the *Vanguardia* for days. The startled councillors reversed their decision. Even before, on 7 March, the town council of Prat de Llobregat, an immigrant suburb, conducted without permission the first council meeting to be held in Catalonia since the war in which both languages were used; the mayor, a native of Valladolid, spoke in Catalan. It seemed that after thirty-six years, the cultural battle with the régime was practically won.

Meanwhile, the political aspects of the Catalan Question arose at national level. The Draft Law to legalize political associations presented by Arias Navarro in December 1974 was so restrictive as to be ostentatiously spurned by almost every significant Spanish political figure. A reminder of the régime's deep-rooted dread of regionalism was the specific exclusion of regional associations – a condition of approval was a minimum membership of 25,000 distributed proportionately in *at least fifteen* provinces. Nevertheless, in his widely publicized travels ostensibly directed towards sounding out the possibilities of founding a 'Democratic Reform' association with the monarchists (Areilza) and the catholics (Silva), Fraga Iribarne felt moved to pay several visits to Catalonia in December and January, meeting both Pujol and Tarragona, and proclaiming without embarrassment 'I am a convinced regionalist. We need men like Cambó nowadays.'[82] In this fluid situation the leaders of the Catalan centre-right kept a foot in both the 'tolerated' evolutionary camp of Fraga, and in the 'semi-tolerated' camp of the moderate opponents of the régime. For on 26 November Canyellas was one of fourteen people arrested and detained for twenty-four hours after an illegal meeting in Madrid between Spanish Christian-Democrat and

Social-Democrat personalities and their Catalan counterparts. The four other Catalans present were Social-Democrats: Casassas, Heribert Barrera (son of a minister of Labour of the Generalitat), Amadeu Cuito (grandson of a leader of *Acció Catalana*), and Josep Pallach (a former member of the POUM exiled until 1970). [83]

On 21 January 1975 Pujol presented his conclusions on the past two months' events at a meeting for eight hundred in the ESADE business school in Barcelona, attended by almost every non-*franquista* political personality in the city. He said that Catalonia had ended the phase of linguistic and cultural recovery; what now remained was a step towards political action. He declared against Arias' political associations, and invited Catalans to form what he termed a 'Centre-left Platform', of 'consensus rather than unity' – but only, he repeated several times to his audience, if the middle class after careful meditation on every implication, were prepared to go all the way along that road without turning back. [84]

It remains to be seen whether the Catalan middle class will take that road, and where it may lead to.

The Catalan Question is still alive in Spain, though in a less strident (and to other Spaniards, probably less virulent) form than it took before the Civil War. It is a microcosm of the larger Spanish Question – and in this it seems to differ from the present situation in the Basque provinces – in that at all levels of Catalan society there exists a specifically regional counterpart to each major political tendency in the rest of Spain. This is however far from saying that all Catalans prefer an autonomist solution. We might make a rough classification as follows:

(i) The haute bourgeoisie, and perhaps even one third of the middle class as a whole, especially the older generation, remain essentially reactionary. Living well and fearing change, they adhere to the régime. Though in some ways they would like to see Catalonia treated more considerately, at heart they have a feeling, inspired by the events of the last sixty years, that a strong hand from Madrid is necessary to prevent catalanism upsetting the social order.

(ii) An increasing proportion of the middle class, larger than the one just mentioned, is dissatisfied with the régime and wants to see evolutionary changes (some of them quite irreconcilable – like a reduction in bureaucracy and lower taxation, at the same time as an expansion of social services to mollify the workers). They are anti-centralist, but stop well short of demanding autonomy. The majority have a real but passive attachment to Catalan culture of a somewhat folklorish type, which becomes active only when Madrid represses its manifestations.

(iii) The remainder of the middle class, including the intellectuals, liberal professions, many technical workers and especially the younger generation, are inclined towards the sort of radical democratic reform that can be achieved only by a political (but not violent social) revolution. Their involvement with Catalan culture is strong (they read and write the language) and has little to do with dancing sardanas. For these, a degree of autonomy is a *sine qua non* of a political solution.

(iv) A large minority among the working class – especially in the newer suburbs of Barcelona – is attracted by promises of immediate material benefits in housing, welfare and education, whatever the political system offering them.

(v) A politically conscious élite of militant workers will settle for nothing less than the overthrow of the capitalist system: regional autonomy is a secondary consideration for them.

(vi) The mass of workers is ignorant of and indifferent to all political programmes at present.

The régime can count on only dwindling support from the conservatives of group (i), and is attempting to woo the reformist 'liberals' of group (ii) by concessions (as in the use of Catalan). These 'liberals' already have a well-publicized leader in Eduardo Tarragona, who has the charismatic virtue of attracting the 'materialist' workers of group (iv). The Christian-Democrats of various shades and Social-Democrats are at present based in the 'progressive' group (iii), but their possibilities for expansion, if realized, must carry them apart. If liberty of association were to be granted in Spain, the Christian-Democrats would become the party of the Catholic sectors of groups (i) to (iii), [85] whilst the future of the *Coalició Democràtica* would depend on its ability to proselytize among the working-class groups (iv) and (vi), though it is doubtful whether it could really compete with the marxists of group (v). [86]

Which of these tendencies eventually predominates in Catalonia will depend, as in 1930, on the future of the Spanish régime. What we now see in Spain in many ways recalls the machinations surrounding the Pact of San Sebastián. Catalan leaders are however much more aware than they were forty years ago of the region's limited possibilities for self-government. The immigrant influx has made separatism unthinkable. A federal solution of the German type would regrettably not seem viable, given the lack of interest in most of the rest of Spain. Yet regional devolution, initially on the lines of the Mancomunitat, but with greatly increased powers to raise local finance, would be quite possible; and, should EEC regional policy ever prove to be more than a pious hope, would give the Catalans an opportunity to fit into a wider European framework in which friction with Madrid could be superseded. Whilst the *Assemblea de Catalunya*, if it exists in any meaningful way, apparently seeks to resurrect the conflicts of the Autonomy Statute, at last a more modern political solution to the Catalan Question may be emerging from the embryonic centre-left movement in the region – provided the rest of Spain will allow it to. Admittedly, it is a middle-class solution; but in Catalonia, the middle class is likely to be dominant long after the Franco régime disappears.

Notes

1. The Falange: An Analysis of Spain's Fascist Heritage

1. Stanley G. Payne states: 'Given authoritarian form, the combination of nationalism with socialism or corporatism usually became known as "fascism" ' (*Falange*, Stanford, 1962, p.1). Bernd Nellessen does not define fascism, nor does he make evident just how 'fascist' he considered the Spanish Phalanx to be (*Die verbotene Revolution. Ausstieg und Niedergang der Falange*, Hamburg, 1963). Juan J. Linz describes *Falange Española* as 'a fascist party', but in his essay 'From Falange to Movimiento-Organización: the Spanish Single Party and the Franco Régime, 1936-1968' (Huntingdon and Moore, *Authoritarian Politics in Modern Society. The Dynamics of Established One-Party Systems*, New York, 1970, pp. 128-201) he does not precisely define his conception of fascism. Hugh Thomas assumes that 'if Nazism in Germany and fascism in Italy are to be regarded as brother movements, the Spanish fascists of the *Falange* are younger brothers still' (his essay 'Spain' in *European Fascism*, ed. by S. J. Woolf, London, 1968, pp. 281-2) but neither does he define fascism.

2. Mussolini defined Fascism in the *Enciclopedia Italiana* with a variety of cloudy phrases, among them the following: 'Fascism is a religious conception of life, in which Man is seen in his inherent relation to a higher law, to an objective will that transcends the individual and raises him to the consciousness of a spiritual community . . .' (as quoted in A. B. Ashton, *The Fascist: His State and his Mind*, London, 1937, pp. 32-3).

3. 'Fascism is the unconcealed terrorist dictatorship of the most reactionary, chauvinistic and imperialistic elements of financial capital', cited in note 33, p. 465, Ernst Nolte, *Three Faces of Fascism*, London, 1965.

4. 'Fascism is anti-Marxism which seeks to destroy the enemy by the evolvement of a radically opposed and yet related ideology and by the use of almost identical and yet typically modified methods, always, however, within the unyielding framework of national self-assertion and autonomy' (Nolte, *op. cit.*, pp. 20-1).

5. In this definition of fascism, it is evident that Japanese militarism in

268

the Second World War, Peronism in Argentina, the régime of the Greek colonels, and the military putschists who overthrew Allende in Chile, are not considered to have been, or to be, fascist. The Portugal of Salazar was not a fascist régime, although it might be viewed as an example of what a fascist régime in decadence might have become: the Empire won, the totalitarian (authoritarian?) State still in power, and the problems of the class struggle still unresolved.

6. Quotations in support of the advocacy of these three methods by Spain's fascists can be found in the basic texts of Spanish fascism, among them, *La Conquista del Estada, Antología* (Barcelona, 1939); *Onésimo Redondo, Caudillo de Castilla* (Valladolid, 1937); *JONS, antología* (Barcelona, 1939); *Arriba* (Madrid, 1942); *F. E.* (Madrid, 1943); Ledesma Ramos, *¿Fascismo en España?* (Madrid, 1935); Ledesma Ramos, *Discurso a las Juventudes de España* (Madrid, 1935); J. A. Primo de Rivera, *Obras Completas,* (Madrid 1954, other editions).

7. José Ortega y Gasset, *España invertebrada* 15th edition (Madrid 1967) *passim.* but especially pp. 55, 63.

8. *Genio de España,* Madrid 1932. Other editions appeared in 1934, 1938, two editions in 1939. The sub-title was: 'Exaltaciones a una resurrección nacional. Y del mundo.'

9. *Discurso a las juventudes de España,* Madrid, 1935, pp. 71-2. Other editions were printed in 1938, 1939, 1942 and 1954.

10. *Genio de España,* Saragossa, 1938, p. 276.

11. This scene is from the prologue to the anthology entitled *La Conquista del Estado,* by Juan Aparicio (Barcelona, 1939, p. xi). It is doubtful that the eleven signatories met and signed at the same time. See Tomás Borrás, *Ramiro Ledesma Ramos* (Madrid, 1971), pp. 248-50.

12. Borrás, *op. cit.,* p. 216.

13. *La Conquista del Estado, op. cit.,* p. xii.

14. *Onésimo Redondo, Caudillo de Castilla* (Valladolid, 1937), pp. 10-11.

15. This fact is taken from Ledesma Ramos' 1935 book *¿Fascismo en España?,* cited by Borrás, *op. cit.,* p. 321.

16. *Onésimo Redondo, Caudillo de Castilla,* pp. 61-70.

17. G. Montes Agudo, *Vieja Guardia* (Madrid, 1939), p. 35.

18. José Antonio Primo de Rivera, *Obras Completas* (Madrid, 1954), pp. 67-8.

19. The most prominent of the deserters at this time was Francisco Moreno Herrera, Marqués de la Eliseda. Concerning his departure, see Southworth, *Antifalange* (Paris, 1967), pp. 81-2. His absence was regretted, because *Falange* headquarters were in his house. Eliseda cut off the gas and electricity, and finally managed to have the Phalanx evicted (Ximenez de Sandoval, *José Antonio,* Barcelona, Juventud, pp. 278-9).

20. Ximenez de Sandoval, *op. cit.,* pp. 249-53. Maximiano García Venero, *Falange en la guerra de España: la Unificación y Hedilla* (Paris, 1967), pp. 52-6.

21. See speech of Primo de Rivera in the Cortes, November 6, 1934 (*Obras Completas,* 1954, p. 333); also his interventions on November 30 and December 11 (*ibid.,* pp. 383-92). The *Falange* insisted that the danger focus of the October rising had been in Catalonia and not in Asturias, that the

peril to Spain was not social and economic change (which the Phalanx also advocated in its fashion) but rather territorial loss and disunity.

22. Francisco Bravo, *José Antonio* (Madrid, 1939), pp. 85-93.

23. Ximénez de Sandoval writes that six thousand people were present in the Círculo Mercantil to hear Primo de Rivera (*José Antonio, op. cit.*, p. 333).

24. Bravo, *op. cit.*, p. 226.

25. Max Gallo, *Cinquième colonne*, 1930-40, pp. 126-31. Stanley G. Payne cites as authority for this story of Italian fascist subventions to Spanish fascism, pp. 40-1 of a dissertation by John F. Coverdale, 'Italian Intervention in the Spanish Civil War', U. of Wisconsin, 1971 (*Iberian Studies*, vol. II, no. 1, note 43, p. 12). Gallo first published this information in a polycopied thesis in 1968, and later in his 1970 book, both antedating Coverdale's thesis. Angel Viñas treats this matter in considerable detail in *La Alemania nazi y el 18 de Julio* (Madrid, 1974), pp. 152-5. See also by Viñás the article, 'José Antonio analiza las fuerzas políticas' (*La Actualidad Económica*, Madrid, 23 November 1974), wherein the Spanish historian states his belief that the subvention given to J. A. Primo de Rivera by the Fascist régime was originally inspired by Count Ciano himself.

26. 'Una noche en casa de José Antonio', by Manuel Aznar, in *Dolor y Memoria de España, en el segungo aniversario de la muerte de José Antonio* (Barcelona, 1939), pp. 190-2; García Venero, *op. cit.*, pp. 265-8.

27. Sancho Dávila, Julián Pemartín, *Hacia la histora de la Falange* (Jerez, 1938), pp. 70-81.

28. Southworth, *op. cit.*, pp. 114-15. Cf. Paul Preston, 'Alfonsist Monarchism & the Coming of the Spanish Civil War' in *Journal of Contemporary History*, Vol. 7, Nos. 3/4, 1972.

29. Ximénez de Sandoval, *op. cit.*, pp. 420-7; Southworth, *op. cit.*, pp. 267-8.

30. J. M. Gil Robles, *No fue posible la paz* (Barcelona, 1968), p. 436.

31. Gil Robles avers that he offered Primo de Rivera three sure seats and three doubtful ones on the electoral list of the Rightist Bloc. This was refused (*op. cit.*, p. 444). For Calvo Sotelo's attitude see, Southworth, *op. cit.*, pp. 113-17). Gil Robles, of course, did not foresee the Popular Front victory and the consequent difficulties of Primo de Rivera.

32. Gil Robles later admitted that 'fascism was gaining ground in a sweeping *arrolador* fashion, in great part at the cost of the CEDA . . .' (*op. cit.*, p. 688, note 25). Primo de Rivera, while in prison in Alicante, June 16, 1936, in his answers to the questions of a journalist, Ramón Blardony, stated that from ten to fifteen thousand young followers of Gil Robles had joined the Phalanx (Agustín del Rio Cisneros, Enrique Pavon Pereyra, *Textos biográficos y epistolario: José Antonio íntimo* (Madrid, 1968, 3rd ed., p. 516).

33. *Onésimo Redondo, Caudillo de Castilla*, pp. 181-99; Ximénez de Sandoval, *op. cit.*, pp. 525-8, 546-8.

34. Ximénez de Sandoval, *op. cit.*, p. 558.

35. *Ibid.*, pp. 543-5; Southworth, *op. cit.*, pp. 106-7.

36. Primo de Rivera, *op. cit.*, pp. 925-9; Southworth, op. cit., pp. 103-5. The imperialist thoughts of Primo de Rivera are evident in this manifesto, where he states: 'The *proposals* of the revolution are clear. The Socialist

Agrupación of Madrid, in the official programme which it has edited, demands for the regions and the colonies an unlimited right of self-determination, even for independence.'

37. Primo de Rivera, *op. cit.*, p. 942.

38. *Ibid.*, pp. 942-3.

39. *Ibid.*, pp. 947-8.

40. *Ibid.*, pp. 951-2; Bravo, *op. cit.*, pp. 243-5; Ximénez de Sandoval, *op. cit.*, pp. 579-81. From these references it appears that this document has but a historical interest, for it was not sufficiently distributed to have played an active role in Phalangist behaviour.

41. García Venero, *op. cit.*, pp. 103-49.

42. *Ibid.* pp. 169-93. Cf. the enthusiastic description by the Irish correspondent Francis McCullagh of the scenes outside Falangist barracks in Burgos, November 1936; McCullagh, *In Franco's Spain* (London 1937) pp. 61-2.

43. Onésimo Redondo, *Caudillo de Castilla* pp. 202-16.

44. Tomás Borrás, *Ramiro Ledesma Ramos* (Madrid 1971) pp. 707-82.

45. Eugen Weber, *Varieties of Fascism* (New York, 1964), p. 73.

46. Eugen Weber writes that Mussolini's ' "March on Rome" would have ended in disaster had the army received orders to oppose it' (*op. cit.*, p. 73). Nolte believes that 'Fascist movements are easily quelled if the State is seriously determined on such a course' (*op. cit.*, p. 320).

47. William Shirer, *The Rise and Fall of the Third Reich* (New York, 1969), pp. 170-1.

48. Serrano Suñer wrote: 'It is a true fact, for which I have no reason to apologize, that I might think with pleasure on a conjuncture which would return to my Patria its geographical plenitude and permit it to recover its rank of other times and acquire the consequent presence in world questions' (*Entre Hendaya y Gibraltar,* Madrid, 1947, p. 202).

49. See Serrano Suñer, *op. cit.*, pp. 85-7, 126-7.

50. Galeazzo Ciano, *The Ciano Diaries* (New York, 1946), p. 94.

51. *The Spanish Government and the Axis* (Washington, D.C., 1946), p. 3. Donald Detwiler, *Hitler, Franco und Gibraltar* (Wiesbaden, 1962), p. 25. Southworth, *op. cit.*, p. 47. J. M. Doussinague, *España tenía razón* (Madrid, 1950), pp. 41-3.

52. Doussinague, *op. cit.*, pp. 43-4. Fernando María Castiella, *Spanish Foreign Policy (1898-1960),* (Madrid? 1961?).

53. This brutal repression was a logical sequence to the class victory by the elements involved in the Republican defeat, and it further accentuated the fact that the Phalanx had not only not won the civil war, but by entering the civil war had lost all chances of realizing its programme. The refusal of a policy of clemency toward the defeated further diminished any possibility of an eventual Conquest of the Empire, but there is nothing in the record to show that the Phalanx – or any of the other institutional victors, such as the Church and the Army – ever advocated an act of mercy toward one of the vanquished. Today, the neo-Franquista historians are seeking to lower the figures for the dead in the Civil War. Ricardo de la Cierva has been active for more than five years in trying to bring down the number of the dead in

the bombing-burning of Guernica to figures that oscillate between 'fewer than a dozen' to around a hundred and fifty (Southworth, *La destruction de Guernica*, Paris, 1975, pp. 363-405). The number of the dead in Guernica was considerably higher, from all known evidence (*ibid.*, pp. 453-75).

The operation attempted on the Guernica dead by La Cierva and others has been extended to all of the war and postwar years (1936-45) by the neo-Franquista historians in an effort to disparage the conclusions on this matter by Gabriel Jackson in *A Concise History of the Spanish Civil War* (London, 1974), pp. 175-6. In *Boletín de orientación bibliográfica* (Madrid, December 1974, p. 27), the editor (Ramón Salas Larrazábal?) diminishes the number of the dead caused by the Civil War to a figure between 225,000 and 250,000. This feat is performed by sociological estimates and weights. The editor adds that the Republicans 'killed more' than did the Rebels. Not only do the total figures given in the *Boletín* seem preposterously low, but the assertion that the Republicans were responsible for more killings than were the Rebels cannot be accepted without more proof than is given. It must be remembered that the Franco people kept on killing from 1939 to at least 1963, date on which Julián Grimau was executed for 'crimes' committed during the Civil War.

The killings by the Rebels can be roughly divided into three parts: 1. those killed in battle, 2. those killed behind the lines during the war, and 3. those 'executed' after the end of the fighting. The second category was probably greater than the first, and I suggest that the third category was greater than the second. This third category could, at any rate, be controlled by a more precise method than sociological speculation: prison records. How many people were taken out from the *Prisión Cellular* of Barcelona and shot, during the three years that followed the capture of Barcelona by the Franco forces, on 26 January 1939? There is a remarkable book on the subject, written by the prison chaplain, Martín Torrent. I say 'remarkable', because of the absolute lack of common humanity shown by the priest, whose sole preoccupation was to get the soul of the condemned in proper shape for a 'Christian' execution. Torrent even considers the man condemned to death to be fortunate for, knowing the hour of his death, he can be prepared to die in a state of grace (*Qué me dice usted de los presos?* Alcalá de Henares, 1942, p. 68). Torrent writes that during the three years he was chaplain of the *Prisión Cellular*, 77, 705 *expedientes* or dossiers were registered at the prison *mibid t1., p. 91);* since some of these were collective, the number of prisoners involved was greater than the number of *expedientes.* phe maximum capacity of the prison was around eleven thousand persons (*ibid.*, p. 156). Father Torrent wrote in 1942 that 35,000 prisoners had been released from the prison on either complete or conditional liberty (*ibid.*, p. 81). If we subtract the figure of 35,000 prisoners, the number who left the prison on some sort of liberty, from 77,705, the total number of *expedientes* (which could be collective, we must remember), we arrive at the figure of 42,705. From this figure we can subtract the number of 10,000, presumed to have been in the prison in 1942, and we find the figure of 32,705. These were not among the freed, and they were not in prison.

Where were they? Had they been shot? I would suggest that a study of the records of the *Prisión Cellular* of Barcelona would be more fruitful than conclusions drawn from speculative statistics.

54. Serrano Suñer wrote in 1947: 'We placed ourselves in conditions whereby we could avoid being crushed by the German advance – something others were unable to prevent – and whereby we could find ourselves situated, in the case of a German victory, in a tolerable position' (*Entre Hendaya y Gibraltar*, p. 203). In simpler words, the position of the Franco government, faced with the prospect of a Hitler-dominated Europe, was pure opportunism.

55. An exposition on this subject can be found in Southworth, *Antifalange*, pp. 38-54.

56. *Op. cit.*, p. 445.

57. In Berlin, in September 1940, Serrano Suñer told von Ribbentrop that Spain wanted to enlarge the hinterland of Spanish Guinea. The German Foreign Minister replied by showing Serrano Suñer a map hanging on the wall, and informed the Spanish envoy that Germany would need naval bases at Agadir and Mogador. This German greed for 'Spanish' territory shocked the traveller from Madrid. But he was to be shocked still more, for the German declared that his country needed a naval base in the Canaries. But the Canary Islands are a part of Spain, cried Franco's minister. See Serrano Suñer, *op. cit.*, p. 182, also Donald S. Detwiler, *op. cit.*, pp. 38-9, *Gibraltar* (Wiesbaden, 1962), pp. 38-9.

58. The evidence for this assertion can be found resumed in Southworth, *Antifalange*, pp. 53-9.

59. Enrique Sotomayor, *Frente de Juventudes*, pp. 37-9.

60. President Truman in his memoirs suggests that at the Potsdam Conference, it was Churchill who argued – just before his electoral defeat – in favour of leaving Franco unmolested, in control of Spain. Any attempt to overthrow Franco would violate the new UN charter, and damage England's trade with Spain (Harry S. Truman, *Memoirs*, I, Garden City, N.Y., 1955, pp. 357-8). Churchill was consistent in his attitude toward Spain, throughout the Civil War and later, keeping two ideas foremost in his mind: the defence of his class and the defence of the British Empire. Had he been a Spaniard, the 'Reds' would have killed him and his (class) friends, he told the Duke of Alba in 1940 (Brian Crozier, *Franco*, London, 1967, p. 332); he told Mrs Roosevelt at a dinner party in London in 1942 that, had the Spanish Republicans won, she and he would both have lost their heads, had they been Spaniards (Eleanor Roosevelt, *This I Remember*, New York, 1949, p. 204); and in 1948 he wrote: 'Naturally, I was not in favour of the Communists [sic]. How could I be, when if I had been a Spaniard they would have murdered me and my family and friends?' (*The Gathering Storm*, London, 1948, p. 214). Pp. 212-13 of this book indicate that this man, for all his great moments in the history of this century, understood nothing about the Spain of 1936. Churchill supported Franco at the beginning of the Civil War, but when he thought that the Germans and Italians in Spain might menace the security of the British Empire, he changed opinions. In 1945, he considered, rightly, that Franco presented no danger to the British Empire, or to Churchill's class; he was insensitive to the fact that the

273

inherent violence of the Phalangist movement was to be turned inward against the Spanish people.

61. Was the Franco régime ever totalitarian? Juan J. Linz appears to consider that since pressure groups have had influence under Franco, his régime is not totalitarian (Linz, *op. cit.*, pp. 146-7). To this perhaps semantic problem, I would contribute two observations. On 15 December 1966, the newspaper *Madrid,* directed in the Spanish capital by the Opus Dei intellectual Calvo Serer, considered the Franco régime at that time to be totalitarian (*Le Figaro,* 15-16 December 1966). Also, a study should be made of the use of the word 'totalitarian' during the Second World War. The Catholic Church, in the United States and elsewhere, did not want to condemn 'fascism' and chose instead to condemn 'totalitarianism' a word which in the catholic vocabulary embraces the Soviet Union and such other régimes which refused to share power with the Church. The Franco régime (and Fascist Italy), under this Catholic definition of 'totalitarianism' were not totalitarian. Certainly, after 1945, the rigid organization of Spanish life, the *Gleichgeschaltung,* needed by the Spanish Phalanx for modern imperial conquest, gradually disappeared.

62. See José Luis de Arrese, *El Estado totalitario y el pensamiento de José Antonio*; Southworth, *op. cit.*, pp. 141-2.

63. 58. *Op. cit.*, p. 159.

2. The Spanish Armed Forces: Poor Relation of the Franco Régime

1. International Institute for Strategic Studies. *The Military Balance* London (Annual publ.)

2. Cf. G. Hills. *Spain,* London, 1970, p. 360.

3. *Las Fuerzas Armadas Españolas,* Dossier Mundo, n. 21, Barcelona, 1971, p. 127.

4. J. Busquets, *El Militar de Carrera en España,* Barcelona, 1971, p. 270.

5. Idem, p. 150.

6. E. Mola Vidal, *Obras Completas,* Valladolid, 1940, p. 968.

7. J. A. Ansaldo, *¿Para qué? Lo que no debe ser y lo que debe ser, de Alfonso XIII a Juan III,* Buneos Aires, 1951, p. 524.

8. *Le Monde,* 12.5.70.

9. Cf. D. Ridruejo, *Escrito en España,* Buenos Aires, 1962, p. 286.

10. J. Busquets, *El Militar de Carrera en España,* p. 270.

11. Cf. F. L. Sepúlveda, 'La Producción Nacional de Armamentos' in *La Vanguardia,* 10.1.75.

12. F. Franco, *Discursos 1955-1959* (Publicaciones Españolas), Madrid, 1960.

13. S. G. Payne, *Politics and the Military in Modern Spain,* Standford, 1967, p. 60.

14. M. Díez-Alegría, *Ejército y Sociedad,* Madrid, 1972, p. 49.

15. J. Pemartín, *Qué es lo Nuevo . . . Consideraciones sobre el momento español presente,* Madrid, 1940, p. 15.

16. Idem, p. 14.

17. *Spanish Labour Charter* (9.3.1938).
18. F. Franco, *Discursos 1955-1959*, p. 181-90.
19. 'El Poder de la Nobleza en España', *La Actualidad Económica, 13.1.73.*
20. C. Moya, 'Las Elites Españolas y el Desarrollo Económico', in S. del Campoed. *La wspaña de los Años 70: La Sociedad,* Madrid, 1971, p. 473.
21. *Organic Law of the Spanish State* (10.1.1967), Title 37.
22. J. Bardavío, *La Estructura del Poder en España,* Barcelona, 1969, p. 207-19.
23. Cf. A. de Miguel, *Sociología del Franquismo,* Barcelona, 1975, p. 160.
24. International Commission of Jurists, *Spain and the Rule of Law,* Geneva, 1962, p. 83.
25. K. Salaberri, *El Proceso de wuzkadi en Burgos,* Paris, 1971.
26. Cf. R. Milliband, *The State in Capitalist Society,* London, 1973, p. 119.
27. S. G. Payne, 'Spanish Fascism in Comparative Perspective', *Iberian Studies,* III.1, 1973, p. 4.
28. R. Ledesma Ramos, *¿Fascismo en España?,* Barcelona 1972, p. 72.
29. P. Preston, 'Alfonsist Monarchists and the Coming of the Spanish Civil War', *Journal of Contemp. History* vol. 7, Nos. 3 & 4, July, 1972, p. 113.
30. E. Mola Vidal, *Obras Completas.*
31. J. de Andrade (F. Franco) *Raza,* Madrid, 1942.
32. R. Salas, *Historia del Ejército Popular de la República,* Madrid, 1973, vol. I, p. 188-9.
33. Cf. R. Serrano Suñer, *Entre Hendaya y Gibraltar,* Madrid, 1947, p. 43.
34. B. Crozier, *Franco,* London, 1967, p. 212-15.
35. E. Comín Colomer, *La República en el Exilio,* Barcelona, 1957, p. 277-311.
36. Stockholm International Peace Research Institute, *The Arms Trade with the Third World,* Penguin Books, 1975, p. 286 & 290.
37. *Documents on German Foreign Policy. 1918-45,* HMSO, 1957, X, no. 326, p. 461-4.
38. R. Proctor, *La Agonía de un Neutral,* Madrid, 1972, p. 150-60.
39. R. Garriga, *La España de Franco,* Puebla, 1971, vol. II, p. 31.
40. G. Hills, *Spain,* p. 245.
41. Cf. S. G. Payne, *Politics and the Military . . .,* p. 426.
42. G. Hills, *Spain,* p. 433-40.
43. T. Cossías, *La Lucha Contra el Maquis en España,* Madrid, 1956, p. 21-5.
44. L. Fernsworth, 'Spain in Western Defence', *Foreign Affairs,* 31.4, July, 1953, p. 653.
45. Cf. Idem, p. 652.
46. Idem, p. 657.
47. R. Serrano Suñer, *Entre Hendaya y Gibraltar,* p. 182.
48. B. Welles, *Spain, The Gentle Anarchy,* London, 1965, p. 290.
49. Junta Interministerial Conmemorativa de los 25 de Paz Española, *Defensa Nacional,* Madrid, 1964.
50. Cf. G. Hills, *Spain,* p. 288.
51. Idem, p. 290.
52. B. Welles, *Spain. The Gentle Anarchy,* p. 239-44.
53. Idem, 292-308.

54. J. Bardavío, *La Estructura del Poder en España*, p. 178-9. *Las Fuerzas Armadas Españolas*, Dossier Mundo, p. 44-6.

55. L. Solana, 'Armamento en Polvo' *Cambio 16*, 6.1.75.

56. *The Times*, 2.3.73.

57. *Cuadernos para el Diálogo*, September, 1972.

58. Minister G. López Bravo's speech to the Cortes in December 1970; in *Actualidad Económica*, 21.11.74.

59. *Las Fuerzas Armadas Españolas*, Dossier Mundo, p. 127.

60. *The Military Balance 1974-75*, IISS London, 1974.

61. Cf. J. Velarde's interview in J. L. Herrero's 'Análisis del Ejército Español', *La Actualidad Económica*, 12.6.71, p. 44-5.

62. J. Busquets, *El Militar de Carrera en España*, p. 155.

63. *La Vanguardia Española*, 10.1.75.

64. *Arriba*, 17.11.74.

65. A. Saez Alba, *La Asociación Católica Nacional de Propagandistas*, Paris, 1974.

66. Cf. D. Ridruejo, *Escrito en España*, p. 287.

67. J. Busquets, *El Militar de Carrera*, p. 264-6.

3. The Church: From Crusade to Christianity

1. On Carlism see G. Brenan, *The Spanish Labyrinth*, (Cambridge, 1943), Ch. IX; R. Carr, *Spain 1808-1939*, (Oxford, 1966) *passim*; R. M. Blinkhorn, *Carlism and the Spanish Crisis of the 1930s* in *Journal of Contemporary History*, vol. 7, nos. 3-4 (1972). A full-length book on this subject is awaited from Dr Blinkhorn.

2. 'Integrism' is used here in its broader sense i.e. that tendency within the Church to defend the 'integrism' or *totality* of traditional Catholic teaching as it had existed since the Middle Ages. Integrism is diametrically opposed to 'modernist' tendencies which attempt to revise doctrine in the light of contemporary trends. For a brief summary see K. O. von Aretin, *The Papacy and the Modern World*, (Eng. Trans. London, 1970) ch. 8: *Modernism and Integrism*. 'Integrismo' in the narrower, Spanish sense, defines the extreme wing of the Carlist movement, as exemplified in the policies of Cándido and Ramón Nocedal. See R. M. Blinkhorn, *Ideology and Schism in Spanish Traditionalism 1876-1931*, in *Iberian Studies*, vol. 1, no. 1 (1972) pp. 16-24.

3. H. L. Matthews, *The Yoke and the Arrows*, (London 1958) p. 121. It is fashionable to regard Leo XIII as a 'progressive' Pope. However, perusal of his writings reveals strong sentiments against democracy, equality and, above all, Freemasonry. The Encyclical *Humanum Genus*, 1884, states that those who advocate equality and the right of people to choose their rulers are animated by Satan. Similar attitudes are expressed in *Quod Apostolici*, 1878, and other encyclicals.

4. Of particular importance was the policy of *desamortización* or disentailment of Church estates held in mortmain. See Brenan, *op. cit.*, ch. III and VI; Carr, *op. cit.*, pp. 172-6.

5. Carr, *op. cit.*, pp. 465 ff.

6. The Encyclical advocates the abolition of strikes and the setting up of vertical syndicates. (Clauses 91-5.)

7. Article 3 declared Spain a secular state, but Article 26 was more controversial. It drastically reduced the legal activities of the regular orders and, above all, forbade them to engage in teaching. Opposing views on this subject can be found in J. Castillejo, *War of Ideas in Spain* (London, 1937) and E. A. Peers, *Spain, the Church and the Orders* (London, 1939).

8. P. Preston, *The 'Moderate' Right and the Undermining of the Second Republic in Spain 1931-1933* in *European Studies Review*, vol. 3, no. 4, (1973); P. Preston, *El 'Accidentalismo' de la CEDA: ?Aceptación o sabotaje de la República?* in *Cuadernos de Ruedo Ibérico*, 41/42 (Paris, 1973); R. A. H. Robinson, *The Origins of Franco's Spain*, (Newton Abbot, 1970).

9. The Catholic rank and file were galvanized by the *Comité Nacional de la Confederación Espanola de Sindicatos Obreros* (CESO) and the *Confederación Nacional Catolico-Agraria*. For a revealing insight into the activities of these organizations following the outbreak of war, see the collection of documents analysed by J. J. Castillo in *Revista Española de la Opinión Pública*, vol. 38, pp. 205-303 (Madrid, 1974).

10. H. Thomas, *The Spanish Civil War*, (London, 1961) 1965 Ed., pp. 575-7; G. Jackson, *The Spanish Republic and the Civil War 1931-1939*, (Princeton, 1965) 1967 Ed., p. 423; N. B. Cooper, *Catholicism and the Franco Regime*, (Beverly Hills and London, 1975) pp. 8-10; G. Hills, *Franco: The Man and His Nation*, (London 1967) pp. 304-5. Many commentaries on the Collective Letter exist in Spanish, the most piquant being that in H. R. Southworth, *El Mito de la Cruzada de Franco*, (Paris, 1963) pp. 104-6, also available in French. A useful summary of the Letter is in J. M. Vázquez *et al., La Iglesia española Contemporánea* (Madrid, 1973) pp. 74-6.

11. Thomas, *op. cit.*, p. 754.

12. For complete text see J. de Iturralde, *El Catolicismo y la Cruzada de Franco*, vol. III, (Toulouse, 1965) pp. 551-3.

13. Translations and useful commentaries are contained in *The Papacy and Totalitarianism between the Two World Wars*, Ed. C. F. Delzell, (New York and Toronto, 1974).

14. S. G. Payne, *Falange*, (Stanford, 1961) pp. 192-4.

15. Accounts of the dilution of the original Falange into the new State party can be found in Payne, *op. cit.*; M. García Venero, *Falange en la Guerra de España* (Paris, 1967) – since re-written under various titles; H. R. Southworth, *Antifalange* (Paris, 1967); J. J. Linz, *From Falange to Movimiento-Organización* in *Authoritarian Politics in Modern Society* (Ed. S. P. Huntington and C. H. Moore, New York, 1970).

16. M. Tuñón de Lara, *El Hecho Religioso en España* (Paris, 1968) p. 152.

17. The formula is as follows: The government would consult with the Nuncio and send to Rome a list of six candidates for a bishopric. The Pope would reduce this to a short list of three from which Franco would make the final choice.

18. The other non-signatories were Bishop Mateo Mugica of Vitoria, whose ambivalent attitude towards the rising placed him in a similar position to that of Cardinal Vidal, Cardinal Segura, who was absent from

Spain, and the Bishop of Orihuela, who was ill. Whether the last-named voted by proxy or not is in dispute. Cooper, *op. cit.*, p. 8.

19. J. Georgel, *El Franquismo,* (Paris, 1970) p. 191, also available in French.

20. J. Martínez Alier, *Labourers and Landowners in Southern Spain,* (London, 1971) pp. 306-11.

21. J. M. Molina (Juanel), *Noche sobre España,* (Mexico, 1958) pp. 114-19.

22. Apart from Molina, *op. cit.*, see V. Alba, *Sleepless Spain* (London, 1948) pp. 40-1, which tells of how prisoners were abused viciously in Alicante jail by the Chaplain Fr. Vendrell. S. J. Primate Plà y Deniel refused to take action against him; if he had, it would have been out of character with the clergy's behaviour in prisons at this time. Isabel de Palencia in *Smouldering Freedom* (London 1946) pp. 127-8, speaks of methods used to convert the 'Reds' by force. See also Martín Torrent García ¿*Qué me dice usted de los presos?* (Alcalá de Henares 1942) quoted by H. R. Southworth, note 53. The most well-known story of clerical violence is that of the impenitent prisoner killed in Burgos jail by a blow from a Crucifix wielded by a furious priest. Arrabal, *Lettre au General Franco* (Paris, 1972) p. 159.

23. A. L. Orensanz, *Religiosidad Popular Española (1940-1965)* (Madrid, 1974), pp. 9-22.

24. B. Barba Hernández, *Dos años al frente del Gobierno Civil de Barcelona* (Madrid, 1948) p. 26; *Catalunya sota el regim franquista: informe sobre la persecució de la llengua i la cultura de Catalunya pel regim del General Franco* (Paris, 1973), pp. 421-7, 431-9; Matthews, *op. cit.*, pp. 40-1.

25. During the Republic the Falange continually spoke out against the 'decadent' orthodox Right. However, falangist thugs always directed their attacks on the Left, and never on rightist groups such as the *Juventud de Acción Popular.*

26. E. J. Hughes, *Report from Spain* (New York, 1947) pp. 54-8.

27. J. J. Linz, *An Authoritarian Regime. Spain.* in *Cleavages, Ideologies and Party Systems,* Ed. E. Allardt and Y. Littunen (Helsinki, 1964). On the history of the ACNP see M. Fernandez Areal, *La política católica en España* (Barcelona, 1970) pp. 91-163.

28. Among its members were Monarchists (Lamamié de Cleirac, Vegas Latapié), Carlists (Victor Pradera), liberal Catholics (Luis Lucía, Giménez Fernández), Basque Nationalists (Aguirre), and Fascists (Onésimo Redondo).

29. On the role of the CEDA see Preston and Robinson, *op. cit.*, quoted note 8. A detailed analysis of the component organizations of the CEDA is given in Robinson pp. 415-24.

30. P. Preston, *Alfonsist Monarchism and the Coming of the Spanish Civil War* in *Journal of Contemporary History,* vol. 7, nos. 3-4 (1972).

31. A. Sáez Alba, *La otra 'Cosa Nostra',* (Paris, 1974) p. XXII.

32. Fernández Areal, *op. cit.*, p. 137. Co-author with Castiella of this grotesque monument to falangist imperialism was Jose Maria de Areilza, Count of Motrico, now given much exposure on the media as a 'liberal' opponent of Franco.

33. Hughes, *op. cit.*, p. 65.

34. The Bishop had refused the sacraments to French citizens resident in Madrid who were not loyal to Vichy, *ibid.*, p. 79. Mgr. Eijo continued to be an embarrassment to the régime. It was not until after his death that the See of Madrid became an archbishopric. B. Welles, *Spain, the Gentle Anarchy,* (London, 1965), p. 142.

35. Orensanz, *op. cit.*, pp. 37-48.

36. It is widely held that Pius XII, then Cardinal Pacelli, Vatican Secretary of State, was the prime instigator of Pius XI's 1937 Encyclical *Divini Redemptoris 'on atheistic communism'*. Spain is specifically mentioned in the document. See Delzell, *op.,cit.*, pp. 160-7; von Aretin, *op. cit.*, pp. 193, 201.

37. Martínez Alier, *op. cit.*, p. 163; M. Gallo, *Spain under Franco,* (London, 1973) p. 227.

38. Gallo, *op. cit.*, p. 222.

39. Hills, *op. cit.*, pp. 413-14. Franco had also negotiated the establishment of the Rota Tribunal, giving Spain independence from Rome in matters concerning annulment of marriage.

40. For the Concordat see Ebenstein, *op. cit.*, ch. 9; Georgel, *op. cit.*, pp. 193-6; Gallo, *op. cit.*, pp. 222-3; Welles, *op. cit.*, pp. 145 ff.; Matthews, *op. cit.*, pp. 122-5; Cooper, *op. cit.*, pp. 15-17; R. Tamames, *La República. La Era de Franco,* (Madrid, 1973) pp. 555-8; G. Hills, *Spain,* (London, 1970) pp. 278-9; A. M. Brassloff, *Church–State Relations in Spain since the Civil War,* in *Iberian Studies,* vol. II, no. 2, 1973, pp. 88-9.

41. R. de la Cierva, *Francisco Franco. Un siglo de España,* (Madrid, 1972-3) vol. II, p. 486.

42. Orensanz, *op. cit.*, pp. 23-4; D. Artigues, *El Opus Dei en España,* (Paris, 1971) pp. 149, 152-3. For Lain's early falangism see H. R. Southworth, *Antifalange*, p. 57.

43. Saez Alba, *op. cit.*, pp. 198-9. It is possible that Fr. Javierre made contact in Munich with Indalecio Prieto.

44. In December 1969 Javierre became Editor of the Seville daily *El Correo de Andalucía*. His inclination to the left was soon reflected in the editorial policy of the newspaper. A controversy followed which ended in his removal from the editorship in April 1972. The case is dealt with in detail by Sáez Alba, *op. cit.*, pp. 174-281.

45. Welles, *op. cit.*, pp. 148 ff.; Ebenstein, *op. cit.*, ch. 7; Cooper, *op. cit.*, pp. 18-20.

46. Welles, *op. cit.*, pp. 148-9.

47. I. Fernández de Castro, *La Iglesia de la Cruzada y sus supervivencias* in *Horizonte Español 1966* (Paris, 1966).

48. For Opus Dei see Artigues, *op. cit.*, a sober account, also available in French. A more sensational view is given in J. Ynfante, *La prodigiosa aventura del Opus Dei* (Paris, 1970). Brief accounts in English can be found in Ebenstein, *op. cit.*, ch. 8; Cooper, *op. cit.*, pp. 20-8; J. Pilapil, *Opus Dei in Spain* in *The World Today* (May, 1971).

49. Artigues, *op. cit.*, pp. 43-51.

50. *Ibid.*, p. 93.

51. *Camino,* Maxims nos. 641, 643, 655.

52. Artigues, *op. cit.*, p. 127.

53. The *Estudio General de Navarra* was found in 1951, recognized as a 'Universidad de la Iglesia' in 1960 and as a full University in 1962.
At Pamplona it has one of the best equipped campuses in Spain and at Barcelona a powerful Business School, the Instituto de Estudios Superiores de la Empresa (IESE) which has established links with Harvard.

54. See chapter eight by Salvador Giner, in this volume.

55. See chapter four by J. M. Esreban in this volume.

56. On the effects of emigration and tourism on Spanish religious attitudes see Vazquez *et al., op. cit.*, pp. 297-344.

57. In a speech on 1 June 1962 in Barcelona. Artigues, *op. cit.*, pp. 209-12. Even Franco himself 'welcomed' the Encyclical. J. W. D. Trythall, *Franco* (London, 1970), p. 233.

58. Fr. González Ruiz was becoming a thorn in the flesh of the hierarchy with his outspoken sermons as Canon of Málaga Cathedral and in writings for periodicals such as the JOC journal, *Juventud Obrera*. See D. Barea, *Sobre el diálogo entre marxistas y católicos* in *Cuadernos de Ruedo Ibérico* (Paris), no. 11, Feb. 1967, pp. 37-58. This issue also contains an article by González Ruiz himself: *El cristiano y la revolución*.

59. A useful summary of proceedings at the various sessions of the Council is *Council Daybook*, Ed. F. Anderson, 3 Vols., (Washington D.C., 1965) (Henceforth C.D.).

60. C.D., vol. II, p. 45.

61. C.D., vol. II, p. 37.

62. C.D., vol. II, p. 45.

63. Georgel, *op. cit.*, p. 222; Tuñón de Lara, *op. cit.*, p. 171.

64. C.D., vol. III, pp. 88-9.

65. C.D., vol. III, pp. 88-9.

66. C.D., vol. II, p. 314.

67. C.D., vol. III, p. 139.

68. A one-volume English translation of the Council documents is *Documents of Vatican II*, Ed. W. M. Abbott, S. J., (London, 1966).

69. This is the figure given by Georgel, *op. cit.*, p. 212; see note 70 below.

70. Welles, *op. cit.*, pp. 149-50; Welles quotes a figure of 335 priests.

71. Saez Alba, *op. cit.*, pp. 78-83.

72. G. Hills, *Franco*, pp. 437-8; Georgel, *op. cit.*, p. 205; Welles, *op. cit.*, pp. 147-8; A. Lloyd, *Franco* (London, 1969) p. 227.

73. Georgel, *op. cit.*, pp. 209-10.

74. *Ibid.*, pp. 198-9.

75. *Ibid.*, p. 225.

76. Survey by Bishop Dorado Soto of Guádix-Baza. See the *Tablet* 3 June 1972. On the Catholic Action crisis see Georgel, *op. cit.*, pp. 222-5; Cooper, *op. cit.*, pp. 31-2; Vázquez *et al., op. cit.*, pp. 184-7; E. Miret Magnalena, *Panorama Religioso* in *España Perspectiva 1968* (Madrid, 1969).

77. *Todo sobre el Concordato*, Equipo Vida Nueva, (Madrid, 1971) p. 117 quoted Brassloff, *op. cit.*

78. Georgel, *op. cit.*, pp. 223-4. Relations between Bishop Gúrpide and his clergy continued acrimonious. Many Basque priests were sympathetic to

ETA and some refused to say Mass unless the red and yellow national flag was removed from churches. Others refused to attend religious services in memory of the death of José Antonio Primo de Rivera. On one occasion pro-Franco nuns demanded that their Chaplain Fr. Julián Ibabi cease to officiate at their services on account of his anti-regime sermons. For an excellent account of ecclesiastical turmoil at this time see Georgel, *op. cit.*, pp. 180-230.

79. See note 69.

80. The priests were Fathers Xavier Amurizar, Jesús Naverán, Alberto Gabicagogeascoa, Julián Calzada and Nicolás Tellería 'Nikola', the last-named released in April 1975 – *Cambio 16,* 5 May 1975.

81. Georgel, *op. cit.*, p. 236.

82. For the text see *Documentos socio-políticos de obispos españoles (1968-1972),* Ed. J. Angulo Uribarri (Madrid 1972) (Henceforth DSP) pp. 114-19.

83. DSP, pp. 41-8; Miret Magnalena, *op. cit.*

84. This idea, of course, has become a cornerstone of the pseudo-liberal 'apertura' policy of the Arias Navarro government.

85. Pildaín had been an opponent of democracy since the time when he sat as a right wing deputy in the Republican Cortes. See Hills, *Spain,* pp. 145, 147; Jackson, *op. cit.*, pp. 49, 58. He resisted attempts in Las Palmas to open a museum in memory of the 'heretic' Pérez Galdós. The Bishop held a similar opinion of Unamuno. See Georgel, *op. cit.*, p. 196.

86. DSP, pp. 53-69.

87. DSP, p. 210.

88. DSP, pp. 141-2, 213, 216.

89. Georgel, *op. cit.*, pp. 211-13.

90. *Catalunya sota el regim franquista,* pp. 439, 445; *Le Vatican et la Catalogne: une affaire de l'après-concile; Le Problème de la Nomination des Evêques dans l'Eglise d'aujourd'hui* (Paris, 1971) *passim.*

91. Georgel, *op. cit.*, p. 216.

92. Vázquez *et al., op. cit.*, pp. 406-28; On religious freedom see also Matthews, *op. cit.*, pp. 133-44; D. Nicholl, *Religious Liberty in Spain* in *Iberian Studies,* vol. I, no. 1, 1972.

93. Miret Magnalena, *op. cit.*, p. 94.

94. Vázquez *et al., op. cit.*, p. 418.

95. DSP, pp. 51-3.

96. Cardinal Tabera was later elevated to the Curia as Prefect of the Congregation of Religious and Secular Institutes. He died on 13 June 1975.

97. Miret Magnalena, *op. cit.*; Vázquez *et al., op. cit.*, p. 382. Cardinal Bueno was, however, quick to deny being a 'progressive', although he favoured the separation of Church and State. *The Tablet,* 27 March 1971.

98. This conservative victory was short-lived. For a penetrating analysis of the real situation see Article by M. Niedergang in *Le Monde,* 14 March 1969.

99. When he resigned, he received recognition for his past services to the State by the award of the Grand Cross of Carlos III, *The Tablet,* 8 August 1970.

100. DSP, pp. 49-50.

101. F. Santos, *1963-73: La memoria de los días,* in *Cuadernos para el Diálogo,* December 1973, p. 547.

102. Vázquez *et al., op. cit.,* pp. 376, 384-5.

103. *The Tablet,* 20 Feb. 1971.

104. Georgel, *op. cit.,* pp. 227-8.

105. DSP, pp. 149-53; Vázquez *et al., op. cit.,* pp. 432-4.

106. DSP, pp. 154-5.

107. DSP, pp. 120-5.

108. DSP, pp. 141-6.

109. DSP, pp. 128-32; *The Tablet,* 1 Aug. 1970, 8 Aug. 1970.

110. DSP, pp. 72-6.

111. *Cambio 16,* 5 May 1973 (see note 80).

112. *The Tablet* 16 May, 13 June, 27 June, 4 July 1970; Sáez Alba states that Cirarda was a reactionary at heart who was forced into action by pressure from militant clergy, *op. cit.,* p. 218.

113. DSP, pp. 133-4.

114. Vázquez *et al., op. cit.,* pp. 431-40.

115. Cf. the article by J. Ll. Hollyman in this volume; Kepa Salaberri, *El proceso de Euskadi en Burgos: sumarísimo 31-69* (Paris, 1971); Federico de Arteaga, *ETA y el proceso de Burgos* (Madrid, 1971); Ortzi, *Historia de Euskadi: el nacionalismo vasco y ETA* (Paris, 1975) pp. 363-73.

116. Santos, *op. cit.,* pp. 551-2; *The Tablet,* 26 Sept. 1970; *Ya* 22 Nov 1970.

117. *Le Monde,* 23 Dec. 1970.

118. DSP, p. 209.

119. *The Economist,* 15 June 1973.

120. DSP, pp. 202-8.

121. P. Preston, *General Franco's Rearguard* in *New Society,* 29 Nov. 1973.

122. Tamames, *op. cit.,* p. 601; *The Tablet,* 24 Jan. 1970. Among defence witnesses was the Auxiliary Bishop of Madrid Mgr. Echarren Ysturiz. Fr. Gamo identified with the struggle of the Madrid working class. He became a symbol of resistance to the régime together with other priests, notably Fr. Jose María de Llanos – see *Le Monde,* 14 Mar. 1969.

123. *The Tablet,* 8 Aug. 1970.

124. Santos, *op. cit.,*p. 551.

125. In the 1907 Encyclical of Pius X, *Pascendi Dominici Gregis,* 'On the doctrines of the modernists' Sec. III, Clause V.

126. DSP pp. 91-101. Only perusal of the completext can give a true idea of the real impact. Among the clauses on civil rights are demands for a fairer distribution of wealth (Clause 9), freedom of association regarding trade unions and political parties (Clause 12), respect for rights of ethnic minorities (Clause 16), equality before the law (Clause 18), right of conscientious objection (Clause 19). Clause 20 stresses the need to protect human beings from torture of body, mind and spirit.

127. Spanish text: '. . . reconocemos humildemente y pedimos perdón porque nosotros no supimos a su tiempo ser verdaderos ministros de reconciliación en el seno de nuestro pueblo, dividido por una guerra entre hermanos.'

128. The words 'no siempre supimos' were substituted for 'no supimos a

su tiempo'.

129. Vázquez *et al.*, *op. cit.*, pp. 364-70.

130. For the 'Wright-Tarancón' affair see *The Tablet*, 11 March, 18 March, 1972; Santos, *op. cit.*, p. 555; Sáez Alba, *op. cit.*, p. LXLIV Note 154; Cooper, *op. cit.*, p. 41. On the Bishops' Conference see K. N. Medhurst, *Government in Spain* (Oxford, 1973), p. 48.

131. *The Tablet*, 18 March, 15 April 1972.

132. *Le Monde*, 22 Dec. 1973; *Información Democrática* (Madrid, Jan. 1974).

133. *Cambio 16*, 24 Feb. 1975.

134. *The Tablet*, 3 Feb. 1973; *Blanco y Negro*, 27 January 1973: Vázquez *et al.*, *op. cit.*, pp. 403-6.

135. *The Tablet*, 14 April, 12 May 1973.

136. *The Tablet*, 12 May 1973; *Blanco y Negro* 12 May 1973.

137. *The Tablet*, 1 Dec., 8 Dec. 1973.

138. *ABC*, 13 Feb. 1974. On the aftermath of the assassination see P. Preston, *Spain in Crisis: The Assassination of Carrero Blanco and its Aftermath* in *Iberian Studies*, vol. III, no. 1 (1974) and *The Tension Mounts* in *The Nation*, 17 Aug. 1974.

139. *Osservatore Romano*, English Edition, 7 Feb. 1974.

140. Mgr. Ubieta López h'een arrested in April 1969 together with six other priests on suspicion of involvement in ETA. He was freed after three days following the intervention of Bishop Cirarda. The other priests remained in prison. Georgel, *op. cit.*, p. 215.

141. *L'Affaire Añoveros*, Pub. CISE (Paris, 1974) p. III.

142. *The Tablet*, 9 Nov. 1974.

143. *The Tablet*, 5 Oct. 1974.

144. *The Tablet*, 7 Dec. 1974; *Blanco y Negro*, 7 Dec. 1974.

145. On the Synod see *Osservatore Romano*, English Edition, 24 Oct., 31 Oct., 7 Nov., 14 Nov. 1974.

146. *The Tablet*, 17 Aug., 24 Aug. 1974; *The Guardian*, 31 July 1974.

147. Cf. the articles by P. Preston cited in note 138.

148. For the *Madrid* case, see Rafael Calvo Serer, *La dictadura de los Franquistas; 1 El affaire del 'Madrid' y el futuro político* (Paris, 1973).

149. *The Times*, 7 March 1975.

150. *The Tablet*, 21 Aug. 1971.

151. *The Tablet*, 15 March 1975; *Cambio 16*, 31 March 1975.

152. *Cambio 16*, 31 March 1975; *Blanco y Negro*, 26 April 1975. For a useful summary in English of the Collective Letter see *The Tablet*, 26 April 1975.

153. An apt distinction between the attitudes of the Bishops and that of the lower clergy is made by the Spanish sociologist Jose Cazorla; he contrasts the overt confrontation by the priests with the gradual lessening of support by the bishops. See J. Cazorla Pérez's contribution on the Church in *La España de los anos 70*, vol. 3, Ed. M. Fraga Iribarne (Madrid, 1974), pp. 383-418.

154. *The Tablet*, 22 March 1975; *Cambio 16*, 31 March 1975.

155. *Cambio 16*, 2 June 1975. For a lengthy analysis of this affair see *Blanco y Negro*, 17 May 1975. See also *The Tablet*, 17 May 1975; *Blanco y Negro*, 24 May 1975.

156. *The Times*, 20 May 1975; *The Tablet*, 24 May 1975; *The Universe*, 30 May 1975.

157. *Cambio 16*, 26 May 1975.

158. *Catholic Herald*, 6 June 1975.

159. *The Tablet*, 21 June 1975.

160. *The Tablet*, 31 May 1975; *Cambio 16*, 2 June 1975.

161. *The Tablet*, 31 May 1975.

162. Sáez Alba, *op. cit.*, pp. LXLII-LXLVI.

163. See G. Hermet, *Reflexiones sobre las funciones políticas del catolicismo en los regimenes autoritarios contemporáneos* in *Sistema*, no. 4 (Madrid, January 1974).

4. The Economic Policy of Francoism: An Interpretation

1. This work owes a great deal to the collective discussions and research materials of a previous study in which I participated together with J. Clavera, A. Monés, A. Montserrat and J. Ros Hombravella – published as *Capitalismo Español: De la autarquia a la estabilización (1939-1959)*, Edicusa, Madrid, 1973. I am also indebted to R. Carr, J. P. Fusi, C. Kayder, F. Lannon, J. Martínez Alier, P. Preston, J. Ros, N. Serra, J. Varela Ortega and J. M[a]. Vegara, who read the first draft and made very helpful comments.

2. See E. N. Baklanoff 'Spain and the Atlantic Community: A Study of Incipient Integration and Economic Development' in *Economic Development and Cultural Change*, vol. XVI, no. 4, July 1968, pp. 588-602.

3. In fact the process of rapid economic growth did not start until 1954. Before that date the régime's argument was: economic stagnation is a reasonable cost for 'social peace'. See E. Fuentes and J. Plaza, 'Perspectivas de la Economía Española', *Revista de Economia Politica*, vol. IV, nos. 1-2, May-Sept. 1952, especially p. 99.

4. Fernández de Castro, I. *De las Cortes de Cádiz al Plan de Desarrollo, 1808-1966*, Ruedo Ibérico, Paris, 1968, and specially, Soler, R., 'The New Spain', *New Left Review*, no. 58, Nov-Dec 1969, and R. Tayà, 'Sobre la Intervenció Estatal i el Creixement Industrial a Espanya de 1939 a 1966' in *Economía Crítica: una perspectiva catalana*, Edicions 62, Barcelona, 1973.

5. See A. Linz, and S. de Miguel, *Los Empresarios ante el Poder Público*, Instituto de Estudios Políticos, Madrid, 1966. See also J. Velarde, 'Sobre la Decadencia Económica de España' *De Economía*, vol. VI, nos. 25-26, Sept.-December 1955, p. 514.

6. A very interesting picture of the actual process of policy-making can be found in J. M[a]. Marcet's memoirs, *Mi Ciudad y yo*, Barcelona, 1963.

7. See C. W. Anderson, *The Political Economy of Modern Spain*, University of Wisconsin Press, (Madison, 1970); see also F. B. Pike, 'The New Corporatism in Franco's Spain and some Latin American Perspectives', in F. B. Pike and T. Stritch (eds.) *The New Corporatism. Social-Political Structures in the Iberian World*, University of Notre Dame Press, Notre Dame, 1974. In fact, Pike goes one step further and argues that corporatism becomes a necessity when resources are scarce.

8. M. Paris Eguilaz, *El Desarrollo Económico Español, 1906-1964*, Madrid,

1965, p. 192; the relevent chapter by J. Velarde Fuertes, in M. Fraga, J. Velarde, and S. del Campo, (eds.) *La wspaña de los años 70,* Ed. Moneda y Crédo, Madrid, 1973, vol. I, pp. 983 and 1031.

9. C. W. Anderson, *The Political Economy . . ., op. cit.*

10. '[Our Régime] . . . will be similar to the Italian and German régimes in so far as hierarchy, love for the Fatherland, social justice and well-being of middle and working classes shall be strengthened', F. Franco, Interview to the *New York Times Magazine,* 26 December 1937. In *Spain, Review of Commercial Conditions,* HMSO, London, 1945, the new controls are referred to as 'modelled partly on German and Italian lines,' p. 23.

11. It was not until 1943 that the new slogan was launched, 'neither fascism, nor communism: national policy', *El Español,* November 1943.

12. Spanish press, 2 October 1936. See also, F. Franco, interview to 'Jornal do Brazil', January 1938. During this period this was clear for all contemporaries. E. Diaz, professor of Law of the University of Barcelona, writes: ' "Everything in the State. Nothing out of the State. Nothing against the State", has said Mussolini, expressing in this way the strong organic unity of the Totalitarian State. Franco's State is like this', *Orientaciones Jurídicas del Nuevo Estado Español,* Barcelona, 1939, p. 13.

13. Preamble of the Decree 23 October 1937. The SNT was responsible for the full commercialization of wheat production; its major aim was to achieve self-sufficiency in wheat. It should be noted that Italy and Portugal also organized the 'battle of grain'.

14. F. Franco, speech in Burgos, 5 June 1939. The previous Junta de Defensa Nacional seems not to have had such strong anti-liberal feelings; see, for instance, Preamble Decree, 11 August 1936.

15. F. Franco, speech at the Consejo Nacional del Movimiento, 18 July 1942. In the same speech Franco argues that one of the causes of the critical state of the Spanish economy before the uprising was that it had been operating in the 'greatest libertinism'. For the extraordinary extent of State intervention before the Civil War see Perpiñá, R., 'De Economía Hispana', appendix to G. Haberler, *El Comercio Internacional,* Labor, Barcelona, 1936.

16. Law (with the rank of Constitutional Law) 9 March 1938. As we shall see later, the Fuero del Trabajo has many points in common with the Italian fascist Carta del Lavoro. See also, *Bases de la Organización Sindical,* Law, 6 December 1940, where it is stated that 'this Law guarantees the subordination of the Syndical Organization to the party, since only the party can communicate the necessary discipline, unity and spirit for the national economy to serve national politics.'

17. Law, 25 September 1941. The INI was the Spanish version of the Italian fascist IRI.

18. Falange's manifesto, for instance, contained many points concerning agriculture and hardly one mentioning industry.

19. *La Nueva España Agraria,* Editora Nacional, Bilbao, 1937, pp. 62 and 66.

20. '. . . the destructive marxism penetrated in workshops and factories . . .', F. Franco, speech, 18 June 1939.

21. Decree, 14 August 1936.

22.

Distribution of Labour Force (Percentages)

	Agriculture	Industry	Services
1930	45.51	26.51	27.98
1940	50.52	22.13	27.35
1950	47.57	26.55	25.88
1960	39.70	32.98	27.32
1970	29.10	37.30	33.60

Sources: Instituto de Cultura Hispánica, 1930-50, and INw, 1960 and 1970.

23. One common topic was the emphasis on Spanish racial values. See, for instance: '. . . from that date [18 July 1936] the purest values of our Army melted together with the racial ideals and virtues of our people', F. Franco, speech at the Consejo Nacional del Movimiento, 18 July 1942; on the Law creating the INI, referring to industrialization as 'the necessary backing for our racial values', Law, 25 September 1941. And for the 'new order', see, for instance, 'We have offered five hundred thousand dead for the salvation and unity of Spain in the first European battle of the new order', F. Franco, speech 18 July 1940; see also R. Serrano Suñer, (minister of Foreign Affairs), speech in Barcelona, 12 January 1941.

24. Preamble, Decree 31 November 1936. One of its articles reads: 'from now onwards, both in restaurants and in private homes, the egg dish will consist of one single egg'.

25. A. Amantia, *Liberalismo Economico e Corporatismo,* Società Editrice Internazionale, Torino, 1938, p. 66.

26. *Ibid.,* pp. 67 and 68.

27. The Fuero del Trabajo is referred to as the 'declaration of principles inspiring the social and economic policy of the National-Syndicalist State', Ministerial Decree 9 March 1939. See also, Preamble of the Law, 3 May 1940.

28. Carta del Lavoro, 21 April 1927 and Estatuto do Travalho Nacional, 23 September 1933.

29. These similarities were already pointed out by contemporary lawyers; see I. Serrano, (Professor of Law, University of Salamanca), *El Fuero del Trabajo. Doctrina y Comentario,* Talleres pipográficos Casa Martín, Valladolid, 1939, pp. 1 and 41. Specifically we have found the following correspondences between these legal documents. The first numbers correspond to the Spanish Law and the corresponding articles in the Italian and Portuguese cases are followed by (i) and (p), respectively. Correspondences:

Preamble: I (i), 1° (p); 1.5: II (i), 21° (p); 1.6: II. 1st par. (i); 1.8: 23° (p); II.1: 24° and 31° (p); II.2: XV (i), 26° 2nd point (p); II.3: XV (i); II.5: XVI (i), 28° (p); II.6: XXX (i); III.1: XII (i), 24° (p); III.3: 7° 3rd point (p); III.6: XXII (i); IV.1: 19° (p); VII: V (i), 50° (p); VIII.2: II, 2nd par. (i); VIII.3: VII, 2nd par. (i); VIII.4: 18° (p); X.1: XXVI (i), 48° (p); X.2: XXVII (i), 49° (p); XI.1: I and II (i); XI.2 and 3: XIX (i), 5° and 9° (p); XI.4: (i), 6° (p); XI.5: 7° 4th point (p); XI.6: VII 1st par. (i), 4° 1st par.

(p); XII.1: 12° and 13° (p); XIII.1: 3° and 7° 4th point (p); XIII.3: VI 2nd and 3rd par. (i), 41° 2nd and 4th par. (p); XIII.5: VI. 4th par. and XIII (i), 43° (p); XIII.6: VIII (i); XIII.7: XXIII (i), 46° (p).

30. The obvious reason for that was that the 'new order' in Spain was established after a civil war and therefore there was no need for compromise with the working class. See w. Diaz, *Orientaciones Jurídicas . . ., op. cit.,* p. 20.

31. Law, 6 December 1940. The preamble states 'syndicalization becomes the political form of the whole Spanish economy'; and art. 1, 'Spaniards, so long as they collaborate in the production process, constitute the National Syndicalist Community as a militant unit under the Movimiento's discipline'; art. 8, 'the socio-economic organization of production will be carried out through the National Syndicates', and art. 19 deals with the role of the party in the syndicates.

32. *Ibid.,* art. 18.

33. J. M ª de Areilza, 'Directrices de la nueva ordenación económica' in *Problemas Técnicos de importancia económica de la nueva organización de España.* Universidad de Barcelona, Barcelona, 1940, pp. 481 and 482.

34. Ministerial Decree, 8 June 1937.

35. Law, 16 July 1938.

36. A more sophisticated expression, authoritarianism with limited pluralism, has been launched by J. Linz, 'An Authoritarian Régime, Spain', in E. Allardt, and Y. Littunen, (eds.), *Cleavages, Ideologies and Party Systems,* Helsinki, 1964.

37. I. Serrano, *El Fuero del Trabajo . . ., op. cit.* (1939), pp. 325 and 326.

38. The point is that this was not an essential feature of fascist régimes. 'Autarchy' did not become a word of generalized use in Italy until 1935 and it does not appear in the *Enciclopedia Italiana* but only in the 1938 appendix; see J. Clavera, *et al., Capitalismo Español . . ., op. cit.,* vol. I, p. 81. This also answers those arguments claiming that after all the régime never did attempt a complete autarchy. Nor did Italy, until it started organizing a war economy; see B..Mussolini, Speech, 23 March 1936.

39. H. Paris, *El Desarrollo Económico . . ., op. cit.,* p. 192, states that attention has been drawn to this issue 'in order to present Spain as a fascist or nazist country to the rest of the world, thereby arousing foreign hostility [towards the Spanish régime].'

40. See J. Velarde, in *La España de los años 70, op. cit.;* H. Paris, *El Desarrollo Económico . . ., op. cit.;* F. Estapé, *Algunos Problemas Actuales de la Economía Española,* Lecture at the Associación Católica de Dirigentes, Barcelona, 1958; J. Clavera *et al., Capitalismo Español, op. cit.;* R. Tamames, *La República. La Era de Franco,* vol. 7 of the *Historia de España Alfaguara,* Alianza Editorial, Madrid, 1973; R. Tayá, 'Sobre la Intervenció Estatal . . .', *op. cit.*

41. R. Perpiña, 'De Economia Hispana', *op. cit.*

42. See F. Estapé, *Política Económica III,* Leccion 38, mimeo, Universidad de Barcelona – Facultad de Ciencias Económicas, Departamento de Publicaciones, Barcelona, 1964, especially anexo n° 4, p. XI.

43. See note 33. The art. 1 of the Law creating the INI clearly states that one of the aims is the creation and financing of industries 'directed to the

development of our economic autarchy', Law, 25 September 1941. See also, L. Alarcón de la Lastra, (Minister of Industry and Trade) in *Problemas Técnicós de Importancia . . . op cit.*

44. See J. M^a. Areilza, *Directrices . . ., op. cit.*, p. 492.

45. See J. M^a. Areilza, *Directrices . . ., op. cit.*, pp. 485 and 486 and L. Alarcón de la Lastra, in *Problemas Técnicos . . ., op. cit.*, p. 580. In 1942 the government publishing house published a book by H. Paris Eguilaz (Secretary of the Consejo de Economía Nacional), *Economía de Guerra*, Editora Nacional, Madrid, 1942, in which the author explains how a country should organize its war economy. Franco himself emphasized this point, stating that preparation for the war 'only brings fruitful goods for the Fatherland, for such preparation means creating our autarchy, striving and exploring our minds, opening new roads, building up new factories', F. Franco, speech at Vigo, 20 August 1942.

46. Autarchy was seen as the ideal solution to problems, limited only by inherent impossibilities. See, for instance: 'Spain has enough resources to solve autarchically the basic problem of housing', F. Franco, interview to M. Aznar, 31 December 1938; 'the possibility of achieving autarchy, in textiles is not very remote', L. Beltran, *La Industria Algodonera Española*, Ministerio del Trabajo, Barcelona, 1943, p. 58; F. Estapé, *Política wconómica III, op. cit.* sees industrial policy as inspired by the aim of autarchy and L. López de Sebastian, *Política Agraria en España, 1920-1970*, Guadiana de Publicaciones, Madrid, 1970, p. 434, reaches the same conclusion with respect to agricultural policy.

47. 'There are many industrialists wasting their time and energies trying to know about all state interventions, puzzled by an alleged incapacity to assimilate all of them, falling into the obsessive monomania of considering it impossible to be completely protected against misfortunes and sanctions they could incur through a lack of awareness or ignorance', J. L. de Campos, *Prontuario de Intervenciones Estatales en las Sociedades Mercantiles*, Ed. Mayfe, Madrid, 1944, p. 13.

48. 'A period of scarcity and inflation always requires an increase in state intervention; but in Spain this happens to coincide with a time in which the bureaucratic staff is disorganized as a consequence of the war of Liberation, and in which there is a lack of important knowledge on economic issues among both old and new civil servants. The result necessarily is a faulty intervention in the economy, susceptible to the spread of favouritism', J. Velarde, *Sobre la Decadencia Económica de España*, Tecnos, Madrid, 1969, p. 133.

49. B. Barba, Governor of Barcelona, accepts that 'should industrialists, who cannot dispose of the essential quotas at the right time, passively accept this situation, instead of obtaining the raw materials by any available means, we would see thousands and thousands of unemployed workers on the streets because of temporary shut-downs or complete bankruptcies', *Dos Años al Frente del Gobierno Civil de Barcelona*, Madrid, 1948, p. 31.

50. J. López de Sebastian, *Política Agraria en España, op. cit.*, p. 75.

51. 'Food conditions were not bad in the country districts, . . . but many of the towns faced starvation', *Spain, Review of Commercial Conditions, op. cit.*, p.

22. An illuminating account of the postwar hunger can be found in R. Fraser, *The Pueblo*, Allen Lane, London, 1973, especially pp. 71-108. In fact, agricultural production per head stood at a level 30 per cent below prewar standards.

	GNP per capita	Agricultural output per capita	Industrial output per capita
1935	100	100	100
1940	79.6	73.5	101.0
1945	70.6	58.2*	95.4
1950	85.3	70.3	118.3
1955	111.0	77.5	171.8
1960	132.8	91.5	264.6
1965	198.1	120.4	396.9
1970	253.6	135.6	549.3

* 1945 harvest has probably been the worst in the twentieth century.
Source: Consejo de Economía Nacional and INE.

52. By 1940 the index of official agricultural prices was 20 per cent above the index for industrial prices, compared with 1935 relative levels. But it should also be taken into account that official index numbers 'included the prices of official markets only; should the essential features of the black market be captured in it, the opinion about the improvement of peasant classes would be reaffirmed', E. Fuentes, and J. Plaza, 'Perspectivas de la Economía Española', *op cit.*, p. 90.

53. The importance of the black market is difficult to assess. J. Walker, *Spain, Economic and Commercial Conditions, Overseas Economic Surveys,* HMSO, London, 1949, p. 2, estimates that the black market supplied as much as 50 or even 60 per cent of demand, although by 1948 it had fallen to 20 or 30 per cent.

54. J. M[a]. de Areilza, 'Presente y Futuro de la Economía Industrial Española' in *Ciclo de Conferencias Económico-Financieras e Industriales,* Escuela de Ingenieros Industriales, Bilbao, 1954, p. 1.

55. The system of relative prices and foreign trade limitations produced an abnormal allocation of resources. The acute petrol shortages and the low price for electricity produced a high increase in the demand for electricity that could not be met by supply. As a result many industries had to install their own electric generators and by 1951 the power of these small generators represented as much as one third or one fourth of total electrical power in Spain. An interesting analysis can be found in F. Estapé, *Política Económica III, op. cit.,* Lección 34. See also, G. Clinton Pelham, *Spain, Economic and Commercial Conditions,* HMSO, London, 1952.

56. By the Decree, 8 September 1939 all new investments required previous ministerial permission.

57. According to Muñoz Linares, C. ('La Concentración de Capital en las Sociedades y Empresas Españolas', *Revista de Economía Política,* January 1952), the situation in 1957 was as follows: the capital of the top 0.55%

industrial firms represented 43.16% of total industrial capital; the top 1.07%, 49.70%, and the top 14.15%, 80.24%. This process towards monopoly was so evident that some radical Falangists turned their attention to monopolies and started a furious attack from the Falangist newspaper *Arriba,* claiming that the 'true task' for the Falange was the destruction of monopolies. Most of these writings are collected in *Notas sobre la Político Económica Española,* ed. del Movimiento, Madrid, 1956.

58. *Spain, Review . . ., op. cit.* (1945), p. 45.

59. See J. Walker, *Spain, Review . . ., op. cit.* (1949). 'Los Salarios durante los últimos veinte años', *Moneda y Crédito,* no. 60, 1957, pp. 49-59; R. Soler, 'The New Spain', *op. cit.,* and R. Tayá, 'Sobre la intervenció estatal . . .', *op. cit.,* M. de Torres ('La Politiça Social y el Desarrollo Económico' in *Juicio de la Política Económica Actual,* Aguilar, Madrid, 1954) argues that the Instituto Nacional de Estadística estimates did not include non-money income, which would put real wages in 1953 20% below prewar levels.

60. F. Franco, Speech at Lugo, 21 August 1942.

61. *Spain, Review . . ., op. cit.* (1945), p. 46.

62. E. Fuentes, and J. Plaza, 'Perspectivas . . .', *op. cit.,* p. 90.

63. See note 52.

64. A detailed analysis can be found in J. Muñoz, *El Poder de la Banca en España,* Zero, Madrid, 1969.

65. Ministerial Decree, 19 October 1939, later developed in the Law 30 December 1940. The entry was not reopened until 1963.

66. 'Either we let the banks dictate the Spanish state's economic policy, or the state will have to nationalize them', J. Velarde, 'Sobre la Decadencia Económica de España', *De Economía,* vol. VI, no. 25-26, Sept.-Dec. 1953, p. 533.

67. The number of banks established in Spain declined from 200 in 1939 to 131 in 1962; see I. Cuesta Garrigós, 'Los Grandes Bancos Españoles. Su evolución. 1922-1943', *Moneda y Crédito,* no. 11, Dec. 1944 (and the annual revisions published in this journal since then onwards).

68. 'In 1956 five of these Banks . . . controlled 51 per cent of the capital in the country', C. W. Anderson, *The Political Economy . . ., op. cit.,* p. 76. This is the impression of contemporary witnesses: L. Olariaga, director of the Consejo Superior Bancario, (*El Dinero,* Ed. Moneda y Crédito, Madrid, 1946 and 1954, vol. II, p. 160) stated that 'Spanish banks have substituted foreign capitalism in the creation of the national industry'; and J. Sardá, former Director of the Servicio de Estudios del Banco de España ('El Banco de España (1931-1962)' in *El Banco de España, Una historia económica,* Madrid, 1970, p. 460), points to the same process. See also T. E. Rogers, *Spain, Economic and Commercial Conditions,* HMSO, London, 1957, p. 4. In fact, the annual increase in industrial shares and bonds held by the six biggest banks throughout the forties represented between 22% and 62% of the new shares issued each year.

69. See R. Soler, 'The New Spain', *op. cit.,* and R. Tayá, 'Sobre la intervenció . . .', *op. cit.*

70. See J. Plaza, *et al., El Ahorro y la Formación de Capital en España, 1939-1968,* Confederación Española de Cajas de Ahorros, Madrid, 1971.

71. The portfolio of Insurance Companies shows that the proportion of real property to industrial shares was 1.4 to 1 in 1942, 2.3 to 1 in 1945 and 3.3 to 1 in 1950; see L. Olariaga, *El Dinero, op. cit.*, vol. II.

72.

	1945	1950	1960	1970
Direct taxes Total tax revenue	41.5	37.7	35.1	30.5
Personal income tax Total tax revenue	1.8	1.9	1.8	1.3

Source: E. Fuentes, 'Política Fiscal y Reforma Tributaria', in *La España de los años 70, op. cit.*, vol. II. 2, pp. 1012-13. As a point of reference, direct taxes in 1970 were more than 50% in countries like Great Britain, France and Germany and more than 60% in USA and Sweden.

73. A detailed analysis can be found in J. Clavera, 'La Politica Económica del Nuevo Estado Español durante la Segunda Guerra Mundial: una aproximación a sus repercussiones en Cataluña', Ph. D. Thesis, Universidad Autonoma de Barcelona, 1974.

74. Relevant evidence about the extent of war damage can be obtained from the balance sheet of the Instituto de Crédito para la Reconstrucción Nacional – official credit institution created by Law, 16 March 1939 with the mission of financing the reconstruction affecting the private sector and corporations. From the total amount of 5,870.6 million pesetas of credits given up to 1952, only 895.6 millions went to reconstruction projects, the rest being credits given to the shipbuilding industry and loans to the Treasury, among others. Moreover, the 895.6 million for reconstruction break down as follows: 48.7 million for agriculture, 88.9 million for industry, 629.4 million for infrastructure, housing and urbanism and 65.6 million for corporations. ICRN, *Memoria*, Madrid, 1952.

75. See for instance J. A. Suanzes, 'Franco y la Economía', in *Ocho discursos*, Centro de Estudios Económicos y Sociales del INI, Madrid, 1963, p. 142.

76. In addition to the evidence we have already produced, it is interesting to consider H. Paris' explanation: '. . . another point which has been subject to controversy is whether or not a nation is capable of recovering its economic prosperity after a long war without a heavy contribution of foreign capital, both for the private sphere, industry and trade, and for the public sector. Generally speaking it can be stated that national economic reconstruction by own means is perfectly possible . . . But, it should be kept in mind that the implementation of an economic policy allowing for a reconstruction by own means cannot be achieved within the general organization characteristic of liberal systems and therefore the transformation and setting of the corresponding state institutions is by all means indispensable for the success'; H. Paris, *Economía de Guerra, op. cit.*, pp. 80 and 81.

77. J. Walker, *Spain, op. cit.* (1949), p. 1 and 38, suggests that had

domestic costs of production not been so high Spain would have been able to export more than it actually did.

78. The régime defends itself about the failure in agriculture by blaming the insufficiency of imported fertilisers, but the value of wheat imports in 1948, for instance, was seven times as much as the value of the imported chemical fertilisers.

Imports (value in million pesetas-gold)

	Average 1931-35	1948
Wheat	7.4	216.5
Chemical fertilisers	60.5	31.1
Tobacco	20.8	66.0
Machinery	55.8	60.8
Electric Appliances	33.7	30.6

This misuse was clearly pointed out in the UNO's 1953 Report.

79. See B. Barba, *Dos años . . ., op. cit.* D. Carceller, Minister of Industry and Trade (1942-45) and well known representative of catalan industrialists' interests, declared before the Cortes that 'the consequences of the present war have intensified the need to follow on this Government's lines . . . and to go with unavoidable interventions, but keeping in mind that they should stop as soon as circumstances allow', *La Situación Económica de España,* Servicio de Propaganda del Ministerio de Industria y Comercio, Madrid, 1943. Even Franco himself recognised in 1947 that 'all countries have need of their foreign trade', Speech at the official closing of the Asamblea Nacional de Hermandades de Labradores y Ganaderos, 10 December 1947.

80. Especially, C. W. Anderson, *The Political Economy . . ., op. cit.*

81. Increasing pressure came from the industrialists' side; P. Gual Villalbi, spokesman of catalan industrialists who later became minister, wrote that 'our economist policy has been suffering for many years from a misleading conception, the belief that Spain can be a country with an intensive agrarian economy . . . Within this presumption, which has misled our staggering economic policy, another commonplace has prevailed, the one that we had to produce all the wheat we need for domestic consumption . . . But, we shall not discuss here to what extent this belief in the Spanish agrarian potential has damaged our economy and blocked our necessary industrialisation', 'Foreword' to E. Sala, *El Problema Mundial del Trigo y el Problema del Trigo en España,* Barcelona, 1947, p. 9. It is also important to note the banks' change of attitude as they started controlling industry. It is significant that the most liberal bank was precisely the only one specialising in long-term industrial financing, the Banco Urquijo.

82. It seems that by 1951 the talks with the US were well in progress. The Agreement signed in 1953 included very clear liberal commitments for the Spanish economic policy, like 'stablize the currency, fix and maintain a

realistic exchange rate, balance the budget as soon as possible, create and maintain domestic financial stability', as well as anti-monopoly policies, free market and liberalized foreign trade.

83. An official statement issued after a Cabinet meeting held by the new government, on 20 July 1951, expressed most of the new points of view. A passionate defence of this ideology can be found in M. Arburua's (Minister of Trade) speeches, collected in M. Arburua, *Cinco Años al Frente del Ministerio de Comercio*, Madrid, 1956. On this particular point, see also Ministerial Instruction 13 January 1953.

84. See M. Arburua, speech, 18 December 1951, speech, 23 February 1952 and speech, 28 June 1952, in *Cinco Años . . .,, op. cit.*, pp. 47, 64 and 76, respectively. See also Preamble of the Decree-Law, 8 February 1952 and Preamble of the Decree, 27 June 1952.

85. See Preamble of the Decree, 5 November 1953, and Decree, 25 March 1952. See also M. Arburua, Interview to the newspaper *Arriba*, 19 January 1954, in *Cinco Años . . . op. cit.*, p. 203.

86. See Arburúa, M., Press Conferences 1 August and 31 October 1951, in *Cinco Años . . ., op. cit.*, pp. 15 and 18.

87. For a detailed analysis of the economic policy in the early fifties see J. Clavera, *et al. Capitalismo Español . . ., op. cit.*, ch. 3.

88. In five years, from 1951 to 1955, agricultural prices fell 26.4 per cent relative to industrial prices. It can be argued that world prices too moved this way, but on the one hand this was an explicit objective by 1951 and on the other this is the expected result after freeing the market and importing large amounts of foodstuff.

89. R. Cavestany, Minister of Agriculture, stated that 'we have to undertake the readjustment of our economic policy with a sense of greater freedom and with a clear orientation towards definite objectives, following a policy of stimuli which makes possible the achievement of our aims by indirect means', and also, 'an agrarian reform is certainly needed, but it must deeply transform rural media, bringing to the land all the capital and technique it requires', in Speech at the Cortes, 18 December 1951 and *Una Política Agrícola*, Madrid, 1958; *cit.* in R. Tamames, *Estructura Económica de España*, 6th ed., Guadiana de Publicaciones, Madrid, 1971, p. 54.

90. See M. Arburúa, speech at the Cortes, 18 December 1951, in *Cinco Años . . ., op. cit.*, pp. 52-3.

91. See Banco Urquijo, *La Economía Española en 1952-1953*, Madrid, 1954.

92. M. de Torres ('La Coordinación de la Política Económica', in *Teoria y Práctica de la Política Económica*, Aguilar, Madrid, 1961, p. 76) suggests that 'it is also true that our industrial development has been partly due to the pressure of circumstances and not to the deliberate action of our economic policy'.

93. *Ibid.*, p. 77.

94. The whole plan seems to have a merely static point of view as if the only problem was the transition from a set of equilibrium prices (in a closed and intervened economy) to another set of equilibrium prices (in an open and free market economy). This static vision of the problem is also reflected in E. Fuentes and J. Plaza's view of the new economic policy: 'It seems

difficult to find among other European economies a case like the Spanish one, with a noticeably balanced structure, in which agriculture, mining, industry and services are pieces conjugating in a mutual economic equilibrium . . .' and therefore they understand that 'the [present] Spanish industrial development [is] a need raised by demographic growth', 'Perspectivas de la Económia Española', *op. cit.*, pp. 25 and 41.

95. See M. Arburúa, speech 31 October 1951, in *Cinco Años . . ., op. cit.*, p. 20.

96. See F. Estapé *Algunos Problemas Básicos de la Económia Española, op. cit.*, p. 15.

97. See M. de Torres, 'La Coordinación de la Politica Económica . . .', *op. cit.*, p. 84.

98. See E. Fuentes, 'La Propensión a Importar', in *Notas sobre Politica Económica Española, op. cit.*

99. By 1953, M. de Torres ('La Coordinación . . .', *op. cit.*, p. 61) had already pointed out the noticeable lack of coordination among ministerial departments, but it soon became an open clash; see M. Arburúa, Interview to *El Español,* January 1956, in *Cinco Años, op. cit.*, especially pp. 324 and 325.

100. It was already clear by 1954 that in spite of the new economic policy 'no change has come about in the principles inspiring monetary policy as against previous years'. Banco Urquijo, *La Economica Española,* 1952-1953, *op. cit.*, p. 12.

101. See J. Sardá, 'El Banco de España 1931-1962', *op. cit.*, p. 466.

102. These were the ministers of Trade, A. Ullastres, and the Treasury, M. Navarro, and the junior minister L. López Rodó, with the support of Carrero Blanco, minister of the Presidency (equivalent to Prime Minister).

103. See M. Navarro (minister of the Treasury), speech at the Cortes, 28 July 1959, in *Nueva Ordenación Económica,* Documentación Económica no. 7, OCYPE, Madrid, 1959.

104. See J. Sardá, 'El Banco de España (1931-1962)', *op. cit.*

105. Marcet, J. M.ª. (*Mi Ciudad y yo, op. cit.*, p. 188) states that 'During the last months of 1956 and the first weeks of the next year the social and political situation in Catalonia was on the verge of a deep crisis, menacing a collapse . . .'.

106. C. W. Anderson, *(The Political Economy . . ., op. cit.)* suggests that other alternative actions were possible at that point and that policy-makers had the ability to choose the right one. But one of the pretended contenders, J. Velarde, stated 'I do not believe that the stabilization plan started in 1959 was convenient, I think it was unavoidable', 'El Plan Nacional de Establización y la Situación de la Economía Española' (1959), in *Sobre la Decadencia Económica de España,* Tecnos, Madrid, 1969, p. 423. Apparently, Dr Anderson read the first part of the sentence only.

107. See the answers to the Questionnaire sent by the Government to different Spanish institutions, like the Chambers of Commerce and Industry, Syndicates, Banco de España, INI, etc. collected in *Contestaciones al Cuestionario Económico del Gobierno,* Documentación Económica no. 5, OCYPE, Madrid, 1959.

108. The answers to the above mentioned Questionnaire show an almost unanimous and enthusiastic support for the liberalization policies.

109. A. Ullastres stated that 'Europe and the world wait for us, and if we go to them it is not for solving an eventual deficit in the balance of payments, but because our vocation is universal', speech at the Cortes, 28 July 1959, in Nueva Ordenación Económica, *op. cit.*, p. 55. Finally, it turned out that these political implications either did not exist or were less immediate than many people expected.

110. Detailed analyses can be found in J. Clavera, *et al. Capitalismo Español . . ., op. cit.*, ch. IV; C. W. Anderson, *The Political Economy . . ., op. cit.;* Banco de España, *Informe Annual, 1959,* Madrid, 1960.

111. Collective bargaining for wage settlements – but still within the 'vertical' syndicates – had been previously allowed by Law, 24 April 1958.

112. See *Nueva Ordenación Económica, op. cit.* The most important were the Decree-Law, 21 July 1959, lifting many market interventions; Decree-Law, 27 July 1959, liberalizing foreign investment; and Ministerial Decree, 29 July 1959, liberalizing foreign trade.

113. The most relevant are: the Law, 6 May 1960 establishing a new Tariff system; Decree-Law, 7 June 1962, nationalizing the Banco de España; Decree, 29 January 1963 freeing industrial investments; Ministerial Decree, 22 February 1963 setting minimum size requirements for new industrial investments; Decree, 5 June 1963 freeing the entry into the banking business; Law, 20 July 1963 creating an anti-monopoly Court; and Law, 11 June 1964 rationalising the tax system but leaving its regressive character unchanged. After this date, the process of structural reforms can be considered closed.

114. Especially a major liberalization of foreign trade, a deep change in the tax system, a serious anti-monopoly action, the liberalization of the labour market and the long-awaited reform in land ownership. See the recommendations of the International Bank for Reconstruction and Development, *The Economic Development of Spain,* The Johns Hopkins Press, Baltimore, 1963.

115. See IBRD, *The Economic Development of Spain, op. cit.*; the reactions of many Spanish economists are collected in E. Fuentes (ed.) *El Desarrollo Económico de España. Juicio Crítico del Informe del Banco Mundial,* Madrid, 1963.

116. Presidencia del Gobierno, Comisaría del Plan de Desarrollo, *Plan de Desarrollo Económico y Social para el periodo 1964-1967,* Madrid, 1963.

117. See L. Gamir, *La Política Económica en los Sesentas,* Guadiana de Ediciones, Madrid, 1974.

118. This point was overtly recognized in the second Plan. To prevent this lack of coordination the second Plan included a 'system of alarm signals', consisting of a set of lower and upper bounds for some key macroeconomic indicators beyond which the long-term objectives were supposed to be in jeopardy, calling for the corresponding short-term counter-measures.

119. Exposition and criticism of the first Plan and its achievements can be found in the special issue 'L' Espagne à l'heure du Développement', *Revue*

Tiers-Monde, vol. VIII, no. 32, Oct.-Dec. 1967. See also R. Tamames, *España ante un Segundo Plan de Desarrollo,* Nova Terra, Barcelona, 1968. During this period the Comisaria published an annual *Memoria Sobre el Cumplimiento del Plan.*

120. This expression and a furious attack on this pretended efficiency can be found in J. L. Sampedro, 'Le Plan de Développement Espagnol dans son Cadre Social', in L'Espagne à l'Heure du Développement, *op. cit.*

121. Presidencia del Gobierno, Comisaria del Plan de Desarrollo, *Plan de Desarrollo Económico y Social para el periodo 1968-1971,* Madrid, 1969.

122. See Banco de España, *Informe Anual 1973,* Madrid, 1974.

123. Compare with the foreign aid obtained from the US during the late fifties and early sixties which stood at an annual average of $170 million. See, Servicio Informativo Español, *Alianza Dinámica,* Documentos Políticos no. 3, SIE, Madrid, 1964.

124. In 1940 the agricultural exports represented 60% of total exports and in 1973 only 17.6%.

125. See, for instance, M. Román, *Los Límites del Crecimiento Económico de España,* 1959-67, Ayuso, Madrid, 1972.

126. See, A. López Muñoz, and J. L. García Delgado, *Crecimiento y Crisis del Capitalismo Español,* Edicusa, Madrid, 1968.

127. The average proportion of Gross Capital Formation to the GNP during this period (1959-74) has been around 23 %.

128. Apart from the traditional industrial centres, Catalonia and the Basque country, towns like Madrid, Valladolid, Pamplona, Zaragoza, Sevilla, Burgos, etc. are now important industrial centres.

129. C. W. Anderson, *The Political Economy, op. cit.,* records his surprise at the fact that some groups, like the Hermandades Agrarias, whose economic interests were clearly contradictory with association to the EEC, urged the Government as soon as 1959 to join the Common Market. An analysis of the economic effects of the association can be found in J. L. Sampedro, *et al., Las Regiones Españolas Ante la Asociación Con Europa,* Sociedad de Estudios y Publicaciones, Madrid, 1966.

130. G. Fernandez de la Mora, (former Minister) has recently stated that 'the ideas put into circulation [by the media], either euphemistically or overtly, are opposed to those upon which the State is based. These ideas are: 1. the Common Market is Spain's economic panacea. If we do not join it we shall miss all the boats. But this requires demo-liberal institutions. The 18 July State does not meet them, therefore we must lay it aside; 2. Ballot boxes are the key for good and truth . . . 3. Syndical pluralism must be accepted . . . – and finally he concludes – Submerged in this persistent and inexorable propagandistic display . . . Can we be surprised that the readers, who mostly belong to the middle and upper classes, have started abandoning the régime?', in the newspaper *ABC,* 16 March 1975.

5. The Peasantry and the Franco Régime

1. This paper derives in part from my doctoral dissertation *Peasants without land: Political Sociology of the Peasantry in Spain,* (Reading, 1975). In it can be

found tables and statistics supporting many of the statements made here.

I would like to thank the following friends: Gwyn E. Jones, for his kindness in reading the paper; Paul Preston, for his unfailing help, encouragement and critical suggestions; and, above all, Salvador Giner, for his crucial help in the development of my ideas and in the present theoretical orientation of my work.

2. For a detailed analysis of Franco's régime as the empirical bases of a broader sociological model within a proper typology of political systems of adequate range, Cf. E. Sevilla-Guzmán and Salvador Giner 'Absolutismo despótico y dominación de clase: el caso de España' in *Cuadernos de Ruedo Ibérico,* no. 43/45 (Paris, 1975).

3. H. R. Southworth, *El mito de la cruzada de France* (Paris, 1963) and his article in this volume.

4. It will be obvious that I have followed here the model elaborated by Barrington Moore Jr., *Social Origins of Dictatorship and Democracy* (Harmondsworth, 1973), pp. 445; pp. 436-7.

5. This concept is used here as it was coined by Barrington Moore, *Social Origins . . . op. cit.,* pp. 433-4.

6. Cf. Daniel Guérin, *Sur le fascime II. Fascisme et grand capital* (Paris, 1971), p. 251. Nicos Poulantzas, *Fascisme et dictature* (Paris, 1974), p. 309. Federico Chabod, *A History of Italian Fascism* (Bath, 1974), p. 50.

7. A vivid and horrifying account of the sheer indiscriminate brutality of some of the reprisals which took place can be found in Larry Collins and Dominique Lapierre, *Or I'll Dress You in Mourning* (St Albans, 1973), pp. 84-91. This is, of course, not a work of formal scholarship. There are few academic sources on this subject. It is obvious that any eyewitness account could only come from one of the terrified and generally illiterate peasants or from the oppressers themselves, who naturally have gone to great lengths to cover their crimes and continue to do so.

Facts about this repression are difficult to find for obvious reasons. However, there is considerable information for the following provinces: Badajoz: Jay Allen, 'Slaughter of 4,000 at Badajoz' in Murray Sperber, *And I Remember Spain* (London, 1974). Cordova: L. Collins and D. Lapierre, *Or I'll Dress . . . op. cit.* Burgos: A. Ruiz Vilaplana, *Doy Fe* (Paris, 1938) Galicia: *Galice sous la botte de Franco* (Paris, 1938). Granada: Ian Gibson, *The Death of Lorca* (London, 1973). Málaga: Ronald Fraser, *In Hiding* (London, 1972).

8. Carmen Nieto, *Precios agrícolas y sus repercusiones* (Madrid, 1961) INIA, Booklet 314. Table no. 5. Cf. also Juan Martínez Alier *La estabilidad del latifundismo* (Paris, 1968), pp. 27-33.

9. In both Hitler and Mussolini's agrarian fascisms migration to the cities was banned by law and land-labourers were in many cases paid in kind to keep them in their rural communities. Cf. Nicos Poulantzas *Fascisme et . . . op. cit.,* p. 319 (Germany), p. 326 (Italy). Daniel Guérin *Sur le Fascisme . . . op. cit.* p. 251.

10. This figure derives from our own estimate using García Barbancho's figures. Cf. the later analysis of internal net migration from areas around provincial capitals. Cf. also Fundación FOESSA, *Informe Sociológico sobre la situación social de España* (Madrid, 1970), p. 549.

11. Francisco Fernández Sánchez-Puerta, *Las clases medias económicas* (Madrid, 1951), p. 368. Speaks of the pagan and materialistic spirit reigning in the cities. The speeches of General Franco during these years are riddled with similar notions. Cf. Speeches of (1) 18 September 1939 in Gijón; (2) 13 December 1947 to Assembly of Labradores and Ganaderos; (3) 12 May 1951 to IV Assembly of Hermandades.

(1) Francisco Franco, *Palabras del Caudillo 19 Abril 1937-7 Diciembre 1942* (Madrid, 1943), pp. 163-7.

(2) *Franco ha dicho 1er. apéndice 1 Enero 1947-1 Abril 1949* (Madrid, 1949), p. 134.

(3) *Discursos y mensajes del Jefe del Estado 1951-1954* (Madrid, 1955), p. 53.

12. The expression is Mussolini's. He wrote in February 1921 'We want the land to belong not to the state but to the cultivator. Whereas social-communism tends to disinherit all, and to transform every cultivator into an employer of the state, we wish to give the ownership of the land and economic freedom to the greatest number of peasants. In place of the sovereignty of a central political caste, we support the sovereignty of the peasant.' Frank M. Snowden 'On the Social Origins of Agrarian Fascism in Italy' in *Archives Européennes de Sociologie*, XIII, 1972, pp. 268-95; p. 279.

13. For the Nazis similarly, the peasant was 'to constitute the new nobility of blood and soil', Franz Neumann, *Behemoth: The Structure and Practice of National Socialism* (London, 1942), p. 321; cf. Karl Dietrich Bracher, *The German Dictatorship* (Harmondsworth, 1973), pp. 198-9.

14. F. Sánchez Puerta, *Las clases medias . . . op. cit.* p. 131.

15. This institute and the policy of internal colonization is far from being an original creation of the Francoism. Its inmediate precedents can be found in the Republic. The Republican Agrarian Reform had foreseen the forced acquisition of *latifundios* and the sharing out of the land among peasants. And the Law of Irrigated Works (*Ley de Obras de Puesta en Riego*) of 1932 had already enforced colonization of the lands set under irrigation by the State.

For a propagandistic vision of it, see A. M. Maqueda 'The National Institute of Colonization, Spain' in A. H. Bunting (ed) *Change in Agriculture* (London, 1970), pp. 505-11. The author is a civil servant of the INC and give the official Francoist view of this institution.

16. INFORME BIR-FAO, *El desarrollo de la Agricultura en España* (Madrid, 1966) p. 89.

17. José López de Sebastian, *Política Agraria en España 1920-1970* (Madrid, 1970), p. 303.

18. The activities of the INC tended to give financial aid to the large land-owners. Cf. the flagrant case of the Duke of Medinaceli who received $1,000,000 for his land, while the position of the peasants living on it remained as desperate as ever, Charles Foltz Jr., *The Masquerade in Spain* (Boston, 1948), pp. 107-8. Víctor Alba, *Sleepless Spain* (London, 1948), pp. 17-26. Cf. Clavera *et al. Capitalismo español 1939-1958; de la autarquía a la estabilización* (Madrid, 1973), p. 107.

19. Jaime Montero y García Valdivia, *Modernas orientaciones de la Colonización agraria en España* (Madrid, 1951), *passim*.

20. In any case, the purely repressive – politically conservative motives of

colonization are clearly revealed in S. J. Martín Brugarola, *El problema social en el campo español* (Madrid, 1950), pp. 70-71. *Fuero del Trabajo* (Madrid, 1972), p. 15.

21. In 1949 only 8 % of the land bought by INC was irrigated. Cf. Martín Brugarol, *El problema social . . . op. cit.*, p. 167.

22. Juan Martínez Alier, 'El reparto' in *Cuadernos de Ruedo Ibérico* June-Sept. 1969, no. 13-14, pp. 47-65; p. 53.

23. For a vivid testimony of the condition of the peasantry, see Eliseo Bayo, *Oración de campesinos* (Barcelona, 1974), pp. 125-35.

24. See note 18.

25. J. L. García Delgado y S. López Roldán, 'Contribución al análisis de la crisis de la agricultura tradicional en España: Los cambios decisivos en la última década' in Manuel Fraga Iribarne *et al.* (eds), *La España de los años 70. II La Economía* (Madrid, 1973, p. 268.

26. Francisco Franco, *Palabras del caudillo . . . op. cit.*, p. 350, where he speaks of the 'victory of wheat that we won for our peasants'.

27. Arturo Camilleri Lapeyra, 'La crisis de la agricultura tradicional' in Alberto Ballarin Marcial, Arturo Camilleri *et al., La crisis de la agricultura tradicional* (Madrid, 1974), p. 55.

28. J. Clavera, J. M. Esteban *et al., Capitalismo español: de la autarqúia . . . op. cit.* pp. 21 and 103-4. Charles W. Anderson, *The Political Economy of Modern Spain* (The Univ. of Wisconsin, 1970), pp. 5 and 27. Esteban Pinilla de las Heras 'España: una sociedad de diacronías' in *Horizonte Español, 1966* (Paris, 1966), pp. 1-12.

29. Both plans arise as a result of the application of the Law of Colonization and Distribution to irrigatable areas (21-IV-1949). In view of the failures of the policies both of colonization (the INC was set up by a 18th-X-1939's Act) and irrigation (Law of large zones liable to irrigaton 26-X-1939): 'The Minister of Agriculture declared in a speech that there were 200,000 Ha which could benefit from the irrigation schemes made by the Government, but that the lack of the landowner's initiative had prevented it from being carried out', Martin Brugarola, *El problema . . . op. cit.*, p. 101.

30. During these years the exaltation of the peasantry continues as a central idea in the public General Franco's speeches concerning the country side. On 12 May 1951 said that in the countryside 'the seed of the race remains purer and people live their problems and they are not polluted with city's depravity.' Similar expressions can be found in his speeches of 12-VI-1951, 27-V-1952, 22-II-1953 and 2-V-1953. Francisco Franco, *Discursos y Mensajes del Jefe del Estado 1951-54* (Madrid, 1955), pp. 53; 80-1; 190; 295 and 320.

31. Rafael Cavestany y de Anduaga, *Una Política Agraria* (Madrid, 1958), pp. 25; 30-6.

32. Xavier Flores, *Estructura socioeconómica de la agricultura española* (Barcelona, 1969), pp. 53 and 57. Cf. J. Clavera *et al., Capitalismo . . . op. cit.* vol. I 'prólogo'. Introduction by preface of Joan Sardá Dexens. Cf. Charles W. Anderson, *The Political Economy . . . op. cit.*, p. 100.

33. Speech made on the occasion of the inauguration of the new

cooperative plant of 'La Daimileña. Daimiel, 19 September 1964. Cirilo Cánovas García, *Agricultura 1957-1965* (Madrid, 1966), pp. 651-2; 356.

34. See the controversial article published in June 1965 by Juan Muñoz, Santiago Roldán and J. L. García Delgado: Arturo López Munõz, 'La visión de los románticos' in *Triunfo*, no. 153 published later in Arturo López Munõz, *Capitalismo españõl, una etapa decisiva* (Madrid, 1970), p. 21-3.

35. R. Cavestany y de Anduaga, *Una política* . . . *op. cit.* p. 89. Author's italics.

36. R. Cavestany y de Anduaga, *Una política* . . . *op. cit.*, p. 94 and 95.

37. Antonio Bermejo Zuagría, 'El futuro agrícola en Castilla la Vieja' in *Información Comercial española* 378, Feb. 1965, pp. 72-85.

38. Cf. Gabriel Jackson, *The Spanish Republic and the Civil War 1931-1939* New Jersey, 1972 1st edition 1965, p. 375; 153-9. G. Jackson, *Breve Historia de la Guerra Civil en España* (Paris, 1974), pp. 47-52. Hugh Thomas, *The Spanish Civil War* (Hardmondsworth, 1971) 1st. ed. 1961, pp. 215-17.

39. The system of local class domination is based on the different forms of dependency created by the latifundios over the peasant community. Such forms of dependency require the loyal assistance by the political institutions on a local level and above all the existence of a more or less efficient 'repressive system of the agricultural labour force' (cf. Barrington Moore, *Social Origins* . . . *op. cit.*, p. 434). Accordingly the power of the latifundistas in the communities takes on more or less despotic forms 'They are in a sense onmipresent, but they are also, for most purposes, outsiders' (Jose Cutileiro, *A Portuguese Rural Society*, Oxford, 1971, p. 50, in a study in which a large part of the key elements of the local class domination system can be found). See also: Ernest Feder, 'Latifundia and Agricultural Labour in Latin America' in Teodore Shanin, *Peasant and Peasant Societies* (Hardmondsworth, 1971), pp. 85-97 and Arturo Warman, *Los Campesinos* (Mexico, 1973), pp. 50-67.

40. It must be remembered that at the end of the previous period, when both the irrigation and colonization policies were closely linked, the settlements of the new peasants were made on only a small part of the estates, which had been completely irrigated.

41. Jose Luis García Delgado and Santiago Roldán López 'Las rentas agrarias en el contexto de la agricultura tradicional española' in A. Ballarin, A. Camilleri *et al.*, *La crisis de* . . . *op. cit.*, pp. 70-104; p. 82. Cf. Ramón Tamames, *Introducción a la economía española* (Madrid, 1972), pp. 1949-55.

42. See Ministerio de Agricultura, *Anuario Estadístico de las producciones agrícolas año 1951* (Madrid, 1953), p. 2 and INE *Primer Censo Agrario de España 1962. Resumenes nacionales,* (Madrid, 1966), p. 96. Cf. Pablo Ortega Rosales 'El problema triguero español' in *De Economía* no. 59, 1959; pp. 508-18. E. Baron, *El final del campesinado* (Madrid, 1971), p. 85.

43. J. L. García Delgado y S. Roldán, 'Contribución al análisis de la crisis de la agricultura tradicional en España: los cambios decisivos de la última década' in Manuel Fraga *et al.*, *La España* . . . *op. cit.*, p. 270. C. Nieto' El Informa BIR-FAO y la tributación en *Información Comercial española* no. 403, 1967, pp. 183-9.

44. Jaime Nosti Nava 'El crédito agrícola' in *Boletín de Estudios Económicos*

(Universidad de Deusto, no. 62, 1964). Xavier Flores, *Estructura socioeconómica . . . op. cit.*, pp. 153-60.

45. Jose Manuel Naredo, *La evolución de la agricultura an España* (Barcelona, 1971), p. 139.

46. The first scholar to make a short but coherent formulation of the crisis of traditional agriculture in Spain was Víctor Pérez Díaz, *Emigración y sociedad en la Tierra de Campos* (Madrid, 1969), pp. 30-2. A more complete interpretation was later made by Jose Manuel Naredo, *La evolución de la agricultura en España* (Barcelona, 1971), *passim*.

47. This 'ideology of agrarian industrialism' will be defined and analysed below. A Round Table of official and semi-official social scientific practitioners held in September 1973 in the 'Valle de los Caídos' was entitled *The crisis of Traditional Agriculture* and the subtitle was *The New Agricultural Enterprise*, which expressively suggests the solution to the crisis.

48. Teodor Shanin, 'The Nature of the Peasant Economy. I.A generalisation' in *The Journal of Peasant Studies*, vol. 1, no. 1, 1973, pp. 63-80; p. 64. For a broader development of this approach to the peasantry see Boguslaw Galeski, 'Social organization and Rural Social Change' in *Sociología Ruralis*, vol. 8, 1968, no. 3 and 4.

49. Jose Manuel Naredo, *La evolución . . . op. cit.*, pp. 128-9.

50. Speech made by the Minister of Agriculture Adolfo Díaz Ambrona *Agricultura 1965-1969* (Madrid, 1970), p. 94.

51. For an excellent theoretical construction of this type of 'modernizing' (*desarrollista*) ideology cf. Angel Palerm 'Ensayo de crítica al desarrollo regional en Mexico' in David Barkin (ed) *Los beneficios del Desarrollo Regional* (Mexico, 1972), pp. 13-62.

52. Karl Marx and Frederic Engels, *The German Ideology* (London, 1970), p. 64.

53. This organisation was created in 1971 and fused both *Servicio Nacional de Concentración Parcelaria* and *Instituto Nacional de Colonización*, whose political role has already been analysed in previous sections. It is to be supposed that this organisation is in charge of carrying on the good work of Francoist agrarian reform.

54. *Ya*, 6 June 1973.

55. Fernando de Elzaburu Márquez 'El nueve empresario' in Alberto Ballerin *et al., La crisis de . . . op. cit.*, pp. 163-269; pp. 163, 165, 169 and 175.

56. Amando de Miguel, *Un futurible para España* (Barcelona, 1969), p. 32.

57. E. Sevilla-Guzmán, *op. cit.* Part II. Tables 2.5 and 2.6.

58. In fact during this period, as a result of the policy of the Minister of Information and Tourism Fraga Iribarne – 1962/1969 – each village acquired a 'tele-club' (a television set in the village bar). In this way even in the most remote areas, peasants were exposed to the temptation of the bright lights of the city.

59. Fundación FOESSA, *Informe sociológico . . . op. cit.*, pp. 1, 151-8.

60. For an excellent analysis of migration as an agent of social homogenization see Víctor Pérez Díaz *Emigración y sociedad . . . op. cit.*, pp. 35-40.

61. I use the notion of 'proletarization' to denote a process through which

the peasant gradually loses his economic independence and becomes a salaried worker, so that new forms of subordination appear in the relations of production in which he lives. Thus, 'proletarization' does not have to be linked to, say, an early industrial and capitalist world, but is a process which may appear at many stages of the economic process, and entail different levels in the standard of living.

62. Javier Rubio *La emigración española a Francia* (Barcelona, 1974), pp. 60-3. This author uses data from the Office National d'Immigration in France.

In 1964 more than 70 % of agricultural workers (*temporeros*) recorded in the census by French sugar beet trade unions were Spanish. Cf. Guy Hermet *Los españoles en Francia* (Madrid, 1969), p. 31. During the following five years (1965-69), 90% of the total seasonal immigrant peasants to France were Spanish, Javier Rubie *La emigración . . . op. cit.*, p. 62.

63. Eliseo Bayo, *Trabajos duros de la mujer* (Barcelona, 1969), *passim*, José M. Naredo, *La evolución . . . op. cit.* pp. 83-91. Eliseo Bayo, *El manifiesto de la tierra* (Barcelona, 1973), pp. 69-70.

64. Enrique Baron, *El final del . . . op. cit.*, p. 147 and ff. Cf. also 'La nueva relación agricultura-industria' in *Cuadernos para el Diálogo: España Agraria* no. extra, XLV March, 1975, pp. 53-6.

65. The protection of traditional crops, normally related to the cultivation system of large estates, such as winter cereals, olive trees, cotton, etc., still remains in the seventies even though these crops are not economically viable for the nation as a whole. Besides, from 1968 there exists a new public body – FORPPA – which has supported the traditional crop policies of the large estates.

66. For an analysis of this process, see Jesus Contreras, *El campesinado español: Transformación y Dependencia*, paper presented at the II Meeting of Spanish anthropologists (Segovia, 18-23 November, 1974) and published later in *Triunfo*, año XXIX, no. 643, pp. 28-30.

67. In Spain, an official agrarian union operates. Its representatives are elected by the government. Belonging to such an organization is compulsory for the peasantry as a whole, since it can then be manipulated within this union, which attempts to create a peasant cooperative movement. In some cases, people who hold high union posts are also presidents of marketing cooperatives which in turn have several marketing branches linked with the cooperatives, whose role in the productive process is rather limited.

It is rather revealing to analyse the contents of 'Hermandad' (Brotherhood) – the agrarian union's newspaper, in which continuous reports from peasant about frauds in feedstuff production are only published when the matter has gone beyond local boundaries, becoming a national scandal. The newspaper's staff, then, publishes it all enclosing a note stressing the fact that they had been waiting *confirmation from Madrid* of such rumours. For reports on frauds in fertilizers, see: *Hermandad* 14, 21 and 28 March; 25 April and 16 May 1974.

68. See *Hermandad*, 11 and 18 July 1974.

69. See *Pueblo* (edition for Castile) 16 March 1974.

70. Cf. *Nuevo Diario*, Madrid, 282 – II and III 1974. *Informaciones,* Madrid

2 and 27 III 1974. *A B C* Madrid 7 III 1974. *Gaceta del Norte* Santander 1 III 1974. *La Voz de España* San Sebastian 28 II 1974. *Ya* Madrid, 23 III 1974. For an account of the 'milk war' see *Hermandad* 6 III, and 25 IV 1974.

71. An account of these wars can be seen in Jesus Contreras 'Las guerras agrícolas' in *Cuadernos para el Diálogo* Madrid, Extra XLV March 1975; pp. 84-8.

6. The Anti-Francoist Opposition: The Long March to Unity

1. I must thank the following friends who made otherwise unobtainable materials available to me: Mariano Aguayo and the *Frente Libertario* group, Miguel García, José Martínez Guerricabeitia and the staff of Ruedo Ibérico, Herbert R. Southworth and Carlos de Zayas. I am also grateful to individual members of the PSOE, the PCE and the MLE who, for obvious reasons, cannot be named and who supplied me with clandestine newspapers.

2. The most malicious account of these is Eduardo Comín Colomer, *La República en el exilio* (Barcelona 1957) which should be tempered with Fidel Miró, *¿Y España cuándo?: el fracaso político de una emigración* (Mexico, 1959).

3. Javier Tusell, 'Teoría e historia de la oposición al franquismo' in *Actualidad Económica* 9 November 1974, p. 57. The concept of *ministrable* is developed by Amando de Miguel in Equipo Mundo, *Los 90 ministros de Franco* 3rd ed. (Barcelona, 1971), pp. 371-9.

4. Cf. Guy Hermet *La politique dans l'Espagne franquiste* (Paris, 1971), p. 9; Juan J. Linz, 'An Authoritarian Regime: Spain' in E. Allardt and Y. Littunen, *Cleavages, Ideologies and Party Systems* (Helsinki, 1964), pp. 291-341.

5. 'Tácito late' in *Cambio 16*, no. 164, 6 January 1975.

6. Cf. Paul Preston, 'General Franco's Rearguard' in *New Society*, 29 November 1973.

7. See the elaborately polite treatment accorded Ruiz-Giménez, Ridruejo and other members of the non-Communist opposition on their recent arrest, *Cambio 16*, no. 160, 9 December 1974.

8. This is virtually admitted by the regime propagandist, Angel Ruiz de Ayucar, *Crónica agitada de ocho años tranquilos 1963-1970* (Madrid 1974) pp. 209-10.

9. Cf. Carlos Semprún-Maura, 'La "oposición" y sus militantes' in *Cuadernos de Ruedo Ibérico* (henceforth *CRI*) no. 33-5, March 1972, 213-16.

10. Luis García San Miguel, 'Para una sociología del cambio político y la oposición en la España actual' in *Sistema*, no. 4, January 1974, p. 106.

11. Sergio Vilar, *Protagonistas de la España democrática: la oposición a la dictadura 1939-1969* (Paris, 1968), p. 25.

12. Luis García San Miguel, 'Estructura y cambio del régimen político español' in *Sistema*, no. 1 January 1973, pp. 101-2.

13. Gonzalo Arias, *Los encartelados* 2nd ed. (Paris 1971). This remarkable 'programme-novel' is a fictionalized account, written before the event, of an attempt to rally non-violent opposition by walking the streets with sandwich-boards calling for elections.

14. See particularly Juan J. Linz, 'Opposition to and under an

Authoritarian Regime: The Case of Spain' in Robert A. Dahl, *Regimes And Oppositions* (New Haven, 1973) pp. 171-259, and Amando de Miguel, 'Tipología de la oposición' in *España, marca registrada* (Barcelona, 1972) pp. 249-53, and the articles by Luis García San Miguel already quoted above.

15. Carlos Semprún-Maura, '¿Quién es y qué pretende Santiago Carrillo' in El Viejo Topo, *De Carrero Blanco a Eva Forest* (Paris, 1975), p. 80-3.

16. For a description of this method, see Eduardo García, 'La organización de las masas' in *Nuestra Bandera*, no. 27, July 1960, pp. 21-8.

17. There is a growing literature on the exiles. The basic works are Antonio Vilanova, *Los olvidados: los exilados españoles en la segunda guerra mundial* (Paris 1969); David Wingeate Pike, *Vae Victis! Los republicanos españoles refugiados en Francia 1939-1944* (Paris, 1969); Alberto Fernández, *Emigración republicana española 1939-1945* (Madrid, 1972); Federica Montseny, *Pasión y muerte de los españoles en Francia* (Toulouse, 1969).

18. See Ian Gibson, *The Death of Lorca* (London, 1973); Anon., *Galice sous la botte de Franco* (Paris, 1938); El Clero Vasco, *El pueblo vasco frente a la cruzada franquista* (Toulouse, 1966); Anon., *Catalunya sota el règim franquista*, vol. I (Paris, 1973).

19. Vilanova, *Los olvidados*, chs. 3-6; Miguel Angel, *Los guerrilleros españoles en Francia 1940-1945* (La Habana, 1971); Alberto E. Fernández, *La España de los maquis* (Mexico, 1973); Vicente Fillol, *Los Perdedores* (Caracas, 1971); Serapio Iniesta, *Flon-flon* (Barcelona, 1972).

20. Comín, *Exilio*, p. 52; Carlos de Baráibar, 'La traición del Stalinismo' in *Timón* (Buenos Aires) no. 7, June 1940.

21. The anti-Communists under Indalecio Prieto controlled the *Junta de Auxilio a los Republicanos Españoles* while the pro-Communists of Juan Negrín had the *Servicio de Emigración de los Republicanos Españoles*. For accounts of the haggling, see Comín, *Exilio*, pp. 67-111; Indalecio Prieto, *Convulsiones de España* 3 vols. (Mexico, 1967-9), vol. III, pp. 97-110; Francisco Largo Caballero, *Mis recuerdos* (Mexico, 1954), pp. 261-5.

22. There is a rather dry account by José Berruezo, *Contribución a la historia de la CNT de España en el exilio* (Mexico, 1967).

23. The issues at stake are discussed in Vernon Richards, *Lessons of the Spanish Revolution* 3rd ed. (London, 1972) and César M. Lorenzo, *Les anarchistes espagnols et le pouvoir* (Paris, 1969).

24. Lorenzo, pp. 350-3; Antonio Téllez, *La guerrilla urbana: Facerías* (Paris, 1974), pp. 33-6.

25. The position of the interior is explained by Juan García Durán, *Por la libertad: como se lucha en España* (Mexico, 1956), pp. 76-8.

26. See the secret report of Abad de Santillán to the sub-delegation of the CNT in Argentina, *Mensaje acerca de la situación actual del Movimiento Libertario Español* (Buenos Aires, 1946).

27. Antonio Téllez, *Sabaté: Guerrilla Extraordinary* (London, 1974), pp. 45, 49-50, 69; *Facerías*, p. 28.

28. This is the view expressed in interviews and articles collected in *CRI* supplement, *El movimiento libertario español: pasado, presente y futuro* (Paris, 1974).

29. Jesús Hernández, *En el país de la gran mentira* (Madrid 1974), pp. 49-60; Enrique Lister, *!Basta!* (n.p., n.d.), pp. 113-8; Enrique Castro Delgado, *Mi fe se perdió en Moscú* (Barcelona, 1964), pp. 28-32; Comín, *Exilio*, p. 229.

30. Enrique Fuentes, 'La oposición antifranquista de 1939 a 1955' in *CRI, Horizonte Español 1966*, 2 vols (Paris, 1966), vol. II, pp. 14-16; Guy Hermet, *Los comunistas en España* (Paris, 1972), p. 46.

31. Andrés Sorel, *Guerrilla española del siglo XX* (Paris, 1970), p. 130; Comín, *Exilio*, pp. 410-11; *Nuestra Bandera*, June-July 1947, April 1950.

32. *!Basta!*, pp. 30, 163-4, 171-3; Fernando Claudín, *La crisis del movimiento comunista: 1 de la Komintern al Kominform* (Paris, 1970), pp. 494-5, note 66, p. 669; Hermet, *Comunistas*, p. 50.

33. Fuentes, pp. 12-15; Hernández, pp. 177-85; Castro-Delgado, pp. 222-5, 246, 289; Antonio Mije, 'Un año de Junta Suprema de Unión Nacional: lecciones y experiencias de un gran órgano de combate' in *Nuestra Bandera*, no. 1, January 1945.

34. Berruezo, pp. 171-81; Lorenzo, pp. 342-5; Fuentes, p. 15; Santiago Carrillo, *Demain L'Espagne* (Paris, 1974) (henceforth *DLE*), p. 19.

35. Ignacio Fernández de Castro & José Martínez, *España Hoy* (Paris, 1963), pp. 4-5; Lorenzo, pp. 345-7.

36. *España Hoy*, p. 7; Lorenzo, pp. 348-55; Juan García Durán, 'La CNT y la Alianza Nacional de Fuerzas Democráticas' in *CRI, MLE supplement*, p. 123.

37. Miró, p. 40; Juan Hermanos, *Fin de la esperanza* (Buenos Aires, 1964), p. 61.

38. Gabriel Kolko, *The Politics of War* (London, 1968), pp. 588-9; Carlton J. H. Hayes, *Wartime Mission in Spain* (New York, 1945), pp. 243-4, 267; García Durán, *Por la libertad*, p. 127; *Le Monde* 15 March 1946.

39. Miró, p. 34-9.

40. Miró, p. 61; García Durán, *Por la libertad*, pp. 106-11; 'CNT y ANFD',

41. Lorenzo, p. 348.

42. Charles Foltz, Jr., *The Masquerade in Spain* (Boston, 1948), pp. 93-8; Gabriel Jackson, *The Spanish Republic and the Civil War* (Princeton, 1965), Appendix D; Herbert R. Southworth, 'The Falange' in this volume, note 53.

43. There is a significant literature on Francoist prisons. See Juan M. Molina, *Noche sobre España* (Mexico, 1958); Melquesidez Rodríguez Chaos, *24 años en la cárcel* (Paris, 1968); Miguel García, *Franco's Prisoner* (London, 1972).

44. Sorel, p. 42.

45. There are numerous cases of Republicans staying in hiding for over twenty years. See Ronald Fraser, *In Hiding* (London, 1972); Prieto, *Convulsiones*, I, p. 128; *Le Figaro* 18 March, 1967; *Oficina de Prensa de Euzkadi* 9 January 1967.

46. Stanley G. Payne, *Franco's Spain* (London 1968), p. 113; Enrique Lister, 'Lessons of the Spanish Guerrilla War' in *World Marxist Review* February 1965, p. 35.

47. Hermanos, p. 28.

48. Tomás Cossías, *La lucha contra el 'maquis' en España* (Madrid, 1956), pp. 60-3; *DLE*, pp. 95-8; *!Basta!*, p. 126; Hermanos, p. 65; Sorel, pp. 55-6.

49. José Gros, *Abriendo camino: relatos de un guerrillero comunista español* (Paris 1971), p. 119.

50. Sorel, pp. 43, 91-9; *DLE*, p. 94; Lister, 'Lessons', 35.

51. Sorel, pp. 141, 158; *!Basta!*, p. 131; Lister 'Lessons', p. 36; Cossías, pp. 142-6.

52. Emmet John Hughes, *Report from Spain* (London, 1947), p. 178; *DLE*, p. 20. For some unconvincing attempts at figures, see Lister, 'Lessons', p. 36; Sorel, p. 10; George Hills, *Spain* (London, 1970), Appendix A.

53. Hermanos, pp. 7, 22, 40, 71; Hughes, pp. 136-8; Bartolomé Barba Hernández, *Dos años al frente del Gobierno civil de Barcelona* (Madrid, 1948), pp. 45-8.

54. Téllez, *Facerías*. p. 64. Cf. the bitter accusations of Lister. *!Basta!*, pp. 127-8, 139, 142; and Carrillo's reply, *DLE*, p. 99.

55. Sorel, pp. 237-41; *!Basta!*, pp. 123-4; Gros, pp. 196-205; 219-223.

56. Sorel, pp. 127-36.

57. For persuasive accounts, see Téllez, *Facerías* and *Sabaté*; Miguel García, pp. 26-42.

58. Téllez, *Facerías*, pp. 68, 101-15; *Sabaté*, pp. 50, 69.

59. Téllez, *Facerías*, pp. 50-5; García Durán, 'CNT y ANFD', pp. 123-8; *Por la libertad*, pp. 78, 106-11, 124-7, 130; Miró, pp. 60-1; Lorenzo, pp. 370-84.

60. Comín, *Exilio*, p. 98; *España Hoy*, p. 12; Carlton Hayes, p. 269.

61. Juan Antonio Andaldo, *¿Para qué . . .? De Alfonso XIII a Juan III* (Buenos Aires, 1951); Benjamin Welles, *Spain: The Gentle Anarchy* (London, 1965), p. 345; Comín, *Exilio*, pp. 251-60; Lorenzo, pp. 384-90.

62. Ansaldo, pp. 392-7, 428-30; Prieto, *Convulsiones* III, pp. 13-16, 63-8; Welles, pp. 351-2; José Gutiérrez-Ravé, *Gil Robles, caudillo frustrado*, (Madrid, 1967), pp. 227-30.

63. *DLE*, pp. 112-13; Fernando Gómez Peláez, 'Santiago Carrillo o la historia falsificada' in *Interrogations* no. 2, March 1975, pp. 61-2. For a more reasonable assessment, see 'El plebiscito de Barcelona' in *El Socialista*, 18 March 1951, Téllez, *Sabaté*, pp. 112-14.

64. 'La lección de Madrid' in *El Socialista*, 31 May 1951; Ricard Soler, 'The New Spain' in *New Left Review*, no. 58, Nov.-Dec. 1969.

65. Lorenzo Torres, 'The Spanish Left: Illusion and Reality' in *The Socialist Register 1966*, p. 69; *!Basta!*, pp. 145-9, 171-2.

66. *Mundo Obrero*, 15 March 1954; Comín, *Exilio*, p. 569; *L'Humanité*, 10 November 1954.

67. Bandera Roja, 'La lutte de classe en Espagne entre 1939 et 1970' in *Les Temps Modernes*, no. 310, May 1972, p. 1,791; Torres, pp. 71-2; Hermet, *Comunistas*, pp. 57-9; Fernando Claudín, *Las divergencias en el partido* (n.p. 1964), p. 9.

68. *Mundo Obrero*, mid-January 1957.

69. *Mundo Obrero*, 15 July 1959; Luis Ramírez, *Nuestros primeros veinticinco años* (Paris, 1964), pp. 169-71; Bandera Roja, p. 1,793; Torres, p. 72; Hermet, *Communistas*, p. 59; Claudín, *Divergencias*, pp. 14-16.

70. Miró, pp. 14, 74; Comín, *Exilio,* p. 10; Ramírez, *25 años,* p. 197; *España Hoy,* p. 25.

71. Miró, pp. 66-8, 212-17; Xavier Flores, 'El exilio y España' in *CRI, Horizonte 1966,* pp. 32-3; *España Hoy,* p. 33.

72. *El Socialista,* 20 November 1958; *España Hoy,* p. 35; *Nuestra Bandera,* no. 30, April 1961, p. 16; Ignacio Fernández de Castro, *De las Cortes de Cádiz al Plan de Desarrollo 1808-1966* (Paris, 1968), p. 285.

73. *El Socialista,* 18 December 1958; *The Times,* 1 January 1959.

74. Vilar, *Oposición,* pp. 577-9; Rafael Calvo Serer, *Franco frente al Rey* (Paris 1972), pp. 25-40; Welles, pp. 352-67; Salvador de Madariaga, *Spain: A Modern History* (London, 1972), pp. 612-13.

75. Ramírez, *25 años,* pp. 198, 203-13; *España Hoy,* p. 25; *El Socialista,* 18 December 1958; Miró, p. 25.

76. Téllez, *Facerías,* pp. 238-67, 299-310; *Sabaté,* pp. 115-64; Octavio Alberola & Ariane Gransac, *El anarquismo español y la acción revolucionaria 1961-1974* (Paris, 1975), pp. 26, 78, 91, 95-6.

77. Ramírez, *25 años,* p. 133, Vilar, *Oposición,* pp. 480-90; *Cambio 16,* no. 187, 13 July 1975.

78. Welles, pp. 194-8; Vilar, *Oposición,* pp. 447-66, 513-20, 559-66.

79. Fernández de Castro, pp. 306-7; Julio Cerón, 'El Frente de Liberación Popular ha sido la gran oportunidad de los últimos años' in *CRI,* no. 13-14 June-September 1967; Pau Costa, 'Organización e iniciativa revolucionaria' in *CRI,* no. 26-27 Aug.-Nov. 1970, 29 note 1; Ramírez, *25 años,* pp. 172-85; Vilar, *Oposición,* pp. 153-9; Julio Sanz Oller, *Entre el fraude y la esperanza* (Paris, 1972), pp. 119-20.

80. *España Hoy,* pp. 235-56; Gutiérrez-Ravé, pp.) 233-95; José María Gil Robles, *Marginalia política* (Barcelona, 1975), pp. 121-4.

81. *España Hoy,* pp. 67-222, contains an excellent anthology of the press on the strikes.

82. *España Hoy,* pp. 383-94; Ruiz-Ayucar, pp. 11-50. Santiago Carrillo claimed that the killing of Grimau was an attempt by the regime to provoke the PCE into abandoning the policy of national reconciliation; see 'Ni Guerra Civil ni revancha: Libertad' in *Nuestra Bandera* no. 36, 1st & 2nd trimestres 1963.

83. Claudín, *Divergencias,* pp. 72-5; Linz, 'Opposition', pp. 219-24.

84. Torres, pp. 75-6; Vilar, *Oposición,* p. 566; Gil Robles, *Marginalia,* p. 189, 124-31, Gil Robles (editor), *Cartas del pueblo español* (Madrid, 1966) *passim.*

85. Vilar, *Oposición,* pp. 447-66; Elías Díaz, *Pensamiento español 1939-1973* (Madrid 1974), pp. 170-83.

86. For Tierno, see Vilar, *Oposición,* pp. 123-31; Díaz, *Pensamiento,* pp. 108-13, 141-8, 189-94. For the PSOE congresses, see *CRI, Horizonte Español 1972* (Paris, 1972), I, pp. 224, 417-18; Carlos Zayas, 'El Socialismo en España' I & II in *Cambio 16,* no. 139, 15 July & no. 140, 22 July 1974.

87. Julius, 'Después del referéndum' & Ignacio Fernández de Castro, 'La eficacia de las consignas' both in *CRI* no. 10 Dec. 1966-Jan. 1967.

88. Santiago Carrillo, 'The Working Class Paves the Way to Freedom for Spain' in *World Marxist Review,* vol. 5, no. 8, 1962, pp. 3, 7.

89. Santiago Carrillo, 'Spain: A New Situation' in *Marxism Today*, Aug. 1962; Carrillo, 'Spain: Opposition to the Dictatorship is growing' in *World Marxist Review* vol. 9, no. 1, 1966; Eduardo García, 'En Espagne: un avant-guarde dans la lutte du peuple' in *Nouvelle Revue Internationale*, no. 103, March 1967; Comité Ejectuvo del PCE, *Huelga nacional y pacto por la libertad* (Madrid, 1972) (clandestine pamphlet).

90. Costa, 'Organización', pp. 29-35; Bandera Roja, pp. 1,797, 1,800-1; Sanz Oller, pp. 66-7, 71, 77, 80, 161; Carlos Prieto, 'La tactique du parti communiste a contribué à l'affaiblissement des "commissions ouvrières"' 'in *Le Monde* 18 February 1970.

91. Claudín, *Divergencias*, pp. 3-5, 94-102; *!Basta!*, pp. 21-8; Antonio Sala & Eduardo Durán, *Crítica de la izquierda autoritaria en Cataluña 1967-1974* (Paris, 1975), p. 163.

92. Eduardo García, 'Espagne: le parti consolide ses rangs' in *Nouvelle Revue Internationale*, no. 120, Aug. 1968, pp. 179-80; interview with Santiago Carrillo in *Le Monde*, 4 Nov. 1970.

93. Claudín, *Divergencias*, pp. 29-31, 43-9, 70-2; 'Dos concepciones de "la vía española al socialismo"' 'in *CRI*, *Horizonte 1966*, II, pp. 66-7, 79-84, 92-6. Carrillo's. reply, *Después de Franco, ¿Què?* (Paris, 1965), already shows concessions to Claudín's reasoning; see pp. 9-44.

94. Sala & Durán, p. 163; Claudín, *Divergencias*, p. 98; Hermet, *Comunistas*, p. 72; *!Basta!*, p. 191.

95. *DLE*, pp. 21-4, 118-21; Santiago Carrillo, *Hacia el post-franquismo* (Paris, 1974), pp. 35-7. (Henceforth *HPF*).

96. Santiago Carrillo, *Nuevos enfoques a problemas de hoy* (Paris, 1967), p. 17; *Le Monde* interview 4 Nov. 1970.

97. Santiago Carrillo, *Libertad y Socialismo* (Paris, 1971), pp. 43-50; *Después de Franco, ¿Qué?*, pp. 75-80, 86-7; *Nuevos enfoques*, pp. 54, 116-34; Enrique L. López, *Carrillo: dos caras de una misma moneda* (n.p., n.d.), pp. 26-9.

98. Fernando Claudín, 'La crisis del PCE' in *CRI*, no. 26-7 Aug.-Nov. 1970, p. 54.

99. Sanz-Oller, pp. 190-1; Sala & Durán, p. 84. Communist militants interviewed by the author claimed to have been physically threatened by FRAP.

100. Hermet, *Comunistas*, pp. 66-71; Bandera Roja, pp. 1,815-17; Sala & Durán, pp. 65-71.

101. *Vanguardia Obrera*, no. 57 Aug.-Sept. 1971; *Acción*, no. 9 Nov. 1972.

102. *Boletín de Información del FRAP*, no. 25, June 1973.

103. Charles Vanhecke, 'Les révisions" du P. C. Espagnol: Deux Ans de Crise' & interview with Santiago Carrillo in *Le Monde* 4 Nov. 1970; *Mundo Obrero* 30 Sept., 7 Oct. 1970; *!Basta!*, pp. 10-41, 62, 83-103; Claudín, 'Crisis', passim; *Mundo Obrero*, 30 Oct. 1974.

104. Alberola & Gransac, *passim*; *Carta abierta del FAI en el exilio* (Paris, 1974); Grupo Primero de Mayo, *Génesis y evolución del activismo revolucionario anarquista en Europa 1945-1972* (n.p., 1973); MIL, *Conspiración Internacional Anarquista* (n.p. 1973).

105. *CRI*, *Horizonte 1972*, pp. 203-12, 381-9; *Mundo Obrero*, 30 March 1972.

106. Paul Preston, 'General Franco's Rearguard' in *New Society* 29 Nov. 1973 & 'The Assassination of Carrero Blanco and its Aftermath' in *Iberian Studies*, vol. III, no. 1, 1974.

107. *Ibid.*

108. Raul Morodo, 'Portugal y España: incidencias políticas' in *Cambio 16*, no. 134, 10 June 1974.

109. *Mundo Obrero*, 24 Dec. 1971, 12 Dec. 1973, 19 June 1974; *HPF*, pp. 57-62.

110. *HPF*, pp. 5-6; *DLE*, pp. 15, 136; *Mundo Obrero*, 8, 22 May, 4 June 1974; *Le Monde* 23-25 June 1974.

111. *HPF*, pp. 29-30.

112. 'El espíritu del Ritz' in *Cambio 16*, no. 134, 10 June 1974; Ramón Tamames, *Un proyecto de democracia para el futuro de España* (Madrid 1975), pp. 7-10. A prominent Catalan banker involved in talks with the PCE told the author that agreement would be reached when he and his associates were sure that the Communists would 'deliver the goods'.

113. *DLE*, pp. 17, 186-7; for the growing PCE links with the PCI, see *Mundo Obrero*, 4th week in June, 1st, 3rd & 4th weeks in July 1975.

114. Carlos Zayas, private report on the future of the PSOE, elaborated under the supervision of the PSOE executive committee at the request of the author.

115. *Mundo Obrero*, 31 July 1974.

116. *Frankfurter Allgemeine Zeitung*, 1 Aug. 1974.

117. IG-Metall-Pressespiegel, *Servicio de Prensa*, no. 479, 12 Aug. 1974.

118. Colectivo 70, 'Interpretaciones políticas en la declaración de la Junta Democrática' & Francisco Lasa, 'La oferta de la Junta Democrática Lenin ha muerto' both in *CRI*, no. 43-45 Jan.-June 1975; *Frente Libertario*, no. 45, Sept. 1974.

119. *Vanguardia Obrera*, no. 90, 2nd fortnight of Aug., no. 91, Sept. 1974; *Servir al Pueblo*, no. 30, Aug. 1974.

120. The special number of *Mundo Obrero*, 13 Oct. 1972, dedicated to the VIII Congress contains hints of how this discontent arose. The Oposition published a newspaper of high intellectual standard, *La Voz Comunista*. Cf. 'Si, Camarada Ardatovski' in no. 7 July-Aug. 1974.

121. Zayas, *Report on PSOE; El Socialista*, 1st fortnight in May, 1975.

122. 'Guerra al FRAP' in *Cambio 16*, no. 190, 28 July 1975.

123. *Mundo Obrero Rojo*, no. 35, 25 March 1975.

7. The Working Class under the Franco Régime

1. Cf. J. M. Maravall, in *Government and Opposition*, vol. 8, no. 4, 1973, pp. 432-54.

2. CEDA: 'Confederación Española de Derechas Autónomas'; an amalgam of right-wing groups formed in 1923 under the leadership of Gil Robles.

3. 'Falange Española y de las JONS' came into being in Feb. 1934 as the result of the fusion of 'Falange Española', led by José Antonio Primo de Rivera, and the 'Juntas de Ofensiva Nacional Sindicalista' of Onésimo

Redondo and Ledesma Ramos. The new organization was fascistic and corporativist.

4. Bandera Roja in '*Les Temps Modernes*', no. 310, May 1972, pp. 1768-826.

5. Cf. Clavera, *et al.*, '*Capitalismo Español de la Autarquía a la Estabilización* (*1939-59*'), 2 vols Edicusa, Madrid, 1973, *passim*.

6. Clavera *et al.*, *op. cit.*, vol. I *passim*. R. Soler, 'The New Spain' in *New Left Review*, no. 58, Nov./Dec. 1969, pp. 3-10.

7. Maravall, *loc. cit.*, p. 437.

8. For a monographic study of the structure and functions of the Spanish Syndical Organization, see C. Iglesias Selgas, *El Sindicalismo Español*, Doncel, Madrid, 1974, *passim*. See also *La Situación Laboral y Sindical en España*, Oficina Internacional del Trabajo, Geneva, 1969, *passim*.

9. The 1937 Law of Unification gave the new body the title 'Falange Española Tradicionalista y de las JONS' otherwise known as the 'Movimiento'.

10. OIT report, p. 126.

11. Article 29 of the Statutes of 'FE y de las JONS' quoted in OIT report, p. 126.

12. *Ibid.* (Article 30).

13. The full text of the XIIIth Declaration is given in the OIT report, pp. 127-8; the 1967 modifications appear on pp. 167-8 of the report.

14. Iglesias Selgas, *op. cit.*, pp. 9-20, 45-6.

15. OIT report, p. 133.

16. Iglesias Selgas, *op. cit.*, p. 67.

17. OIT report, p. 144.

18. For detailed exposition of the struction of the Organization, see OIT report, pp. 134-54 and Iglesias Selgas, *op. cit.*, pp. 45-52, 82-7, 94-134, 212-32, 264-300.

19. B. Barba Hernández, *Dos Años al Frente del Gobierno Civil de Barcelona*, Javier Morata, Madrid, 1948, p. 55.

20. *Ibid*, pp. 58-9.

21. Cf. M. Gallo, *Spain Under Franco*, Allen & Unwin, London, 1973, pp. 169-70.

22. L. Ramirez, *Nuestros Primeros 25 Años*, Ruedo Ibérico, Paris, 1974, p. 64. Gallo, *op. cit.*, pp. 176-7.

23. Clavera, *et. al.*, vol. II, *passim*.

24. Cf. A. de Miguel, *Sociología del Franquismo*, Barcelona, 1975, *passim*.

25. For theories of neo-imperialism and international monopoly capitalism which help to explain Spain's role vis-à-vis the US see articles by F. H. Cardoso, in *New Left Review*, no. 74, July 72, and E. Laclau, in *New Left Review*, no. 67, 1971.

26. OIT report, pp. 150-3. J. Amsden, *Collective Bargaining and Class Conflict in Spain*, Weidenfeld & Nicholson, London, 1972, p. 70.

27. Maravall, *loc. cit.*, p. 440.

28. J. Sanz Oller, *Entre el Fraude y la Esperanza*, Ruedo Ibérico, Paris, 1972, pp. 268-70.

C. Prieto, in a letter to 'Le Monde', Paris 18.2.70 quoted by *'Servicio de Prensa'*, no. 302, 23.3.70 ' I.G.M. Pressespiegel, Frankfurt, p. 3.

29. See, e.g. Barbancho, *Las Migraciones Interiores Españolas: Estudio Cuantitativa desde 1900,* 2 vols, Estudios del Instituto de Desarrollo Económico, Madrid, 1967, passim.

30. Soler, *loc. cit.*, p. 5.

31. Sanz Oller, *op. cit.*, pp. 61-2.

32. *Ibid.*, p. 66.

Gallo, *op. cit.*, pp. 226-7.

33. Cf. Clavera *et al., op. cit.*, vol. II, pp. 144-5.

34. Sanz Oller, *op. cit.*, pp. 85-6.

See also Bandera Roja, *loc. cit.*, p. 1812.

35. *The Economist,* February 1957, p. 566.

36. Cf. J. Blanc, 'Las Huelgas en el Movimiento Obrero Español' in *Horizonte Espanol,* 1966, vol. II, Ruedo Ibérico, Paris.

See also, I. Fernandez de Castro, J. Martínez, *España Hoy,* Ruedo Ibérico, Paris, 1963, p. 29.

37. I. Fava, M. Compta, & J. M. Huertas Claveria, 'Conflictos Laborales que Dejaron Huella' in *Cuadernos para el Diálogo,* extra XXXIII, Feb. 73, p. 36.

38. For details and full analysis of the legislation see Amsden, *op. cit.*, ch. 7, and OIT report, pp. 200-35.

39. OIT report, p. 213.

40. Maravall, *loc. cit.*, p. 441.

41. Report of the IV Plenum of the Syndical Congres, p. 381-2, quoted in OIT report, p. 214.

42. G. Germani, in M. Tumin, *Social Stratification,* Prentice-Hall, 1967, p. 97.

43. Fernandez de Castro & Martinez, *op. cit.*, p. 34.

44. Cf. Clavera *et al., op. cit.*, vol. 2, p. 145.

45. Prieto to 'Le Monde', *loc. cit.*, p. 2.

46. For a collection of declarations made by the Workers Commissions from 1966-71 see *'Spain: the Workers Commissions'* the Canadian Committee for a Democratic Spain, 1973. See also *Cuadernos de Ruedo Ibérico,* nos. 8, 9 20/21. The Principles quoted here were stated in a declaration by the Madrid Comisiones, 1966.

47. Fernández de Castro & Martínez, *op. cit.*, p. 39.

48. See: A. Villanueva, 'Causas y Estructura de la Emigración Exterior' in *Horizonte Espanol,* 66, vol. II, pp. 377-408.

49. Cf. Maravall, *loc. cit.*, p. 436.

50. On the Opus Dei, see, for example, J. Infante, *La Prodigiosa Aventura del Opus Dei,* Ruedo Ibérico, 1970, *passim,* and D. Artigues, *El Opus Dei en España: 1928-57,* Ruedo Ibérico, 1968, *passim.*

51. See Sanz Oller, *op. cit.*, pp. 66-7 and Guy Hermet's reply to Prieto, *Le Monde,* Paris, 25.2.70.

52. E. García 'El Movimiento Obrero en Madrid' in *Cuadernos de Ruedo Ibérico,* no. 30, pp. 97-102.

53. I. Fernández de Castro, 'Tres Años Importantes, 1961-62-63' in

311

Cuadernos de Ruedo Ibérico, no. 16, pp. 79-97.

54. *Ibid.*

55. J. Blanc, 'Asturias: Minas, Huelgas y Comisiones Obreras' in *Cuadernos de Ruedo Ibérico,* no. 1, pp. 70-4.

56. For details of the aims, provisions and failure of the 1st Development Plan, see A. López Muñoz, & J. L. García Delgado, *Crecimiento y Crisis del Capitalismo Español,* Edicusa, Madrid, 1968, *passim.*

57. Re migration, emigration and re-imigration, see A. Pascual *El Retorno de los Emigrantes,* Editorial Nova Terra, Barcelona, 1970, *passim.*

58. See Iglesias Selgas, *op. cit.,* pp. 49-50, 90, 125-30. OIT report, pp. 148-50.

59. Maravall, *loc. cit.,* p. 442.

60. See, e.g. Bandera Roja, *loc. cit.,* originally published in Spain in 1970. Prieto and Hermet letters *loc. cit.,* 'Comisiones Obreras' declarations printed in vols. 8 and 20/21 of 'Cuadernos de Ruedo Ibérico'; Sanz Oller, *op. cit., passim.*

61. Cf. Iglesias Selgas pp. 54-5. This author states that it was the Falangist circle 'Manuel Mateo' which initially provided the premises for these meetings, subsequently withdrawing this facility on the grounds of excessive Communist infiltration of the group.

62. See R. Bulnes, in *Horizonte Espanol,* '66, vol. II, pp. 300, 309-19.

63. Prieto, *loc. cit.*; Hermet, in his reply, maintains that only part of the CP, the 'Communist Movement', was pro-infiltration of the official syndicates and that Catholic adhesion to the Comisones was very tardy.

64. Prieto, *loc. cit.,* p. 3.

65. See OIT report, pp. 160-7.

66. Prieto, *loc. cit.,* p. 3; see also: Bulnes in *'Cuadernos de Ruedo Ibérico'* no. 21/2, Aug.-Nov. '68, p. 31, n.4.

67. For a full account of the strike see *Nuestra Huelga* written by the strikers of 'Laminación de Bandas Echevarri' (distributed by Ruedo Ibérico).

68. Gallo, *op. cit.,* p. 345.

69. See López Muñoz & García Delgado, *op. cit., passim,* esp, pp. 40-2.

70. 'Arriba', 1 Nov. 1967.

71. See R. Bulnes, in *'Cuadernos de Ruedo Ibérico'* no. 21-22, Aug.-Nov. '68; p. 24.

72. Cf. J. M. Maravall, *Trabajo y Conflicto Social,* Edicusa, Madrid, 1967, pp. 204-19.

73. The potential in this direction, with regard to Professional Associations, contained in the 1967 Fuero del Trabajo has still not been fully developed in practice.

74. Cf. *'Horizonte Español'* 1972, vol. 1 pp. 189-418.

75. For details of strikes, demonstrations etc. and government and employer reaction to them, see e.g. *Cuadernos de Ruedo Ibérico,* nos. 26-27, Aug.-Nov. 1970; pp. 97-111 and 36, April-May 1972, pp. 43-5.

76. Quoted by Equipo, IEL, 'Los Conflictos Laborales' in *Cuadernos Para el Diálogo* extra XXXII, p. 33 (emphasis of text).

77. For detailed accounts and analysis of the Law and the Professional

Associations see: Iglesias Selgas, *op. cit.*, pp. 94-157, and *Revista Internacional del Trabajo*, vol. 85, no. 3, March 1972, OIT Geneva, *passim*.

78. Saña, in *Sindicalismo,* no. 1, April 1975, Madrid, p. 20.

79. In the same article Saña suggests that such a reversal will not in fact occur and that the number of migrants to Germany who are redundant or have returned is between 10,000 and 15,000.

80. On 20 December 1973, coincident with the assassination of Admiral Carrero Blanco, ten men were given prison terms ranging from 12-20 years for their alleged participation in Workers' Commissions, among them, Marcelino Camacho and a worker priest. The trial was so-called because it was number 1,001 in the records of the court. In February 1975, an appeal was heard and the men were ultimately released. The case raised considerable international as well as national interest and several demonstrations, stoppages and petitions were organized in favour of the prisoners. See, e.g. *The Times* reports, Jan.-Feb. 1975.

81. *The Times* 1 Nov. 1974 – Basque priest fined £1,880 for 'objectional sermons'; 4 Feb. 1975 – 19 priests fined total of £28,000 for sermons sympathetic to Pamplona strikers.

82. *The Times,* 5 Feb. 1975 – Police raid a church meeting and make 37 arrests; 17 March 1975 – The '1st Christian Assembly of Vallecas' called by Cardinal Enrique y Tarancón to discuss conditions in the industrial suburb of Vallecas, banned by government order. See also: *Cambio 16,* no. 173, 31.3.75, p. 10.

83. For example a group of miners staged a 14-day sit-in at the bottom of a potassium mine in Navarre, in protest against employer intransigence following a break-down in Collective Contract negotiations. See: *Cambio 16,* no. 167, 27 Jan.-2 Feb. 1975, pp. 10-13 and *The Times* 20 and 23 Jan. 1975.

84. *The Times,* 21 March 1975 – Details appear in the same report of other disturbances in Northern Spain – 'police wielding truncheons' chased mourners from a Requiem Mass for six miners killed in an accident in Pamplona, following the shouting of 'subversive remarks'; the Pamplona labour court dismissed the Potasas de Navarra strikers plea for reinstatement; 14 people were arrested in Bilbao – 'five for painting "subversive" slogans on walls and nine for attending an illegal meeting'.

8. Power, Freedom and Social Change in the Spanish University, 1939-75.

1. I have already published a brief study of the first three periods mentioned here in M. S. Archer, ed. *Students, University and Society* (London, Heinemann, 1971) pp. 103-26. Inevitably a substantial part of the present chapter expands and develops what was said there.

2. I am grateful to Imma Julián, University of Barcelona, for facilitating access to important documents issued by the non-professorial staff (PNN) over the recent years. Eduardo Sevilla and Paul Preston, University of Reading, and José M. Elizalde, University of London, have been very helpful with comments and criticisms.

3. Juan J. Linz, 'An Authoritarian Regime: Spain' in Erik Allardt and Stein Rokkan (eds.), *Mass Politics: Studies in Political Sociology* (New York,

313

Free Press, 1970); H. Thomas, 'Spain' in S. J. Woolf, ed. *European Fascism* (London, Weidenfeld, 1968) pp. 280-31; J. Solé-Turà, 'The Political "Instrumentality" of Fascism' in S. J. Woolf *The Nature of Fascism* (London, Weidenfeld, 1970) pp. 42-50 and S. G. Payne 'Spanish Fascism in Comparative Perspective' in *Iberian Studies,* vol. II, no. 1, 1973, pp. 3-12.

    4. D. Jato, *La Rebelión de Los Estudiantes* (Madrid, 1967), pp. 130-2.

    5. M. Valdés, Introduction to D. Jato, *op. cit.*, pp. 12-13.

    6. *Ibid., loc. cit.*.

    7. D. Jato, *op. cit.*, p. 422.

    8. *Ley de Ordenación de la Universidad Española,* article 40.

    9. A. Sáez Alba *La Otra 'cosa nostra': La ACNP* Paris, Ruedo Ibérico, 1974, pp. xxxi, ix-xliv.

    10. Took place at the Escorial, from 4 to 8 Jan. 1940.

    11. Comrade José Maria Guitarte. D. Jato *op. cit.* pp. 427-8.

    12. D. Jato, *op. cit.*, pp. 428-9. And *Ley de Ordenación* etc. art. 3, 34, 40.

    13. I.e. Srs, Fernandez Cuesta, Ruiz Gimenez, Romeo Gorria.

    14. The 'fascist' *Milicia Universitaria* was disbanded after 1945; instead, students entered special army units for NCO Training.

    15. A. Peña, *'Veinticinco años de Luchas Estudiantiles',* in *Horizonte Español 1966* (Ruedo Ibérico, Paris, 1966), vol. II, pp. 169-212.

    16. D. Jato, *op. cit.*, pp. 448-9.

    17. On 14 Aug. 1942. The intended victim was General Varela.

    18. A Peña, *op. cit.*, p. 171.

    19. Until 1952, in exile. In 1947 it had been severely damaged by repression and political trials.

    20. Quoted by D. Artigues, *El Opus Dei en España* (Ruedo Ibérico, Paris, 1968), vol. I, p. 37.

    21. A. Saéz Alba, *op. cit.* pp. xlv-xlvi.

    22. Barrington Moore, *The Social Origins of Dictatorship and Democracy.*

    23. J. Clavera *et al., Capitalismo español: de la autarquía a la establización,* Madrid, Edicusa, 1973, vol. I.

    24. Various, *Catalunya sota el régim franquista,* Paris, Edicions catalanes, 1972.

    25. R. Tamames, *Estructura económica de España* Madrid, Guadiana, 1969, 4th ed. p. 592.

    26. This statement is based on personal experience and on discussion with Professor José Maria Maravall. In two papers jointly submitted by us at the London School of Economics (1971-and-1973) we have stressed the importance of Republican intelligentsia families as breeding grounds of early opposition groups against the régime.

    27. Such as *Alcalá,* the Madrid SEU review; or *Revista,* a magazine published in Barcelona by the ex-Falangist poet Dionisio Ridruejo.

    28. For the theory of Hispanic *caudillaje* see the work of Professor Javier Conde and that of the other totalitarian disciples of Professor Carl Schmitt.

    29. A. Fontán, *Los Católicos en la Universidad Española Actual* (Punta Europa, Madrid 1961), p. 114.

    30. For a description of the 1956-57 situation see A. Peña, *op. cit.* (note 13), pp. 169-212.

31. Cf. F. Claudin, *Las Divergencias en el Partido* (privately published, no place given, 1964, *passim*).

32. The SUT survived several years in a subdued form.

33. Others were the FUDE (*Federación Universitaria Democrática Española*) founded in 1961 and centred in Madrid: The CUDE (*Confederación* . . .) later embraced both organizations.

34. For a good account of these events see 'Chronicle' in *Minerva,* vol. III, no. 3 (Spring 1965), pp. 420-8: Also E. Tierno 'Students' opposition in Spain'; in *Government and Opposition,* vol. I, no. 4, 1966, pp. 467-86.

35. Professors Aranguren, Tierno, García Calvo, Aguilar Navarro, Montero Díaz. Professors Valverde and Tovar resigned as a gesture of solidarity.

36. Quoted by M. Jiménez de Parga 'Nuestra Universidad y nuestra sociedad', in *Cuadernos para el dialogo,* 5th special issue, May 1967, p. 13.

37. A. Martín 'Estudios de Filosofia, 1960-1971' in *Teorema,* vol. IV, 2, 1974, p. 279.

38. For a suggestion as to why this might be so, see A. de Miguel, *Manual, op. cit.,* p. 443.

39. For class percentages cf. J. Rubio *La enseñanza superior en España* (Gredos, Madrid, 1969). The author claims that children of the poorest strata achieve 8 or 9 per cent of the student body of the higher technical schools, certainly a 'European' average. In the universities percentages have been abysmally low – less than 2 per cent – although important changes have been reported for 1968 and 1969. One critical author puts the percentage of students of working-class origin at 4.69 per cent.; R. Conte, 'Universidad' in J. M. Areilza *et al., España, Perspectiva 1969* (Guadiana, Madrid 1969) p. 128 For *clasismo* in general cf. O. Bohigas *Les escoles tècniques superiors i l'estructura professional* (Nova Terra, Barcelona 1968).

40. Cf. J. L. Pinillos, 'Actitudes sociales primarias: su estructura y medida en una muestra universitaria espanola', in *Revista de la Universidad de Madrid,* no. 7, 1953; J. F. Tezanos, M. A. Dominguez, 'Los universitarios y la religion, in *El Ciervo,* no. 142, December 1965; J. L. Pinillos, *Actitudes sociales de los universitarios madrileños,* unpublished research, although cf. *Time* magazine, vol. 67, no. 3, 16 Jan., 1956. Cf. also *Revista española de la opinión publica, passim,* since 1965, amongst other sources.

41. N. J. Smelser and S. M. Lipset, 'Social Structure, Mobility and Development', in N. J. Smelser and S. M. Lipset (eds), *Social Structure and Mobility in Economic Development* (Routledge & Kegan Paul, London, 1966), p. 32.

42. Such growth and development have been erratic and still present many dangerous features (cf. J. M. Muntaner, 'Los altibajos del desarollo economico espanal' in *Destino,* no. 1696, 4 April 1970, pp. 16-17), but this is quite another matter.

43. Ministerio de Educacion y Ciencia. *La Educacion en España: Bases para una politica educativa* (Official publication, Madrid 1969) *passim.*

44. Article in *España Económica,* quoted by R. Tamames, *op. cit.* (note 19), p. 723. Yet a report from a commission in the Cortes claims that the expenses incurred by the Educational Reform Act discussed by that body

will be yearly on 15 per cent. of the state budgetary credits (see *Noticiero Universal*, 12 March 1970, p. 10).

45. Turkey excluded.

46. The incompetence and inexactitudes of government planners can be measured by the several criticisms which have appeared on the two development plans. Cf. Tamames, *op. cit.* (note 19), pp. 779-800 and A. López Muñoz and J. L. G. Delgado, *Crecimiento y Crisis del Capitalismo Español* (Edicusa, Madrid, 1968), *passim*.

47. M. Niedergang, in *Le Monde,* 31 Oct. 1969, p. 2.

48. Cf. Artigues, *op. cit.* (note 18), *passim,* for this purpose; also his 'Qu'est-ce que l'Opus Dei? in *Esprit,* November 1967, no. 11, pp. 707-44, and especially J. Infante, *La prodigiosa aventura del Opus Dei* (Ruedo Ibérico, Paris, 1970).

49. Probably the earliest open clash between Opus Dei students and others (in this case Falangists) occurred during the academic year 1949-50, at the Colegio Mayor César Carlos.

50. It first took over the Consejo's learned journal *Arbor:* its first publishing house, Rialp, was founded soon after.

51. Although their students had to sit final examinations in State Universities in order to be granted degrees.

52. D. Artigues, *op. cit.* (note 18), p. 155.

53. *J. Ynfante op. cit.* (note 39), pp. 60-2.

54. When the participants in a free assembly of students, teachers and intellectuals, held in the Franciscan Sarrià Monastery, were locked in by the police. Mass arrests followed.

55. A. Latorre, *Universidad y Sociedad* (Ariel, Barcelona, 1964); P. Laín, *El Problema de la Universidad* (Edicusa, Madrid, 1969); A. Tovar, *La Universidad en la Sociedad de Masas* (Ariel, Barcelona, 1968); all *passim*.

56. *Cuadernos para el Diálogo,* June-July 1966, nos. 33-34; May 1967, special issue no. 5; Oct. 1969, special issue no. XVI.

57. Cf. S. Giner 'La Ciencia y la Sociedad Española', in *Diario de Barcelona,* 7 March 1965, p. 15; 'La Universidad y el diálogo', *Diario de Barcelona,* 4 April 1965, p. 14.

58. Cf. A. De. Miguel's articles contained in his *Diagnóstico de la Universidad* (Madrid, Guadarrama, 1973). They represent a liberal reformist view of the situation. A more conservative view (but still in the liberal and democratic camp) is represented by the economist professor Jesús Prados Arrarte; cf. for instance his article in *Blanco y Negro* 'El. problema de la Universidad', 10 March 1973.

59. Cf. Editorial Nova Terra, Barcelona: *Dossier Universitario* series; and *La Universidad* (Ciencia Nueva, Madrid, 1969) *passim*.

60. Manuel Fraga Iribarne *La famila y la educación en una sociedad de masas y máquinas* (Madrid, Congreso de la Familia Española, 1960).

61. Madrid: Alianza Editorial, 1971 and Barcelona; Edicions 62, 1971, respectively. Cf. also J. Xiran *Manuel B. Cossio y la educación en España* Barcelona, Ariel, 1969. I. Fernández de Castro *Reforma educativa y desarollo capitalista*, Madrid, Edicusa, 1973. General essays on the 'student rebellion' in the modern world (widely read) have also appeared, such as E. Tierno *La*

rebelión juvenil y el problema en la universidad Madrid, Seminarios y Ediciones, 1st. ed., 1972.

62. FOESSA Suplemento March 1970, p. 20.

63. Obviously this statement is not aimed at those competent and distinguished scholars or scientists who have obtained chairs during this period. Scandals during *oposiciones* have often accompanied nominations to chairs when it became clear that the appointment was rigged. This may be a hopeful sign that the system will be challenged in the future. On nepotism in the Madrid Faculty of Medicine, see *Sábado Gráfico* 31.7.1971, p. 9.

64. J. A. Aguirre, *et al.*, *Así está la Enseñanza Primaria* (Gaur, San Sebastián, 1969), *passim;* FOESSA 'Informe sobre Educación Superior' cf. *La Vanguardia*, 25 March 1970, p. 7.

65. Out of the 2,372 who graduated (M.A.) in pure physics over nineteen academic years, by 1969 only forty-two worked in their field in Spain; 1,730 worked abroad (75 per cent): 700 had other jobs; and 20 only were in higher research Cf. *Ibérica*, vol. 17, no. 6, 15 June 1969.

66. *Información 1975, Universidad Nacional de Educación a Distancia*, Madrid UNED, 1974, for details, numbers of students (about 25,000 by 1974) courses taught, careers (10 by same year), etc.

67. I. Fernández de Castro, *De las Cortes de Cádiz al Plan de Desarrollo* (Ruedo Ibérico, Paris, 1968), p. 356. On the professional strikes of engineering students, cf. ABC., Weekly Supplement, 18 Jan. 1970, pp. 28-33; and constant reports in the Spanish press, Spring 1970. Cf. especially discontent in the Autonomous University of Barcelona, Faculty of Medicine.

The *numerus clausus* problem is of course related to the monopoly certain professional bodies have over sectors of the state apparatus. On this cf. V. M. Gonzales-Haba 'Las minorias burocráticas' in *Triunfo* no. 636, 7 Dec. 1974, pp. 52-6.

68. M. Tuñón de Lara 'Le Problème universitaire espanol' in *Esprit*, Mai 69, no. 381, p. 848. The most important local branches of SDEU have been inevitably Barcelona (SDEUB) and Madrid (SEDUM); for a chronology of its first years of existence, its vicissitudes ant the political struggles and problems going on within it cf. S. León 'Notes sobre el movimiento estudiantil en Espana' (pp. 157-78) and D. Formentor 'Universidad: cronica de siete años de lucha' (pp. 179-236) in *Horizonte español 1972*, Paris, Ruedo Ibérico, 1972. Another important chronology of events appears in *Universitat*, no. 6, Dec 1974-Jan 1975 pp. 6-17, published by the Catalan branch of the CP.

69. G. Hermet, 'Les Espagnols devant leur régime', in *Revue française de science politique*, vol. XX, no. I, Feb. 1970, p. 27.

70. R. Conte *op. cit.*, p. 116.

71. For the Decree see *Gaceta de Madrid BOE*, 21 Oct. 1975.

F. Bayon 'Elecciones en la Universidad' in *Posible*, no. 2, 1-15 Dec. 1974, pp. 38-39. Same opinion expressed by Amparo Moreno 'Participacion en la ensenanza' *Destino* no. 1939, 30 Nov. 1974, p. 19.

72. For a case study of the new subculture in the University of Valencia, cf. Salvador Salcedo *Integrats, rebels i marginats* Valencia L'Estel, 1974, and my own preface to it.

73. The problem of clasismo which of course directly refers to the question of class hegemony has been the subject of serious renewed debate through the introduction of entrance selection procedures (*selectividad*) by the authorities. On this matter cf. *Dossier* of the 'Colegio Oficial de Doctores Y Licenciados', Barcelona, 3 April, 1974 and Alberto Moncada 'Selectivaded y enseñanza post-secundaria' in *Sistema,* no. 8, Jan. 1975 pp. 111-24.

74. That Francoists should think otherwise is not surprising. For a late attempt at developing a theory according to which all evils are due to Marcuse and other godless spirits, cf L. Gómez de Aranda *Las ideologías y la universidad* Madrid: Ediciones del Movimiento, 1972. Certain sociologists who would not subscribe to such grotesque nonsense have nevertheless engaged in futurology in which 'educational reform' covers 1970-1980, (at least half of it therefore under Francoism) and the University is understood as a service body in a 'service society' leading to a 'scientific society' propelled by an 'industry of ideas'. I find this approach highly objectionable on grounds which are certainly not only sociological but perhaps ethical. Cf. A. Almarcha, J. Martin Moreno and A. de Miguel 'El sistema educativo español en los treinta próximos años' in the *Revista Española de la Opinión Pública,* April-June 1974, no. 36 pp. 7-19.

75. It was only after this essay was completed and revised that I had access to Professor Carlos París' interesting article on the Spanish University in M. Fraga Iribarne *et al. La España de los Años 70,* vol. III, 1974, pp. 509-620.

9. Basque Revolutionary Separatism: ETA

1. ETA – the initials of Euskadi Ta Askatasuna, meaning Basque homeland and Freedom.

2. Julen Agirre, *'Operación Ogro'. Cómo y por qué ejecutamos a Carrero Blanco.* Ediciones Mugalde/Ruedo Ibérico, Hendaye and Paris, 1974. This book contains details of the planning of the assassination including a transcribed interview with the commandoes concerned and documentary material. For a full and extensive justification in political terms of the assassination, see *Zutik,* no. 64, May 1974, the theoretical organ of ETA. This number develops the theme of the parallel development of working class popular action with minority activism. ETA-6a's magazine is also called *Zutik* but is clearly designated as such.

3. Similar, more justified explanations are given for the bomb-blast which killed eleven people in a restaurant in the Calle de Correos in central Madrid on 13 September, 1974. ETA denied the attack after accusations by the police, which stated that the act was carried out jointly by ETA and the Communist Party – a clearly far-fetched possibility to all except the police.

4. For a response by an anarchist to charges of irresponsible involvement in direct action by an ETA (6a) leader see 'El anarquismo y la ETA' by Eguzki, in *Frente Libertario,* año 3, no. 25, Paris, Nov. 1972. Exiled militants of ETA in Belgium have anarchist tendencies and were influential in the

pressure towards decentralization of ETA's leadership in 1972. Their magazine is *Gataska*. (See Ortzi, *Historia de Euskadi: el nacionalismo vasco y ETA*, p. 390 (Ruedo Ibérico, Paris, 1975). Another Basque anarchist broadsheet is *Askatasuna*, occasionally published in Brussels. 'Dentro del contexto vasco actual (esencialmente en lo que se refiere a las actuales corrientes de ETA) nos sentimos distanciados de ambas corrientes principales' Askatasuna, no. I (no date).

5. For the immediate reaction in Spain to the assassination, see Paul Preston, 'Spain in crisis: the assassination of Carrero Blanco and its aftermath' in *Iberian Studies*, vol. III, no. I, Spring 1974.

6. For a study of the problems of state – and nation-building in Spain within the sphere of political sociology see Juan Linz 'Early state-building and late peripheral nationalisms against the state: the case of Spain' in S. N. Eisenstadt and Stein Rokkan (eds), *Building States and Nations, vol. 2*, ISSC 1973. On the same theme, see W. Bell and W. E. Freedman (eds.) *Ethnicity and Nation Building, Comparative, International and Historical perspectives*, Sage, 1973, which has a chapter on Spain and the Basque country. For a wide-ranging study towards a definition and comprehensive typology of nationalism, see A. D. Smith, *Theories of Nationalism*, Duckworth, 1971.

7. See M. García Venero, *Historia del nacionalismo vasco*, Editora Nacional, Madrid, 1969, now outnumbered by histories written outside Spain from a sympathetic point of view.

8. Baroja was attracted by the nationalism not of the PNV but of the ANV, its a-confessional counterpart. See Ortzi, *op. cit.*, p. 177.

9. K. Medhurst, *The Basques*, Minority Rights Group, report no. 9, London, 1972.

10. Sartre's opinions highlight one of the long-standing political arguments within ETA, namely whether the movement can be said to represent a country that is a subject colony despite its geographical position or whether its claims and therefore its activity should be more like those of the Palestinians, the Breton liberation movement, parts of Welsh nationalism, etc. Sartre writes the preface to G. Halimi, *Le procès de Burgos*, Gallimard, Paris, 1971, and reveals sympathy for ETA-5a. The preface is translated into English in *Planet*, 9, Dec. 1971, Jan. 1972, Llangeitho, Tregaron, Wales, under the title *The Burgos trials*.

11. Medhurst, *op. cit.*, p. 7.

12. See Ned Thomas 'Self-help nurseries can save Basques' in the *Times Educational Supplement*, 4 Jan. 1974 and C. A., 'Las ikastolas' in *Cuadernos para el diálogo*, extra XXXIV, April 1973.
See *Berriak*, no. 14, Feb. 1973, the news organ of ETA 6a. '. . . sólo en el marco de la realización de la revolución socialista es posible el desarrollo pleno del euskera y de la cultura popular euskaldún . . . sólo mediante la unidad de todas las ikastolas populares y la coordinación de sus luchas con las del movimiento popular y obrero . . . podremos obtener conquistas importantes en el terreno de . . . la implantación del bilingüismo en toda la enseñanza.'

13. For accounts of the incident and its repercussions, see A. Brassloff 'Prelate caught in the crossfire', *The Guardian*, 8 March 1974, and 'Franco

319

relents on expelling rebel bishop', The *Sunday Times,* 10 March 1974. See also Ortzi, *op. cit.,* pp. 404-7.

14. The 'anonymous leader' gives this information in G. Halimi, *op. cit.,* p. 152 and it is repeated in J-L. Davant, 'Lutte nationale et lutte des classes dans le mouvement basque, *Les Temps Modernes,* Aug./Sept. 1973. Other informed sources suggest that the intention to derail the train was serious and that the plan simply misfired.

15. The organizational structure was divided into four areas of responsibility – political, economic, military and cultural – held by Julen Madariaga, Benito del Valle, Imaz Garay and Txillardegui respectively. (Ortzi, *op. cit.,* p. 300). See also Txabe, 'ETA y la cuestión nacional vasca' in *Horizonte Español 1972,* vol. 2. p. 78.

16. A work by one of ETA's founding members, Federico Krutwig, is of particular interest for this early period in ETA's development. See Fernando Sarrailh de Ihartza, *Estudio dialéctico de una nacionalidad: Vasconia,* Norbait, Buenos Aires, 1962. See also Iñaki Goitia, Algunas precisiones sobre Euskadi', in *Cuadernos de Ruedo Ibérico,* no. 25, June/July, 1970, p. 40.

17. See Ortzi, *op. cit.* for the best account of this and earlier periods; also the following: 'Nacionalismo y lucha de clases en Euskadi. (V y VI Asambleas de ETA)' by Iker in *Cuadernos de Ruedo Ibérico,* no. 37/38, June/Sept. 1972; 'Algunas precisiones sobre Euskadi' by Iñaki Goitia, in *Cuadernos de Ruedo Ibérico,* no. 25, June/July 1970.

18. This view is well expressed by Martín Zugasti in 'El problema nacional vasco' in *Horizonte Español, 1966,* vol. II, Ruedo Ibérico, Paris, 1966. See also Patxi Isaba, *Euskadi Socialiste,* Editions du Cercle & Editions de la Tête de Feuilles, Max Chaleil, Paris, 1971.

19. There is little consolation for sympathisers with the Basque cause in the programme of the Junta Democrática set up in July 1974 which includes this sentence: 'La Junta propugna: el reconocimiento, bajo la unidad del Estado español, de la personalidad pública de los pueblos catalán, vasco, gallego, y de las comunidades regionales que lo decidan democráticamente.' (Ortzi, *op. cit.,* p. 411).

20. See Iker, *op. cit.,* p. 20;

21. See *Cuadernos vascos,* no. I: 'De Santoña a Burgos', Euskal Elkargoa, St Jean de Luz, 1972, pp. 42-3.
This group of socialists constitute what is now known as the 'Branka' group from the name of the magazine which they produce regularly. A full description of the kind of programme this essentially culturalist and, (within the context of ETA) right-wing group espouses can be found in the special number of *Branka* entitled *Proyecto de manifiesto vasco,* Editions Hordago, Ciboure, 1973. There are figures relating to the economic situation of Euskadi contained in this booklet as well as clear indications of irredentism. 'Sería absurdo que nosotros, patriotas vascos, no pensaramos desde ahora en despertar la conciencia vasca de las comunidades desgajadas del tronco nacional por el imperialismo' (p. 63).

22. In 1972 this group was joined by a group from Valencia; its trotskyism, extended into Maoist sympathies, found allies with ORT (Organización Revolucionaria de Trabajadores). (Ortzi, *op. cit.,* p. 352).

23. See Halimi, *op. cit.*, pp. 159-62.

24. See Ortzí, *op. cit.*, pp. 361-77.

25. Apart from Halimi, Federico de Arteaga, *ETA y el proceso de Burgos*, Madrid, 1971 and Kepa Salaberri, *El proceso de Euskadi en Burgos*, Ruedo Ibérico, Paris, 1971, deal with the trial from a hostile and a sympathetic view respectively.

26. See Max Gallo, *Historia de la España franquista*, Ruedo Ibérico, Paris, 1971, pp. 370-88.

27. See Martín Zugasti, 'Aberri Eguna' in *Cuadernos de Ruedo Ibérico* no. 6, April/May, 1966.

28. The document appears in Ortiz de Zárate, *op. cit.*, p. 159.

29. See *Langile*, the ETA (former 5a) labour pamphlet that is aimed at analysing labour problems and future programmes in Euskadi. No. 1, July 1974 sets the tone of the series and is a mixture of theoretical pieces and diary accounts of strike action undertaken in Tolosa and Lesaka.

30. In addition to *Zutik*, 64 and its extensive justification of the necessary interlinking of minority activism with mass action, see ETA Va's news pamphlet *Hautsi* (various numbers) which regularly lists the activist deeds of commandos of ETA such as robberies of banks, burnings of informers' property, attacks on police and Civil Guard posts and so on. See no. 3, April, 1973 for an elucidation of the significance of the kidnapping of the industrialist Zabala in the context of the workers' struggle (p. 30).

31. See ETA (6a)'s *Zutik* no. 54 for a long and often indigestible account of this evolution.

32. See *Red Weekly*, II Jan. 1974 and also various numbers of *Inprecor* (International press correspondence) especially nos. 7 and 9, Sept. and Oct. 1974.

See also *Zutik* no. 61, Nov. 1973 ('Resoluciones de la 7a Asamblea') 'La decision tomada por la VIIa Asamblea de unir en adelante nuestras fuerzas con las de la LCR supone un paso importantísimo . . . hacia la construcción de un partido revolucionario centralizado a nivel estatal . . . la fusión con la LCR se basa en la coincidencia sobre la vía que ha de conducir a la victoria de la revolución socialista en nuestro país; frente a la vía pacífica, la vía revolucionaria; frente a la línea de alianza de clases, la vía de la independencia política del proletariado.'

33. The fullest description of Enbata's genesis and philosophy is in Davant, *op. cit.*, p. 288.

See also *Mouvement Enbata: Objectifs et stratégie*, (bilingual manifesto of Enbata) Bayonne, 1972.

10. The Catalan Question Since the Civil War

1. The term 'catalanist' is resented by some autonomists who prefer to be called simply 'Catalans'. I have nevertheless used the word, without any pejorative sense, as a portmanteau label for those Catalans who are not merely conscious of Catalonia's differences from the rest of Spain but wish to see them given formal institutional recognition. The term has a long

history of use by Catalans, from the *Unió Catalanista* of 1891 to the *Partit Catalanista Republicà* of 1933.

2. This proportion was significantly higher in the city of Barcelona: 32 per cent at the advent of the Republic. M. Ramírez Jiménez *Los grupos de presión en la Segunda República Española,* Madrid, 1969, p. 289.

3. Ernest Lluch *Les lliçons d'una regionalització econòmica* in *Serra d'Or,* November, 1970.

4. It must be remembered that even the Generalitat was scarcely autonomous, being merely the delegate for the ministries in Madrid in most of its functions such as education, social policy, communications, justice and police; practically the only fields in which it was genuinely independent were culture and public health.

5. Díaz Reitg, *España bajo el nuevo régimen,* p. 227, quoted in J. Pabón, *Cambó,* Barcelona, 1969, vol. II, *primera parte,* p. 510.

6. *Palabras del Caudillo,* Barcelona, 1939, p. 226, quoted in *Catalunya sota el règim franquista* (henceforward *CSRF*), Paris, 1973, p. 98.

7. *Manchester Guardian,* 27 July 1939, quoted in *CSRF,* p. 241.

8. *CSRF,* p. 458. 1714 was the date of the capture of Barcelona and the suppression of traditional Catalan institutions by Philip V.

9. Mateu y Pla was soon afterwards the object of an investigation involving racketeering in foodstuffs. As a member of Falange's National Council, he was protected by Serrano Súñer and the case against him was dropped. (L. Ramírez, *Nuestros primeros veinticinco años,* Paris, 1964, p. 63.)

10. The Count of Ruiseñada (Julio Claudio Güell, head of the foremost family of the Catalan manufacturing oligarchy) and Abadal's son, Ramón Abadal i Vinyals, were two *lligueros* who became prominent members of Don Juan's *Consejo Privado,* joining traditional Catalan monarchists such as Santiago Nadal and Ignacio Villallonga. The *Lliga* was one of the components of the 'Confederation of Monarchist Forces' which negotiated the 'Pact of St Jean de Luz' with the exiled socialists in 1948. On the other hand Manuel Bastos, a *Lliga* member of the Cortes who spent the war working as a surgeon at the Norwegian hospital in Alcoy, was sentenced to twelve years' imprisonment (and served four).

11. D. Ridruejo, *Escrito en España,* Buenos Aires, 1964, p. 177.

12. In 1970 the Barcelona Exchange represented 18 % of the total Spanish stock market; its operation in futures had still not been regularized. J. Planasdemunt, *Gran Enciclopedia Catalana* (henceforward *GEC*) Barcelona, 1971, vol. III p. 752.

13. F. Cabana *et al. GEC,* vol. III pp. 127-33. The share of Catalan banks in total Spanish bank capital was:

1925	1930	1935	1940	1945	1950	1955	1960	1965	1969
11.5%	10%	7.25%	6.75%	6.25%	3%	3%	3.5%	4.5%	5.75%

14. Ironically *Destino,* now a progressive and catalanist magazine, was born as a falangist periodical in Burgos during the war.

15. *CSRF* p. 295.

16. *CSRF* pp. 326-9.

17. *CSRF* p. 158.

18. *CSRF* p. 150. The Catalan language is approximately as different from Castilian – lexically and morphologically, though not syntactically – as Chaucerian from modern English. In the common speech of Barcelona it is adulterated by many borrowings from Castilian.

19. *CSRF* pp. 170, 340, 136.

20. *CSRF* pp. 138-47. R. Trias Fargas, *Introducción a la economía catalana,* Madrid, 1974, pp. 28, 48.

21. *CSRF* p. 198.

22. *CSRF* pp. 261-5. The philologist Fabra, who had standardized Catalan orthography and compiled its definitive dictionary, was a favourite target of the *españolistas,* who accused him of 'having invented the Catalan language in his study with the help of a French dictionary' – a reference to his elimination of castilianisms.

23. *CSRF* pp. 360-7.

24. *CSRF* pp. 369-86.

25. *CSRF* pp. 411-52.

26. They were Pompeu Fabra, Santiago Pi i Sunyer, Josep Pous i Pagès, Antoni Rovira i Virgili, and Jaume Serra Hunter – all of them originally sympathizers with the centre party *Acció Catalana* rather than the *Esquerra.* (M. Ferrer, *GEC,* vol. V, p. 514).

27. At a 'First National Conference' held in Mexico in 1953 the federalists re-created the Consell Nacional Català, headed by Salvador Armendares. In 1964 it moved its headquarters to London: the present secretary is the octogenarian Batista i Roca. (M. Ferrer, *ibid.*; F Miró *¿Y España cuándo?* Mexico 1959, pp. 103-9.)

28. J. Carner i Ribalta *De Balaguer a Nova York,* Paris, 1972, p. 144. An interview with Josep Cornudella, a former FNC militant, is included in S. Vilar, *Protagonistas de la España democrática,* Paris, 1968, pp. 326-30.

29. The MSC (*Moviment Socialista de Catalunya*) was founded in Toulouse in 1945 by ex-members of the PSUC and POUM. It was a reversion to the Fabianism of the pre-1933 *Unió Socialista.* Its leader, Serra i Moret, was a former USC figure and an ex-minister of the Generalitat (1931-32). He remained a member of Alvaro de Albornoz's Government of the Republic in Exile until 1951, four years after it had been abandoned by the PSOE.

30. The Generalitat still lingers on, an archaeological survival located at St Martin-le-Beau (Indre), presided by – and practically consisting only of – the now venerable Taradellas.

31. A. Téllez, *La guerrilla urbana: Facerías,* Paris, 1974, p. 262.

32. Téllez, p. 104.

33. The *Unió Socialista* had seceded from the PSOE in 1923 after quarrelling with the Spanish party over its lukewarm attitude to regional autonomy. Originally moderate and reformist, it had veered sharply leftwards after Comorera became its president in 1933.

34. Comorera himself was a catalanist *sui generis,* having edited a bilingual weekly *Nación Catalana* in Argentina during the twenties. The underlying catalanism of the PSUC was reinforced by the enormous expansion of its membership during the first year of the war, only partially

accounted for by the influx of frightened members of the middle class (*v.* B. Bolloten *The Grand Camouflage* ch. VI); the PSUC also recruited many blue-collar workers, especially in the hinterland – Sabadell, Terrassa, Manresa – who had been members of Pestaña's *Opposition Syndicates*. Vidiella remarked, in an article in *Leviatán* in October 1935, that almost all the unskilled workers in Barcelona were immigrants and consequently 'the language used in the *Opposition Syndicates* is almost exclusively Catalan and in the CNT preferentially Castilian'. (A. Balcells, *La polèmica de 1928,* Barcelona, 1973, p. 16.)

35. G. Hermet, *Les communistes en Espagne,* Paris, 1971, p. 80; C. Lorenzo, *Los anarquistas españoles y el poder,* Paris, 1972, p. 318. The coincidences between the Generalitat's Collectivisation Decree of October 1936 and the Yugoslavs' decentralized economic system has often been remarked (v. foreword by Velarde Fuertes to A. Pérez Baró, *30 mesos de collectivisme a Catalunya,* Barcelona, 1970, p. 10).

36. J. Gros, *Abriendo camino,* Paris, 1971, p. 205.

37. Comorera secretly re-entered Spain in 1951, intending to rebuild his influence in the underground PSUC. In 1954 he was arrested in Barcelona and died in Burgos prison four years later (Hermet, p. 80; Vilar, p. 246; F. Bonamusa in *GEC* vol. III p. 402). There were rumours that he had been betrayed by the Stalinists, who regarded the former USC members of the PSUC as semi-bourgeois 'parasites of the *Esquerra*' (J. M. Huertas, interview with Rafael Vidiella in *Triunfo* 19 April 1975, p. 51).

38. Hermet, p. 57.

39. Lorenzo, p. 286.

40. A. Manent, *Literatura catalana a debat,* Barcelona, 1969, p. 136. J. Roig, *Veinticinco años de movimiento nacional en Cataluña* in *Horizonte Español,* Paris, 1966, vol. II, p. 119.

41. Vilar, pp. 405, 411, 423, 280.

42. The monastery of Montserrat had been a spiritual home of catalanism since the mid-nineteenth century. In late 1938 Escarré, a thirty-year-old member of the community in exile in Italy, travelled to Zaragoza and, in advance of the National army by several days, returned to Montserrat and took possession, giving himself the title of prior, in order to forestall the intervention of an ecclesiastical commissioner already appointed by Salamanca. The old abbot Marcet confirmed Escarré as prior, and passed the direction of the community to him in 1941. Thereafter Montserrat assumed the moral leadership of the Catalan Church, in constant opposition to the 'foreign' episcopacy. (A. Manent in *GEC* vol. VI, p. 747).

43. The *minyons* (nowadays usually called *nois escoltes*) had been founded by Batista i Roca in 1927, and were organized on a parish basis.

44. J. Solé Turà, in *Las ideologías en la España de hoy* Madrid 1972, pp. 197-8.

45. Leaflets scattered in the streets stressed the injustice of a rise in fares in Barcelona but not in Madrid – 'Spain is one? Then the same for everyone.' (M. Gallo, *Historia de la España franquista,* Paris, 1971, p. 225) Actually fare increases were pending in Madrid too; anti-castilian sentiment

evidently still counted for as much in Barcelona as appeals to proletarian unity.

46. Lorenzo, p. 320; Vilar, p. 235. Gallo (p. 227) claims that the Barcelona employers encouraged the strikers, as a way of pressing the government to liberalise the economy.

47. *El año del Congreso Eucarístico de Barcelona* in *La Actualidad Española*, 7 Nov. 1974.

48. Vilar, pp. 399-401.

49. Roig, p. 120.

50. Gallo, p. 292; Roig, p. 123.

51. Vilar, pp. 299, 411; Solé Turà, p. 201; S. Giner, *Spain* in M. Archer, *Students, University and Society* (1972) p. 110.

52. The text was later published by Marcet in *Mi ciudad y yo,* Barcelona, 1963, quoted by Roig, p. 122.

53. Few catalanists hoped to see teaching *in* Catalan; they sought the lifting of the prohibition on the teaching *of* Catalan – i.e. how to read and write the regional language.

54. The refounded *Institut* corresponded with foreign learned institutions, and its publications were even included in official Spanish exhibitions abroad, though booksellers were forbidden to put them on public display in Spain. After a scandal in 1960 when police broke up a reception given by the *Institut* at a private house, at which foreign diplomats were present, Martín de Riquer (almost the only Catalan scholar close to the régime) proposed to the Ninth General Council of the *Movimiento Nacional* that the *Institut* should be placed under the control of the provincial *diputación* 'to remove its political character'. (J. Melià *Informe sobre la lengua catalana*, Madrid, 1970, pp. 234-7).

55. *Catalunya Avui*, Toulouse 1973, pp. 31-2.

56. Meliá, p. 172.

57. Various presentations of figures for immigration are given in E. Lluch, *La minva relativa de la immigració* in *Serra d'Or* March 1966; F. Candel, *Els altres catalans*, Barcelona, 1964, pp. 155-61; *GEC* vol. IV pp. 715-16; Banco Urquijo report quoted in J. Linz, *The Case of Spain* in R. Dahl, *Regimes and Oppositions*, Yale, 1973, p. 246.

58. B. Welles, *Spain, the gentle anarchy*, 1965, pp. 84-5; L. Ramírez, *Nuestros primeros veinticinco años*, Paris, 1964, pp. 219-32; Roig, p. 123; Vilar, p. 275. Welles wrongly places the events in December 1960.

59. Montserrat does not come under the authority of any Spanish bishop. Nevertheless – as Pérez de Urbel, the abbot of that other Benedictine institution and shrine of *franquismo*, the Valle de los Caídos, enthusiastically pointed out, Rome had once before, in the sixteenth century, placed Montserrat under the authority of the Benedictines of Valladolid.

60. The Palau de la Música, home of Barcelona's prime Orpheus Choir, had a special significance, since it was one of the institutions decatalanized in 1939.

61. After a Catalan song won first prize at the Mediterranean Song Festival of 1963, the government prohibited J. M. Serrat from representing Spain at the Eurovision contest and banned the broadcasting of Raimon's records.

62. Vilar, p. 275.

63. Escarré's authoritarian ways had also created certain difficulties within his community. His exile lasted from 1965 until October 1968, when he was allowed to return in the terminal stage of fatal illness. His funeral at Montserrat was the occasion of a large catalanist demonstration, those present singing 'We shall overcome'.

64. According to a story current at the time, a peasant from a remote village visited the city and, seeing the slogan 'Vint-i-cinc anys de pau' everywhere, asked 'Es una película que fan a Barcelona?' 'No,' was the caustic reply, 'és una comédia que fan a Madrid.'

65. The Vatican yielded to the demands, first by nominating four Catalans as auxiliary bishops; and later, in 1971, by moving González to Toledo and promoting the Catalan Jubany to Barcelona.

66. The figures are given by Melià p. 214. One should remember, however, that any immigrant who has lived in Barcelona for twenty-five years arrived when the linguistic environment was much more Catalan than nowadays. It is very uncertain that one third of the immigrants *now* arriving will speak Catalan within twenty-five years.

67. J. Amsden, *Collective bargaining and class conflict in Spain,* 1972, p. 96.

68. Reprinted in English translation by the Canadian Committee for a Democratic Spain, *Spain: the Workers' Commissions,* Toronto, 1973, pp. 51-7.

69. *Frères du Monde,* no. 60, Bordeaux 1969, pp. 53-5.

70. Franco Estadella, *El Señor Tarragona,* Barcelona, 1971, p. 68.

71. Trias Fargas, p. 139.

72. Trias Fargas, pp. 70, 134. Local authorities in Spain are empowered to raise only small amounts of local taxation and effectively depend on Madrid for most of their budget (v. K. Medhurst, *Government in Spain* 1973, p. 205.

73. Franco Estadella, p. 58.

74. The 'Civic Union' was described as an association to promote social, cultural and economic development in Catalonia, specifically mentioning housing, town planning, working conditions, medical services and schooling. This was turned down as 'too vague in its objectives'. On the same day, the government approved the constitution of the *Club Siglo XXI,* created to 'promote cultural welfare and favour social harmony within order', whose sponsors included Arias Navarro, Barrera de Irimo, Pío Cabanillas and Samaranch.

75. '*Vota Tarragona que llama al pa, pa, y al vi, vi.'* Samaranch's slogans were 'We shall achieve the forty-hour week' and 'No one ever did so much for sport'.

76. This time there was no technocrat candidacy – reputedly as a result of a 'Pacto de Gijón' between Opus and *Movimiento,* by which the Opus undertook to present no candidates in Madrid or Barcelona.

77. In Cornellà, Tarragona had 71 % of the poll and Samaranch 18 % (figures from a confidential report on the election sent to supporters of Barenys and Casassas).

78. A. M. Badia i Margarit *La llengua dels barcelonins,* Barcelona, 1969, p. 145.

79. *Informe sociológico sobre la situación social en España* Madrid, 1970, tables 18.45, 61, 44, 62; p. 1265.

80. *Mundo,* 17 Nov. 1973, p. 15.

81. *La Vanguardia,* 23 Jan. 1975, p. 36.

82. *La Vanguardia,* 8 Dec. 1974, p. 6.

83. *Triunfo,* 7 Dec. 1974, p. 115.

84. *Mundo,* 1 Feb. 1975, p. 16.

85. This is already becoming evident: Pujol's *éminence grise* is the technocrat Duran Farell.

86. Public opinion surveys show that most workers have never even heard of the names of the leaders of the centre-left (*Mundo,* 24 April 1975).

327

Index

331

132; defeat, 20, 133
Hospitalet, 257
'huidos', 133, 134 (*see also* guerrilla)
Hurtado, Amadeur 246

IESE (Instituto de Estudios Superiores
de la Empresa) 60n53
ILO, 161
IMF, 97, 165
INI (Instituto Nacional de Industria)
creation, 86; purpose of, 89n43; 87,
89, 90; military in, 28; public
investment in, 94, 159
Ibabi, Fr. Julián; 65n78
Ibáñez Martin; José; 58, 59, 187
Ibarruri, Dolores; leader of PCE, 130,
131; speech at V. congress, 139; on
Czechoslovakia, 150; and Partido
Comunista Vasco, 214
Igualada, elections at, 258, 260
'ikastolas', *see* Basque country
industry; attitude to rebellion, 86;
problems in 1940s, 91n55;
industrialization, 90, 91, 93;
expansion in 1950s, 94; excess
production, 95; control by
industrialists, 102; migration to, 104,
109, 117, 118; monopolies, 91, 91n57
Infantes Florido, Mgr. Antonio; 67, 69,
70, 80
Iniesta-Cano, General Carlos; 43, 45
Iniesta Jiménez, Mgr. Alberto; 79
Institut d'Estudis Catalans; 241, 252,
254
Instituto Español de Estudios
Mediterráneos; 241
Instituto Nacional de Colonización; *see*
'colonization, internal'
Instituto Nacional de Previsón; 92
Instituto Nacional de Reforma y
Desarrollo Agrario (INRYDA); *see*
colonization, internal
Iraurgui, Fr. Félix; 80
Irla, Josep; 242, 243
Izquierda Democrática Cristiana; 248
Izquierda Republicana; 243
International Red Aid, 161
Iraurgui, Fr. Félix, 80

JOC (Juventud Obrera Católica), 57, in
strikes, 58, 165; and Opus Dei, 60, 65
Jaén, scheme of, 109, 109n29
Javierre, Fr. José María, 56, 57, 57n44
Jesuits, Deusto university, 60, 202;

Faculty of Chemistry, Barcelona, 205;
Fr, Arrupe Jiménez, Alberto, author
of 'Historia de la Universidad
Española', 203
Jiménez-Fernández, Manuel, 142, 145,
249
John XXIII., Pope, 61, 'Mater et
Magistra', 60; 'Pacem in Terris', 60;
63; 67; 'Aggiornamento', 68
Joint Assembly (Asamblea Conjunta),
see Catholic Church
Jornet Ibara, Sister Teresa, 76
Juan de Borbón, Don, 327n10; attack on
Franco, 35; talks with Franco, 137,
142; declaration on 'Movimiento', 141
Juan Carlos de Borbón, Prince, 24;
education 141; transition, 151; as
King, 155, 232, 233, 260
Jubany Arnau, Narcis, Cardinal, 72, 77,
78, 256n65
Junta Castellana de Actuación
Hispánica, La, *see* Redondo, O.
Junta de Auxilio a los Republicanos
Españoles 129n21
Junta Democrática, creation, 153, 154;
PCE in, 129
Junta Española de Liberación (JEL),
128, 132
Junta para Ampliación de Estudios, 59
Junta Suprema de Unión Nacional, *see*
'Communist Party of Spain'
Juntas de Ofensiva
Nacional-Sindicalista (JONS), 6, 7,
159
Justice and Peace Commission, 80, 255
(*see also* 'Justitia et Pax)
Juventud Obrera, 61n58

Kemen, 259, *see also* 'ETA-Sexta'
Kindelán, General Alfredo, 26, 35
Komunistak, *see* ETA-berri
Krutwig, Federico; 219n16

labour legislation; 28, 85, 87, 88, 159,
160, 163-172 *passim*, 179
Labour University; 204
Laín Entralgo, Pedro; separation from
Falange, 19; *España como Problema*, 56,
57; rector Madrid university, 190
Landera, Fr, Román, 76
Ledesma Ramos, Ramiro, 4; *Discurso a
las juventudes de España*, 5; 'La
Conquista del Estado', 6; separation
from Falange, 8; death, 13, 31

control of labour under, 104
Mutualidades Laborales; 92

Nadal, Santiago; 237n10
National Commission of Justice and
  Peace; *see* Vatican
National Conference of Young Writers;
  190
National Council of the Movement; *see*
  Falange
Navarra, university of; 60, 60n53, 202,
  205, 202n51; CCOO in, 221; ETA in,
  230; strikes in 181n83
Navarro Rubio, Mariano; minister, 60
Naverán, Fr. Jesús; 66n80
Negrín, Juan; 236, 129n21
North Africa, Spanish designs on, 16, 18;
  Italian interests, 18; German interests,
  18n5 allied landing, 17; loss of
  colonies in, 30, 39; defence of Ifni and
  Sahara, 39
Nueva Izquierda Universitaria, 191

Opi, *see* Communist Party of Spain
  (PCE)
Oficina de Coordinación y
  Programación Económica (OCYPE);
  97
Olwer, Nicolau d'; 242
Omnium Cultural; 254
Open University (Universidad Nacional
  de Educación a Distancia), 205
Oposición Sindical Obrera, *see*
  Communist Party of Spain (PCE)
Opposition; definition, 125, 126, 127,
  anti-communism of, 128, 138;
  weakness of, 137
Opposition Sindicates; 244n34
Opus Dei; 48, 53, ideology, 57; economic
  philosophy, 57; in CSIC, 54, 58; into
  universities, 59, 202, 203; into
  government, 59, 60, 96, 110, 200, 201;
  and Falange, 60, 126, 202n49;
  economic development under, 60, 169;
  'Europa Press' 74; Wright-document,
  75; attack by Bishops' Conference; 76;
  departure from government, 78, 204
  (*see also*, Navarra university; IESE;
  Arbor; Rialp)
Organización Revolucionaria de
  Trabajadores; *see* Trotskysts
Orgaz, Luis, General; 26
Orihuela, Bishop of, 51n18
Ortega y Gasset, José, 4, 190

Otaegui, Angel; 232
Otones, Manuel; 176

PCE-Internacional; 149
PCE-ML; 149, 154
PCOE; 150
PNV (Partido Nacionalista Vasco); 213,
  216; and ETA, 217, 220, 221, 223,
  230, 231, 233
PNN (Profesores no numerarios); 210
POUM (Partido Obrero de Unificación
  Marxista), 265, 243n29
Pacelli, Cardinal, *see* Pius XII
'Palau de la Música', 253, 253n60, 254
Pallach, Josep, 265
Pamplona; 1957 strike at, 165; Bishop
  of, 216
'Papers', academic journal, 209
Partido Comunista Vasco; 214, 226, 228
Partido del Trabajo de España; *see*
  'PCE-Internacional'
Partido Socialista Popular; 154
Partido Socialista Unificado de Cataluña
  (PSUC); origins, 244; October 1948
  meeting, 135; 'Unidad' group, 149;
  250; in Asamblea de Cataluña, 263
Partit Socialista d'Alliberament
  Nacional (PSAN); 207
Paul VI.; Pope, 64; 'Populorum
  Progressio', 64; speech at Bogotá, 66;
  letter to Franco, 69; Wright
  document, 75; loyalty, 68; speech to
  College of Cardinals, 69; Spanish
  bishops' delegation to, 76; Spanish
  government delegation to, 76
'Pax', *see* Montero Moreno, Fr. Antonio
'Pax Christi'; *see* Ruiz-Giménez, Joaquín
'Pax Romana'; *see* Ruiz-Giménez, J.
peasantry; *see* agriculture
Pemán, José María; 239
Pereleda, castle of, 249
Pérez de Urbel, Fr., 64
Pérez Galdós, 67n25
Pérez Viñeta, R., General; 43
Pestaña, Angel; 244n34

Pi i Sunyer, Carles, 242
Picasso, Pablo, 73
Pildaín y Zapaín, Bishop, 62, 67, 67n85
Pino Gómez, Mgr. Aurelio; 62, 241
Piñar López, Blas, 65, 67; *Fuerza Nueva*,
  73, 76
Pius XI., Pope; 'Quadragesimo Anno',
  49, 50n6; 'Divini Redemptoris', 54n36

337